APOCALYPSE

THEN, NOW, AND SOON

BRENT LAUDER

STORIED
publishing

Copyright © 2023 Brent Lauder

All rights reserved.

No part of this book may be reproduced in any form or by any electronic or mechanical means, including information storage and retrieval systems, without written permission from the author, except for the use of brief quotations in a book review.

Unless otherwise indicated, Scripture quotations are from the ESV Bible (The Holy Bible, English Standard Version), copyright 2001 by Crossway, a publishing ministry of Good News Publishers. 2011 Text Edition. All rights reserved.

ISBN: 978-1-951991-35-7

Edited by Doug Serven

Cover design by Sean Benesh

Published by Storied Publishing

CONTENTS

Acknowledgments ix
Why Reading This Book Will Do You Good xi

PART 1
PROLOGUE AND CHRIST AMONG THE LAMPSTANDS 1:1–3:22

1. Welcome to the Apocalypse — 3
2. Son of Man, Seven Lampstands — 10
3. Jilted Love, Jealous Christ — 18
4. The Cross Before the Crown — 27
5. Hidden Manna, White Stone, New Name — 35
6. Intolerant, Redemptive Love — 42
7. Sleepers Awake! — 50
8. The Unclosable Door — 58
9. He Stands at the Door — 67

PART 2
THE HEAVENLY THRONE AND THE SEVEN SEALS 4:1–8:5

10. The Glorious Ancient of Days — 77
11. The Lion, The Weeper, and the Worshipers — 86
12. The Four Horsemen — 94
13. Sovereign Over Seals — 104
14. Those Who Stand — 113
15. Silence in Heaven, Fire on Earth — 122

PART 3
THE SEVEN TRUMPETS 8:6–11:19

16. Sound Judgment — 133
17. War and Peace — 142
18. The Conqueror and the Commissioned — 152
19. Fire and Rain — 161
20. The Unending Jubilee — 171

PART 4
THE WOMAN, DRAGON, AND TWO BEASTS 12:1-15:4

21. Silent Night, Frightful Sight	181
22. The Beast from the Sea	192
23. The Beast from the Earth	203
24. The Lamb's Army	213
25. The Eternal Gospel	221
26. Judgment and Jubilee	230

PART 5
THE SEVEN BOWLS 15:5-16:21

27. Seven Bowls Outpoured (Part 1)	243
28. Seven Bowls Outpoured (Part 2)	252

PART 6
THE FALL OF BABYLON 17:1-19:21

29. Beauty? And the Beast	265
30. Come Out, My People	275
31. The Marriage Supper of the Lamb	284
32. The Macabre Supper of Defeat	292

PART 7
THE NEW JERUSALEM, THE GREAT CONSUMMATION, AND EPILOGUE 20:1-22:5

33. One Bound, Countless Emboldened	303
34. The Great White Throne	313
35. All Things Superabundantly New	323
36. Here Comes the Bride	332
37. They Will See His Face	343
38. "So What?"	351
About White BlackBird Books	363
Also by White Blackbird Books	365

IN PRAISE OF APOCALYPSE: THEN, NOW, AND SOON

Western Culture is in upheaval, and many of our social institutions are self-destructing–the family, the church, the state, and the individual. As darkness seems to roll over society, people turn every which way for a solution. But to whom shall we turn? Jesus! And Dr. Lauder's commentary on Revelation is a helpful guide to point the Church to him. Written in an accessible manner, it will serve well every member of the church. Beyond exegetical insights, Brent is the finest illustrator I have heard preach, bringing that gift to bear throughout the commentary. Each section is well illustrated, bringing the passage to life. Brent's pastoral wisdom and affection for the Lord are evident throughout the book. Christians need a clear revelation of Jesus and our historical situation, and Brent Lauder's work sets Jesus Christ before our eyes.
Keith Darrell
Campus Preacher, Whitefield Fellowship

Like fortune tellers and palm-readers, many pundits have spilled tons of ink on Revelation, telling you why these events or those catastrophes are proof that Jesus is returning next week (or month, or year) and if you purchase their book, you'll get it all figured out. But not Brent Lauder. He sees the Revelation of Jesus Christ as the story of Jesus, from his crucifixion and crowning to his return, told seven-fold. Lauder and I could quibble on some details. Nevertheless, this work will bring you to adore the Lord who saved you more and come to fear the world and your moment in it far, far less. *Apocalypse: Then, Now, and Soon* will guide you deeper into the heart, work, and triumph of Jesus."
Michael W. Philliber
Pastor, Heritage Presbyterian Church

It is a privilege to recommend Dr. Brent Lauder's commentary on the Book of Revelation. Why? It is timely, accessible, faithful, well-written, and yet insightfully challenging. Use it and enjoy it!
Harry L. Reeder, III
Former Pastor, Briarwood Presbyterian Church

If you have ever wondered what the practical, devotional, or pastoral relevance of John's apocalyptic Book of Revelation could possibly be, wonder no more. In this deeply refreshing look at a seemingly arcane and mysterious prophetic book, Pastor Brent Lauder reveals its beauty, comfort, and delight with Gospel clarity and charity. Highly recommended.

George Grant
Pastor of Parish Presbyterian Church
Founder of Franklin Classical School
Director of King's Meadow Study Center

Lauder's work on Revelation is masterful. The exegesis is incisive, the pastoral care is palpable throughout, the illustrations are illuminating, and the applications are excellent. Pastor Lauder demonstrates that the book of Revelation is not a maze that requires a PhD or a decoder ring to interpret, but that it is given by Jesus to strengthen his faithful disciples in the good fight of faith with confidence that our King has won the victory. The study questions at the end of each chapter are thought-provoking and will stimulate more than surface-level conversations in small groups and one-to-one discipleship.

David Sunday
Teaching Pastor, New Covenant Bible Church
President of WordPartners

Brent Lauder's study of the Revelation of John presents us with an accessible apocalypse. His writing is clear and compelling with delightful illustrations. His interpretation is scholarly yet fully within the reach of regular Bible readers. Designed for personal study and discussion, this book belongs in pastor's libraries and in the hands of those who love the word of God.

Peter A. Lillback
President, Westminster Theological Seminary

I wish I had this book when I preached through Revelation! Dr. Lauder's penetrating insight and thorough exegesis would have undoubtedly enriched my sermons. Lauder takes readers on a thought-provoking journey through the book of Revelation. With meticulous attention to detail and a keen theological perspective, Lauder unveils the profound truths embedded in this often perplexing text, offering clarity and wisdom for believers today. I also appreciate the carefully crafted study questions at the end of each chapter which encourage deep reflection, meaningful discussions, and personal application of the biblical truths explored throughout the book. Whether you are a seasoned pastor or a curious seeker, this book will

undoubtedly deepen your understanding of Revelation and ignite a renewed passion for God's Word. Dr. Lauder's book is a valuable resource that every Christian should have on their shelf.
Lucas Tanner
RUF Campus Minister, Florida Gulf Coast University

Christians around the world, convinced of the book of Revelation's contemporary importance, are simultaneously enthralled and perplexed by it. The full-plated pastor and earnest layperson alike often stand paralyzed before the mountain of scholarship written on Revelation, needing reassurance that *"blessed is he who reads and those who hear the words of this prophecy"* (Rev. 1:3). Brent Lauder's commentary on this blessed prophecy provides such reassurance. It takes the reader on deep dives into Old Testament background at the appropriate points, interweaves insights from relevant cultural background, moves seamlessly from the discussion of context to observation to meaning, and provides both convicting and comforting points of application. The complex is made simple. Ancient promises are championed with contemporary faithfulness. And the heart of Christ for His pilgrim people revealed in the Apocalypse shines through brilliantly. I didn't want to put it down, nor will you.
Jeffrey M. Scott
Pastor, Covenant Grace Presbyterian Church

The apostle John bore witness to the reality of Christ's now-and-future reign in the book of Revelation to cut through the fog of chaos and hostility that first-century Christians were experiencing. As a faithful pastor, skilled preacher, and incisive writer, Brent Lauder follows John's example by making plain John's great book of comfort and confidence to Christians experiencing the same today. Dr. Lauder clears the air of the cacophony of confusing interpretations to make plain sense of Revelation and, in the voice of a seasoned pastor and preacher, brings its message home with engaging illustrations and heart-aimed application. For the reader hungry and thirsty to find God's protection and provision in this chaotic and hostile world without having to wade through the tortuous gymnastics of much of the popular teaching on Revelation, *Apocalypse: Then, Now, and Soon* is written for you.
Mike Glodo
Associate Professor of Pastoral Theology, Reformed Theological Seminary-Orlando

Although younger than I, Brent Lauder has accomplished a feat that I have yet to attempt. He has preached through the entirety of the book of Revelation in his church. With the publication of *Apocalypse: Then, Now, and Soon*, Dr. Lauder now offers the fruits of his exegetical studies and pastoral skills to the Church at large. While wisely avoiding interminable controversies and fantastic speculations, the author has obviously done his homework. (Hint: Make sure you read the footnotes). Remarkably, Pastor Lauder's work is useful for a range of audiences. For example, with its accessible language, thoughtful application, and concluding reflection questions, his book is appropriate for individual or group Bible studies. Also, with its careful exegesis, theological analysis, and (again) thoughtful application, his work will help preachers land the plane in teaching Revelation to their churches. With Brent Lauder's help, it may be time for me to plan a sermon series on the entire book of Revelation.

Larry Trotter
Pastor, Florida Coast Church
Adjunct Professor, Knox and Westminster Seminaries
Author, *How to Speak a Sermon*

In *Apocalypse: Then, Now, and Soon*, Brent Lauder unpacks the essential message the book of Revelation has for all Christians as we await the glorious return of Christ. This well-researched, yet accessible volume convincingly argues that John's apocalypse is God's often-challenging, always-gracious message for his Church in every age as she lives in a hostile world. In these pages, find a faithful, clear, steady guide through one of the Bible's most misunderstood books.

Peter Stonecipher
Assistant Pastor, Providence Christian Church

ACKNOWLEDGMENTS

Special thanks belong to the Providence Christian Church congregation, whom I've been honored to serve for over a decade. The constant encouragement, love for God's word, and honor they show their pastor fills my heart with gratitude. I thank the Fox family for their early support, which got this book off the ground. In addition, Peter Stonecipher's careful reading and suggestions for the manuscript were invaluable. I also serve a Session that joyfully supports their pastor's side projects for the cause of Christ. For each of those men, I am grateful.

Thank you also to Doug Serven, this work's editor, who patiently walked this rookie writer through the process. I gave him a hundred reasons to forfeit working with me, but he capitalized on none. Thanks, Doug.

This book is for Jennifer, Job, Miriam, Ethan, and Lydia. Every moment given to this book was time away from you. I hope it will bring you joy in the Savior as you read through its pages.

Soli Deo Gloria!

WHY READING THIS BOOK WILL DO YOU GOOD
FOREWORD BY C. JOHN COLLINS, COVENANT THEOLOGICAL SEMINARY

Brent Lauder is one of those students whose work and life reassures teachers that the grind of teaching is worth it if we can teach people like him. The ground for that reassurance is fully on display in the book you are now reading. Not only did he sit in my classes, he and his wife sat in the same pew with my family while he was in seminary, and we became very fond of them.

But my gratefulness for his family isn't a good enough reason for *you* to read his book. Let me explain how you can profit from what Dr. Lauder has written.

What can this book do for you? I'll let the incomparable C.S. Lewis provide the guidance. In 1941, he began a series of lectures on John Milton's *Paradise Lost* with this:

> The first qualification for judging any piece of workmanship from a corkscrew to a cathedral is to know *what* it is—what it was intended to do and how it is meant to be used.[1]

Our answers to these three questions—What is it? What was it intended to do? How is it meant to be used?—will show why going on from this Foreword to Dr. Lauder's text will do you good.

What is it?

Well, the obvious reply is that it's an exposition of the New Testament book called *The Apocalypse (or Revelation) of John*, a book that has been the occasion of all manner of controversy. But we have to say more than that. Dr. Lauder is a *pastor*, whose exposition reflects what a good and conscientious pastor will do. He has done a fine job of consulting quality sources, whether of scholars who have written on the New Testament text, or of writers on theological and spiritual topics, or of insightful cultural commentary.

But not only has he consulted them, he has sifted them, using his own judgment, and offering good reasons for the conclusions he draws. You will find all of his discussions helpful—and even if at times you come to a different conclusion than he does, you will have learned something worth learning in the process.

Dr. Lauder has also written this to be understood: he is clear, and that clarity obviously shows that he has wrestled with his material to the point of understanding it himself. But he never wields his clarity as a weapon to belittle anyone; he's never overbearing as he explains his conclusions. It's really nice to have someone talk to you clearly, who knows what he's talking about, who takes it to his own heart, and who cares for his readers.

Above all, in this book, you will meet a person worth meeting: someone whose faith has made him thoughtful, irenic, careful, and genuinely interested in helping you to love and serve Jesus truly.

What was it intended to do?

At the very least, Dr. Lauder intends to share with us what he's learned from his own study of this often baffling book. He's certainly worked hard, but it's not just that—he wants you and me to serve Jesus in our own era with confidence. We all know that there are many voices out there calling for our loyalty, or aiming to silence us, or trying to alter the historic Christian faith.

And there are many in the Church who find all kinds of things in the book of Revelation. Dr. Lauder can help us to sort through all these who clamor for our attention. By his telling—which I find persuasive—we can stand firm in our faith and call our neighbors to believe, without fear of them and without fear that loving them and speaking attractively means watering down our message. If you follow along with Dr. Lauder, you'll find that this ancient book, with all of its strange passages, has much to say to us right here, and right now: it's about *life*, real life.

How is it meant to be used?

I can think of several ways to use this book. First, as I've suggested already, by reading this you will find yourself in contact with a person who is worthy of your attention. He can help you to think clearly and to live courageously. Second, if you are a preacher or teacher, you will find this a valuable resource—not only for its content but for its style as well. Dr. Lauder is an excellent example of the kind of diligent, careful, and thoughtful study that a pastor can do, and he shows how all of this promotes sound piety. May his tribe increase many times over!

If you're not a preacher or teacher, you can give this as a gift to someone who is, to encourage and challenge him to similar thoughtfulness, clarity, and charity.

Dr. Lauder has offered to do you good. I'm going to move aside so that you can receive the blessings he has for you. And just before I do that, let me record my gratitude at the honor of commending this fine piece of work.

---

1. C.S. Lewis, *A Preface to Paradise Lost* (London: Oxford University Press, 1942), 1.

PART 1

PROLOGUE AND CHRIST AMONG THE LAMPSTANDS 1:1–3:22

1

WELCOME TO THE APOCALYPSE

REVELATION 1:1-8

How do you hide a twenty-thousand-ton battleship in the middle of the ocean? That was a question plaguing many in the armed forces of World War I. Before the days of advanced radar detection, the newly-designed German submarine, capable of hovering unseen just below the surface of the water, torpedoed  countless Allied civil and military boats to a watery grave. Several suggestions came forward to address the problem. One recommendation brought forth was to conceal the ships through clever paintwork. Perhaps, it was reasoned, if the vessel matched the colors of the midday sky, detection by German periscopes would be more difficult. The Allied Forces soon abandoned this practice, however, as no static color could effectively blend the vessels into the ever-changing environment of the sea.

So they employed a new tactic. Instead of using paint to hide the ships from submarines, they painted the vessels to bring attention to the craft while simultaneously disorienting the observer. Artists added contrasting shades of blue, orange, and red paint to the traditional black, white, and gray. Moreover, they also added geometric patterns of squares, circles, and triangles overlapping intersecting horizontal and vertical lines. The hope of this new paint scheme, called "Dazzle Camouflage," was to make the ship look so odd and bewildering that determining the ship's size, direction, speed, and type was nearly impossible.

While the advent of advanced sonar made the use of Dazzle Camouflage no longer necessary, the idea of looking at something that causes disorientation is familiar to anyone living in this world and endeavoring to be faithful to Jesus. The book of Revelation was given to a group of people looking out on a world over which Jesus claims all authority (Matt. 28:18), yet what they observed was troubling. Some of John's[1] audience suffered for following Jesus (Rev. 2:9, 13), and the question arose: "Why is God allowing this?" Others looked out at a hostile Roman Empire, and they avoided persecution by blending in with their surrounding culture (Rev. 2:14–15, 20). "What's wrong with a little compromise?" they wondered. "As long as we hold to the essentials, what's a little incense to the emperor going to hurt?" And then some associated with Jesus, but their hearts were far from him. They went to church, sang the songs, and recited the creeds, but deep in their hearts, they didn't make much of him (Rev. 3:15). They don't deny Jesus' claims; they just don't give them free rein. They want to be saved from their sins and go to heaven when they die. But a king over every aspect of their lives doesn't interest them. Disorientation plagues them.[2]

So, in these ways, we find this book of contemporary relevance. Sometimes we have an idea of how our lives should look and proceed forward trusting Jesus. But when covenant kids walk away from Jesus, when we're slandered for our faith, or inoperable tumors grow, we wonder if anyone's in charge. At other times, we find that the doctrines of our faith put us far outside of the convictions of our neighbors and coworkers, and in the name of living quiet and peaceful lives (1 Tim. 2:2), we give in a little here and there, becoming less vocal about eternal truths.

And then there are those times when we are neither excited nor indifferent toward Jesus. We can enter a kind of spiritual cruise control[3] in which we do our best to avoid the big sins of lying, adultery, and theft while maintaining a lax, easy approach toward the other areas over which Jesus asserts his authority.

John's diverse audience needed the same thing every generation of mixed and marred Christians needs. In a world where we find ourselves easily disoriented, the Lord gives us an apocalypse and an assurance.

Apocalypse

The word "apocalypse" conjures images of zombies, earthquakes, and world wars. But the Greek word that John uses (*apokalupsis*) to open this letter means to unveil or uncover, hence the English translation of "revelation." But what exactly is John telling us will be revealed or uncovered in this book? The fuller phrase that John uses to start the book is "the revelation of Jesus Christ" (Rev. 1:1). Does John mean that in the following pages, Jesus will reveal and uncover secrets? Yes, on the one hand, he does suggest that. Jesus will show us a worship service in heaven (Ch. 4). He'll disclose a dragon pursuing the Church and how he will save his people (Ch. 12). He'll unveil the danger of being allured by the riches and promises of a harlot (Ch. 17). He'll also show us how we can and must resist her seduction. Page after page, Jesus reveals previously undisclosed secrets about the world in which we live, the heavenly world under which we live, and the future world toward which we strive.

But John is perhaps telling us more in "the revelation of Jesus Christ." He's indicating that this Revelation unveils or discloses Jesus Christ himself. That is to say, Jesus Christ is the secret, the presently hidden One revealed throughout the book. Jesus will be presented as one who walks among the churches (Rev. 1:12–13) while also enthroned in heaven (Ch. 5). John is fond of the double meaning of words in his Gospel.[4] He seems to be taking the same tack here. This book is a revelation of unknown secrets and a presently unseen Christ.

John's audience needed this apocalypse. And we need it now. For those of us who are compromising our faith, giving up what we know is true for fear of sticking out in an increasingly anti-Christian culture in our workplaces, schools, and even around the dinner table, we need an unveiling. We need to see Jesus as the one who says, *"I am ready to spit you out of my mouth"* (Rev. 3:16) and to hear with those same lips, "It's not too late. I'm standing at the door, knocking. Open the door, and we will feast together."

For those of you suffering for your faith, being called "judgmental," "arrogant," "bigoted," or "full of hate" because you refuse to let go of eternal truths entrusted to you in Scripture, you, too, need a disclosure. You need to see the Wonderful Counselor who has kept track of all your sorrows, collected all of your tears, and recorded them all in his book (Ps. 56:8). The Lord will open those books, and every wrong will be made right (Ch. 20).

But recognizing this book as an apocalypse does more than simply describe the book's function. Just as necessary, the word indicates the type of book we are studying. Revelation is a type of literary genre we call an apocalypse.[5] Knowing the sort of book that John wrote will be crucial, as it not only shapes our expectations of what lies ahead but also informs how we read and understand the book's uniqueness.

An example might help us here. Suppose I handed you a document and asked you to read what was on the page. If the page opened with "Once upon a time, in a land far away," you might guess you were reading the beginning of a fairy tale or myth complete with fire-breathing dragons, talking unicorns, witches, and so forth. Suppose I handed you another document, and this time it began with these words: "Four score and seven years ago, our fathers brought forth on this continent a new nation." You would not expect this document to include any fairy tale elements at all. Instead, you would anticipate a historical retelling of past events, just as Lincoln did in his Gettysburg Address. We recognize the distinguishing characteristics among the different genres, or types, of literature, and those distinctions help shape how we read them. John tells us right from the beginning how to read this book. It's an apocalypse.

John was not the first biblical author to compose this type of writing. Old Testament books like Ezekiel, Zechariah, and Daniel all fall into this literary genre or at least contain some apocalyptic elements within their pages. While we could say much more about the genre, it's important to note that apocalyptic literature heavily uses symbolism.

Think back to the book of Daniel where we find pictures of a four-part statue, toppled over by a stone (Ch. 2), four beasts rising from the sea, and then overthrown by the son of man figure (Ch. 7). Both the statue and the beasts are symbols of historic realities. From Daniel's time, four more kingdoms would arise, and then the Lord would establish the Kingdom of God.[6]

Therefore, in the pages to come in Revelation, much of what we will encounter is not intended to be taken literally. For example, Jesus is not a seven-eyed, bronze-footed lion/lamb with fire for eyes perpetually carrying a sword in his mouth. Instead, each of those symbols points to realities about Jesus Christ.

We should also note apocalyptic literature's use of numbers.[7] One only needs to look at 1:4–5 to see how he will use numbers. John composes a benediction from the Father, Son, and the *"seven spirits who are before his throne."* Surely John isn't suggesting that the Holy Trinity consists of nine persons! Instead, seven is a number used throughout this book to represent fullness or completeness.[8] John says many things on the opening page of his revelation that has perplexed and puzzled many, many people over the years. But he makes an important declaration: the fullness of Almighty God—the Father, the Son, and the full outpouring of the Holy Spirit—is bestowed upon those who hear, and are shaped by, the contents of this book.

Therefore, this is not just an apocalypse, unveiling Jesus and otherwise unseen realities; it's also an assurance of God's richest blessing upon those shaped by its contents.

Assurance

We will find many assurances in the pages to follow, but we must begin with the heart of God, which beats with love for his people. For all of the mysteries we'll encounter together, there is no mystery behind the origin of this message. John tells us that the Father who so loved the world that he gave up his only son gave this Revelation to Jesus (Rev. 1:1). Jesus then gave it to an angel, who gave it to John.

The book of Revelation is a love letter from the One whom John tells us is love (1 John 4:8), and who so loved the world that he gave his son, that those who believe in the son would have life everlasting (John 3:16). And the Son, who has come to show us what the Father is like, loves you.

Revelation 1:5 tells the Christian that Jesus loves you and has freed you from your sin by his blood. We all need to hear the present tense (*loves* you, not *loved* you) of his love. If you're persecuted and maligned for your faith or if the Spirit of God is pointing to areas of compromises or indifference from which you must flee, you need to hear that Jesus loves you. We have to be confident of his love for us. And we must also be convinced of his sovereign control over the events of our short lives.

The Father, who loves you, reveals that when Jesus ascended into the clouds, he approached the Father. The Father gave all dominion, glory, authority, and power to Jesus to rule over the details of your life (Dan. 7:13–14). Jesus is not a king in exile, awaiting the moment he can take control of the events of history. Instead, as John tells us, Jesus is *"the ruler of kings of the earth"* (Rev. 1:5). The assurance of his present rule makes all the difference we need when we go through difficult circumstances, faith-staggering events, and painful trials. While we may not understand how those trials glorify God or work toward our good (Rom. 8:28), we're assured that those occurrences must first go through the nail-scarred hands of the ruler of the kings of the earth, who loves us. The same one who calls me his friend (Luke 7:34), the apple of his eye (Ps. 17:8), and his bride (Rev. 19:7) discloses to us that all that we encounter passes first through hands that promise never to loosen their grip upon us (John 10:28).

To shore up the assurance of the Lord's loving care for his people, I'll end this section with a promise made to us by the Father. We will only hear the Father speak twice in this book: once at the beginning of the book and once again at the end (Rev. 1:8, 21:5–8).[9] The first time, he calls himself the "Alpha and the Omega" (Rev. 1:8), declaring his unaltering supremacy over history. Since Alpha and Omega are the first and last letters of the Greek alphabet, an English equivalent would be "I am the A to Z," the first and the last, the beginning and the end. The God who greets us in these pages is the maker, sustainer, and goal of all creation. God authors history from beginning to end. This book opens then with our Father assuring us he is God over all we will "see" in this book, and then once more, at its close, he will declare that all of his purposes for the world, his Christ, and his people have been accomplished, saying in the end, "It is done!" (Rev. 21:6).

Several years ago, I met up with an old pastor friend. While catching up, I asked about his son, who I knew suffered from extreme autism. In response, he told me about a terrible storm that rolled through his neighborhood in St. Louis that took out the power grid in the area. His son, who feared nothing more than a dark bedroom, woke the entire home screaming, "Daddy! I'm scared. Come get me, Daddy!" My friend jumped from his bed and made his way down a dark hallway to his son's room, where the agony in his son's screams was interrupted only when he tried to catch his breath.

Having come to the side of the bed, grabbing his son's hand, he assured him, "Son, I am right here. Don't be afraid. Daddy is right here." "But I can't see you, Daddy! I want to see you," pleaded the boy. "You can't see me right now. Your eyes are full of tears, and the lights are out. But I can see you. Just listen to my voice. I'm right here. Daddy sees you." My friend spent the rest of the night on the floor of his son's room, holding his hand and praying with him. Then, just as the boy was falling asleep, the last words my friend heard him say were, "Daddy, you see me."

In this book, Jesus will show us some glorious, joyful, hope-filling, worship-inducing truths that will whet our appetite for the glorious consummation of the age. But he will also show us some sinister, dark, malicious, and, at times, sobering things that disorient us and make us ask ourselves, "What's going on?" But in all of this, we are more than conquerors through him who loves us. And he promises us, especially when we cannot see him, that he can see us and that he will never leave or forsake us until we see him face to face.

Study Questions

1. In what ways do you see the needs of John's original audience as our own?
2. In which of the three groups that John addresses do you see yourself?
3. Why is it important to understand the genre a writer uses? Think of the resurrection of Jesus. How would you answer the critic who suggests that we should not regard the gospel's record of that event literally?

---

1. I regard the apostle John, the writer of the Gospel of John, as the author of Revelation. For detailed discussions on authorship, one should consult the commentaries. For a defense of my position, see G.K. Beale, *The Book of Revelation: A Commentary on the Greek Text* (Grand Rapids, MI: Eerdmans, 2013), 34–36.
2. Revelation is sometimes wrongly characterized as a book written for the comfort of persecuted Christians. However, while there is comfort for the oppressed, the letters to the seven churches will show Jesus warning some with severe consequences for compromising and others still with the disaster that awaits those maintaining a tepid allegiance to him. See Richard Bauckham, *The Theology of the Book of Revelation* (Cambridge University Press, 2012), 15.
3. Jerry Bridges often used this metaphor. See Jerry Bridges, *The Disciplines of Grace: God's Role and Our Role in the Pursuit of Holiness* (Colorado Springs, CO: NavPress, 1994), 116.
4. See the commentaries on John's use of *logos* in Chapter 1:1 of his Gospel.
5. More accurately, Revelation is an apocalypse (1:1), a prophecy (1:3), and a circular letter (1:4), or in the words of Bauckham, "an apocalyptic prophecy in the form of a circular letter." For our purposes, I am keeping the description of the genre simple while not neglecting the book's prophetic nature addressed to the churches. See Bauckham, *The Theology of the Book of Revelation*, 2.
6. Daniel 7 and the coming of the son of man is sometimes regarded as a description of the "second coming" of Jesus. Attention to the text, with the direction of the son of man coming toward the Ancient of Days and not to the earth, would suggest otherwise. Daniel saw what the disciples only wondered about on the other side of the clouds that gathered their Savior into Heaven. Through the clouds, the ascended, glorified son of man came to the Ancient of Days to take his place on David's vacant throne. For more on this, see R. T. France, *The Gospel of Mark: A Commentary on the Greek Text* (Eerdmans, 2009), 341–343.
7. For an extended treatment of the symbolic use of numbers, see G.K. Beale, *The Book of Revelation: A Shorter Commentary* (Eerdmans, 2015), 14–16. In addition, the symbolic use of numbers will heavily influence other sections of this book, such as the meaning of 666, 144,000, 10 horns on the heads of beasts, the 1,000-year binding of Satan, and so forth.
8. Bauckham, *The Theology of the Book of Revelation*, 26.
9. See also Bauckham, *The Theology of the Book of Revelation*, 25.

2

SON OF MAN, SEVEN LAMPSTANDS
REVELATION 1:9–20

Robert Louis Stevenson tells the true story of a boat caught in the middle of a terrible storm. As the wind and the waves caused the vessel to list from side to side, waves crashed over the boat's sides. Wave after wave brought hundreds of gallons of seawater onto the deck and down into the hold, where crew and passengers huddled in prayer.

During a prayer break, the group selected one man to go up on the deck to assess their chances of survival. Fighting through knee-high water and blasts of wind, the passenger made his way to the boat's bridge, where, to his surprise, he saw a figure standing behind the wheel. When he got closer, he could see the boat's Captain holding onto the wheel and wiping saltwater from his eyes.

As the passenger looked on, the Captain caught sight of the terror-stricken man and gave him a reassuring smile. The passenger returned to the ship's hold and announced to the frightened passengers, "I have seen the face of the Captain, and he smiled. All is well."[1]

In this world, you will have trouble. And even more problems will find you if you follow Jesus Christ. And if the promise of trouble in the world feels impersonal, Jesus fortifies it with the assurance that the world will hate you because of your allegiance to him (John 15:18–19). Going further still, Jesus warns his disciples in this book (Rev. 3:10) that severe suffering will soon come upon them and some will lose their lives for him. And like us, their temptation in the face of that kind of suffering is to ask, "Why is this happening? (cf. Ps. 6:3, 13:1; Jer.12:1) How much longer until you bring justice?" (Rev. 6:10).

Sometimes those questions are accompanied by the temptation to make compromises and little sacrifices of truth and behavior here and there to avoid bringing attention to our faith. During such storms, we need to see the face of our Captain. And he tells us we've nothing to fear.

Before we look at the text itself, I'll share an outline of how we should best approach the book. Many of us were taught that Revelation deals primarily with future things. The preachers and teachers I followed early in my faith taught that Chapters 1 through 3 of Revelation deal with issues in the first-century church. But once you approach Chapters 4–22, we read about possible-near-but-definitely-future events. Additionally, well-meaning teachers argued that Chapters 4–22 unfold sequentially as a road map to the world's end.

That's not the best way to view the book, and I'll share why in the pages ahead. Instead, we should see the book as a collection of seven portraits, all of which give a picture of the same time period—the time between the ascension and return of Jesus—but from different angles. Imagine that John is holding up a diamond and describing what he sees. He sees events that will occur between the ascension and the return of Jesus Christ. Then, he turns the diamond—the angle now changed and the light bouncing off differently—and describes it again. John does this seven times,[2] and each time he does, his descriptions will move progressively toward the end of this present age.[3] So, instead of treating the Book of Revelation like a continuous movie about the distant future, running sequentially to the end of the world, we should treat it like seven portraits in an art gallery, often showing the same subject but from different angles.[4]

The first portrait John paints for us covers the book's first three chapters, showing us the face of our Captain, who stands in the midst of the church, saying, "Fear not." What did John see and how does it remove our fears? John sees the person and the provision of Jesus Christ.

Person

Before John describes his vision of Jesus, he tells us that he was on the island of Patmos, where Rome would often place their political misfits. John was sent there because he refused to stop preaching and teaching about Jesus. It was there, one Sunday morning (1:10), that he received a vision,[5] which makes up the bulk of what follows in the book. But before John sees anything, he hears a voice behind him instructing him to record all he was about to hear and see. At the sound of the voice, John turns around, and the drab penal colony of Patmos falls away. A veil of sorts is pulled back, and what he sees nearly kills him (Rev. 1:17).[6] The same Jesus, upon whose chest John once reclined, stands before him in glory, honor, and terrible majesty. We read:

> Then I turned to see the voice that was speaking to me, and on turning I saw seven golden lampstands, and in the midst of the lampstands one like a son of man, clothed with a long robe and with a golden sash around his chest. The hairs of his head were white, like white wool, like snow. His eyes were like a flame of fire, his feet were like burnished bronze, refined in a furnace, and his voice was like the roar of many waters. In his right hand he held seven stars, from his mouth came a sharp two-edged sword, and his face was like the sun shining in full strength. (Rev. 1:12–17a)

But before John sees Jesus, seven golden lampstands appear, representing the churches to whom John will send this apocalypse. More on that in a moment because the sight of Jesus overwhelms John. John describes a figure standing in the middle of the seven lampstands as "one like a son of man" (v. 13). This title is a clear reference to the figure Daniel observed (Dan. 7:13–14) and described as "a son of man," who would bring an end to the world-dominating kingdoms of men and establish the Kingdom of the Lord. The shadowy, vague[7] figure in Daniel's vision of the future, stands before John in the present and with greater clarity. John even knows his name: Jesus.

John describes Jesus's hair as white as wool, suggesting purity and the wisdom that comes with age.[8] His eyes, blazing with fire,[9] peer through the excuses people make for rebellion. His bare feet[10] are like bronze glowing in a furnace, suggesting that this one will come to judge and trample down his enemies.[11] His voice is like listening to the roaring ocean,[12] and in his mouth, he holds a sword with which he will purge his Church of imposters (Rev. 2:16) and cut down his enemies (Rev. 19:15).

This presentation of Jesus is a corrective to nonsensical, weak portrayals of a meek and mild Jesus who hopes we will answer when he taps outside the door of our hearts. That's not who John saw, and it's not the Jesus we should see.

Some time ago, I read the story of Tom Skinner,[13] a former street gang leader in Harlem during the 1960s. The Lord later transformed Tom and made him an evangelist. But initially, he rejected Jesus because he'd always thought of him as a weak, effeminate White guy from the suburbs. Tom would often think about that one-dimensional Jesus, concluding that the suburban Jesus wouldn't last an hour in his neighborhood. But once he began to read the Bible, he encountered a bronze-footed Jesus who will pummel his enemies. He also met a warrior messiah who brandished a sword and will conquer his enemies with just a word. Tom realized he had Jesus all wrong. Consequently, he changed his tune and started saying, "My neighborhood couldn't last an hour if he showed up."

If you're not a Christian, you must see the Jesus that John encountered. He is not to be toyed with or treated lightly. Jesus will not bargain with you. Instead, he commands what you must do at some point, joyfully or with deep regret (Phil. 2:10): Bow the knee to him. Come to him with all of your doubts, anger, guilt, and excuses. But you must come. Receive from him the pardon, love, and care that only he can provide.

If you are a Christian, Jesus says to you, "Fear not." I need the command to be courageous when I think about the future of the country that my children will inherit. We live in a time where people who hold to the Christian faith are becoming more marginalized. It's no longer a laughable proposition, one best left in dystopian novels, to think that people who adhere to the Bible's essential teaching on marriage, sexuality, and identity will be persecuted and maybe put in jail. When I listened to preachers in the 1980s speak of persecution, I thought their warnings were hyperbolic. Now I'm not so sure.

Jesus encourages us, saying, "Fear not." Consider the person of Christ and also the promise of his provisions.

Provision of Sustaining Grace

John tells us that Jesus stands as a warrior king among the lampstands, representing the Church (Rev. 1:20). But another image emerges as we examine Jesus' clothing. John describes Jesus wearing the garb of a high priest: a long robe with a sash (Ex. 28:8). However, the sash differs because it's made of gold, signifying the wealth, beauty, and purity of this unique high priest.[14] So the picture John shows is a king-priest who stands among the lampstands.

This isn't the first time one of God's prophets had a vision of a lampstand. It seems that John saw something that the Old Testament prophet Zechariah also saw but with a few variations.

Zechariah lived about 500 years before the birth of Jesus. Zechariah ministered to those who had returned from Babylonian exile with the instruction to rebuild the ruined temple. After some time of working on the renovation project, the people grew discouraged, and the work came to a halt. The Lord sent a vision to Zechariah (Zech. 4) to encourage his people. Zechariah saw a golden lampstand with seven flames, and on both sides of it stood an olive tree. Zechariah asked about the vision's meaning. The Lord explained that the golden lampstand represented the temple and that his Spirit would fuel the seven flames on the lampstand.

This is where that great verse *"Not by might, nor by power, but by my Spirit"* comes from (Zech. 4:6). The Lord was telling Zechariah, "I will build my temple, and the gates of hell (or any "great mountain" (cf. Zech. 4:7) would not prevail against it" (Matt. 16:18). Zechariah then asked about the two olive trees on either side of the golden lampstand. The Lord told him, "These are the two anointed ones'" (Zech. 4:14), with one tree representing Joshua, the high priest, and the other, Zerubbabel, the King of Jerusalem."[15] In short, the Lord said that he would rebuild the temple. He would pour out his Spirit upon the king and the priest, and no person, power, or political upheaval would stand in the way.

Fast forward 600 years, and John sees not one but seven lampstands, representing the holy, universal Church of all ages and nations. And John sees not two men but one, who is both king and priest, walking among the lampstands.

Through this vision, Jesus says, "I am the King and Priest who tends to the churches. I am the King-Priest upon whom the Spirit has been poured out in full measure. And I will build my church. Not by the might of people, politicians, political parties, or social reform, but by my Spirit. And to those who look to me and walk in my ways, I will give a fresh supply of oil so that they may burn as lights in a dark world."

Do you hear the promise of Jesus to you in this vision? He says, "If you entrust yourself to my care and do not compromise or become cowardly in your witness, no matter how fierce and frightening the storm, your lamp will burn."

My friend, with Jesus you are on a side that cannot lose, and you are called to burn brightly in a dark world that cannot win. Don't let Satan cripple your witness through compromise or cowardice in a world that hates you. Jesus promises that some will despise us for his name's sake. But he shows us that our lamp will continue to burn if we hold on to him.

See him as he provides sustaining grace among the lampstands and listen to him as he sets before you the depths of his love, shown in the provision of his life.

Provision of Gospel Assurance

Seeing Jesus terrified John—a typical response throughout the Bible when sinful people come close to a Holy God. One thinks here of Isaiah, Ezekiel, and Daniel (Isa. 6:5; Ezek. 1:28, 3:23; Dan. 8:17, 10:10) in the Old Testament as well as Peter, James, John, and Paul (Matt. 17:6; Acts 9:4, 26:14) in the New, all of whom collapsed as though dead when the veil of this world was pulled back just enough to see the Almighty.

But Jesus preaches the Gospel to John, and by extension, to you. In verse 17, Jesus tells John not to be afraid. He then announces his authority to proclaim peace to John because he is the *"first and the last,"* uttering this with the equal authority of his Father, who declared in verse 8, *"I am the Alpha and the Omega," "who is and who was and who is to come."* Jesus, Almighty God himself, charges John, *"Do not be afraid of me."* Jesus could command this because of the Gospel, which Jesus shares with his dear disciple in verse 18: "I am... the living one. I died, and behold I am alive forevermore, and I have the keys[16] of Death and Hades," meaning that he has not only triumphed over death but also has full authority over those who shall be victorious and be freed from its grip. Before the resurrection of Jesus, death kept men and women in lifelong slavery to fear (Heb. 2:15). But now, as John sees the risen and glorified Jesus who has conquered death and will eradicate it at the great consummation (Rev. 21:4), Jesus proclaims that he has full sway over Death and Hades. It is as though Jesus says to John and any who are united to him by faith, "I have died for you, and I've been raised for you. And as the risen Son of God, I put Death to death, rendering it powerless over my people. Therefore, you have nothing to fear, whether it be trials, persecution, or the end of your earthly life. I hold the keys, and I hold my people. Fear not."

Count Nikolaus Zinzendorf (1700–1760) was a German religious leader in the 1700s and bishop in the Moravian Church. In his youth, he studied law and planned a life of great affluence. But one afternoon, he visited an art museum, where he encountered a painting of Jesus, head crowned with thorns, blood running down his face, and love in his eyes. As he examined the image, his eyes fell upon the artist's words just below: "This have I suffered for you; now what will you do for me?" Zinzendorf responded, "Anything!"[17] Think of the person and provision of Jesus Christ as you have seen him today, and say to him, "I will do anything for you."

Study Questions

1. Consider John's visions as one event presented to us from multiple vantage points. How does that differ from how you have read this book before?
2. How does reading Zechariah 4 alongside John's vision of Jesus in the lampstands help to understand this passage?
3. When Jesus shows up without the Gospel, he is rightfully terrifying. However, Jesus doesn't allow John to remain terrified. So how does Jesus preach the gospel to John? What is Jesus saying to you?

---

1. This story is recounted in E.M. Bounds, *E.M. Bounds on Prayer* (Peabody, MA: Hendrickson Publishers, 2006), 255.
2. I offer here a slightly modified outline from the one found in William Hendriksen, *More than Conquerors* (Baker Books, 1998), 16–19:
    Ch. 1:1–8 Prologue
    Ch. 1:9–3:22 Christ in the 7 Lampstands
    Ch. 4:1–8:5 Heaven and the 7 Seals
    Ch. 8:6–11:19 The 7 Trumpets
    Ch. 12:1–15:4 The Woman, Dragon, and the Beasts
    Ch. 15:5–16:21 The 7 Bowls
    Ch. 17:1–19:21 The Fall of Babylon
    Ch. 20:1–22:5 The Great Consummation
    Ch. 22:6–21 Epilogue
3. This interpretive approach is called "recapitulation" or "progressive parallelism" and adopted by commentators such as Gregory Beale, William Hendriksen, Vern S. Poythress, and B.B. Warfield. See G.K. Beale, *The Book of Revelation: A Shorter Commentary* (Eerdmans, 2015), 48–49; Hendriksen, *More Than Conquerors*, 16–43; Vern S. Poythress, *The Returning King: A Guide to the Book of Revelation* (P&R, 2000), 27–37; B.B. Warfield (2000), "The Millennium and the Apocalypse" *Biblical Doctrines*, 645.
4. One could think of Daniel Chapters 2 and 7, which are two different symbolic presentations (a four-part statue and four beasts of the sea) of the same historical period.
5. Some suggest that John saw four visions, each preceded by the words "in the Spirit" (1:10; 4:2; 17:3; 21:10). Others, such as Bauckham, suggest that John saw one sustained vision from 1:10 to 22:6. One's opinion on this matter will not influence the overall interpretation or approach to the book.
6. The allusions here to Daniel's vision of a terrifying man are unmistakable. See Daniel Chapter 10.
7. "The Son of Man" was Jesus' favorite title of self-identification. Jesus rarely referred to himself as the *Christ* or the *Messiah*, as, it seems, these terms were so heavily burdened with political overtones. On the other hand, "Son of Man" was a title rarely used in the first century for the coming one, which left this self-identification as a more moldable character. See O. Palmer Robertson, *The Christ of the Prophets* (P&R, 2008), 257.
8. Note also that the white hair, like pure wool, matches Daniel's description of the Ancient of Days in Dan. 7:9, thus showing how Christ and God are described with the same terms.

9. See 19:2, where the same phrase describes Christ as the judge of the wicked.
10. Like the priests of the tabernacle and temple, Jesus stands among the lampstands barefoot. This practice of shoeless ministry in the presence of the Lord goes back to Moses' sandal-free moment at the burning bush. See Richard Bauckham, *Who is God? Key Moments of Biblical Revelation* (Baker Academic, 2020), 38–39.
11. See Poythress, 79 and Hendriksen, 56. Alternatively, Beale, 48, suggests the bronze feet represent a foundation of moral purity.
12. A voice like the sound of many waters also describes the Lord God found in Ezekiel 1:24; 43:2.
13. Interested readers can find some of Tom's story at https://urbana.org/message/us-racial-crisis-and-world-evangelism.
14. Poythress, 79.
15. On the identity of the two "anointed ones," see Beale, ibid., 577 and Joyce G. Baldwin, *Haggai, Zechariah, Malachi* (InterVarsity Press, 1972), 119.
16. More on these keys when we examine Rev. 3:7.
17. http://zinzendorf.com/pages/index.php?id=ecce-homo

3

JILTED LOVE, JEALOUS CHRIST
REVELATION 2:1-7

Several years ago, a Learjet took off from an airport in Orlando, Florida. It was supposed to fly to Dallas, but it never arrived. The jet carried professional golfer Payne Stewart and a few of his friends.

Before departure, anyone observing the Learjet on the tarmac would have marveled at its sleekness and style. After takeoff, one could have commented on its speed and how nice it must be to travel in such style. But despite outward appearances, something inside the jet would wreck all of our perceptions. Shortly after the plane took off, experts suspect it lost cabin pressure, dropping the internal temperature below freezing and killing all the passengers. And because the aircraft was set on autopilot, it flew a ghostly journey of 1,400 miles for four hours until it finally ran out of fuel, crashing in a South Dakota field.

That tragic event is a heartbreaking image of what can happen to us. From all outward appearances, our lives can look complete, in order, and under control. But on the inside, something can be incredibly wrong. Worry, addictions, consuming thoughts about money, and secret sins can be easily hidden from the view of others. Perhaps the problem is more subtle but just as dangerous. Maybe on the outside, your life looks fairly good. But inside, your soul has gone from a zealous pursuit of Jesus to lax, duty-driven obedience, lacking joy, warmth, and intimacy with the Savior.

We desperately need this letter to the church in Ephesus. Ephesus was one of seven churches that received this revelation. But we have already seen that the number seven carries symbolic significance. Seven is the number of completion, wholeness, or totality. While these letters address seven ancient actual churches in Asia Minor, they are relevant for the churches of every region and in every time period.[1] Each letter, after all, ends with the refrain, *"He who has an ear, let him hear what the Spirit says to the churches."* So as Jesus spoke to the Ephesians, he also addressed the other six churches and anyone in the Church today with ears to hear.

The first letter comes to the church in Ephesus, located in the city closest to Patmos, where John was imprisoned.[2] According to church tradition, the Apostle John was arrested and exiled to Patmos while pastoring the church in Ephesus. One wonders if John's heart skipped a beat as he anticipated what the Lord would say to the church under John's charge. What John heard must have both thrilled him and broke his heart. Jesus praised this church for their intolerance of false doctrine but also rebuked them for lacking love, the most important thing. The Ephesian church, like that Learjet, which on the outside looked impressive, concealed a terrible situation on the inside.

Before we examine the Ephesian church, notice that, just like the other six, this letter is addressed to the "angel of the church" (Rev. 2:1). The word John uses for angel, *angelos* in Greek, is sometimes used in the New Testament to refer to a human messenger, like John the Baptist (Matt. 11:10). This leads some to assume these letters address each of the churches' pastors, who are the messengers of the Gospel.[3] Others, however, note that whenever John uses the word "angel" in Revelation, he always refers to the otherworldly messengers we know as angels. Therefore, we should not look to find an alternative here.[4] If forced to choose, I would opt for the latter interpretation. If this is correct, the point is that we already partake of heavenly existence. As citizens of heaven (Col. 3:1), each time we gather for worship, we are reminded that we join our voices with the innumerable host above,[5] to give glory, honor, and praise to Jesus.

The focus, however, here and in the other letters, falls upon Jesus and the churches addressed and not the angels (or pastors). Jesus had a message for the Ephesian Christians. He commended them for their intolerance of false doctrine and practice. But he also rebuked them for having abandoned love.

Praise for Intolerance

Ephesus[6] was a significant city in the ancient world with an estimated population of 300,000 people, about the same number of people living in Orlando, Florida. And like Orlando, Ephesus had an attraction that drew people from all over the world. Everyone wanted to see the temple for the Greek fertility goddess Artemis. Equivalent in size to an American football field, the temple ranked as one of the largest in the ancient world. Tourism thrived in the city, providing steady revenue. Ephesus was home to hotels, restaurants, and souvenir shops which sold miniature models of the temple made of silver and terra-cotta as keepsakes.[7] Sound like Orlando? Imagine Orlando without Disney influencing you—a difficult task, to be sure. The pastors in Ephesus needed to guard their parishioners from the ever-present, influential pull of paganism. Jesus praises them for doctrinal purity:

> I know your works, your toil and your patient endurance, and how you cannot bear with those who are evil, but have tested those who call themselves apostles and are not, and found them to be false. I know you are enduring patiently and bearing up for my name's sake, and you have not grown weary. (Rev. 2:2–3)

The Ephesians didn't compromise by removing the Gospel's offense to make it more palatable to the culture. Jesus particularly commends them for having no tolerance for the practices of a group called the Nicolaitans: *"Yet this you have: you hate the works of the Nicolaitans, which I also hate"* (Rev. 2:6).

Details regarding the teaching of the Nicolaitans remains a matter of speculation, both in the ancient and modern church. They'll be addressed again in the letter to Pergamum. Based on what we'll observe in that letter, they probably taught that Christians shouldn't be so uptight about participating in or vocally opposing the pagan rituals common to Ephesus.[8] They might have said, "Why invite hostility toward the faith by refusing to participate in the festivals to Artemis?" Or perhaps they would challenge their congregations with, "Why refuse to call the Roman Emperor 'Divine'? How will we reach the world for Jesus if we come off as backward, uneducated, and opposed to the city's prosperity?" To their credit, whatever the Nicolaitans taught and practiced, the Ephesians would have nothing to do with them.

While the Nicolaitans died out quickly, Solomon tells us there is nothing new under the sun (Eccles. 1:9). In the first century and in our own, there are those who dilute, distort, or suppress the fundamental truths of the Gospel. For example, consider how often we hear Christians affirm multiple paths to God even though the Scriptures explicitly tell us that there is *"one God, and there is one mediator between God and men, the man Christ Jesus"* (1 Tim. 2:5). Some Christians say, "Jesus is the way to God for me, but who am I to judge another's path?"[9]

Often driven by the fear of what people will think (John 12:42–43) or ignorance about what the Bible says, statements like this compromise our testimony and tarnish the name of Jesus. The Ephesians understood that compromise of doctrine or practice robs the Savior of the glory due to his name. Consider, Christ lauds the Ephesians in verse 3 for guarding the worth of his name through the refusal to give in to the pressure to compromise: *"I know you are enduring patiently and bearing up for my name's sake, and you have not grown weary"* (Rev. 2:3).

Let me give you an example of how the compromise of doctrine maligns the person and work of Jesus. Former seminary professor Roger Nicole used to tell a story to demonstrate the cost of compromise.[10] Imagine your house is burning down, and you manage to go in a few times to remove everything of value: the children, the photo albums, the family dog, important papers., etc.

While you're terrified at the flames, your neighbor walks over and says, "I want to show you how much I love you." Then he runs into the burning house, you hear screams, and the house falls on him, killing him. Afterward, you would not say, "What love that man showed me!" No. You would say, "That was insane!"

Now imagine the same scenario, and one of your children can't get out of the house because of the fire. No one can get in to save her. Your neighbor says, "I want to show you how much I love you." He goes into the burning house, and the next moment, your child emerges safe, and you hear screams from inside the house, which falls on and kills your neighbor. What would you say about your neighbor in the days, weeks, and years ahead? That he was crazy? Insane? No. You'd say, "How deep that man's love for us!"

What's the point of the story? If Jesus died on the cross when other options or pathways to God were available, his death was not honorable, necessary, or even sane. Instead, his death was foolish and embarrassing. On the other hand, if he is the only way, then what he has done is not only necessary and logical but the most beautiful and powerful act of love ever done on earth. He ran into the fire of his Father's wrath against our sin so we might emerge safe from the flames.

Does this drama still move you? Does your heart still leap with joy and wonder at the thought of Christ hanging on a cursed tree to give you access to the Tree of Life (Rev. 2:7)? Maybe your heart has grown cold. Perhaps you've lost your hunger for him. Possibly the zeal for Jesus that once moved you to tell anyone who would listen to you about Jesus has been replaced by vague guilt that you should be sharing your faith. This cooling-off happened in the hearts of the Ephesians. Once on fire for the Lord, their hearts had iced over even though they were doctrinally precise and contested false practices. And Jesus, still in love with the Ephesians, pursues them with a rebuke.

Pursues for Intimacy

Jesus' words in verses 4 and 5 must have broken the heart of John, the Apostle of Love, who heard Jesus tell his beloved people that they have lost their first love for him:

> But I have this against you, that you have abandoned the love you had at first. Remember therefore from where you have fallen; repent, and do the works you did at first. If not, I will come to you and remove your lampstand from its place, unless you repent. (Rev. 2:4–5)

Maybe your heart breaks at these words because they describe you. You remember the appetite you once had for knowing Christ. You can recall sweet times in prayer when you talked Jesus' ear off, telling him how grateful you were for his grace, but now you find yourself throwing up occasional prayers for a health need, a good day at work, or a meal. Perhaps you remember the thirst you had looking forward to gathering with God's people to worship. But now Sunday feels like one more thing to do in an already busy schedule.

Let me offer a word of encouragement that will lead us into the words of Jesus. If you are dissatisfied with what you are offering to God in terms of witness, worship, and finding deep, satisfying love for Jesus, that is a good thing. A changed heart recognizes that Jesus is worth far more than what we give him. Even wanting to have our hearts fully caught up and saturated with the loving, living waters of Jesus, should be considered a small but important act of worship (cf. Ps. 42:1–2; 63:1). Guy Prentiss Waters offers a helpful word on this topic worth quoting here:

When the believer finds himself grieved over the presence and power of remaining sin and his inability to serve God the way that he wants, the believer should recognize this grief as evidence of the grace of Christ in his life. When the believer is sincerely committed to Christ's lordship and, in spite of himself, finds himself engaged in sin and even, as it were, in the vice grip of sin, it is then that he may and ought to redouble his efforts to fight sin with confidence. How can he do so? He must first remind himself that he belongs to Christ, that there is no condemnation for those who are in Christ Jesus, and that Christ has won for him the resources he needs to wage well the war against sin.[11]

Does your heart long for him today? Then be encouraged, and then: remember, repent, and redo the things you did at first.

Remember

Remember therefore from where you have fallen. (Rev. 2:5)

What does Jesus command the Ephesians and us to remember? Remember the reason you had a first love for Christ in the first place. You loved him because he first loved you (1 John 4:19). Knowing your love for him would fluctuate, before the foundation of the world the Father set his deep affection on you (Eph. 1:4–5). And Jesus, who walks among the lampstands today,[12] *"loves us and has freed us from our sins by his blood"* (Rev. 1:5). And the Spirit, who loves you, grabs you and tells you to remember the love we once had and why that love was there at all. You loved him because the Father, Son, and the Holy Spirit loved you. They still love you. Remember this truth.

Repent

repent (Rev. 2:5)

Secondly, the loving Jesus says, "Repent." In the Bible, repentance is more than a call to stop doing something. Instead, repentance means to turn away from one behavior, thought, or action to another. In this case, Jesus says, "Set your affection back upon me. Don't just *remember* my love for you and the love you once had for me. Seek my face again." Why does Jesus insist upon a sincere love for him? Because he is a jealous God. That can be an odd thing to consider, but when the Lord appeared as fire and smoke at Mt Sinai, he introduced himself to Israel as a jealous God (Ex. 20:5). In fact, the Lord goes even further than the description "jealous," saying in Exodus 34:14 that his name is Jealous. It feels off to describe Jesus as jealous because we typically think of jealousy, as a sign of weakness. Sinful jealousy is rooted in self-doubt, inadequacy, envy, resentment, or frustration with our position.

But what of a jealous God? The Lord is not needy, inadequate, or lacking in self-worth. Moreover, God's jealousy is not a byproduct of a wounded ego. Instead, God's jealousy for his people comes from his holy love for us.[13] While sinful jealousy often leads to the destruction of a relationship, God's holy jealousy for his people is the zealous protection of a relationship ever on the watch for intrusions.

If you're married, you understand that true love for your spouse carries a zeal to protect and keep the relationship. Human marriage is designed to mirror Christ's relationship with his Bride, the Church (Eph. 5:22–33). And just as a husband has a holy jealousy for the love of his wife, so Christ, in calling us to love him afresh, is jealous for your love. J. I. Packer writes about the jealousy of God, saying, "It is his holiness reacting to evil in a way that is morally right and glorious.... It is a praiseworthy zeal on his part to preserve something supremely precious."[14] God is jealous for us not because he is fragile but because we are. And we are easily lured away from "something supremely precious," namely, Jesus Christ. Our need to remember and repent is so serious that Jesus warns the Ephesians, *If not, I will come to you and remove your lampstand*" (Rev. 2:5).[15] He effectively told the Ephesians, "I will un-church your church. Your building may be standing and there may be people in the pews and music in their ears, but I will not be found among you if there is no love for me."[16]

Remember, repent, and finally, redo the things you did at first.

Redo

Jesus commands the Ephesians, and us by extension, to "do the works you did at first" (Rev. 2:5). This counsel, to do the things you did at first, mirrors the very same behavior marriage counselors often suggest to those in struggling marriages. The counselor will encourage you to think about what you did with your spouse when you first met. They'll often ask, "When you two first met how did you show love to one another? Did you buy her flowers? Write him notes? Plan time together? If so, do those things again." I've been that marriage counselor and given that advice. A few times, the couples reported back excellent results. But other couples have given different responses, like "We can't go back again. The trust is gone. There is too much pain. The marriage is so violated that we can't go back again."

Do you hear what Jesus is saying to you? He says to you, his bride, "We can go back again. We can start over. My love has never ceased for you; my mercies never come to an end; they are new every morning" (Lam. 3:22–23).

And maybe you think you can't go back again. But as long as there is an empty tomb in Jerusalem and a Christ who still stands among the lampstands, you can go back. You have been loved extravagantly by the Father, the Son, and the Holy Spirit. A jealous God loves you. And by keeping that love before you, you will never cease to love and worship him.

Study Questions

1. How are the Ephesians' struggles similar to those the Church faces today?
2. 42 percent (footnote number 9) is an alarming number of self-proclaimed evangelicals who believe there are many ways to God. If there are many ways to God, what does that suggest about the cross of Christ?
3. Remember—Remember how you felt the first time you realized Jesus ran into the flames of his Father's wrath so that you might emerge unscathed. How did it change the way you lived?
4. Repent—In what ways have you forgotten your first love for Jesus? What would genuine repentance look like for you? What would you need to turn away from to turn back to Jesus?
5. Redo—What things could you begin doing again that you once did in your love for Jesus? Do you trust that he will give you the very thing he commands?

---

1. Richard Bauckham, *The Theology of the Book of Revelation* (Cambridge University Press, 2012), 16.
2. The order in which the cities are addressed probably reflects the route the messenger traveled around the province of Asia, beginning in Ephesus. See Bauckham, *The Theology of the Book of Revelation*, 12.
3. William Hendriksen, *More than Conquerors* (Baker Books, 1998), 58.
4. G.K. Beale, *The Book of Revelation: A Commentary on the Greek Text* (Grand Rapids MI: Eerdmans, 2013), 218–219; Vern S. Poythress, *The Returning King: A Guide to the Book of Revelation* (P&R, 2000), 85.
5. Angels representing nations and even individuals find expression in the Book of Daniel

(10:20–21; 12:1) and Matthew (18:10), respectively. While purely speculative, John may be suggesting that each church has an angelic representative before the Lord.
6. For an overview of Ephesus, see Harold W. Hoehner, *Ephesians: An Exegetical Commentary* (Baker Academic, Grand Rapids, 2002) 78–89.
7. I. Howard Marshall, *The Book of Acts: An Introduction and Commentary* (Grand Rapids MI: Eerdmans, 1980), 317. See also Acts 19:24, in which one such vendor (Demetrius) saw Paul's preaching as a threat to his business.
8. See G.K. Beale, *The Book of Revelation: A Shorter Commentary* (Eerdmans, 2015), 57. Also, for an educational and enjoyable historical novel set in the late 90s Ephesus, see David A. deSilva, *A Week in the Life of Ephesus* (IVP Academic, Downer's Grove, Illinois, 2020).
9. In the 2020 Ligonier Ministries' State of Theology survey, researchers discovered that nearly half (42 percent) of those professing to be Evangelical Christians believe that "God accepts the worship of all religions." For more results, see https://thestateoftheology.com/
10. This story is recounted by Tim Keller in "Boasting in the Cross," Redeemer Presbyterian Church, New York City, May 24, 1998.
11. Guy Prentiss Waters, *The Life and Theology of Paul* (Reformation Trust Publishing, Samford, Florida, 2017), 89.
12. Jesus's description of the one who walks among the seven golden lampstands suggests an intimate awareness of all that is happening in the churches. See Beale, *The Book of Revelation: A Shorter Commentary*, 55.
13. God's jealousy is not limited to his relationship with his people. Instead, he is also jealous for his glory and honor (Ex. 20:5; Isa. 48:11).
14. J. I. Packer, *Knowing God* (InterVarsity Press, Downers Grove, Illinois, 1973), 169–170.
15. The moving of the lampstand may be an allusion to the historical reality of Ephesus having been "moved" several times due to the gradual silting up of its river, the Caÿster. See Poythress, 85.
16. David E. Aune, *Revelation 1–5*, Word Biblical Commentary (Nashville TN: Thomas Nelson, 1997), 155.

4

THE CROSS BEFORE THE CROWN
REVELATION 2:8-11

How do you get the attention of a fully-distracted Air Force pilot? The United States and British Air Forces sought to solve this situation years ago. It's incredibly difficult to communicate with pilots in combat with all of the sounds, lights, and instruments vying for their attention.

Many pilots naturally tune out messages from weapons systems, flight systems, and air traffic control to focus on flying.

However, tuning out signals and voices comes at a cost; essential and crucial warnings about incoming missiles or plane malfunctions cannot be ignored. But in complex combat situations, even the most focused pilots often miss crucial communications. The British Air Force tried to solve the problem by adding a lovely female voice called Nagging Nelly that would override all communication in the cockpit with warnings like "You are about to stall" or "Incoming missile." But Nagging Nelly was less effective than what the United States Air Force initiated. Instead of piping in a female voice, they discovered that a child's voice is far more attention-grabbing.

But not just any child's voice works—it must be the voice of the pilot's own child. When a pilot hears his or her own child say, "Daddy! You are about to stall the plane" or "Mommy!! Check your fuel," it works. When all the other warnings, voices, and flashing lights fail to get the pilot's attention, the voice of a relationship breaks through.[1]

We live in a very chaotic and trying time, not only in our nation but also in world history. At times we can feel like distracted pilots with incoming alarms from talking heads on television, toxic voices in social media, and our own conflicting responsive voices. These can all compete like so many warning signals vying for our attention. Those noises can cause anxiety, uncertainty, anger, or fear. Or we might tune them out and become numb to the chaos.

To break through the noise, we need to hear the voice of a relationship, of one who loves us. We need to hear Jesus. If we listen to him today, he'll instruct us to endure with him to the end faithfully.

How does this passage help us to endure? It calls us to set our eyes on Jesus, embrace the inevitable, and ask for boldness.

Set Your Eyes on Jesus

In each of the letters to the churches, Jesus introduces himself with an element from John's initial vision of Jesus (Rev. 1:17–18). For example, Jesus presented himself to the church in Ephesus as the one who walks among the lampstands. In each case, the attribute that Jesus recalls at the beginning of each letter suits each church's need. To the Smyrnans, Jesus reminds them that he is *"the first and the last, who died and came to life"* (Rev. 2:8).[2]

In short, Jesus says he is the Divine Sovereign over all history. He transcends time and governs all that comes to pass in human history. Therefore, whatever the church in Smyrna faced came as no surprise to Jesus, nor, as we will see momentarily, apart from his own will for them (Rev. 2:10b).

The church in Smyrna faced the challenges of both economic hardship and imprisonment[3] for their faith:

> *I know your tribulation and your poverty (but you are rich) and the slander of those who say they are Jews and are not, but are a synagogue of Satan. Do not fear what you are about to suffer. Behold, the devil is about to throw some of you into prison.* (Rev. 2:9–10)

A little history here will help us understand Jesus' words. Smyrna had a reputation for fierce patriotism and devotion to the prosperity of the Roman Empire. Even before Rome rose to the strength and renown that it possessed at the end of the first century, Smyrna stood as a solid ally for Rome. The faithfulness and loyalty of the Smyrnans to Rome became legendary.[4] Smyrna's patriotism included the worship of Emperor Domitian (81–96), who not only thought of himself as divine but also demanded that he be addressed as "lord and god" by everyone in the Roman Empire.[5]

There was one group, however, the Romans exempted from showing this type of honor: the Jews. They knew the Jews were very particular about their monotheism and the use of the names of Lord and God. Therefore the Romans didn't force the Jews to participate in the standard requirement of emperor worship. Instead, they mandated that the Jews pray for the emperor—not to him—and imposed a tax on the Jews, which funded other projects.[6]

For a time, Christians were also safe from required emperor worship under the umbrella of Judaism. But as the Church continued to grow and more Gentiles were added to the mix, it became clear to the Romans that Christians should no longer be viewed as a sect of Judaism. As a consequence, Rome removed the exception to emperor worship the Church once enjoyed. Additionally, it appears from the words in verse 9 that the Jews in Smyrna sought out Roman authorities to expose the Christians. They might have said, "These Christians are not Jews. They are enemies of the State. They are anarchists! Make them participate in emperor worship and the feasts honoring the gods, or put them to death."[7]

Jesus said to the Smyrnans, "I know the slander heaped upon you." My friend, Jesus knows when you are maligned for his name. He knows that you're told you are close-minded for saying there is one way of salvation, judgmental for talking about sin in our culture, and homophobic because you testify to the Lord's design for men and women. Jesus says, "I know."

And he reminds us that behind such labels, accusations, and slander is the enemy of your soul:

> *I know your tribulation and your poverty (but you are rich) and the slander of those who say that they are Jews and are not, but are a synagogue of Satan.* (Rev. 2:9)

We must not take Jesus' words as anti-Semitic. Jesus was, and remains, a Jewish man, just like John, Peter, and Paul. Jesus is not anti-Semitic—he is anti-sin. In calling the Jews of Smyrna a "synagogue of Satan," he pulls back the veil to disclose what is genuinely behind any organization, individual, or piece of legislation that denies the lordship of Jesus Christ or slanders his people—Satan. Satan's name means "the accuser," and whenever you are falsely accused for standing with Jesus, behind that accusation stands the enemy of your soul. Keep that in mind when you're tempted to compromise truth to avoid labels and accusations. When you compromise, you cede territory to the accuser.

Jesus is the first and the last, the sovereign Lord of history. He knows what you are facing. If they hated him, they will hate you. If they persecuted him, they will do the same to you. (cf. John 15:18–20) These are promises Jesus makes to us. Thus, if we are to endure, we must embrace the inevitable.

Embrace the Inevitable

As a consequence of their faith, some Christians in Smyrna were incarcerated:

> *Do not fear what you are about to suffer. Behold, the devil is about to throw some of you into prison, that you may be tested, and for ten days you will have tribulation. Be faithful unto death, and I will give you the crown of life.* (Rev. 2:10)

Jesus particularizes a general promise to the Smyrna Christians which he makes to us all: follow me, and the world will hate you. We could also turn to the promise made by the Apostle Paul: *"All who desire to live a godly life in Christ Jesus will be persecuted"* (2 Tim. 3:12). We must be clear on this point: as the cross went before the crown for Jesus, so the cross goes before our crown as well. Jesus first commands us to take up our cross (Matt. 16:24). Only later does he promise *"I will give you the crown of life"* (Rev. 2:10).[8]

For some Smyrnan Christians, their cross included imprisonment for ten days. Jesus appears to allude to an event in the book of Daniel when he and three of his fellow Jews were tempted to eat and drink food dedicated to the gods of Babylon. They refused to participate in the pagan festivities and were tested for ten days to see if they could live on just vegetables and water (Dan. 1:8–14). Perhaps Jesus places Daniel and his companions before the Smyrnans' minds, who likewise carried a cross before being crowned.

You and I may not get thrown into prison for the Gospel, but this doesn't mean we're free from the threat of persecution. There are severe forms of persecution that many Christians have faced, like prison, torture, and murder. But Jesus tells us that persecution can come through those who revile you and utter evil against you for his name's sake (Matt. 5:11). Your cross may not look or feel like the one the Smyrnans took up. But you'll bear a cross first if you will later receive the crown (Luke 9:23). Jesus warns us of the inevitable hatred that will find you if you are public in your testimony for Christ. This promise should shape our expectations for our brief time in this world.

But notice that Jesus promises to make use of whatever befalls us. He tells the Church not to fear because he has an overriding purpose in all of their trials:

> *Do not fear what you are about to suffer. Behold, the devil is about to throw some of you into prison, that you may be tested, and for ten days you will have tribulation. Be faithful unto death, and I will give you the crown of life.* (Rev. 2:10)

Jesus opened this letter with the reminder that he is the sovereign Lord over all of history: *"I am the first and the last"* (Rev. 1:17). Therefore, even if Satan targets you through malicious deeds of men and women, you must not fear. As the sovereign Lord over that hatred, Jesus overrides the Devil's purposes. That's what Jesus wants us to understand when he tells the Smyrnans that their trial is used by the Lord *"that you may be tested"* (Rev. 2:10). The Lord frustrated Satan's plan of destroying Jesus on Good Friday. In the same way, the Lord frustrates the wicked design behind Satanic attacks on the Church by blessing those who respond in obedient faith. Peter, James, and John all tell us that the Lord tests his people through adversity, and these tests are to be regarded as a blessing (1 Pet. 4:12; Jas. 1:12; John 6:6).

Why does the Lord test his people? It is certainly not because he wonders how we might respond; his knowledge is infinite and infallible. Jesus can tell the Smyrnans that their trial will be severe but brief (ten days) because he is the all-knowing, sovereign Lord over their suffering.

Therefore, the Lord sends tests to us, not for his enlightenment but for ours. How do you know if your faith is genuine? You know when you are forced to exercise it.

For example, how do you know if you trust the Lord with your future? He will test our faith through adversity. That adversity has many forms: sometimes he puts a politician you differ with into the Oval Office, sends a frightening health diagnosis, allows the loss of income, or permits a child or grandchild to wander from the faith. Through these tests, we may know if we genuinely believe in the Lord's care for us.

Another example: how do you know when you are more grounded in what the Lord says about you than what our culture says about you? Your answers to questions like "What do you believe?" or "Are you a Christian?" will show you something about your heart. And when the Lord reveals areas where we aren't trusting him, we fall at his feet saying, "I believe; help my unbelief" (Mark 9:24).

And when he reveals that we have passed a test, we take comfort in our soul because it means God is at work within us. And we give him all the glory, praise, and honor due to his name. In this world, you will have trouble. Jesus directs us to cast our gaze on his sovereign hand, which has his purposes in our adversity, and therefore calls us not to fear and to be faithful to the end (Rev. 2:10). To do so, you will need to be bold.

Ask for Boldness

Most readers will recognize the seismic shift in our country's attitude toward Christians and Christianity.[9] A generation ago, our society had a generally positive view of Christianity. In the 1980s, church attendance was fundamental to the definition of an upstanding citizen. At that time, basic Judeo-Christian moral norms were the bedrock of our society's moral norms.

During the 1990s and early 2000s, Christianity fell from having a positive reputation to a neutral one. Christianity no longer had a privileged position in the culture but was not highly disliked either. In an increasingly postmodern, pluralistic society, faith in Jesus was regarded as an allowable option.

However, around 2014, just before the Supreme Court of the United States ruled on the Obergefell decision that granted same-sex couples the right to marry, the attitude toward Christianity shifted from neutral to negative. Now, fewer than ten years later, people generally view Christianity as a social negative, especially in elite circles of society. The traditional Christian values that once formed the bedrock of our country are now rejected and viewed as a threat to the public good. Again, much of this you already know.

Many Christians remain silent about their faith or have abandoned core biblical teachings because they fear being disliked, shunned, or hated by their fellow citizens. What would Jesus say to us today? He certainly wouldn't tell you to pity yourself or adopt a defeatist or victim attitude. Perhaps he would tell us: "For such a time as this, I have you right here, right now. Don't be afraid, don't retreat, and certainly don't pity yourself."

Christian, you are on the winning side. You live for a king who cannot lose, and you are to burn as light in a dark world that cannot win. There is absolutely no room for Christians to adopt a victim mentality. Christ's victory over death is your victory.[10] Christ's victory over Satan and his minions will be yours as well. You will share Christ's inheritance of the renewed heaven and earth. What are we to fear, then? In what way shall we pity ourselves? None! We are more than conquerors through him who loved us (Rom. 8:37). Jesus tells us not to fear. To be faithful unto death. And we respond by asking him to make us bold so that the name of Jesus would be marvelous in the eyes of those who hate us (Acts 4:23–31). The Lord will always answer such prayers in the affirmative.

About 260 years after Jesus addressed the church in Smyrna, another Roman Emperor came along who hated Christians. His name was Julian. As emperor, one of his goals was to eliminate Christianity from Rome and reinstate the pagan practices of former rulers.

One story[11] from Julian's time is about a Christian man named Agathon. Julian knew Agathon was a Christian, so he mocked him, saying, "How is your carpenter god doing nowadays? The one from Nazareth? Is he still finding work to keep himself busy? Does he ever cease to build mansions in the sky?" Agathon responded, "He will only cease to build a mansion long enough to build a coffin for your empire."

No one intimidated Agathon. He knew what side he was on—a side that could not lose—and that his adversaries could not win. So may you, likewise, speak and live boldly.

Study Questions

1. Look at Jesus. He is the first and the last, overseeing what we are suffering, and he has a purpose in it. What does this do to your heart's posture toward Jesus?
2. The phrase "synagogue of Satan" may sound strange or harsh to our ears, but consider who is behind the people and organizations opposed to Christ. Think about to whom you are giving ground when you compromise. In what ways does this sober and encourage you?
3. Embrace the inevitable: Assessing your own heart, how have you responded to the hard promise that you will be hated for Jesus' sake?
4. The Lord tests his people through adversity. So why is this a blessing?

5. Ask for boldness: Do not pity yourself; you are on the winning side. Instead, spend time in prayer asking the Lord to make you bold for Jesus.

---

1. Story told by Bryan Chapell, "I Am the Good Shepherd," Grace Presbyterian Church, Peoria, Illinois, December 22, 2013.
2. Jesus' description as the "first and last" are explicit references to the Lord's self-designations in Isa. 41:4, 44:6, and 48:12.
3. The localized persecution the Christians in Smyrna faced fits well with what we know about the localized persecutions under Domitian (81–96 AD). Severe persecutions occurred under Nero in AD 64–65, but we have no record of them outside Rome. Therefore, it seems best to place the date of John's Revelation during the reign of Domitian. For a brief overview of the issue of dating, see Vern S. Poythress, *The Returning King: A Guide to the Book of Revelation* (P&R, 2000), 49–53. For a more extensive examination, see G.K. Beale, *The Book of Revelation: A Commentary on the Greek Text* (Grand Rapids MI: Eerdmans, 2013), 4–27.
4. William Hendriksen, *More than Conquerors* (Baker Books, 1998), 63.
5. Vern S. Poythress, *The Returning King*, 50.
6. And especially the upkeep of the temple of Jupiter Capitolinus in Rome. See Ibid., 52.
7. See Acts 13:45, 50; 14:2–7, 19 for examples of how the Jews would incite Gentile leaders to prevent Christianity's spread.
8. The offer of a crown may be an allusion to the prominent topographical features of Smyrna's buildings atop the hill Pagos, which was called "the crown of Smyrna." See Hendriksen, *More than Conquerors*, 63. Additionally, Smyrna was home to the goddess Cybele who was pictured on coins with a mural crown atop her head. In contrast to these crowns, Jesus offers to impart the true crown of life. See Poythress, *The Returning King*, 87.
9. Much of this cultural analysis is a summary of Aaron M. Renn's article "The Three Worlds of Evangelicalism" in *First Things* no. 320 (February 2022): 25–31.
10. Jesus promises the Christian that they will not be *"hurt by the second death"* (Rev. 2:11). At this point in Revelation, the "second death" hasn't been explained. But in 21:8, it will be revealed as those whose *"portion will be in the lake that burns with fire and sulfur."*
11. While this story is regularly reported as "source unknown" and therefore may be apocryphal, it is powerful nonetheless. Agathon is also sometimes listed as Agaton. I do hope the story is true.

5

HIDDEN MANNA, WHITE STONE, NEW NAME

REVELATION 2:12-17

One of my favorite books is John Bunyan's classic, *The Pilgrim's Progress*, the famous allegory of the Christian life. It tells the story of a man named Christian, who travels from his home city, the City of Destruction, to another called the Celestial City. Along the way, Christian traveled through a village called  Vanity, which held a year-long festival called Vanity Fair. The festival was called Vanity Fair because the merchants sold their products along with false promises of long-lasting happiness. They offered a wide range of items including new homes, satisfying jobs, prestigious titles, and various forms of pleasure. Some merchants sold prostitutes; others peddled a perfect spouse, healthy children, and good health.

No matter what anyone thought would solve their inner emptiness, a vendor at Vanity Fair could offer an empty promise of satisfaction, such as an item, person, title, possession, or state of being. Many of the items at Vanity Fair were good: homes, a faithful spouse, loving children, a positive reputation, and health. But gifts from our Creator were presented as ultimate things. The merchants sold God-substitutes that attempted to fill voids that only the Creator can.

In Bunyan's story, Christian faces the same challenge as anyone striving to reach Jesus—only one path leads to the Celestial City, and it goes through Vanity Fair (1 Cor. 5:9–10; John 17:15). As we make our way toward our eternal home, we often encounter vendors who try to distract us from our path. They shout, "Buy from us! You need a new home! A better spouse! Respect at work! More money in the bank! You're miserable because you lack this one thing!" Vanity Fair resides both on outside of us as well as on the inside. Each of us has that one dangling carrot right out in front of us, always just out of reach, saying to us, "If only you had this one last thing, you would be happy."

Going back to Bunyan's tale, Christian recognized that he was veering off the path, tempted to believe the lies of Vanity Fair's vendors. So he put his fingers in his ears and, with the words of the psalmist, prayed, *"Turn my eyes from looking at worthless things"* (Ps. 119:37). That should be every Christian's prayer when he or she feels the temptation to turn good things into ultimate things: *"Turn my eyes from looking at worthless things."*

But it is not enough to look away from these things; we must set our eyes on something better. After all, you're designed for joy, pleasure, intimacy, safety, and friendship. So, we cannot simply turn away from the empty promises of these things. Instead, we must turn to the one who alone can fulfill them.[1]

Before we consider how Jesus sets himself as the provisional presence the church in Pergamum needs, we will first consider the problem they faced.

The Problem

A large city with an estimated population of 120,000, built atop a high, rocky elevation, Pergamum proudly boasted numerous temples to various pagan gods.[2] The city hosted an enormous altar to Zeus, shaped to look like a throne.[3] In addition to Zeus, the pagan cult of the serpent god of healing and medicine, Asclepius thrived in Pergamum. Artisans depicted Asclepius carrying a serpent-entwined staff, which remains one of the primary symbols of medicine today often affixed to hospital buildings, medical staff uniforms, and ambulances. Pergamum also housed the first and most important temple built for Roman Emperor worship. Pergamum has been called the Washington, DC of the region,[4] not only because of its firm allegiance to Emperor worship but also due to the high concentration of Roman soldiers and politicians in the city. From Pergamum, Rome's wishes were made clear and enforced in Asia Minor. These three features of Pergamum —the altar to Zeus, the worship of the serpent god Asclepius, and the center of imperial worship—probably stand behind Jesus' words in verse thirteen:

> *I know where you dwell, where Satan's throne is. Yet you hold fast my name, and you did not deny my faith even in the days of Antipas my faithful witness, who was killed among you, where Satan dwells.* (Rev. 2:13)

It's important to appreciate the challenges that Christians in Pergamum faced in maintaining their public faith in Jesus while also inviting conflicts with non-Christians.

The usual practice and expectation of these Greek cities were that each city resident would honor the local gods. People celebrated the gods in different ways, including an annual festival that honored local deities known for blessing different professions. These annual feasts to the gods often concluded with ritual fornication.[5] To refuse to participate in these feasts signaled indifference, ingratitude, and treason against Rome and ushered in severe economic and social consequences. One of Pergamum's own, Antipas, about whom we know nothing except what we read in verse 13, was put to death for not renouncing his faith in Christ.[6] And Jesus honors Antipas by calling him "my faithful witness," the same descriptor of Jesus in Revelation 1:5. Jesus honors Antipas for his witness, and he will honor us as well.

So what is the problem in Pergamum? After all, Jesus commends them for not renouncing their faith, even when persecution took the life of one of their own. The problem is that they were tolerating some within the church who advocated ways of avoiding persecution through assimilation:

> *But I have a few things against you: you have some there who hold the teaching of Balaam, who taught Balak to put a stumbling block before the sons of Israel, so that they might eat food sacrificed to idols and practice sexual immorality. So also you have some who hold the teaching of the Nicolaitans.* (Rev. 2:14–15)

Jesus refers to an Old Testament story involving a false prophet named Balaam (Num. 22–24). The book of Numbers tells us that when Israel was traveling to the Promised Land from Egypt, the King of Moab, Balak, feared the loss of his Kingdom. So, he hired a prophet, Balaam, and promised him a small fortune to curse Israel. Not wanting to miss out on an easy payday, Balaam agreed to the deal, but when he tried to curse Israel, the Lord filled his mouth with benedictions for them. Now angered at Balaam, Balak offered him more money to curse Israel, but again, Balaam tried, and the Lord filled his mouth with blessings. Balaam attempted to curse Israel four times, and he gave out four blessings instead.

Finally, Balaam convinced Balak to try another tactic: send in some prostitutes to lure the men of Israel away from fidelity to the Lord (Num. 25:1–2; 31:16). Balak followed through, and consequently, numerous individuals in Israel engaged in idol worship, celebrated other deities, and committed acts of promiscuity. By the time we reach the first century, Balaam's name had become associated with those who teach ungodly practices for financial gain.[7]

It seems probable that a faction within the church of Pergamum taught the flock that they could avoid being ostracized, thrown into jail like the Smyrnans, or killed like Antipas by dulling their public witness. Perhaps they said, "There is no need to stick out. How will we reach unbelievers if we refuse to go where they are and do the things they do? We know what is true in our hearts. Jesus is Lord. Not Zeus, Asclepius, or the emperor. Go to the feasts and burn the incense. Otherwise, you might lose your livelihood." These false teachers functioned like the vendors at Vanity Fair: protect yourself from sticking out, guard your reputation, preserve your income, and maintain your social circles. You need to blend in. I'm sure their arguments sounded reasonable, plausible, and sophisticated.

And that's precisely why we need to hear Jesus' stern words for these false teachers:

> *And to the angel of the church in Pergamum write: "The words of him who has the sharp two-edged sword.... Therefore repent. If not, I will come to you soon and war against them with the sword of my mouth." (Rev. 2:12, 16)*

There is no point in trying to blunt Jesus' words. Jesus threatens the sword against those who teach or practice half-hearted allegiance to him.[8] In the end, it is not Rome that they should be concerned about, but Jesus. He warns:

> *For whoever is ashamed of me and of my words, of him will the Son of Man be ashamed when he comes in his glory and the glory of the Father and of the holy angels. (Luke 9:26)*

While few of us today are invited to participate in feasts dedicated to pagan gods, we know the same temptation to soften our witness to protect ourselves. Sometimes we blunt our witness to remain in certain social circles. Or to preserve business relationships. I, too, hear the vendors of Vanity Fair calling out to me at times: If you want to maintain your reputation, don't say there is only one way of salvation. That's narrow-minded.

Don't say God created all things. That's anti-science. Don't say that a Creator has designed sexuality to be used in one way. That's judgmental.

I've been called all of those things, either to my face or through email, and I wouldn't say I like hearing any of them. I don't like rejection any more than you do. So I need to listen to the warning from a sword-wielding Jesus. But I also need to see him extend the offer of hidden manna, a white stone, and a new name.

The Provision

> *He who has an ear, let him hear what the Spirit says to the churches. To the one who conquers I will give some of the hidden manna, and I will give him a white stone, with a new name written on the stone that no one knows except the one who receives it.* (Rev. 2:17)

Just as the Lord sustained his people in the Old Testament wilderness through the miraculous provision of manna, Jesus promises to do the same. The Lord sustained his people for forty years as they made their way to the Promised Land through this daily provision of bread. Jesus promises here to feed the one who comes to him hungry for boldness, courage, and faithfulness to him. Jesus assured the crowds, *"I am the bread that came down from heaven"* (John 6:41). He still faithfully feeds hungry pilgrims who look to him. Are you asking him for opportunities to be a faithful witness, like your brother Antipas? Are you asking for boldness and courage? Are you making use of the opportunities when they present themselves?

Jesus also promises a white stone. What is this white stone? Jesus may be blending two ancient practices into one with this promise. The first practice consisted of casting a white or black stone as a vote in court cases.[9] If you judged the defendant accused to be innocent, for example, you would cast a white[10] stone; if guilty, black. Jesus assures his people that he'll reverse the guilty verdict the world has placed on his faithful witnesses.

In addition, another practice also used a white stone. When kings or dignitaries invited people to a special event like a wedding or a feast, guests would often be given a white stone with their name written on it.[11] The Christians in Pergamum were tempted to go to elaborate feasts to pagan gods, but the promise of a white stone invited them to the great messianic banquet called the *"marriage supper of the Lamb"* (Rev. 19:9). To the one who overcomes, Jesus will grant admission to a feast that will be unending and ever-satisfying.

And what is a marriage without giving the groom's name to the bride?[12]

Just as a groom from antiquity to the present day shares his name with his bride, Jesus will place his name upon us.[13] In this world, you will be hated, reviled, and called all sorts of names for Jesus' sake. However, Jesus promises that those who hold fast to him will bear his name for all eternity and be constantly bathed in his delight (Isa. 62:4).

Christian, from whom do you seek acceptance? What shapes your identity? The temporary approval of man or the eternal embrace of God? Be wise, and feed on the manna Jesus gives until he hands you a white stone, admitting you to the eternal marriage supper, where you will be crowned eternally with Jesus' name.

Study Questions

1. Consider the road to the promised land that leads straight through Vanity. Do you hear the merchants calling out to you? "The perfect spouse, right this way! More money than you can imagine down this path! Stop at this booth for obedient children!" What do the vendors call to you? What is that one thing that completes your thought, "If only I had _____, I'd be happy."
2. The Problem. The people of Pergamum would've faced immense pressures to blunt their witness to protect themselves from risk. How are they similar to the pressure Christians face today? In what ways have you advocated, or participated in, compromise to avoid being ostracized?
3. The Provision. Hidden manna, a white stone, a new name. Meditate on these three promises, and write down how they inform your thoughts, adjust your feelings, and change your actions.
4. Hidden manna—the Lord is promising to sustain you. He will feed you with courage, boldness, and confidence!
5. A white stone—when you stand accused, the Lord has cast your verdict and pronounced you innocent!
6. A new name—the name on the stone serves as your invitation to the wedding feast! And more than that, you are the bride!

---

1. Otherwise, as Peter tells us, we will be like the dog that returns to its vomit and the sow, who, after washing, returns to wallow in the mire (2 Pet. 2:22).
2. David E. Aune, *Revelation 1–5*, Word Biblical Commentary (Nashville TN: Thomas Nelson, 1997), 194.

3. G.K. Beale, *The Book of Revelation: A Commentary on the Greek Text* (Grand Rapids MI: Eerdmans, 2013), 246.
4. Michael Wilcock, *The Message of Revelation* (InterVarsity Press, Downers Grove, 1975), 47.
5. G.K. Beale, *The Book of Revelation: A Commentary on the Greek Text*, 248–249.
6. Legend suggests that Antipas was roasted alive inside the torture device called a brazen bull. See Leon Morris, *Revelation* (Grand Rapids MI: Eerdmans, 1984), 67.
7. G.K. Beale, *The Book of Revelation: A Shorter Commentary* (Eerdmans, 2015), 66.
8. Jesus' use of a sword here may allude to the original threat Balaam heard from the Angel of the Lord, who, while holding a sword, told Balaam to cease opposing Israel (Num. 22:23, 31). Additionally, it was with the sword that Balaam's life was eventually taken (Num. 31:8). See G.K. Beale, *The Book of Revelation: A Shorter Commentary*, 67.
9. See Acts 26:10. See also Ben Witherington III, *The Acts of the Apostles: A Socio-Rhetorical Commentary* (Grand Rapids MI: Eerdmans, 1998), 741–742 footnote 481.
10. White is the color associated with purity, innocence, and righteousness in Rev. 3:4; 6:2; 19:8–9; 14.
11. G.K. Beale, *The Book of Revelation: A Shorter Commentary*, 68.
12. Cf. 3:12; 21:12; 22:3–4 for further developments of the promised name given to Christians.
13. See Isa. 62:2; 65:15, where the Lord promises to wed himself to Israel, thus giving her a new name.

6

INTOLERANT, REDEMPTIVE LOVE
REVELATION 2:18-29

When I was in elementary school, my family moved from the urban sprawl of Chicago to a small, rural town in Indiana. In one of the first projects my father and I did at our new home, we made a chicken coop. While neither of us knew what the chickens' maintenance would demand, we both wanted an opportunity for me to raise and tend to a few animals on my own. We completed the building, fenced off a small section where the chickens could free-range, and filled the yard with several hens and one very happy rooster.

Everything went well for months until I left a few eggs behind for the hens to sit on, hoping their work would bring new chickens. I remember waiting and checking daily for signs of life inside the eggs. My waiting paid off when, one morning, I noticed one of the eggs had a small hole on the surface. I could see a tiny beak moving back and forth, and nothing could contain my excitement.

However, I soon felt frustrated and impatient because, in my opinion, the chick took too long to free itself from the shell. Ten minutes of watching and waiting turned to twenty, thirty, and then forty-five minutes of what appeared to be fruitless struggling for the chick. Then I made the foolish decision to help the chick. Piece by piece, I picked away fragments of the surface entrapping this little life until I saw its fully formed body before my eyes. Free at last!

At first, the chick looked satisfied at the outcome. But it turns out I had made the situation far worse. That long process of chipping away at the eggshell develops the chicken's lungs and leg and wing muscles. When I took away that work, I drastically reduced its chance of survival outside the shell. In the end, eliminating what I perceived as an unpleasant or harmful experience irreparably damaged the animal, and it died.

So too, the gospel message suffers damage when Christians attempt to avoid, water down, or explain away what they regard as harsh, unpalatable doctrines in the Bible. In an effort to make the Gospel more attractive, many people pick away parts and pieces of God's word, doing irreparable damage, to the Church and its witness.

In this letter to the Christians in Thyatira, we encounter a group of people unwilling to do hard things. They have chosen a path that, on the surface, appears kind and loving but will lead to destruction. Jesus sets himself before this church to warn and rebuke them. Jesus is so angry that he threatens to kill several people in the congregation if they do not repent. Jesus shows us a type of love that refuses to tolerate certain behaviors, lifestyles, and worldviews. Therefore, for the church to reflect its Savior and faithfully speak on his behalf, it must exercise a love that can definitely seem intolerant. But the aim of our Lord's intolerant love is always redemptive.

Intolerant Love

We've noticed that each of the letters to the seven churches recalls the vision of Jesus that John saw in Chapter 1. And each opening description of Jesus is in some way relevant to each church's particular need. As we'll see, the church in Thyatira tolerates immoral teaching and lifestyles. Therefore, Jesus introduces himself with eyes of fire, representing the flames of judgment,[1] and feet of burnished bronze,[2] with which he will trample his enemies:

> *And to the angel of the church in Thyatira write: "The words of the Son of God, who has eyes like a flame of fire, and whose feet are like burnished bronze."* (Rev. 2:18)

Before Jesus addresses what's wrong in Thyatira, he commends them for many things: labor in works, love, faith, service, and patient endurance. They sound like a friendly, caring congregation that loved and served one another. I imagine they warmly greeted newcomers and encouraged them to get plugged into the life and community of the church. He's not dismissive of what he finds commendable in the Thyatirans, nor does he ignore it. He doesn't crush their spirits by rushing past the fact that they are known for their works, love, faith, and service to others.

Christian, remember that this is the same Jesus who meets you today. He knows about your service to others, your many prayers, and your desire to love and serve him. Keep that in mind when he corrects, convicts, or disciplines you. And bring that same Christ-like charity to others when we confront or disagree with one another. Let's work to cultivate the ability and practice of publicly celebrating commendable things in each other, even when navigating complicated matters.

The Thyatiran Christians loved people, but they also blindly affirmed or ignored immoral behavior and false teaching. Somewhere along the line, their warm hearts overtook clear minds. John writes:

> *But I have this against you, that you tolerate that woman Jezebel, who calls herself a prophetess and is teaching and seducing my servants to practice sexual immorality and to eat food sacrificed to idols. I gave her time to repent, but she refuses to repent of her sexual immorality.* (Rev. 2:20–21)

It's probable that this false teacher, described here as Jezebel, mirrored the famous Jezebel of the Old Testament, the wife of King Ahab, who gained notoriety for introducing Baal worship to her husband and later to all of Israel (1 Kgs. Chps. 16–22).

Coming back to Thyatira, a false teacher instructed the church, in the words of Jesus, to *"practice sexual immorality and to eat food sacrificed to idols"* (Rev. 2:20). The exact nature of her teaching is unknown,[3] but most likely like the false teachers in Pergamum, she taught a person could avoid being hated and ostracized in the community by going with the flow, to fit in with the crowds: "Go to the feasts and honor the emperor as a god." Perhaps she even taught that Christians need not be such prudes regarding sexuality:[4] "What matters is what's in your heart, not what we do with our bodies." Therefore, she may have encouraged participation in the ritual prostitution common to these feasts.

Additionally, based on verse 24, she may have called her teaching *"the deep things of God,"* believing that God had enlightened her, making her teaching profound and far more agreeable. But Jesus, more accurately and with biting sarcasm, traces her teaching back to a different entity: *"the deep things of Satan."*[5] But sadly, for all the love the Thyatirans showed, they erred in tolerating Jezebel and her teaching.

Today, people often regard tolerance as the ultimate embodiment of love and the most esteemed of all principles. Many churches, with their ministers, have been caught up in the tolerance wave, longing to be known as those who will make no evaluation or judgment of others' lifestyles. They believe that a wholesale tolerance of all opinions and worldviews is the supreme expression of love, and they proudly advertise themselves as affirming, non-judgmental, and welcoming to all.

We do well to remember that the Church belongs to Jesus (Eph. 1:22–23; Col. 1:18). As the king and head over the Church, Jesus has all authority to establish expectations for his community. He never instructs us to be a community known for embracing all behaviors, worldviews, and opinions.

Instead, he forbids lax attitudes toward sinful mindsets and behaviors. Paul wrote to the Corinthians, teaching that those who consider themselves Christians but refuse to repent of unchecked greed, idolatry, lying, and sexual promiscuity, are not welcome in the church (1 Cor. 5:1–2, 11. See also, Matt. 18:17; Tit. 3:10–11). To welcome such people, as Thyatira did, failed to love them enough to warn them of the disaster that awaits any who live and die in rebellion against Jesus.

We shouldn't drive away sinners from the Church in an effort to rid it of sin. That would leave no one in the pulpit or pews. Instead, it is dangerous to bear the "Christian" and refuse to repent of sin. And love demands a clear warning to those in danger. If someone refuses to stop sinning, the Church must show love by expelling them from the community. When the Church exercises that drastic measure—often after long months of meetings, prayers, and tears—they mirror what is true of Jesus; namely, he resists the proud but gives grace to the humble and the broken in spirit (Jas. 4:6; 1 Pet. 5:5).

Sadly, Jezebel's time was up. Verse 21 indicates that Jesus gave her time to turn away from her behavior and be healed (Isa. 6:1), but she refused to repent. Therefore, Jesus tells the church:

> *Behold, I will throw her onto a sickbed, and those who commit adultery with her I will throw into great tribulation, unless they repent of her works, and I will strike her children dead. And all the churches will know that I am he who searches mind and heart, and I will give to each of you according to your works.* (Rev. 2:22–23)

Notice that Jesus gives a severe judgment but not a hasty or haphazard one. We don't know how Jesus warned her—perhaps through preaching or a private confrontation with another Christian—but she heard his rebuke. Instead of turning toward him in repentance, she turned away in disobedience. And Jesus says he will warn her no more.

My friend, we are reminded that while God is infinite in mercy to those who turn to him, his patience with those who refuse is finite. Today, if you hear his voice, calling to turn to him, don't harden your heart against him (Ps. 95:7–11). Jesus doesn't promise another offer of mercy to those who proudly refuse it. Jezebel hardened her heart, and Jesus gave her an ironic punishment that seemed to fit the crime. On Jezebel's bed, she looked for life. On that same bed, death looked for her.[6]

I don't know how Jesus' words strike you, but they make me tremble because I don't have any reason to believe that Jezebel's heart was any harder than my own has been at times. I, like Jezebel, have heard warnings that I've ignored. I've listened to clear rebukes from Jesus that I discarded. Like Jezebel, I know enough about Jesus to know better than to continue in specific patterns of thought or behavior, but I chose to make excuses for why I couldn't or shouldn't repent. I tremble before the image and words of Jesus here because Jezebel doesn't appear strange to me. In many ways, she looks just like me.

But I also rejoice because his love is also redemptive.

Redemptive Love

Let's not miss the fact that Jesus appealed not only to Jezebel but also her followers to repent. His words indicate that the time to turn and to live had not passed them by:

> *And those who commit adultery with her I will throw into great tribulation, unless they repent of her works, and I will strike her children dead. And all the churches will know that I am he who searches mind and heart, and I will give to each of you according to your works.* (Rev. 2:22–23)

The reference to her children being struck dead may refer to literal children, but it's more likely a term for her spiritual offspring, disciples who followed her teaching. And consider the indescribable mercy which attends the call to repent. Jezebel's children had tarnished Jesus' name, hurt themselves, and created turmoil for his flock. These are dreadful sins against Jesus and his bride, which cannot be dismissed by the Lord lest he be guilty of the same indifference of the Thyatirans. Instead, when he says, "Repent," he also says, "I will assume the debt." Perhaps for months, even years, Jesus appealed to Jezebel, saying, "Repent! I'll be mocked for you and have my back opened by a whip for you. I'll be nailed to a tree for you. I'll assume your debt. Jezebel, repent!"

We see in Jesus here what John will see in a few chapters (Rev. 5:5–6), namely, one who has the ferocity of a lion, threatening to tear sinners into pieces, but also the gentleness of a lamb, willing to be torn apart for those seeking refuge in him. I tremble before the Lion, who will not tolerate the evil in my own heart and life. But I rejoice before the Lamb, slain for sinners just like me. God loves to show mercy. He's not stingy with his compassion or kindness. He desires to do good to his people (Jer. 9:24). He is slow to anger—as he was with Jezebel—and abounding in steadfast love to those who turn to him—which she would not (Ex. 34:6). Remember, he never grows weary toward the sinner seeking refuge in Jesus. The Father's magnification of his mercy in the person of Jesus never bores him. His anger moves at a glacial pace. But his mercy comes with lightning speed to those who ask.

Jesus ends his letter to the Thyatirans with two promises. The first assures his people that they will rule with him:

> *The one who conquers and who keeps my works until the end, to him I will give authority over the nations, and he will rule them with a rod of iron, as when earthen pots are broken in pieces, even as I myself have received authority from my father.* (Rev. 2:26–27)

Jesus quotes from the second Psalm (Ps. 2:8–9), in which the Lord promises the Messiah universal rule.[7] Every knee will bow, and every tongue will confess that Jesus Christ is Lord, to the glory of God the Father. And those who entrust themselves to his care will reign with him when he comes in glory. You will be instrumental in the process of making all things right in the world. That is the first promise, and the second is that you will receive the morning star: *"And I will give him the morning star"* (Rev. 2:28).

In the letter to the church in Pergamum, Jesus mentioned that there were some who *"hold to the teaching of Balaam"* (Rev. 2:14). Balaam, you'll recall, was hired by a pagan king to curse Israel, but with every attempt to do so, the Lord filled his mouth with blessings upon Israel. For example, consider one of the forced blessings the Lord made Balaam utter: *"I see him, but not now; I behold him, but not near: a star shall come out of Jacob, and a scepter shall rise out of Israel."* (Num. 24:17).

Later in Revelation, Jesus identifies himself as the bright morning star (Rev. 22:16). Here, Jesus says, *"I am the ultimate reward for those who over-*

come." As the embodiment of God's promises to do good to his people, Jesus Christ will stand before you and say, "All that I am, I give to you. And all that I have, I share with you. Well done, good and faithful servant. Enter into the joy of your master." Christian, until then: *"Serve the LORD with fear, and rejoice with trembling. Kiss the Son... blessed are all who take refuge in him."* (Ps. 2:11–12)

Study Questions

1. Our culture loves tolerance. How does this idea of Jesus showing an intolerant love sit with you? In what ways is it unsettling? In what ways is it encouraging?
2. How can you emulate Christ's example of commending the commendable, even while confronting sin? Why is this important?
3. How does the world define love regarding tolerance of all lifestyles, choices, and worldviews? How does the Bible describe love? What danger do we present to the world when we choose to love people in a worldly way?
4. The intolerant love of Jesus terrifies the impenitent, but he is patient and merciful to those who repent and seek him. For a moment, consider the areas of your life that Jesus could call you by that terrible name, Jezebel. Is there an area of your life in which repentance is commanded, but you withhold trusting in the Lord's goodness, and wisdom?
5. If you are a Christian, one day Jesus will say to you, "All that I am, I give to you. And all that I have, I share with you. Well done, good and faithful servant. Enter into the joy of your master." Meditate on this and spend some time in prayer, thanking the Savior who is fierce like a lion, ready to tear apart sinners, but also gentle like a lamb, ready to be torn apart for you in his great intolerant and redemptive love.

---

1. See Rev. Ch. 19:12, where the exact phrase describes Christ's role as judge.
2. Thyatira was known throughout the region for its famous bronze products. Jesus' self-description would have uniquely impacted Thyatiran ears.
3. Because this false prophetess' teaching overlaps with the Nicolaitans, she may have been among their number.
4. It's possible the sexual immorality advocated and practiced by this woman wasn't literal but metaphorical, for spiritual unfaithfulness to Christ (cf. Jas. 4:4). See G.K. Beale, *The Book of Revelation: A Shorter Commentary* (Eerdmans, 2015), 72.

5. David E. Aune, *Revelation 1–5*, Word Biblical Commentary (Nashville TN: Thomas Nelson, 1997), 214.
6. Leon Morris, *Revelation* (Grand Rapids MI: Eerdmans, 1984), 72.
7. The use of Psalm 2, which refers to the coming one as the Son of God (vv. 7, 12), brings us back to Jesus' introduction to the Thyatirans with the same title.

7

SLEEPERS AWAKE!

REV. 3:1-6

What would your city look like if Satan were in complete control? Reverend Donald Grey Barnhouse asked this thought-provoking question in a sermon preached last century. What images come to mind for you? Perhaps satanic control of your city would cause wide-  spread mayhem on a massive scale: violence in the streets, rampant deviant sexual practices, pornography on every billboard, and Christians rounded up and thrown into jail. We could all agree that such a scenario would trace its origin to a dark, sinister source.

Pastor Barnhouse offered his thoughts on the question and proposed a different picture of what a satanic-controlled city might look like. He imagined that every bar in town would be closed, every strip club made illegal, and the streets would be clean and occupied by polite, smiling pedestrians. Marriages would thrive; divorce would be a thing of the past. Every church in town would be filled to the rafters with people every Sunday. But from the pulpit would come this message: you are all doing just fine!

If Satan were in control of your city, the message of Jesus Christ, crucified for sinners would not be preached in pulpits, nor would the sermons ever mention the wrath of God. Instead, week after week, service after service, parishioners would hear "You are all doing just fine."[1]

The church in Sardis esteemed themselves highly and had a reputation for being a group of Christians doing just fine. Jesus doesn't mention major heresies like he does in the other churches. He doesn't talk about any sexual scandals or teachers of wanton promiscuity. They're thinking, "We are doing just fine. Thank you" when asked about the state of the church.

But they are not fine. And in utter kindness and through sheer grace, Jesus stands in the path of this church to tell them that they're in trouble. Jesus describes some of them as dead, and others as asleep. They were whitewashed tombs that outwardly looked good, fresh, and tidy but whose external beauty concealed dead men's bones.

In his mercy to the church in Sardis and the Church of every age, Jesus comes as the Great Physician not only to diagnose the nature of a dead, sleepy church but also to offer his surgical hand to get us on the path that leads to life.

How is your spiritual life? Do you have one? You must be born again to see the kingdom of God. Do you have this new life and awake to Jesus's voice? It seems to me that every church, from time to time, falls asleep. A church may be numb to the call Jesus places upon them even though major scandals and infighting are absent. Is your church awake? Are you? When we find ourselves in spiritual slumber, we need a spiritual solution.

Spiritual Slumber

To understand the situation in the Sardis church requires some detective work. In contrast to the Pergamum and Thyatira churches, the Sardinians are not charged with tolerance for false doctrine. Additionally, nothing indicates the church experienced external opposition from Jewish or Roman authorities, as seen in Smyrna, Pergamum, and Philadelphia. Finally, no evidence suggests this church engaged in pagan celebrations, unlike the Christians in Pergamum and Thyatira. In fact, the absence of such charges may be the reason they have a good reputation: *"I know your works. You have the reputation of being alive"* (Rev. 3:1).

This positive reputation probably came from other Christians in the area. Visitors to the Sardis church may have noted the absence of theological compromise and championed "Those Sardinian Christians don't tolerate the teachings of the Nicolaitans or Balaam. And the promiscuity of Jezebel has no place in their ranks." The conclusion of visitors may have been "The church in Sardis is alive!" But Jesus, the one who walks among with lampstands, peered beyond the veneer of spiritual activity and theological accuracy and reported: *"But you are dead"* (Rev. 3:1).

From the outside, the Sardis church looked like a living, faithful, and generous model church. But with blunt honesty, Jesus tells them they're dead. But why does he say that? We need to examine the text for clues, the first of which comes at the end of the letter, where Jesus promises to the one who conquers: *"I will confess his name before my Father and before his angels"* (Rev. 3:5).

In Matthew, Jesus attaches a warning to this promise: *"So everyone who acknowledges me before men, I also will acknowledge before my Father who is in heaven, but whoever denies me before men, I also will deny before my Father who is in heaven"* (Matt. 10:32–33).

Perhaps Jesus made this promise to the Christians in Sardis because they refused to confess him publicly as Christ. Maybe they bravely confessed Jesus within the friendly confines of the church, but fear set in once they left the assembly. Why would they be afraid to proclaim Jesus openly? We have a second clue, in a second promise Jesus made to the conqueror, saying: *"I will never blot his name out of the book of life"* (Rev. 3:5).

Before we consider the meaning of this promise, a reminder of the historical situation will help us. At this time, the Romans required all citizens to show their political loyalty to the empire by worshiping the emperor, who was addressed as "god and lord."[2] Only the vigorously monotheistic Jews were exempt from this law. The Romans provided a special tax the Jews could pay to support the empire and not break their faith. For a time, we think Christians avoided emperor worship under the protection of their strong association with Judaism. But as the church continued to grow, adding more and more Gentiles, this infuriated non-Christian Jews. Sadly, many Jewish leaders reported Christians as "non-Jews"[3] to Roman authorities, bringing pressure upon the young Christian community.

But we don't find any pressure placed upon the Christians in Sardis. We know that Sardis had numerous Roman pagan temples and was also home to a sizable Jewish community which met in a massive synagogue large enough to host one thousand people.[4]

Why is there no mention of Roman or Jewish pressure upon this church of outstanding reputation? When they were in public, it seemed they found a way to conceal their faith, perhaps by remaining associated with the enormous synagogue in town. Just as one can hide on the membership rolls of the contemporary mega-church today, Christians in Sardis probably did the same with the mega-synagogue in the city. After all, ancient synagogues did keep a register of its members. And if at any point you were found to be unfaithful or a heretic, the elders would remove your name from the membership rolls, thus removing you from the protection Judaism provided from Rome's laws.⁵ This information may serve as a background for Jesus' promise to never blot the names of his people from the membership roll that matters. To the overcomer, not ashamed of Jesus, he promises, *"I will never blot his name out of the book of life"* (Rev. 3:5).

The force of this promise asks each of us, "What is your priority? What is more important to you? Is it the temporary, human verdict of your peers who find Jesus offensive or the eternally divine affirmation of Jesus, who calls you his beloved?" I am wondering which affirmation makes your heart beat faster. If it's the approval of man, Jesus grabs you by the shoulders, shakes you, and warns:

> *Wake up, and strengthen what remains and is about to die, for I have not found your works complete in the sight of my God. Remember, then, what you received and heard. Keep it, and repent. If you will not wake up, I will come like a thief, and you will not know at what hour I will come against you.* (Rev. 3:2–3)

This threat would have been potent to the church in Sardis because Jesus described something that happened numerous times in their city's history. Sardis was constructed on a steep, seemingly impregnable hill. As a result, Sardis residents arrogantly and overconfidently felt safe from enemy invasion. But in 549 BC, Cyrus the Persian took forces into the city. In 334 BC, Alexander the Great conquered the city, as did Antiochus III in 218 BC. On several occasions, enemy troops scaled the steep walls at night, finding the over-confident Sardinians asleep, having set no guards.⁶

Jesus warns the Sardinian Christians to wake from their spiritual slumber, or he, like a thief in the night, will come against them. This threat isn't a reference to the second coming of Jesus. Instead, Jesus often "comes" to a church group through external persecution, internal collapse, church splits, or simply by allowing a church to sleep until they quietly fade away in inoffensive irrelevance.⁷

Let's acknowledge that all of us sometimes find ourselves asleep. We fall into a spiritual slumber, forgetting that we are called to be priestly people to *"proclaim the excellencies of him who called [us] out of darkness into his marvelous light"* (1 Pet. 2:9). The Christian's call to priestly service may serve as the background to Jesus' description of unsoiled, white garments: *"Yet you have still a few names in Sardis, people who have not soiled their garments, and they will walk with me in white, for they are worthy. The one who conquers will be clothed thus in white garments"* (Rev. 3:4–5).

The ordinary attire of the priest was a white turban, a white coat, and a white sash.[8] Christian, you are part of *"the chosen race, a royal priesthood, a holy nation, a people for his own possession"* (1 Pet. 2:9), which means every person you meet in this world is either a missionary or a mission field. Every man, woman, and child either possesses the Good News and, therefore, called to give it away, or they need the Good News and commanded to embrace it.

Maybe you've fallen asleep and need to wake up. I sometimes fall asleep. The earliest signs that I am dozing off toward my responsibilities show up in my prayers. I listen to myself asking the Lord for comfort, good health, safety, and success in certain areas, and avoiding failure in others. These desires and requests are not inherently wrong. But if these things are all that we seek from the Lord, we may be asleep. After all, those are the same things a non-Christian prays for—when they do pray.

The prayers of a living, awake church—and the individuals who embody them—don't dismiss such things, but they also do not make them the priority. Instead, those awake and ready to serve as priests pray as Jesus taught them, "Father, bring glory to your name through my life. Usher in your kingdom here on earth, as it is in heaven. Use me to proclaim the excellencies of your name. Strengthen me to bear up the cross so I might honor the Savior." I confess my prayers don't always begin here and, tragically, sometimes never arrive. I wonder if my prayers for comfort, family, health, and success sometimes sound like loud snoring to the Lord. Sometimes we all fall asleep and need to wake up, which requires a spiritual solution.

Spiritual Solution

As in the other letters, Jesus introduces himself to the Church in Sardis with an attribute witnessed by John in the opening vision (Rev. 1:9–20). And each time, knowing the particular situation of the church addressed, Jesus opens with something immediately relevant to their need. Sardis has lost its power to witness to the world. Though they have a reputation for being alive, they are dead. So Jesus presents himself as the only one who has the solution to their problem: *"And to the angel of the church in Sardis write: 'The words of him who has the seven spirits of God and the seven stars"* (Rev. 3:1).

As you'll recall, seven is used throughout this book to symbolize completeness, wholeness, and totality.[9] Jesus says to every individual and every sleepy church, "You lack nothing if you come to me." He has the fullness of the Spirit of the Living God and will pour it out upon those seeking it.

So, do you want to wake up for the first time or again this week? You must go to Jesus. Ask him to open his hand to give you a new heart or to jumpstart the heart previously made alive that's now only faintly beating. But how can we take advantage of his offer? That is to say, how can I grow in my love of, boldness for, and service to Jesus? Thankfully, we are not left to guess, nor given an answer too complicated for any to understand. Jesus gives us three things to do, and, my friend, there are no three sweeter instructions than these in all of Holy Scripture: *"Remember, then, what you received and heard. Keep it, and repent"* (Rev. 3:3).

This passage drips with the mercy, patience, and kindness of Jesus, and I hope your soul will absorb its life-giving power. The first instruction Jesus gives to dead and sleepy people is, "Remember... what you received and heard." This language of receiving and hearing figures prominently in John's writings, and each time it refers to the beginning point of the Christian faith (John 1:12; 3:11, 32–33; 5:43;12:48; 13:20; 17:8).[10] To the dead and the sleepy, Jesus says, "Remember the Gospel." And what is the Gospel? The sweet and glorious truth that God so loved the world—so loved *you*—that he did not spare his Son, but gave him up to die, that you might live. So remember the Gospel first. Beat that truth into your head and heart over and over again, and then: *"Keep it"* (Rev. 3:3).

What does this mean: to keep the Gospel? It means to believe, trust, and embrace it from the heart. After all, this is where we part ways with the demons—they know the Gospel; they know that God is One; they know that Jesus is the Son of God, crucified and raised for sinners (Jas. 2:19). But they don't embrace it. The demons know what you have received and heard but do not keep it for themselves. They don't let those eternal truths trickle down into their hearts to give them life and wake them from their demonic slumber. They know the Good News, but they don't keep it. They don't make it their own through submission to Jesus. Jesus effectively says, "Don't just remember what is true; believe it is true for you. Believe not just that God so loved the world, but that he so loved, and still loves—you." And he also loves the person he is putting on your mind right now, who needs you to come to them as a priest. Remember, first, the Gospel. Second, believe it. And then, third: *"Repent"* (Rev. 3:3)

Repentance isn't simply a call to stop some behavior or thought pattern. Instead, a repentant person turns away from one behavior or thought pattern to another. So Jesus says, "You have taken your light and hidden it under a basket. Therefore, first, remember that the Light of the world has shown you what God is like and what he requires of you. Second, believe that the Light of the world has come to live, die, and be raised triumphantly for you. Third, turn away from hiding this truth. Let your light shine before men, that my God and Father would be glorified through you."

No one preaches the Gospel like Jesus! Did you notice that the order of his commands is perhaps different from the order that your soul might believe? Sometimes we fall into the trap of thinking that if we clean ourselves up and get certain things right, then the Lord will receive and delight in us.

Sadly, this performance-based thinking often underlies our approach to the Lord. But Jesus turns it around for our souls: "Remember that God is love. And so great was his love that he sent his Son. Now believe it! It is true for you. Dig the fingernails of your soul into this truth and never let it go. Then repent! Turn away from your folly, cowardice, and love of people's approval and turn toward me." Maybe he's calling you to come to him for the first time to receive new life. Or perhaps you're already alive, but sleeping. Jesus calls you too. He is the lover of your soul, in whose hands are all the resources you need to serve him with joy until you see him face to face, when you will walk with him, in white, for all eternity.

Study Questions

1. Spiritual Slumber—the church in Sardis is seemingly doing well, but Jesus delivers the surprising verdict: *"But you are dead."* This evaluation should serve as a wake-up call to us all. In what areas of your spiritual life are you asleep?
2. We must guess at the specific problems in Sardis based on the promises Jesus delivers to the faithful ones there who are awake. If Jesus came to you today, what promises would he make to you based on your spiritual problems?
3. Spiritual Solution: Jesus gives us three things to do. What are they? Does the order of remember, keep, and repent differ from your usual approach to Jesus?

---

1. Slightly adapted from the language used in Michael Horton, *Christless Christianity* (Baker, Grand Rapids, 2008), 15.
2. Vern S. Poythress, *The Returning King: A Guide to the Book of Revelation* (P&R, 2000), 50.
3. The argument over who is a "real" Jew appears to underlie the words of Jesus in Revelation 2:9, *"I know your tribulation and your poverty (but you are rich) and the slander of those who say that they are Jews and are not, but are a synagogue of Satan."*

4. David E. Aune, *Revelation 1–5*, Word Biblical Commentary (Nashville TN: Thomas Nelson, 1997), 218.
5. I owe my construction of the situation in Sardis to the insights found in James M. Hamilton Jr., *Revelation: The Spirit Speaks to the Churches* (Wheaton IL: Crossway, Illinois, 2012), 103–110.
6. Leon Morris, *Revelation* (Grand Rapids MI: Eerdmans 1984), 75.
7. See G.K. Beale, *The Book of Revelation: A Shorter Commentary* (Eerdmans, 2015), 79.
8. This outfit also applied to the High Priest, who, on the Day of Atonement, would set aside his ornate, colorful garments to don a set of white linen garments for the two times he would enter the Holy of Holies. See Lev. 16:4.
9. Michael Wilcock, *The Message of Revelation* (Downers Grove, IL: InterVarsity Press, 1975), 62. See our chapter on Rev. 2:1–7 for a brief discussion on the seven stars.
10. For a more developed argument, see David E. Aune, 221.

8

THE UNCLOSABLE DOOR
REV. 3:7-13

A few chapters back, I set John Bunyan's *The Pilgrim's Progress* before you. I want to do that again but take you to a different scene. Christian, the main character traveling from the City of Destruction to the Celestial City, comes to a home called the House of the Interpreter. The building provides travelers with the necessary information to navigate their way to the eternal city.

As Christian walks through the front door, he's met by one called Interpreter, who escorts Christian around the residence. In one of the rooms, he sees a fireplace burning hot with flames that continue to grow in strength, even though a man close by throws water on the fire. Christian asks Interpreter, "What does this mean; why is this man throwing water on the flames? And why do they continue to burn?"

Interpreter answers, "The fire burning in the fireplace is your faith. The man trying to extinguish the flames is the Evil One. But you see, the fire will not go out. Let me show you why."

Interpreter walks Christian around the wall to the other side of the fireplace, and there they see a man pouring oil on the flames, keeping them fueled. "Who is this man?" inquired Christian. "This man is Christ," answers the Interpreter, "who always pours the oil of his mercy on the flames of faith so that they should never be extinguished."

There is an enemy of your soul who will always try to extinguish your faith. He continually throws the waters of cynicism, temptation, anxiety, guilt, and doubt onto your heart. But you're not alone. Though he stands out of sight, Jesus has oil to pour on the hearts of weary travelers. He maintains the flame of hope.

As we come to the letter to the Christians in Philadelphia, we meet with a small group targeted by a larger, more powerful group of people. I envision the Christians here as those drenched with the hostile waters of persecution, rejection, and slander for Jesus' name. But Jesus meets with them with the oil of his mercy to remind them that he has the power to save, sustain, and secure them for all eternity.

Power to Save

Coming to the church in Philadelphia, we should imagine a faithful little church doing all it can to keep going. There's no suggestion in this letter of any theological or behavioral compromise as we find in some of the other letters. Additionally, they appear to have been vocal in their faith:

> *I know your works. Behold, I have set before you an open door, which no one is able to shut. I know that you have but little power, and yet you have kept my word and have not denied my name.* (Rev. 3:8)

Like the letter to Smyrna (Rev. 2:8–11), Jesus' words to the Philadelphian church contain no rebuke or call to repentance. Instead, they were commended for their faithfulness. A few clues in this letter suggest that they shared the same struggle with Jewish authorities that the Smyrnan church faced. After all, both letters speak of "those who say they are Jews and are not," and in both letters, the Jews are identified as a "synagogue of Satan" (Rev. 2:9; 3:9).

The strife most likely revolved around an issue we have already examined: who has the rightful claim to be called "the Jews"? This question had significant practical implications as citizens of the Roman Empire were obligated to pay tribute to Caesar as their "god and lord" unless they could demonstrate Jewish identity.

And many Christians, both ethnically Jewish and Gentile, believed that they were the true children of Abraham and, therefore, in a real sense, genuinely Jewish. Paul instructed these early Christian communities that the genuine people of God consist of those who, like Abraham, believe and trust in the Lord (cf. Rom. 2:28–29; 9:6–9; Gal. 3:7; 6:15–16). Regardless of ethnicity, Christians are "the Israel of God," (Gal. 6:16), citizens of the Jerusalem "above" (Gal. 4:26). Paul was not introducing a new idea. According to Jesus, the unbelieving Jewish crowds would demonstrate their true descent from Abraham through faith in Christ. Consequently, the crowd's rejection of Jesus revealed their inauthenticity as the true Israel of God (John 8:39–44).[1]

The consequences of this theological debate had real, everyday repercussions. As long as Christianity remained under the protective umbrella of Judaism, Christians were exempt from Rome's idolatrous feasts and participation in the Imperial Cult. But when the Jewish authorities denounced the Christians to the Romans as non-Jews (cf. Acts 18:12–17), the refusal to participate in Roman idolatry came at a heavy cost. Once excluded from the protection afforded by the local synagogue, Christians were subject to Rome's cruelty.

Perhaps the closed door of the synagogues provides the backdrop for Jesus' introduction to the church in Philadelphia:

> *And to the angel of the church in Philadelphia write: 'The words of the holy one, the true one, who has the key of David, who opens and no one will shut, who shuts and no one opens.*
>
> *"'I know your works. Behold, I have set before you an open door, which no one is able to shut. I know that you have but little power, and yet you have kept my word and have not denied my name.* (Rev. 3:7–8)[2]

Jesus' self-description as the one *"who has the key of David"* would have sounded familiar to Jewish ears. The *"key of David"* would have brought to mind an incident from the book of Isaiah (Ch. 22), where Hezekiah, a godly king in Judah, carried out several reforms, including changing his staff members. One of those who had to go was a crooked, money-hungry assistant named Shebna, who used his place of power for self-indulgence. In his place, Hezekiah installed a faithful godly man named Eliakim.

The Lord commanded Eliakim to wear a special robe and sash as emblems of Eliakim's authority. Moreover, he had a key, called the key of David, which he would wear on his shoulder.[3] Concerning Eliakim, the Lord said, *"He shall open, and none shall shut; and he shall shut, and none shall open"* (Isa. 22:22). We don't know whether the key literally locked and unlocked doors or represented his power. Nevertheless, the message was clear—Eliakim had all authority to give entry or refuse admission to the city of David. To the church in Philadelphia, excluded from the synagogue and told they have no place in the kingdom of God, came the one to whom Eliakim pointed, he who truly wears the key of David. Only Jesus has the authority to receive people into the kingdom and forbid entrance to others.

Like many Christians today, perhaps you believe that Jesus is only one way to God. You think that many paths lead to the summit, and they all go to the same place. But Jesus tells us, *"I am the way, and the truth, and the life. No one comes to the Father except through me"* (John 14:6). To continue the metaphor, Jesus has the Key of David, and has not unlocked other doors to God; therefore, they are un-openable.

Or maybe you acknowledge that Jesus is the only way, but you also recognize that you have not lived in a manner becoming a follower of Jesus. Perhaps you have strayed away and fallen into a pattern of sinful living. Maybe you know you've not been brave for Jesus. And what you hear are not synagogue authorities pronouncing curses over you,[4] but your own heart rising to condemn you: "You do not love Jesus! Christians don't sin like this! You've committed an unpardonable sin! And now you wonder, 'Is the door locked?'"

You must listen to Jesus. He has the key of David. He has the power to save. And he can sustain you.

Power to Sustain

Jesus tells the Philadelphian Christians that he'll sustain them through the trials coming upon the whole world:

> *Because you have kept my word about patient endurance, I will keep you from the hour of trial that is coming on the whole world, to try those who dwell on the earth. I am coming soon. Hold fast to what you have, so that no one may seize your crown.* (Rev. 3:10–11)

Scholars disagree on the sure identification of the "hour of trial" to come upon the Philadelphian church. Some[5] think it refers to the great difficulties and punishments that God sends upon the world in the chapters to come, while others[6] suggest a more localized conflict with the Jews and Romans of the first century. What is clear is that Jesus has the power to sustain Christians both then and now during a great struggle. The promise to keep us from the hour of trial doesn't ensure personal comfort or freedom from persecution. Instead, Jesus promises protection from spiritual, eternal dangers.[7] Some of those who first received this letter had already lost friends, and their freedoms (Rev. 2:10), and at least one man lost his life (Rev. 2:13). In the midst of difficult situations, Jesus promises his sustaining presence. Even if someone causes harm to us, he will not let us go.

Maybe it's not the external threats that trouble you but the internal ones. That voice of self-doubt that speaks poisonous accusations and paints caricatures of God, saying:

> You have not kept up your end of the bargain. The command is to love the Lord with all of our heart, soul, mind, and strength, which you've failed. The command is to forgive as you've been forgiven, but we both know you still hold a grudge. The fruit of the Spirit includes self-control, and here you are again, losing your temper, running to an addiction, and falling into old patterns of sin. You're not a Christian or at least not anymore.

We can become convinced of these accusations because we think Jesus has placed limits on what he will tolerate from the brokenhearted sinner seeking refuge. As John Calvin once said, "There is nothing that troubles our consciences more than when we think that God is like ourselves."[8] How long would we show patience and love to someone who continually violates our expectations? We sometimes put up a relational wall, distancing ourselves from such people. And then, as Calvin said, we fear God is like us in this way, and our souls are left troubled, floating aimlessly upon waters of uncertainty.

Perhaps you're suffering an internal "hour of trial" because you entertain a caricatured version of the Lord. Jesus tells you, *"All that the Father gives me will come to me, and whoever comes to me I will never cast out"* (John 6:37).

This promise was one of John Bunyan's favorites. For Bunyan, these words were oil on the fire of his sometimes-smoldering, faintly-burning flames of faith. But no matter how unworthy he felt or how heinous his sinful thoughts or deeds were, he clung to the words of Jesus: "Whoever comes to me I will never cast out." Bunyan gives us a picture of his dialogue with Jesus, writing:

> But I'm a great sinner, I say.
> "Whoever comes to me, I will never cast out," Jesus responds.
> But I'm an old sinner, I say.
> "I will never cast you out," he responds.
> I've backslidden, I protest.
> "I will never cast you out," says Christ.
> But, Jesus, you don't understand. I've really messed up! I say.
> "I do understand," he responds.
> I don't know if I can break free of this sin.
> "I have not come for the righteous," he reminds me.

I'm crushed with guilt, I lament.
"Cast your burden on me," he responds.
If you see just how ugly my sin is, you'll turn away, I cry.
"Whoever comes to me, I will never cast out," he promises.⁹

My friend, Jesus holds the key of David, not you. So bring to Jesus whatever fear, doubt, one-off sin, or even long periods of backsliding that troubles your soul. No matter what makes you question the perseverance of his mercy, he has already answered your objection when he said, *"Whoever comes to me, I will never cast out."* He opened this letter as *"the holy one, the true one"* (Rev. 3:7), reminding us that he's not only morally pure, but he's also trustworthy. He's opened a door you have no power or authority to close. He says, *"Come to me, all who labor and are heavy laden, and I will give you rest"* (Matt. 11:28). He alone has the power to save and sustain you. And he alone can secure a place for you.

Power to Secure

Jesus promises the Philadelphians that he has the power to secure a dignified eternity for them in the very presence of God. He promised to make them a pillar inscribed with three names:

> *I am coming soon. Hold fast to what you have, so that no one may seize your crown. The one who conquers, I will make him a pillar in the temple of my God. Never shall he go out of it, and I will write on him the name of my God, and the name of the city of my God, the new Jerusalem, which comes down from my God out of heaven, and my own new name.* (Rev. 3:11–12)

In the ancient world, people showed honor and appreciation to loyal servants, public officials, or clergy members by having a unique pillar added to one of the temples. Then, on that same pillar, you would inscribe the name of the person you wished to honor.¹⁰ Jesus says to those temporarily dishonored in this world for his name, that he will eternally honor them in the world to come. Notice, too, that Jesus says, *"Never shall he go out of it"* (Rev. 3:12), referring to the presence of God in the temple. This assurance would've been an exceptional promise to those in Philadelphia because few people felt secure in the city. Philadelphia experienced numerous catastrophic earthquakes over the years due to its location above a seismic fault.

The earthquakes were so severe and frequent that few people lived in the city itself. New cracks appeared in the city's walls every day.[11] The promise of never having to flee the city to come was of utmost importance to a people whose day-to-day life knew constant instability and uncertainty.

Does this lift your heart? In this world, you'll be temporarily dishonored for Jesus' sake. But in the world to come, eternal honor will be showered upon you so that all will marvel at how he loved his people.

But it will not be your name that Jesus inscribes upon you:

> *And I will write on him the name of my God, and the name of the city of my God, the new Jerusalem, which comes down from my God out of heaven, and my own new name.* (Rev. 3:12)

Three names will be inscribed upon us: first, the *"name of my God,"* signifying ownership, eternally belonging to the Father; second, the *"name of the city"* of God, ever dignified as a member of the Jerusalem from above, and; finally, Jesus promises to write his "own new name" upon you. If the first name denotes ownership and the second citizenship, the third points to intimacy. The bride of Jesus will have his name placed upon her at the wedding to come (Rev. 19:9).

The one who has all authority in heaven and earth pours the oil of mercies upon you, saying, "I not only have the power to save and sustain you. I also intend to honor you for all eternity." Do these promises stoke the flames of your faith?

One of my colleagues[12] tells the story of a life-changing encounter one of his parishioners had at a restaurant. As he made his way into the restaurant, he noticed an older, hunched-over man shuffling across the parking lot with a cane. As the man shuffled past, he unknowingly dropped a pen, which the other man picked up and handed back to him. But what he saw and heard in response forever changed him.

What he heard from the lips of the old man was, "Thank you, friend." What he saw was one of the most recognizable faces in the world, the face of Muhammad Ali, self-proclaimed "The Greatest." That man went home boasting, "Muhammad Ali called me 'Friend!' 'The Greatest' knows me!"

When the adrenaline of the moment subsided, he reflected, "What's wrong with me? I serve the true Great One!" Almighty God, through the magnificent person of Jesus, knows you. He not only knows you, but he also loves you. And he calls you not only Friend but also his Beloved, his Bride, and the Apple of his Eye (Isa. 41:8; Jer. 12:7; Rev. 21:9; Ps. 17:8).

Let the oil of his mercies fuel your heart for love, service, and bravery for him until you see him face to face.

Study Questions

1. Imagine your faith is like that fire burning in the hearth, with water poured on you from all directions. Now picture Jesus standing on the other side of the wall, pouring oil on your faith to keep it burning. Does this image make you bold? Does it comfort you? Maybe it fills you with gratitude. Whatever it is, take some time to journal your thoughts and ask the Lord to shape you with his assurances.
2. We see the closed door of the synagogue as the backdrop to what Jesus says to this little church in Philadelphia. How does the intimate particularity with which Jesus addresses the church a comfort for us? How might Jesus address you today? How would he speak to your church?
3. What is your "hour of trial from which you must be kept"? Is it internal or external?
4. Three names will be inscribed eternally upon us: first, the "name of my God," denoting ownership, forever belonging to the Father; second, the "name of the city" of God, eternally dignified as a member of the Jerusalem from above, and; finally, Jesus promises to write his "own new name" upon you. The first name indicates ownership, the second citizenship, and the third points to intimacy. The bride of Jesus will have his name placed upon her at the wedding that is to come (Rev. 19:9). Take some time to journal your reaction to this and give thanks to the Lord of all creation who promises this to you!

---

1. For an excellent book-length treatment of this topic see, O. Palmer Robertson, *The Israel of God: Yesterday, Today, and Tomorrow* (P&R, 2000).
2. Many good commentators (i.e., Beale, Hendriksen, N.T. Wright) regard the open door Jesus sets before the Philadelphian Christians as a description of opportunities to evangelize versus my understanding which suggests it means full access to God and the salvation he grants. It seems that the Christians in Philadelphia are facing problems with non-Christian Jews because they are *already* vocal and public about their faith in Jesus. Consequently, they have been eliminated from the synagogue and need to hear from their Lord that this doesn't mean that a door to the kingdom of God has been closed to them. In support of this understanding of the open door, see David E. Aune, *Revelation*

1–5, Word Biblical Commentary (Nashville: Thomas Nelson, 1997), 236; Leon Morris, *Revelation* (Grand Rapids MI: Eerdmans 1984), 79; Vern S. Poythress, *The Returning King: A Guide to the Book of Revelation* (P&R, 2000), 91.

3. For a fascinating examination of Eliakim as a type of Christ, see G.K. Beale, *The Book of Revelation: A Shorter Commentary* (Eerdmans, 2015), 83–84.
4. Around the time John sent this letter to Philedelphia, the "curse of the Minim" (the heretics) was added to the 18 Benedictions, which Jews in the ancient world prayed daily. "The curse of the Minim" reads, "May the Nazarenes and the Minim suddenly perish, and may they be blotted out of the book of Life and not enrolled with the righteous." See James M. Hamilton Jr., Revelation: The Spirit Speaks to the Churches (Wheaton IL: Crossway, Illinois, 2012), 106.
5. Poythress, 92.
6. Beale, 86.
7. The only other occurrence of "I will keep from" (*tereō ek*) in the New Testament is in John 17:15. There, Jesus prayed, *"I do not ask that you take them out of the world, but that you keep them from the evil one."* Jesus didn't expect his people to be free from the trials and painful suffering that attend to those living in the world. Instead, his prayer was that, amid such things, the Father would protect his people from the spiritual damage Satan intends. See Aune, 239; Beale, 86.
8. Quoted in Dane Ortlund, *Gentle and Lowly* (Crossway, 2020), 155.
9. Slightly adapted and amended from the version in Ortlund, 62–64.
10. A. F. Johnson, "Revelation" *The Expositor's Bible Commentary* XII (Zondervan, 1981), 455.
11. As noted by the historian Strabo (64 BC–21 AD). See Aune, 234.
12. George Robertson, "Come to the Waters," First Presbyterian Church, Augusta, GA, August 28, 2016.

9

HE STANDS AT THE DOOR
REVELATION 3:14-22

"You are supposed to be different."

These words have haunted my friend for thirty years. A group of his friends including his brother were all telling off-color jokes. Everyone knew that my friend was the only Christian in the group. Wanting to fit in, he listened  to the highly offensive jokes and offered up one of his own. His joke was far more offensive than the others. He received a roar of laughter from everyone—except for one person, his brother.

Later that evening, my friend asked his brother what was bothering him and if he was angry. He didn't laugh at the joke. His brother responded, "Why are you acting like us? Why are you telling those jokes? When I look at you, I see the only hope of ever being a different person. I'm sad. You are supposed to be different."

Jesus comes to the seventh and final church with the same message: you are supposed to be different. But it's an understatement to say Jesus was sad; he was disgusted with this church. Jesus urged the Laodicean congregation to fulfill the same obligation as every other Christian: to serve as a positive influence in society, akin to salt and light (Matt. 5:13-14). Salt, a commonly used preservative in ancient times, functioned as a metaphor for the preservative quality of his people in the world. Additionally, we must strive to be a beacon of light in the darkness, radiating God's love through our actions (Matt. 5:16).

Sadly, the Laodicians were neither salt nor light. No one was living an observable Christian lifestyle. No one was willing to take a stand for Jesus in their city; consequently, they had become indistinguishable from the culture in which they lived.

As we'll see in this letter, the Laodicean church is distracted. Instead of pursuing the Lord with all of their heart, soul, mind, and strength, the Laodiceans gave their energy to seeking comfort, wealth, image, success, family, and personal networking. When Christians in Laodicea got up in the morning, their goals were no different than those of their pagan neighbors: make money, secure comforts, and put a little more in the bank. Like the church in Ephesus, the Laodiceans' love for Jesus had grown cold.

And unlike the church in Sardis, which still had a few faithful Christians in a primarily dead church, Laodicea had no such remnant. The spiritually dead filled the Laodicean church and stands alone as the only church with no commendations from Jesus. But this dead church does have one thing going for it: a living Savior who still loves them and sets before them the life-giving hope of the Gospel.

Perhaps as you consider the Laodicean problem—a distraction from pursuing the Lord to the pursuit of the things of this earth—you recognize your tendency to wander from the God you love. Maybe you know what a Laodicean relationship with Jesus looks and feels like. You don't deny him, but you're not making much of him at the moment. Maybe if someone were to listen to your prayers, he or she might conclude that you care much more about your physical comfort and safety than the needs of your soul. Or perhaps your prayers suggest that you care more about your political party's success than the coming of the Kingdom of God.

This letter speaks to us regardless of what distracts us away from the Lord. Jesus' words to this church may prevent you from spiritual drift or deliver you if you have already begun. Either way, we turn to his words which are a severe warning to the church, and also a sweet wooing of his bride.

Severe Warning

To understand Jesus' words to the Laodiceans, we'll benefit from examining some of the city's characteristics.[1] First, Laodicea was an extremely prosperous city and one of the wealthiest commercial centers in the world. Founded upon the crossroads of several trade routes, Laodicea soon became an industrial powerhouse for the region. The city served as a crucial center for banking in the area and was known for housing a considerable amount of gold reserves. In AD 60, an earthquake caused significant damage to Laodicea. Despite the destruction, the city had such an abundance of gold that they refused financial assistance from the empire to rebuild. When the city was rebuilt, the Laodiceans boasted that they required no outside help.

Second, Laodicea was also known for producing and exporting expensive garments made from black wool. The local farmers near the city had developed a particular breed of black sheep with wool of the highest quality.[2] From this unique wool, they produced black, shiny garments that became a fashion trend worldwide, a trend eagerly embraced by the Laodiceans. The third noteworthy detail concerning Laodicea is a contemporary medical district that focused on ophthalmology. People would come to Laodicea from all over the empire to acquire a popular powder for eye and vision care.

Putting these things together—the abundance of wealth, a prosperous textile industry, and world-famous medical facilities—draws a portrait of a highly affluent, self-sufficient group of people who only needed themselves to get by. And it appears from Jesus' words to the Christians in Laodicea that they, too, had taken advantage of the affluent economic opportunities the city afforded: *"For you say, I am rich, I have prospered, and I need nothing, not realizing that you are wretched, pitiable, poor, blind, and naked"* (Rev. 3:17).

The problem here isn't that the Christians had flourished and become wealthy. Nowhere does the Bible forbid the accumulation of wealth. Abraham, David, Solomon, and Joseph of Arimathea (the man who provided a grave for the body of Jesus) were all wealthy people. However, Scripture consistently emphasizes that wealth should be handled with care and used to glorify God. Otherwise, it may end up consuming its owner. Jesus warns us that we cannot simultaneously live for the accumulation of wealth and the Lord. You can only be devoted to one or the other (Matt. 6:24).

While material prosperity isn't inherently sinful, it can be dangerous because the more you accumulate, the greater the temptation to find your meaning, value, identity, and joy in what it can provide. But wealth is also dangerous because the more you have, the more it can dull your sense of dependence on and gratitude to the Lord. Consider one of the wisest prayers regarding money ever uttered:

> *Two things I ask of you; deny them not to me before I die... give me neither poverty nor riches; feed me with the food that is needful for me, lest I be full*

and deny you and say, "Who is the LORD?" or lest I be poor and steal and profane the name of my God. (Prov. 30:7–9)

Could you offer that prayer right now? It would go something like:

Father, preserve me from riches if they would cause me to forget you. Keep me from too much wealth, lest it cloud my vision and I become dull in my dependence upon you. Free me from pursuing anything that will function as a counterfeit joy.

Unfortunately, it appears the Laodicean Christians didn't pray like in this way. Instead, they ran past the warnings and, like their pagan neighbors, set their heart on wealth, and, as Paul tells us:

It is through this craving [desire to be rich] that some have wandered away from the faith and pierced themselves with many pangs. (1 Tim. 6:10)

The craving for wealth led the Laodicean Christians to wander far from the faith because they felt satisfied with themselves. Notice the local flavor of Jesus' command to them in verse 18, remembering that Laodicea was known for its vast gold reserves, a black garment industry, and facilities devoted to the health of the eye:

I counsel you to buy from me gold refined by fire, so that you may be rich, and white garments so that you may clothe yourself and the shame of your nakedness may not be seen, and salve to anoint your eyes, so that you may see. (Rev. 3:18)[3]

These three items—gold refined by fire, white garments, and salve for the eyes—all point to one remedy for the Laodicean problem: Jesus Christ.[4] We are created and redeemed for true riches, clothing, and spiritual sight that can only be found in him.

Therefore, Jesus stands in the way of these wayward people with the command to come back to him—to buy true spiritual riches from him.

If they refuse, Jesus issues a severe warning in verses 15–16. Before we consider those words, one more detail about Laodicea will help us understand the warning. For all that Laodicea had going for itself, it lacked a fundamental resource: drinkable water. They did have some water in the area, but its muddy consistency made it undrinkable. But Laodicea's neighbors, Colossae to the east and Hierapolis to the north, had good water. Colossae had access to a source of pure, icy-cold water originating from the snow-capped mountains in the area, so Laodicea financed a significant aqueduct project to bring the cold water to their city. On its eleven-mile journey through the pipes, the cold water turned lukewarm and dirty.

The Laodiceans also tried to import water from their neighbors to the north in Hierapolis. They had hot water that bubbled up from springs for medical baths. So they built another aqueduct to transport the hot water. And the hot water also became lukewarm by the time it arrived in Laodicea. To make matters worse, the water from Hierapolis contained high levels of calcium carbonate which made people vomit. We should consider Jesus's words in verses 15–16 with this information in mind:

> I know your works: you are neither cold nor hot. Would that you were either cold or hot! So, because you are lukewarm, and neither hot nor cold, I will spit you out of my mouth. (Rev. 3:15–16)

Given the background we have just considered, I don't think Jesus is saying they would be better off being cold than lukewarm in their faith. Nor is he saying that he would rather they be one extreme or the other. Instead, he communicates that their pursuit of comfort, wealth, and status has neither the refreshing qualities of cold water nor the healing properties of hot water. Their faith had become worthless and sickening to Jesus because they abandoned their priestly duty of being salt and light in Laodicea. The city's lukewarm and contaminated waters were a fitting comparison to their lack of commitment.

The water that reached Laodicea had lost its value because of its distance from its source. Similarly, the Christians in Laodicea had strayed far from their Savior and his teachings, making their faith appear useless to the non-believers in the area. What hope did they have? Recall that Jesus introduced himself to the Laodicean church as "the Amen" and "the faithful and true witness" (Rev. 3:14). These descriptions point to his trustworthy and accurate assessment of the Laodiceans. But he also calls himself the "beginning of God's creation" (Rev. 3:14).[5] This title doesn't mean that Jesus was the first created being. Instead, as the rest of the New Testament attests, Jesus is the origin of all creation. All things, visible and invisible, were created by Jesus (Col. 1:16); therefore, he is uniquely qualified to descend into the mess of Laodicea to recreate her.

Jesus' stern warning to the Laodicean church is coupled with an equally powerful desire to reconcile with his bride.

Sweet Wooing

Jesus woos his bride to himself with a command, an invitation, and a promise. The command is found in verse 19: *"Those whom I love, I reprove and discipline, so be zealous and repent* (Rev. 3:19).

Few phrases hold as much significance and encouragement for those seeking restoration as this one: *"Those whom I love, I reprove and discipline."* Of the seven churches studied, this church least deserves the very thing that gives them hope: Jesus loves them. He doesn't say that he once loved them or that if they become zealous and repent, he will again love them. Instead, he loves them.

And he loves you. The command to be zealous and to repent is a call to go to the One who already loves you. Repent, because he loves you, not because you think his love is earned. The command comes with an invitation:

Behold, I stand at the door and knock. If anyone hears my voice and opens the door, I will come in to him and eat with him, and he with me. (Rev. 3:20)

To appreciate this picture of Jesus standing outside of the door knocking, we do well to see it as an allusion to an incident in the Old Testament book Song of Solomon (5:2). The Song of Solomon depicts the intimate and passionate dialogue between a married couple as they ardently express their affection toward one another. In Chapter 5, the wife has retired to her bedroom and readied herself for sleep when a knock from her husband comes upon the latched bedroom door. With the knocking, she hears, *"Open to me, my sister, my love, my dove, my perfect one,"* coming from her wet-haired lover, covered with the morning dew. The wife hesitates because she has already readied herself for a comfortable night's sleep. But then she comes to her senses, remembering that that was her husband out in the dew, her beloved, her perfect one, her dearest friend. It would be foolish to let this opportunity pass!

Do you see the picture Jesus sets before you today? So often, people use this verse for evangelistic purposes, inviting non-Christians to receive an eager, at-the-door Jesus, into their hearts. While not a terrible application of this passage, the context suggests something altogether different.[6] Christ stands at the church's door as a husband calling his bride to return to the intimacy they once enjoyed. Few passages in Holy Scripture are as sweet as this one for a person who feels they have strayed too far, too long, or in a manner too egregious to be restored to Jesus. Jesus' invitation to the

Laodiceans is also for you. He effectively says, "No matter how far you have wandered, I am right at the door if you turn around. No matter who you are, what you have done, or how far you have fallen, I am right at the door."

No matter where you are or who you are, don't hesitate to open that door which can only lead to spiritual life and refreshment. And if you do, he promises that whatever you lose in this life for his sake will be more than compensated for in the next:

> *The one who conquers, I will grant him to sit with me on my throne, as I also conquered and sat down with my Father on his throne.* (Rev. 3:21)

True and eternal riches await you at the side of Jesus. There, seated on Jesus' throne with him, you'll wear the beautiful garments of salvation. Your eyes will see the deep love and wonders of the Savior's glory.

Until then, Jesus stands at the door knocking as a husband longing for his bride. Let him who has an ear hear the Savior knocking at the door. And let it be opened for the first or for the thousandth time.

Study Questions

1. The Laodiceans lived lives indistinguishable from their non-christian neighbors. Is the Lord putting his finger on areas in your life where you need to entrust yourself to Jesus?
2. Read Proverbs 30:7–9. Is this a prayer you'll submit to the Lord? What risk comes with pursuing wealth for wealth's sake?
3. In what three things do the Laodiceans place their hope and trust? What's the significance of Jesus calling them lukewarm? How does his warning to spit them out of his mouth register in your heart? Is he warning you in this way too?
4. The order in which Jesus woos the Laodiceans is essential. What do you notice about it? How does the assurance of Jesus' love shape our response to his command to "be zealous and repent"? (Rev. 3:19).
5. How is this picture of Jesus knocking at the door in the Song of Solomon different from how you have heard it taught? Why does this matter?

---

1. For an extensive overview of Laodicea, see David E. Aune, *Revelation 1–5*, Word Biblical Commentary (Nashville, TN: Thomas Nelson, 1997), 249–250.
2. N.T. Wright, *Revelation for Everyone* (Louisville, TN: John Knox Press, 2011), 37.

3. A few textual clues suggest that the nature of the Laodicean problem involved participation in the annual feasts we've examined in previous chapters. The first clue comes from verse 17, where Jesus, speaking for the Laodiceans, alludes to a passage in Hosea 12:8. There, Hosea condemns Israel's self-congratulatory attitude that uttered, *"And Ephraim said, 'Surely, I have become rich, I have found wealth for myself... they will find in me no iniquity'"* (Hos. 12:8). Throughout the book of Hosea, Israel is charged with prosperity through dishonest measures, giving credit to the idols for their success. Jesus appears to be likening the Laodicean Christian to the idol-worshiping Israelites. A second clue suggesting participation in idol feasts is found in the description *"the shame of your nakedness"* (3:18). Uncovering the *"shame of nakedness"* is an Old Testament threat upon those who participate in idolatry (Isa. 47:3; Ezek. 16:36, Nah. 3:5). The repetition of the idiom here suggests that the Laodicean Christians are in some way involved with local idols. For this insight, see G.K. Beale, *The Book of Revelation: A Shorter Commentary* (Eerdmans, 2015), 91–92.
4. The offer of gold, white garments, and eye salve correspond to the initial vision of Christ, who wore a golden sash, white hair, and whose eyes were like a flame of fire.
5. There is some disagreement among commentators regarding the phrase *"the beginning of God's creation."* Some argue that this points to Jesus' resurrection as the beginning of the Old Testament promise to make all things new in the eschaton. In other words, with the resurrection, Jesus has inaugurated the beginning of the new heavens and the new earth. Others suggest that the phrase points to Jesus' creative role in Genesis 1. For a persuasive argument for the latter, toward which I lean, see Richard Bauckham, *The Theology of the Book of Revelation* (Cambridge University Press, 2012), 56–57.
6. Additionally, the language in verse 19 of reproof and discipline versus judicial wrath suggests that this letter is written to the children that he loves and not those he has rejected. For more on this point, see Gregory Beale, *The Book of Revelation: A Commentary on the Greek Text* (Grand Rapids, MI: Eerdmans, 2013), 307.

PART 2

THE HEAVENLY THRONE AND THE SEVEN SEALS 4:1–8:5

10

THE GLORIOUS ANCIENT OF DAYS
REVELATION 4:1–11

I enjoy the daily summer rains in South Florida. Not a single drop of water falls for about six months, but once the rainy season sets in, you can plan on an early afternoon shower nearly every day. Not only do the rains provide refreshment to the area, they often provide an added bonus—rainbows. Like most people, looking at a rainbow brings me joy. But, the truth is, I have never seen a full rainbow because there's always something in the way. It's not trees and buildings that obscure the view. Instead, the earth gets in the way.

After reading about the Pilot's Halo, I realized I had only ever seen a portion of a rainbow. If you get up high above the earth's surface on a mountain or in an airplane, you'll see more than a half-circle shape, starting and ending on either side of the horizon. Instead, you will see fully circular rainbows, unobstructed by the earth.

Think of John's vision of the throne room of God as someone giving us a perspective from above the earth to show us the fullness of God's plan for the world. John's audience needed this vision just like we do.

After all, Jesus Christ ended each of his letters to the seven churches with a promise to the *"one who conquers."* Jesus told the Ephesians, *"To the one who conquers I will grant to eat from the tree of life"* (Rev. 2:7). To the

Smyrnans, Jesus promised that those who conquered would not be hurt by *"the second death"* (Rev. 2:11). He promises hidden manna, a white stone, a new name to the conqueror in Pergamum.

What will shore up their hope? To be transported high above the earth, where, in the next chapter, we'll see a Savior who has already conquered (Rev. 5:5).

From the earthly perspective of John's audience and our own, sometimes we only see a world out of control, ruled by evil men and women. In John's day, Rome controlled the world, and the emperor sat on a wicked throne, demanding to be called a lord and a god. The emperor ruled with severe oppression founded on conquest and maintained by violence, which started to target this young community of Christians.[1] The seven churches of John's day, as well as our own, need this front-row seat, high above the earth, to see another important seat—the throne of the true Lord and God.

This vision has a powerful message for both Christians and non-Christians. For those who believe, it inspires awe, wonder, and steadfast hope in Jesus. For those who do not, it serves as a warning of what is to come and an invitation to embrace Jesus. While the vision is mysterious and intricate, some things are certain: it emphasizes the centrality of God's glory, the certainty of judgment, and the confirmation of our joy.

The Centrality of God's Glory

When we began our study of Revelation, I noted that well-meaning teachers instructed many of us to read this book in a way that creates difficulties. A popular approach to this book suggests that Chapters 1–3 deal with matters pertaining to the first-century church, while Chapters 4 to the end describe events of an as-yet unreached future time. As we move forward, I think the problems with that view will present themselves.

I suggested that we treat this book as a collection of seven portraits, all of which give us a picture of the same time period—the time between the ascension and return of Christ—but from different angles. I asked you to imagine that John held a diamond and described what he saw. Then he turns the diamond and describes the same object, but from another angle, with the light bouncing off it differently. I bring that up here because we are entering into the second portrait of the period between the ascent and return of Jesus.

I don't believe this chapter describes unmet, future events. Some of the picture is unfulfilled, but much of it occurred long ago. In the next chapter, I hope to show that the events of Chapter 5 occurred 2,000 years ago. Likewise, the Four Horsemen of the Apocalypse of Chapter 6 were released about the same time, and they still ride upon the earth.

This second portrait begins here and will conclude in Rev. 8:1, and once again, John will turn the diamond.

The first thing we see in this fresh portrait is the centrality of God's glory. John tells us that he saw a door standing open in heaven, and heard the same voice from the initial vision (Rev. 1:10). Once again, Jesus spoke to John inviting him to see what is, what has been, and what must happen before he returns. At once, he was in the Spirit,[2] and he saw a throne in heaven, on which the Lord of Glory sat:

> *At once I was in the Spirit, and behold, a throne stood in heaven, with one seated on the throne. And he who sat there had the appearance of jasper and carnelian, and around the throne was a rainbow that had the appearance of an emerald.* (Rev. 4:2–3)

We'll look at a few more details shortly, but we should address two items to begin. First, God and his glory are the all-important, all-powerful center of the vision. John sees a throne and someone seated on it. The scene he depicts radiates outwards, with crowds of individuals proclaiming the immense glory and honor that is rightfully due to God's name.

Closest to the throne, four strange creatures with six wings and full of eyes ceaselessly praise the Lord. We read:

> *And around the throne, on each side of the throne, are four living creatures, full of eyes in front and behind: the first living creature like a lion, the second living creature like an ox, the third living creature with the face of a man, and the fourth living creature like an eagle in flight. And the four living creatures, each of them with six wings, are full of eyes all around and within, and day and night they never cease to say,"Holy, holy, holy, is the Lord God Almighty, who was and is and is to come!"* (Rev. 4:6–8)

What are we to make of these four-winged creatures? In the church's earliest days, some thought the four creatures represented the four gospels. The lion-faced creature represents Matthew because, in his gospel, we discover Jesus as the Lion of Judah. The man-faced creature was Mark because of his emphasis on the humanity of Jesus. The ox represented Luke with his focus on the sacrifice of Jesus. And the eagle represented the Gospel of John, which, like the eagle, soars with a lofty presentation of the divinity of Jesus.[3]

John's revelation doesn't tell us what these four living creatures represent. But a few clues suggest they symbolize the created order. The whole creation, day to day and night after night, proclaims the glories of the One who fashioned it. Psalm 19 tells us, *"The heavens declare the glory of God,"* the sky above *"proclaims his handiwork"* (Ps. 19:1–2). Creation ceaselessly attests to the wonder, the majesty, and the power of the Lord.

Psalm 103:22 calls on the created order to bless the Lord. Perhaps the four living creatures are a symbolic representation of what is constantly occurring, minute by minute, hour by hour, and night after night. Creation points away from itself to the one who made it. The Apostle Paul tells us that creation communicates specific knowledge about its Creator to the observer. God shows us something whenever we observe a tree, a flower, or even something as mundane as our hands.

What knowledge about God does creation give to us all? The Apostle answers: creation shows us the invisible attributes of God, especially his eternal power and divine nature (Rom. 1:20). The four creatures may point to the invisible attributes of God: the lion represents the nobility of God, the ox his divine power, the man the wisdom of God, and the eagle, the highly exalted position of the Creator. The eyes that cover these living creatures may suggest that wherever creation looks, the glory of its Creator is on display.[4]

Whatever these four living creatures are, they serve to bring glory to the One on the throne. As the circle moves out from the four living creatures, John sees twenty-four elders on twenty-four thrones, casting their crowns before the Lord, proclaiming God worthy of all glory (we will focus on these elders soon). Moving further out, in the next chapter, we'll discover thousands and thousands of angels proclaiming the worth and glory of God.

Here is the first takeaway from the vision's design: God's glory is central in heaven. And at this book's end, God's glory will be foremost on earth, as it is in heaven. One writer has said that the book of Revelation shows how the Lord will fulfill the first three petitions of the Lord's Prayer: *Hallowed be thy name, your kingdom come, your will be done, on earth as it is in heaven.*[5] At present, we don't see God's name honored by everyone in every place, nor do we enjoy the fullness of God's kingdom. But we will. For God sits unshakable upon his throne. The first item of note, then, is that the glory of God is central in heaven and will one day cover the earth (Num. 14:21; Hab. 2:14).

The second thing we should address is the whole idea of glory. What does the word mean, and why is God's glory foremost on the minds and lips of those in heaven? What does it mean to speak about the glory of something?

Throughout the Old Testament, "glory" refers to what makes up the essential aspects of something. The glory of something "is its mass, its bulk, its worth, what makes it up, what its all about–indeed, what makes it *itself.*"[6] The root of the word "glory" (Hebrew: *kābôd*) refers to weight or heaviness.

If you put all the pieces of a being together, its collective weight is its glory. So, for example, the glory of a person who lives for money is money. If money drives a person, money is his glory, essence, and what makes him tick. Psalm 49 says:

> *Be not afraid when a man becomes rich, when the glory of his house increases. For when he dies he will carry nothing away; his glory will not go down after him.* (Ps. 49:16–17)

For some people, their glory is their money. For others, it's their careers, politics, children, sex, image, etc. Glory refers to someone's essence, what they are all about.

What about God's glory? Recall this was the very thing Moses asked of God, *"Please show me your glory"* (Ex. 33:18). The Lord replies, and listen for his answer to Moses' request:

> *I will make all my goodness pass before you and will proclaim before you my name 'The* Lord.*' And I will be gracious to whom I will be gracious, and will show mercy on whom I will show mercy.* (Ex. 33:19)

Moses asked the Lord about his glory, the essence of what makes God, who he is. Did you notice the Lord's answer? *"I will make all my goodness pass before you"* (Ex. 33:19). So what do we mean when we talk about the glory of God? He gives us the answer! God's glory, which is his goodness, and fills all of heaven today, will one day cover the earth as the waters cover the sea (Hab. 2:14).[7]

This is one of the reasons why the glory of God is often manifested in the Bible in the form of light. The glory of God manifests *"like radiant light, shining out, enlightening and giving life."*[8] The Father created the world to give it to his Son (Heb. 1:2). In so doing, the glory of the Father—his goodness—shines out. The Son came into the world not to do his own will, but the will of his Father (John 6:38). The glory of the Son—his goodness—shines out. The Holy Spirit, described as the *"seven spirits of God"* (Rev.

4:5) came into the world, not to bring attention to himself, but to bring glory to Jesus (John 16:14). The glory of the Spirit—his goodness—shines out in that way. In other words, "the beautiful glory of the triune God is radiating, self-giving and loving."[9]

When Ezekiel, like John, saw the throne of God and the one seated on it, he described it as gleaming metal, fire, and *"brightness all around"* (Ezek. 1:27). When Jesus was born, an angel of the Lord appeared to the shepherds and *"the glory of the Lord shone around them"* (Luke 2:9).

When Jesus was on the Mount of Transfiguration, Peter and his companions saw his glory. Matthew tells us about the glory displayed in Jesus' face, which *"shone like the sun, and his clothes became white as light"* (Matt. 17:2). John also described what he saw when he looked at the figure on the throne:

> *And he who sat there had the appearance of jasper and carnelian, and around the throne was a rainbow that had the appearance of an emerald.* (Rev. 4:3)

John doesn't attempt to give a physical form to the one on the throne. God is a spirit. He doesn't have a body, so John doesn't describe one. Instead, he writes about the glorious light he saw through the colors of the ancient world's most precious and costly gems. The idea here is that God's beauty is magnificent and the most precious thing to behold. The rainbow brings to mind the days of Noah when God flooded the earth but then "recreated" it and set his rainbow in the sky as the sign of the new creation. This emerald-colored rainbow may function as a reminder of the Lord's commitment to renew the heavens and the earth at the end of the age.

Also forward looking are each of the gems described—jasper, carnelian, and emerald. Each of these precious stones form parts of the walls and foundation of the New Jerusalem, which John will later see (Rev. 21:11, 18-20). The precious jewels speak to the infinite worth and beauty of the glory of God that will fill all of creation. The glory of God, which is central within the throne room of heaven, must—as Jesus told John (Rev. 4:1)—take place on earth.[10] So must the judgment of God.

Certainty of Judgment

We will have plenty of opportunity to address the wrath and judgment of God coming upon those who refuse to trust his Son. We won't address these matters in detail here. But we do get a glimpse the coming judgment in

John's description of what he saw and heard coming from the throne itself: *"From the throne came flashes of lightning, and rumblings and peals of thunder"* (Rev. 4:5).

John seems to be alluding here to the thunder, lightning, and rumbling, which accompanied God's self-manifestation at Mount Sinai (Ex. 19:16, 20:18).[11] We shouldn't understand the wrath and anger of God, so prevalent in the chapters to come, as an awkward aside from his goodness. God's wrath does not represent a divine temper tantrum coming from an easily provoked, irritable deity.

Instead, his wrath and terrible judgments that we'll witness only serve to magnify his glorious goodness. His wrath arises out of his love and reacts to evil. The Father loves his Son and therefore he is angry with those who reject him. He also loves his people and therefore is angry with those who mistreat them. God's wrath demonstrates the sincerity of his loving-kindness rather than an unfortunate side issue reluctantly acknowledged. When Christ returns, his light will drive out darkness; his truth will drive out lies; his goodness will drive out all evil.

And then, our joy before and in the Lord will be cemented forever.

Confirmation of Our Joy

We see this in the twenty-four elders seated on the twenty-four thrones:

> *Around the throne were twenty-four thrones, and seated on the thrones were twenty-four elders, clothed in white garments, with golden crowns on their heads... And whenever the living creatures give glory and honor and thanks to him who is seated on the throne, who lives forever and ever, the twenty-four elders fall down before him who is seated on the throne and worship him who lives forever and ever. They cast their crowns before the throne, saying, "Worthy are you, our Lord and God, to receive glory and honor and power, for you created all things, and by your will they existed and were created."* (Rev. 4:4, 9–11)

Who are these twenty-four elders on twenty-four thrones? They represent the perfect, embodied people of God. They symbolize those who looked forward to the coming of the Messiah in the Old Testament and those of us who look back to his arrival in the New Testament. Numbers in Revelation typically carry a symbolic meaning. The number twenty-four may not mean much to us until John describes the coming city of God by bringing two groups together, which counts twenty-four:

> *It had a great, high wall, with twelve gates, and at the gates twelve angels, and on the gates the names of the twelve tribes of the sons of Israel were inscribed.... And the wall of the city had twelve foundations, and on them were the twelve names of the twelve apostles of the Lamb.* (Rev. 21:12)

The twelve gates representing the twelve tribes with the twelve apostolic foundations gives us twenty-four. Consider also a few details suggesting that the elders represent the Old and New Testament saints.

First, Jesus promised the Laodiceans (Rev. 3:21) that those who conquered would sit on thrones. The elders are sitting on thrones. Next, Jesus promised the church in Sardis (Rev. 3:5) that those who conquered would be dressed in white. White garments clothe the elders. Finally, Jesus promised the conquerors in Smyrna (Rev. 2:10) a crown. The elders possess crowns which they cast at the feet of the Lord. It appears, then, that the twenty-four elders represent all of God's people, eternally dressed, crowned, and seated upon the very promises of God.

Why do we need this vision of heaven? Not only because it shows us what must happen: the knowledge of the glory of the Lord will cover the earth as the waters cover the sea (Hab. 2:14). But also, this vision shows us ourselves. Jesus Christ will keep every promise he has made to us. You will sit on thrones. The beauty of Jesus' righteousness will cover you like a garment. You'll wear a crown of life, which you'll cast back at the throne, declaring God's worth, glory, honor, and power. On that day, you will undoubtedly see that everything the Lord walked you through on this side of heaven was for our good (Rom. 8:28). The painful things, the hard providences, and the trials that at times cause our faith to stagger will be shown to magnify the goodness of God.

Christian, the day is coming when you'll see the Savior face to face and the fulfillment of each of his promises. Now we see only a piece of the rainbow. But on that day, its fullness will be unobscured. See yourself in John's vision clothed in the fulfilled promises of Jesus, and live today for the glory of God.

Study Questions

1. What is God's glory? Why does this matter?
2. As we define glory, take an honest assessment of your life. What is your glory? What makes up who you are?
3. "His wrath arises out of his love and reacts to evil." We tend to

shy away from the judgment and wrath of God. Why is it important to leave all of God's characteristics intact?

4. If this vision shows us the glory of God, his judgment, and our assurance that Jesus will keep every promise, how does this inform our emotions? Our anxiety? Our fear? Our sorrow?

---

1. For more on the brutality of the Romans, see Richard Bauckham, *The Theology of the Book of Revelation,* (Cambridge University Press, 2012), 35.
2. We could argue that John has four visions, each opening with John *"in the Spirit"* (1:10, 4:1, 17:3, 21:10). Throughout these four visions, seven portraits emerge.
3. The above designations were the most common in the early church, but some offered alternative assignments for each creature to different gospels. For the most common and alternate views, see William Barclay, *The Revelation of John* (Westminster Press, 1960) vol. 1, 202–204.
4. Additionally, in support of seeing these four living creatures as symbols of the created order, the number four is used throughout the book of Revelation to represent creation. Rev. 7:1 reveals four angels standing at the earth's four corners, holding the earth's four winds back. Chapters 5:13 and 14:7 divide the created order into four parts. The first four judgments of the seals, trumpets, and bowls affect the world (6:8; 8:7–12; 16:2–9). For more on the number four in Revelation, see Richard Bauckham, *The Theology of the Book of Revelation,* 66–67.
5. Bauckham, *The Theology of the Book of Revelation,* 40.
6. Michael Reeves, *Delighting in the Trinity* (InterVarsity Press, 2012), 121.
7. I owe this insight into the nature of the glory of God to D.A. Carson, who writes, "God's glory, then, is supremely his goodness." See D.A. Carson, *The Gospel According to John* (Grand Rapids, MI: Eerdmans, 1991), 129.
8. Reeves, *Delighting in the Trinity,* 123.
9. Ibid, 123.
10. The sea of glass before the throne of God may represent the certainty that the Lord will subdue and eradicate all evil from creation. The seas of the earth in Revelation are places of chaos, from which the people of God must be delivered (15:2), and the location from which the dragon summons the first beast (12:17–13:1). But the sea of glass in heaven, and the lack of a sea in the New Jerusalem (21:1), may represent the promise that these things are temporary.
11. For more on this, see Bauckham, *The Theology of the Book of Revelation,* 40–43.

11

THE LION, THE WEEPER, AND THE WORSHIPERS

REVELATION 5:1–14

Some time ago, I read about Darwin Smith, the one-time CEO of the Kimberly-Clark Corporation. During his tenure, the corporation lost revenue, stock values dropped, and the once-loyal base of customers drifted to their competitors. In response, Darwin Smith called a meeting with all his corporate officers and surprised them by standing behind his chair. He said, "I want everyone to rise in a moment of silence."

The officers around the table were confused, and they whispered, "Has someone died? Why a moment of silence?" Dutifully, each executive stood and reverently stared at the floor. Then, after an appropriate pause, Darwin Smith said in a somber tone, "That was a moment of silence for [our competition]." Everyone immediately broke out in celebration because they needed a leader with a vision right in that moment.[1]

This dramatic event united people under one vision. Though clever, did Darwin have what it would take to make sure his corporation would beat the competition? After all, he couldn't control the markets, see into the future, or be present in the boardrooms of the competition. So, while it was a clever leadership tactic, the outcome still remained uncertain. But those who followed him were re-energized.

Jesus' throne room vision should energize us even more. John shares what he saw when he peered into the boardroom of the CEO of the universe! He went to great effort to depict the Ancient of Days, Creator of heaven and earth, surrounded by four living creatures, twenty-four elders seated on twenty-four thrones, and the seven spirits of God. All of them praised the Lord for his eternal existence and the created world's wonders. John saw God's glory—which referred to his essential goodness—issuing from the throne of God, which must come into all the earth.

In this chapter, we'll watch as a drama plays out. The Ancient of Days has a scroll in his hand. Like an architect with blueprints or a general with a map containing the battle strategy, an angel asks who can carry out the Lord's plan. We can see how, and through whom, the Ancient of Days will spread his glory.

John's first audience needed this vision, and we do too. We need it because it's easy to let the immediate circumstances of our lives—like political elections, inflation, troubled relationships, or our health—crowd out the bigger picture: our God reigns over all history, including elections, relationships, and health. But he doesn't reign over this world as an indifferent machine, pushing forward the wheel of history from one generation to the next.

Instead, he showcases the splendor of his glory. That means our ups and downs, trials and victories, good days and bad ones don't hinge on the brute forces of the universe. Instead, they come to us through the hands once nailed to a cross. Revelation 5 gives us this assurance by showing us that Jesus Christ, the lover of your soul, reigns over history. And his reign calls us to respond with obedient trust.

Reigns Over History

The scene opens with attention falling on a scroll in the hands of the Lord:

> *Then I saw in the right hand of him who was seated on the throne a scroll written within and on the back, sealed with seven seals. And I saw a mighty angel proclaiming with a loud voice, "Who is worthy to open the scroll and break its seals?" And no one in heaven or on earth or under the earth was able to open the scroll or to look into it, and I began to weep loudly because no one was found worthy to open the scroll or to look into it.* (Rev. 5:1–4)

What is this scroll, and why can no one open it? Reviewing a few events that occurred long before John's vision helps us to understand the scroll. The first one happened in the life of Ezekiel, an Old Testament prophet. Like John, Ezekiel saw a vision of the Lord. In that vision, Ezekiel received a scroll with writing on the front and back (Ezek. 2:9–10), matching the description of the scroll John saw. Ezekiel's scroll contained words of judgment, lamentation, and woe. As we proceed in

John's vision, we will also see and hear messages of judgment, suffering, and lament.

The second event that helps us understand the scroll happened in the life of Daniel, another Old Testament prophet. Like Ezekiel, Daniel received messages of judgment, followed by the salvation of God's people. Daniel sometimes became confused and overwhelmed with what the Lord told him (Dan. 8:26–27; 12:8) about the coming judgments. At the end of Daniel's book, the Lord instructs him to "seal the book" until the end times (Dan. 12:4).

The scroll John saw in the hand of the Ancient of Days was sealed shut. Putting these two events together, the scroll of John's vision appears to blend Ezekiel's scroll of judgment with Daniel's sealed scroll of judgment and salvation, to be opened in the end times.[2]

An angel cries out with a loud voice, *"Who is worthy to open the scroll and break its seals"* (Rev. 5:2). In other words, "Who can carry out the plan of the Ancient of Days—the plan of judgment and salvation?"

Sadly, no worthy candidates were found. But why? We must return to the Garden of Eden to find the answer. In the Garden, we discover God's plan for people: to rule over the earth as God's delegated representatives. God made people in his image and told them:

> *Be fruitful and multiply and fill the earth and subdue it; and rule over the fish of the sea and over the birds of the heavens and over every living thing on the earth.* (Gen. 1:28)

In other words, Adam and Eve were designed and charged to reflect the kingly rule of God.[3] This was God's original plan—that people rule over the earth. So, the angel's question could be rephrased as "Is there a man or woman who has perfectly reflected the Creator?" But unfortunately, none were found because all have fallen short of God's glory and contributed to this world's sin and misery.[4]

John begins to weep. And if we consider the consequences of this book of judgment and salvation not being executed, we might join him! If the scroll remained sealed, the promises of the Bible wouldn't come true.

- Jesus wouldn't be acknowledged as innocent of all sin (Rev. 5:9).
- The slain martyrs wouldn't receive justice (Rev. 6:10).
- The prayers of God's people would go unanswered (Rev. 8:4).
- The wicked wouldn't be judged (Chps. 16–18).

- Jesus wouldn't return (Chps. 19–20).
- Every tear would remain unwiped from our eyes (21:4).

In short, evil would win. Your life would have no meaning, significance, or value. If no one opened this scroll, heaven would be empty of all humans, and image-bearers would be stacked to the rafters in hell. Of course John weeps. We would have too.

Thankfully, John hears a worthy candidate has been found. And even before we look, we know who it is:

And one of the elders said to me, "Weep no more; behold, the Lion of the tribe of Judah, the Root of David, has conquered, so that he can open the scroll and its seven seals." (Rev. 5:5)

These titles, "the Lion of the tribe of Judah" and "the Root of David" echo Old Testament promises of the great Messianic figure who would come to crush the enemy and deliver God's people from oppression (Gen. 49:9; Isa. 11:1–10). John hears about a ferocious messianic warrior, perhaps expecting to see the Lion just described or a mighty champion like David. Instead, he saw a picture of weakness and vulnerability:

And between the throne and the four living creatures and among the elders I saw a Lamb standing, as though it had been slain, with seven horns and with seven eyes, which are the seven spirits of God sent out into all the earth. And he went and took the scroll from the right hand of him who was seated on the throne. (Rev. 5:6–7)

John sees not a lion but a lamb. And not just a lamb, but one that, though living, gave evidence that it had been slain. Most likely, the Lamb's throat showed signs of having been opened with a knife. A slain-but-living lamb pictures not only the crucifixion of Jesus Christ but also his triumphant resurrection back to life. The elder tells us that the Messiah has conquered (Rev. 5:5).

And here we see how he conquered: the judgments in the scroll, which hung over the heads of his people, fell upon him. John also sees that the Lamb has seven horns and seven eyes. In the Bible, horns signify power (Deut. 33:17; Ps. 89:17, 24; Dan. 7:8, 11, 20–21). We've learned that seven is the number of fullness or totality. This vision depicts Jesus as someone who has great power and uses it to serve others. The Lamb's seven eyes point to his omniscience. Nothing escapes his notice.

Before going further, does your understanding of success, victory, and conquering revolve around the image of Jesus Christ as a lion and a lamb utilizing his power and authority to serve others? Recall that each of the seven letters to the churches contained promises for those who conquered.

Here we see the basis for all of those promises. A lamb that appears to have been slain is what conquering looks like. The one who conquers takes up their cross, lives for the glory of God, and seeks the good of others. This picture of Jesus—dying to self for others—is a foretaste of what those who follow him will be called to do in the chapters ahead. So take up your cross and "follow the Lamb wherever he goes" (Rev. 14:4).

Returning to the vision, the Lamb approaches the throne, takes the scroll, and the worship in heaven transforms as soon as he does. The Lamb becomes the new focus of worship.[5] The four living creatures bow before the Lamb as the twenty-four elders sing a new song:

Worthy are you to take the scroll and to open its seals, for you were slain, and by your blood you ransomed people for God from every tribe and language and people and nation, and you have made them a kingdom and priests to our God, and they shall reign on the earth. (Rev. 5:9–10)

The elders are not only singing, but they also hold harps in their hands (Rev. 5:8). As far as we can tell, Israel's worship didn't include musical instruments until King David introduced them.[6] In the same way, adding musical instruments with the arrival of David's offspring transforms heaven's worship. John also sees an even greater host of worshipers enter the picture. Myriads of angels sing in a loud voice: "*Worthy is the Lamb who was slain, to receive power and wealth and wisdom and might and honor and glory and blessing!*" (Rev. 5:12)

And then praise ripples to the very edge of creation until the worship of heaven echoes over all the created order:[7]

And I heard every creature in heaven and on earth and under the earth and in the sea, and all that is in them, saying, "To him who sits on the throne and to the Lamb be blessing and honor and glory and might forever and ever!" And the four living creatures said, "Amen!" and the elders fell down and worshiped. (Rev. 5:13–14)

Do your best to set the whole scene before your mind's eye. Jesus draws near to the Father to take his place as the King. This King will reign over the salvation of God's people and the judgment of those who refuse him. Some well-meaning Bible teachers suggest that this drama describes an unreached future time.[8]

I don't believe that is the best way to understand what we have just studied. Instead, John saw and described what happened when Jesus ascended to heaven. He took his seat upon the throne of God and, from there, he exercises all rule and authority in heaven and earth.[9] If you've ever wondered what happened when Jesus ascended into the clouds, Revelation 5 gives us the answer. At the ascension, he presented himself as the slaughtered lamb, now raised, having completed the will of his Father, ready to take his place far above all earthly powers (Mark 10:45; Eph. 1:20). Paul tells us that when Jesus ascended to heaven, the Lord *"put all things under his feet and gave him as head over all things"* (Eph. 1:22).

Response of Obedient Trust

Do you see why this vision would have been as crucial for the first-century church as it is for us? If we know that Jesus Christ, who has all power, is presently ruling over the details of our lives, our perspective changes. In the first century, Emperor Domitian demanded to be called lord and god, and he started systematically killing Christians for refusing to worship him. Some of us have people in our lives who intimidate and mock us for our faith. I've been told that I preach "outdated fairy tales."

What do we see in verse 13? A picture of the future. Somewhere in Heaven or Hell, Emperor Domitian is on a bent knee today, acknowledging that Jesus Christ is Lord. So too, will the knees of the one who intimidates you be bent before Jesus. Be not afraid!

This vision also shows us that the one who holds the blueprints of our lives knows the difficulties of trusting the Lord when his love appears mysterious. Look at the neck of the Lamb. John says the Lamb was alive but bore the appearance of having been slain.

Perhaps John saw that the neck of the Lamb was cut and had blood stains on its chest. Even before you look at his neck, look at Jesus in the garden of Gethsemane (Mark 14:32–42). Look at him pleading with his Father for another way. Look at his terror in facing the wrath of God. Look at him weeping with tears on his cheeks and repeatedly falling to the ground. Look at him as he had a request from his Father denied for the first time in eternity.

Christian, you serve a Savior who understands the deep pain and confusion that often comes from God's plans. We follow a Savior who knows the disorientation when we ask for things we think we need and believe are for our good, only to have the Lord say "No." Look at his neck. And then look at him in the garden, who for the joy set before him—the joy of serving His Father and redeeming his bride—he endured the cross and is now seated at the right hand of the throne of God (Heb. 12:2). This is the one whose nail-scarred hands hold the blueprints of your life and mine. This assurance calls for bold trust.

Recently, I read a story by Ernest Gordon, who spent three years in a Japanese POW camp during the Second World War. He and several fellow prisoners were forced to build a railway through the jungle. Gordon recalls an event that occurred at the end of a long, painful day of construction. The prisoners had to turn in their shovels, which were counted to ensure none were missing. As the men were ready to be dismissed for the day, a Japanese soldier started yelling in broken English that a shovel was missing. He insisted that one of the prisoners had stolen the shovel and that if the guilty man didn't confess, he would kill the entire group of prisoners. "All die! All die!" he shrieked. Then, to show he was serious, he cocked his rifle, put it to his shoulder, and looked down the sights, ready to fire at the first man at their end.

Suddenly, a prisoner stepped forward, stood at attention, and said, "I did it." The Japanese captor was so enraged at the man that he beat him with the stock of his rifle until the man was dead. The next day, the prisoners returned to work, and it was found that there had been a miscount the day before. All the shovels were there; none were missing. Refusing to allow his fellow prisoners to die, that man courageously stepped forward and took the blows for his people. Gordon later said that that incident was the turning point in the morale of the prison camp. That man's unspeakable sacrifice gave them the hope they needed to endure imprisonment.[10]

How much more hope do we have when we think of Christ, who, for the joy of purchasing his people for himself, took the blows owed to us so that we might live? That same one, who loves you, has been exalted above all earthly powers, and he will bring the glory of God to this earth. Therefore, give him the fullness of your trust.

Study Questions

1. Everything that comes to you passes "through the hands of the one who is love." How does this shape how we live on both good and bad days?
2. We take comfort as we look at the neck of the slain Lamb and see him in Gethsemane, falling and pleading. How does this image of the Savior as slain comfort you? How does it shape our definition of conquering? Success?
3. Jesus reigns over history, which demands a response of obedient trust. In what areas of your life are you not trusting him? Ask the Lord to reveal them to you and repent of your unbelief. "I believe! Lord, help my unbelief."

---

1. This story is recounted in Jim Collins, *Good to Great* (New York, NY: HarperCollins, 2001), 81.
2. See G.K. Beale, *The Book of Revelation: A Shorter Commentary* (Eerdmans, 2015), 111; Vern S. Poythress, *The Returning King: A Guide to the Book of Revelation* (P&R, 2000), 108.
3. For more on this theme, See G.K. Beale, *The Temple and the Church's Mission* (Interarsity Press, 2004), 81.
4. Psalm 14 attests to the dreadful situation we've created: *"The LORD looks down from heaven on the children of man, to see if there are any who understand, who seek after God. They have all turned aside; together they have become corrupt; there is none who does good, not even one"* (Ps. 14:2–3).
5. Additionally, there is a shift in the focus of worship from chapters four to five. While the worship of chapter four focused on God's actions in creation, Chapter 5 shifts attention to redemption and re-creation. See Vern S. Poythress, *The Returning King: A Guide to the Book of Revelation*, 107.
6. Peter J. Leithart, "Lamb Ascendant," *First Things*, Web Exclusive (June 6th, 2014), https://www.firstthings.com/web-exclusives/2014/06/lamb-ascendant.
7. Most commentators understand this last circle of praise as a glimpse into the future where *"every knee should bow, in heaven and on earth and under the earth, and every tongue confess"* that Jesus Christ is Lord (Phil. 2:10). See G.K. Beale, *The Book of Revelation: A Shorter Commentary* 118; Vern S. Poythress, *The Returning King: A Guide to the Book of Revelation*, 112.
8. Donald Grey Barnhouse suggested that the Book of Revelation "is entirely concerned with the future from the beginning of the fourth chapter." Donald Grey Barnhouse, *Revelation: An Expositional Commentary* (Grand Rapids, MI: Zondervan, 1971), 192.
9. Crucial to this interpretation is recognizing Daniel 7:9ff as the model behind Revelation Chapters 4–5. It lies outside the scope of the present work to tease out all the details. I encourage readers to consult Beale's exhaustive commentary and France's treatment in his commentary on Mark. See G.K. Beale, *The Book of Revelation: A Commentary on the Greek Text* (Grand Rapids MI: Eerdmans, 2013), 311–369; R. T. France, *The Gospel of Mark: A Commentary on the Greek Text* (Eerdmans, 2009), 341–343.
10. Ernest Gordon's story can be found in his autobiography, *Through the Valley of the Kwai*.

12

THE FOUR HORSEMEN
REVELATION 6:1-8

I'll never forget the World War II Air Force veteran's story about how he learned to fly. Long before computer-simulated flight training, instructors took young pilot candidates into the sky to experience anticipated scenarios. An element of the training included a night-time flight, where the instructor and student would fly the aircraft into a  heavy, thick layer of clouds, and they couldn't see anything—no stars, moon, or any visible landmarks. Once the cloud cover obscured everything outside the craft, the instructor would ask, "What direction are we flying?"

Sometimes the student would look out the window and offer up a guess like, "I think we're flying South." "Wrong," the instructor would respond. "No guessing. Check your compass." After several minutes, the instructor asked, "Are we ascending or descending?" If the student looked out the window again, the instructor would say, "No guessing. Check your instruments." By the time the training was over, those who went on to fly planes had learned to rely on the surety of the instrument panel, not upon their unreliable senses.

In our lives, we are called to live by faith. Sometimes, we feel like we're flying through thick, dark clouds at night. At some point in your life, if you're not already there, you'll encounter circumstances that seem to contradict the character and promises of God. Jesus promises us: *"In the world you will have tribulation"* (John 16:33). It's not a question of "if," but "when" tribulation comes.

For some, that tribulation manifests itself in worry about the future, our country, and finances. For others, hardship is more relational: troubled marriages, prodigal children, rejection by a family member because of your faith. For others still, as they look out on a world that appears to be out of control and filled with meaningless chaos, they can be tempted to tune out, fall into hopeless despair, or become emotionally numb to it all.

As we've already seen, John's first audience faced many dreadful tribulations. They suffered economically because they wouldn't attend the feasts to pagan gods (Rev. 2:9). They suffered relationally as the objects of slander for their faith (Rev. 2:9). Some went to prison for Jesus (Rev. 2:10). Others were murdered for their testimony (Rev. 2:13). Those within the seven churches had no shortage of tribulation. And perhaps, they wondered, "Is Jesus really on the throne? How can we square the awful calamities we see on earth with the idea of a sovereign, holy, and good God?" John's first audience needed this chapter of Revelation as much as we do. It shows us that Christ reigns over all of history and even over the trials that sometimes cause our faith to stumble.

Like the instructor to the pilot candidate, this chapter discourages guessing about what is happening in the world. Instead, it encourages us to set our eyes on the one who holds the scroll and breaks its seals, and in so doing, carries out his purposes in the world.

Purposes

The previous chapter examined what happened when Jesus ascended into Heaven. In John's vision, he saw a Lamb, who appeared to have been slain, approach the throne of God. The Lamb took a scroll from God, one sealed with seven seals. The scroll represents God's plan for the judgment of evil and the salvation of his people. We suggested that when Jesus ascended to his Father, he took his place on the throne. Taking the scroll into his hand symbolized what the Apostle Paul wrote to the Ephesians. Paul asserted that when God raised Jesus from the dead and seated him at his right hand, it was *"far above all rule and authority and power and dominion... not only in this age but also in the one to come"* (Eph. 1:20–21). Continuing, Paul confirmed that "All things" have been put "under his [Jesus'] feet" and he is "head over all things."

That is to say, Revelation 5 gives us a glimpse of the Father's reception of his Son back into heaven, and God grants Jesus all authority to carry out God's judicial and redemptive plans for the world. Revelation 6 gives us a glimpse of what we should expect during this time between the ascension of Jesus and his return. And perhaps if we were writing the script, we might hope or expect a very different picture to emerge, one with suffering eradicated, evil punished, death done away with, and the earth restored to its pre-fall glories. And to be sure, God's people will realize those longed-for dreams in the end. But before that great and glorious day, four horses gallop across the globe between Jesus' ascension and return.

To understand these four horses, we must return to Zechariah's Old Testament book. The prophet Zechariah describes (Zech. 1:7–17) a vision of four groups of horses with different colors patrolling the earth. The four horsemen report to the Lord that the surrounding nations have persecuted his people and that, from all appearances, they've done so without any consequence. The horsemen ask the Lord, *"How long will you have no mercy on Jerusalem?"* (Zech. 1:12). The Lord assures the patrolmen that he is jealous for his people (Zech. 1:14) and angry with the nations oppressing them (Zech. 1:15).

Fast forward several chapters. Zechariah sees the multi-colored four horsemen again. This time, they pull chariots, the ancient equivalent of tanks. In Chapter 1, the patrollers question "How long?" is answered with the command to the horses, *"Go, patrol the earth"* (Zech. 6:7), meaning they must destroy the nations that have oppressed God's people. Two chariots go North, the direction from which the Babylonians and Persians came upon the Lord's people. Two chariots go south toward Egypt, the other great threat to Israel.[1] The Four Horsemen of Zechariah represent the Lord's judgment upon any nation, or people groups, that oppose and oppress his people.

With that Old Testament background in mind, we return to John, who also sees multi-colored horses that Christ sends out through the breaking of the first four seals. Cooperating with the horses of Zechariah, we should see the horses here as serving the same purpose: to punish those who oppress and oppose the people of God. But there is another reason for these horses, which is hinted at in verse 8:

> *And I looked, and behold, a pale horse! And its rider's name was Death, and Hades followed him. And they were given authority over a fourth of the earth, to kill with sword and with famine and with pestilence and by wild beasts of the earth.* (Rev. 6:8)

The summary statement offered at the end of verse 8—killing with the sword, famine, pestilence, and wild beasts—is a quote from the book of Ezekiel (Ezek. 14:21). There, the Lord threatens all of Israel with these four judgments for their rampant idolatry. But even so, through those same terrible judgments, which will fall on every member of Israel, the Lord will purify his people. Put another way: Terrible things are coming upon all of Israel—sword, famine, pestilence, and wild beasts—that will punish those who don't follow the Lord. But at the same time, those judgments will also affect and refine the faith of those who love the Lord.

Putting these backgrounds together—Zachariah's four horses of punishment and Ezekiel's four judgments of punishment and purification—we're left to view John's four horses as having a dual purpose: to punish those who oppress God's people while simultaneously refining the faith of those who trust in the Lord.[2]

Turning to the horses themselves, we first see a white horse:

Now I watched when the Lamb opened one of the seven seals, and I heard one of the four living creatures say with a voice like thunder, "Come!" And I looked, and behold, a white horse! And its rider had a bow, and a crown was given to him, and he came out conquering, and to conquer. (Rev. 6:1–2)

For good reasons, some have identified this horse with Jesus himself. There are weighty reasons for doing so. First, later in Revelation (19:11–16), John will see Jesus atop a white horse, wearing crowns on his head, coming to conquer his enemies. Second, in the book of Revelation, white typically symbolizes the holiness of God, Christ, or his people. Third, the theme of conquering in the book thus far is associated with Christ (Rev. 5:5), who makes promises to those who likewise conquer (Rev. 2:7, 11, 17, 26; 3:5, 12, 21).[3]

Strong as these reasons appear, I think it's better to understand that this white horse represents Satan-inspired, man-centered empires that charge to and fro, conquering others and oppressing God's people. There are three reasons for this assertion.[4]

First, the four horsemen of Zechariah each work together to bring suffering and woe. Zechariah's horses function as one unit; we should probably see John's horses similarly. Second, as we'll see in the coming chapters, Satan-inspired forces often manifest themselves through the imitation of Christ. A beast rising out of the sea will appear to have been wounded, like the Lamb, but then healed (Rev. 13:3), imitating Christ. Again, a second beast will appear with the horns of a lamb and perform miracles (Rev.

13:11–14), another gross caricature of Jesus. This rider on the white horse is an inadequate substitution for the white horse Jesus rides in the later chapters of this book. And third, while the theme of conquering has thus far been associated with Jesus and his people, John will later tell us in two different places that the beast will make war on Christ-followers and conquer them (Rev. 11:7; 13:7). To summarize, the white horse probably refers to any Satan-inspired nation, empire, or people group that seeks to conquer people and oppress the people of God.

John's audience surely would have thought of the Romans who sought to maintain the *Pax Romana* through military might. This white horse would have reminded them of Roman generals returning from a military victory. They would lead processions through the streets of Rome on chariots pulled by white horses with enslaved people following behind. The white horse was a symbol of victory for the Romans.[5]

But at the same time, we shouldn't treat the white horse, or any of the horses, as a one-time event fulfilled in the past or an as-yet unreached future occurrence. Instead, these four horses ride across the globe to this very day. For some of our brethren, the white horse represents the Chinese government. In North Korea, the Kim family gallops like a white horse on Christians. For others, the anti-Christian Indian government embodies the white horse. This horse represents any and every Satan-inspired empire or people group that seeks to conquer others and persecute Christians as they go.

The second horse, the bright red one holding a sword, would also have reminded John's audience of their Roman oppressors:

> *When he opened the second seal, I heard the second living creature say, "Come!" And out came another horse, bright red. Its rider was permitted to take peace from the earth, so that people should slay one another, and he was given a great sword.* (Rev. 6:3–4)

The red horse and the great sword its rider wields point to warfare, but more particularly to the persecution of Christians. Jesus' words to his disciples are alluded to here: *"Do not think that I have come to bring peace to the earth. I have not come to bring peace, but a sword."* (Matt. 10:34). The second horse wielding a sword and taking peace from the earth, symbolizes what Jesus promised to those who follow him. Some would face a literal sword, as John's audience did and as many Christians worldwide do today. In fact, in the fifth seal, examined more closely in the next chapter, martyrs cry out to God from under an altar. Those who cry are the ones killed for the word of God and their unwavering testimony to Jesus (Rev. 6:9).[6] But all

Christians who don't compromise or hide their faith will know the sword of division.

Jesus tells us he'll set sons against fathers, daughters against mothers, and in-laws against in-laws. A person's enemies will often live in the same home (Matt. 10:35–36). Maybe you know what that sword of family division feels like, as I do. Faithfulness to Jesus will sometimes bring you loss. This second horse reminds every generation of the church that persecution should not surprise us as though something strange is happening (1 Pet. 4:12).

And sometimes, persecution comes from an economic angle. Consider the black horse:

> *When he opened the third seal, I heard the third living creature say, "Come!" And I looked, and behold, a black horse! And its rider had a pair of scales in his hand. And I heard what seemed to be a voice in the midst of the four living creatures, saying, "A quart of wheat for a denarius, and three quarts of barley for a denarius, and do not harm the oil and wine!"* (Rev. 6:5–6)

The black horse carries a rider holding a pair of scales in his hand. In the ancient world, particularly in times of limited resources, people rationed food by weight through scales.[7] In addition to the scales, a voice sounds from the throne that a quart of wheat would cost a denarius and three quarts of barley for the same. A denarius represented about a day's wage for the ordinary laborer, and a quart of wheat could feed one person for the day. However, this horse brings extreme inflation and food chain supply issues. The price listed for wheat and barley amounts to eight to ten times the average price in the Roman Empire at the time. In 2023, the equivalent would be spending $25 for a loaf of bread or $40 for a gallon of gas. The order not to harm the oil and wine—considered non-essentials and more luxurious items—probably suggests a picture of the wealthy, generally unaffected by the shortages. While everyone else struggles just to eat, the rich still have all the wine and oil they desire.[8]

John's audience would have felt the sting of these words. We've already examined how Christians paid an economic price for refusing to participate in the annual feasts. Only through participation in the Roman cults did people prosper socially and economically. Refusing to participate often led Christians down the road to social and economic poverty (Rev. 2:9). Thus, in times of famine, they were the first to be affected.

This is still the case today. I recently read a report produced by a Christian advocacy group called Open Doors. The report detailed how secular governments worldwide used the Covid pandemic to increase pressure on Christian minorities. In China, they've not only increased surveillance of the general population but also started putting facial recognition cameras in state-approved churches. In India, the Hindu nationalist government has blocked all incoming funding designated for Christian-run hospitals, schools, and church organizations. In Nigeria, Christian families receive only one-sixth of the Covid-relief rations allocated to Muslim families.[9]

Perhaps you've been passed over for a job because of your integrity. Maybe you work in an environment where a transparent testimony for Jesus would cost you your job. Perhaps your public faith excludes you from certain social circles that would bring you greater opportunity for financial gain. The black horse was released at the ascension of Jesus, and the horse still gallops across the globe, pounding its hooves down hard in some areas, softer in others. But still, he rides.

As does the final horse, described as a pale one:

When he opened the fourth seal, I heard the voice of the fourth living creature say, "Come!" And I looked, and behold, a pale horse! And its rider's name was Death, and Hades followed him. And they were given authority over a fourth of the earth, to kill with sword and with famine and with pestilence and by wild beasts of the earth. (Rev. 6:7–8)

This horse symbolizes death, just as its rider is named. Behind the horse follows Hades, the abode of the dead. Death cuts people down, and Hades gathers them in. The fourth horse summarizes and stands as the consequence of the preceding three.[10] We know that all men and women die. But not all die in old age or because of what we'd call natural causes. Instead, John heard that the fourth horse is given authority "over a fourth of the earth." This partial authority suggests that a sizable portion of those who die do so due to wars, famines, plagues, and the social disasters accompanying the white, red, and pale horses.

Why does the Lord give us this vision of the four horsemen and the terrible calamities they bring? The most important part of this vision is not simply communicating the nature of the time before Christ returns—a time of wars, bloody conquests, famines, and persecutions. Rather, our faith buoys up with the assurance that Christ reigns over them all.

Christ opens each of the seals. Not Satan. Not John. Only Jesus is worthy to carry out God's plan of judgment and salvation. Four times (vv. 1, 3, 5, 7), we hear a command given: "Come!" And four times, the riders obey. Representing terrible suffering and God's judgments, these riders have no authority on their own. Christ summons them for his purposes.

Knowing this makes all the difference in the world when you face painful relational, economic, and physical trials that can make your faith stagger. When we wonder why these things happen, we might ask, "Does chaos reign?" The answer given in the four horses is a firm "No."

Christ shows us that in everything that comes our way—when sinners and Satan beat us up or when we catch Covid and lie in a hospital bed—he is not a passive observer. He rules over sinners, Satan, economies, supply chain issues, inflation, and, as we saw in Chapter 1, even over Death and Hades (Rev. 1:18). He is sovereign over all. The ups and downs, the good days and the bad, pass first through the hands of Jesus, who loves us and has freed us from our sins by his blood (Rev. 1:5).

A friend recently told me of a failed prank many Halloweens ago. He loves to play practical jokes on his kids. This year, he wanted to scare his oldest son, who bragged that he wasn't afraid of anything. So he decided to take his kids to a house in the neighborhood where he knew the owner of the home—Mr. Johnson—liked to dress in frightening costumes. He had heard Mr. Johnson had picked the Grim Reaper, complete with a skull mask, a long flowing black robe, and a sickle in his hand.

His son had never seen the Grim Reaper, so he knew that as soon as his boy saw this terrible creature, he'd run for his life. They made their way to the Johnsons' home with all his plans in place. Up the sidewalk, his son walked toward the front door. Before he could ring the bell, Mr. Johnson jumped through the door screaming, "I'm going to get you! You better run!" To my friend's surprise, his son smiled and said, "Hello, Mr. Johnson! Trick or treat." After the boy returned to his father, my friend asked him, "Why weren't you afraid?" The boy said, "I knew who it was. I saw his hands. I would recognize Mr. Johnson's hands anywhere, and I saw them when he opened the door. So, I wasn't afraid."

When the ways of the Lord mystify, disorient, and even bring us to doubt, we must look at the hands of Jesus, the ones that hold the scroll and break the seals open. Remember that those same hands were nailed to a tree for you. Even if we can't understand what he is doing now through our trials, we can look at his hands and know his love for us. Come to him. Trust him. God is at work in ways that will one day astonish you.

Study Questions

1. At some point in your life, if you're not already there, you'll know circumstances that seem to contradict the character and promises of God. How do we reconcile what we see in the world and our lives with the idea of a holy, sovereign, and good God?
2. Is it difficult for you to see Jesus behind the sending of these horsemen? How does the Lord's total control over these events change how you view your circumstances?
3. The White Horse: in what ways do we hear and feel the thundering of the white horses' hooves today?
4. The Red Horse: this symbolizes what Jesus promised to those who follow him. How has this horse thundered through your life?
5. The Black Horse: it brings "persecution from an economic angle" as it rips through the world. Where do we see this horse in our own lives? What about the lives of Christians around the world?
6. The Pale Horse: "Death cuts people down, Hades gathers them in." This horseman is the consequence of the first three. What is the significance of this horseman's authority over a fourth of the earth?
7. "When the ways of the Lord mystify, disorient, and even cause us to doubt, the instruction is to look at the hands of Jesus." What difference would beholding the hands of Jesus make when you face hard trials?

---

1. See C. F. Keil and F. Delitzsch, *Commentary on the Old Testament*, 10 vols., *The Minor Prophets* (Hendriksen, Peabody, Massachusetts, 1996), 10:552.
2. For an exhaustive examination of the Zechariah and Ezekiel backgrounds, see G.K. Beale, *The Book of Revelation: A Commentary on the Greek Text* (Grand Rapids MI: Eerdmans, 2013), 372–374.
3. For what I regard as the best argument for seeing Christ as the white horse, see William Hendriksen, *More than Conquerors* (Baker Books, 1998), 93–99.
4. I owe these arguments to the insights of G.K. Beale, whose exhaustive commentary gives these three reasons for rejecting Christ as the white horse, along with several more. See G.K. Beale, *The Book of Revelation: A Commentary on the Greek Text*, 372–377.
5. William Barclay, *The Revelation of John* (Westminster Press, 1960) vol. 2, 4.
6. That Christian persecution is particularly in mind is also suggested by the use of the word "slay" used by John without exception to refer to the death of Christ or his followers. See G.K. Beale, *The Book of Revelation: A Commentary on the Greek Text*, 379.

7. Additionally, the scale is used in the Old Testament as a metaphorical symbol of famine. See Ibid., 381.
8. A mandate given by Domitian in AD 92 ordering the reduction of land dedicated to vines and a corresponding increase in land devoted to grain may be behind the cry not to harm the wine or the oil. However, Domitian's edict was so unpopular in Asia Minor, the region where the seven churches resided, the wealthy landowners staunchly refused to abide by the proclamation and eventually won an exemption. Some suggest that it's the voice of the wealthy landowners echoed from the throne, who are effectively saying: "Whatever you do, don't touch our wine and oil!" See David A. DeSilva, *A Week in the Life of Ephesus* (Downers Grove Academic, IL: IVP Academic, 2020), 72–73.
9. https://www.opendoors.org/en-US/
10. G.K. Beale, *The Book of Revelation: A Shorter Commentary* (Eerdmans, 2015), 129; Vern S. Poythress, *The Returning King: A Guide to the Book of Revelation* (P&R, 2000), 116.

13

SOVEREIGN OVER SEALS
REVELATION 6:9–17

Rico Tice, Anglican clergyman and co-author of the evangelism course *Christianity Explored*, tells the story of visiting a friend in Australia.[1] While visiting, the two of them traveled to a beach on a hot sunny day, and Rico decided he would jump in the water for a quick swim.

When his friend saw Rico planning to head for the waters, he asked him, "What are you doing?" "I'm going for a swim," Rico said. The other man responded, "What about those signs?" pointing in the direction of clearly posted signs on the beach that read: Danger: Sharks!

With bravado, Tice shrugged at the warning and said, "Don't be ridiculous! I'll be fine." His local friend warned him that shark attacks had already killed two hundred Australians, many of whom were at that very beach. "You've got to decide," he said, "whether those shark signs are there to save you or to ruin your fun." Rico looked at the water, looked again at the signs, considered his friend's warning, and decided a casual swim might not be his best decision for the day.

The passage before us issues several warnings of the impending doom and destruction of everyone and everything opposed to Jesus Christ. We have to decide whether this warning saves us or ruins our fun. The wise will heed these warnings and find them to be their encouragement and motivation to lovingly warn others of what lies ahead. On the other hand, the foolish will ignore the warnings and walk headlong into the waters of destruction, thinking that even if there are sharks, they will be fine.

May God make us wise.

In the last section, we considered the first four seals that Jesus broke off the scroll, releasing the four horsemen on the earth. The four horses represent the Satanic-inspired, man-centered empires and the consequent disasters they bring upon the world, primarily upon those who follow Jesus. Coming to the fifth seal, we hear from the people of God who have suffered under the pounding hooves of the four horses. The scene shifts from the conquest of the horses on the earth to the moving appeal from the martyrs in heaven who ask the Lord to visit their oppressors with judgment. In the sixth seal, the Lord executes the judgment requested.

This passage comforts those afflicted in this world for the sake of Jesus. But it also serves as an instrument to afflict those comfortable with their disregard for Jesus. Under those two thoughts—comfort for the afflicted and affliction of the comfortable—we'll examine seals five and six.

Comfort for the Afflicted

When Jesus released the four horses, he gave the second horse authority to slay men with the sword (Rev. 6:4). In the fifth seal, John witnesses those killed for the sake of the Gospel:

> *When he opened the fifth seal, I saw under the altar the souls of those who had been slain for the word of God and for the witness they had borne. They cried out with a loud voice, "O Sovereign Lord, holy and true, how long before you will judge and avenge our blood on those who dwell on the earth?"* (Rev. 6:9–10)

John sees and hears the voices of martyrs coming from under the altar. What is this altar, and who are these martyrs?

We'll consider the altar first. In the mobile Tabernacle, and later in the permanent Temple of Jerusalem, an altar of incense stood before a curtain that separated the priests from the room containing the Ark of the Covenant. After the priest sacrificed animals for sin, he would enter this room to burn incense on the altar, whose smoke would rise, representing the prayers of the people ascending into heaven.

So why are the saints said to be under the altar? It's an allusion to the once-a-year Day of Atonement ritual, where the priest poured blood on the altar of incense, which would then flow down the sides and gather underneath.[2] This image symbolizes those who, in the words of the Apostle Paul, presented their *"bodies as a living sacrifice, holy and acceptable to God"* (Rom. 12:1). While literal martyrs may be in mind here, likely these martyrs represent all of Christ's people who suffer for his name.[3]

Jesus informs those who follow him that he or she must die and "take up his cross" to the place of death (Mark 8:34). For *"whoever would save his life will lose it, but whoever loses his life for [Jesus'] sake will find it"* (Matt. 16:25). Every Christian is called to everlasting life. But that call to life begins with a call first to die. In the words of Dietrich Bonhoeffer, "When Christ calls a man, He bids him come and die."[4]

How do we die for Christ? In the case of these martyrs, sometimes it's by carrying out the two greatest commandments: to love the Lord and our neighbor (Mark 12:29–31). For, as Jesus instructed, there are no other commandments greater than these. The martyrs had been slain for *"the word of God and for the witness they had borne."* They loved God and their neighbor by refusing to compromise their testimony. If we love God and our neighbor, then we must be willing to die: sometimes literally, always metaphorically.

Consider how our culture defines love.[5] People throw around the slogan "Love is love" to excuse and celebrate any number of practices and worldviews which the Bible calls evil. Many told us "Love is love" before and since the Supreme Court ruled in 2015 that same-sex couples have the right to marry. "Who are we to judge? Love is love." My city recently made the news because a middle school art teacher self-identified as pansexual and discussed her sexual attraction with her students without parental consent.

You can guess how some of the pushback has manifested itself—who are you to judge? Who are we to say pansexuality shouldn't be practiced and celebrated? After all, love is love.

But Christians must not agree with this slogan and must oppose its application to evil practices. God is love. (1 John 4:8,16). And there are some things that he hates: a proud heart, a tongue that lies, and hands that shed the blood of the innocent (Prov. 6:16–19), to name a few. In Revelation 2:6, Jesus told the Ephesian church that he hates the teachings of the heretics. Therefore if we define love according to its divine source, we cannot accept that every expression of love offered by men and women pleases our Creator.

Writing to the Christians in Rome, Paul said, *"Let love be genuine."* And immediately after calling for genuine love, he writes, *"Abhor what is evil; hold fast to what is good"* (Rom. 12:9). That means that if we're to carry out the two greatest commandments—loving God and loving our neighbor—we must love them with a genuine love, which abhors evil.

That might look like saying, "I love you, and therefore I can't celebrate this. You may be angry with me and think I'm being judgmental. But your life is more important to me than my interests." We do not hate people; we abhor the behavior. Loving people may lead to being "slain" for the Word of God and the testimony you bear.

However, two comforts exist in our passage for those maligned in Jesus' name. First, white robes are gifted to the martyrs. These robes represent the divine reversal of the world's judgment upon them.[6] Just as the white horse symbolized Roman victory, so the white-clad martyrs represent those covered with heaven's triumph. This comfort presents us with the question: for whose verdict are you living? The world's or the Lord's?

There's a haunting verse in the book of John about a group of people who saw and believed in Jesus, but, they feared the authorities and didn't confess their faith. John adds this editorial comment, *"for they loved the glory that comes from man more than the glory that comes from God"* (John 12:42–43). Which glory are you prioritizing??

God comforts his afflicted people with the promise of his vindication and that he will bring justice to those who have maligned them. The martyrs asked, *"How long before you judge and avenge our blood?"* He doesn't answer with a rebuke but with encouragement to patience:

> *Then they were each given a white robe and told to rest a little longer, until the number of their fellow servants and their brothers should be complete, who were to be killed as they themselves had been* (Rev. 6:11).

To see how this comforts the afflicted, consider an alternative scenario. You have been slandered, thrown out of the synagogue, refused to participate in feasts to foreign gods, and continued to tell people about Jesus though it came at a social and financial cost. And then like Antipas (Rev. 2:13), your refusal to compromise leads to the loss of your life. Imagine now you are in the presence of God, under the altar, and you ask the Lord what he will do in response.

You'd be deflated if the Lord responded by telling you that wrath and anger have no place in his world. And that he's not in the business of punishing people or repaying men for their actions. Many of our friends and loved ones maintain this sad caricature of the Lord.

But there would be no comfort for the afflicted and maligned if this caricatured version of God represented reality. Instead of comfort, it would send the afflicted in one of two directions—either toward despair or revenge. If God does not care about injustice, why should we? If God does not care about what happens to us when we live for truth, why should we? That's the direction of despair. The other approach is revenge. If God is not going to right this wrong, I will! If God does not repay this evil, then someone should.

God would not leave his people to despair or to seek vengeance. Instead, as Paul writes to the Romans:

> *Beloved, never avenge yourselves, but leave it to the wrath of God, for it is written, "Vengeance is mine, I will repay, says the Lord." (Rom. 12:19)*

Vengeance belongs to the Lord because he is holy, true, and cares for his people. Therefore, he exhorts the martyrs to patience while donning robes of vindication, which point to God's coming justice.

Justice unfolds in the sixth seal, ushering in unimaginable affliction to those who've disregarded Jesus' summons to be saved.

Afflict the Comfortable

> *When he opened the sixth seal, I looked, and behold, there was a great earthquake, and the sun became black as sackcloth, the full moon became like blood, and the stars of the sky fell to the earth as the fig tree sheds its winter fruit when shaken by a gale. The sky vanished like a scroll that is being rolled up, and every mountain and island was removed from its place. (Rev. 6:12–14)*

Here, John witnesses the end of the present world. However, there are other places John observes this same event repeated. For example, in a later chapter (16), we'll see not only another earthquake but also another instance of islands and mountains removed. And then again in Chapter 20, earth and heaven flee from the throne of God.[7] The repetition of this cataclysmic event doesn't mean there are numerous ends of the world.

Instead, as I suggested early on, John paints several portraits of the time between the ascension and return of Jesus, and here we are coming close to the end of the second of seven images. Chapter 6 ends with the sixth seal—the undoing of creation and judgment upon the wicked. Chapter 7 is a long, beautiful, and necessary interlude followed by the seventh and final seal of Rev. 8:1, which concludes the second portrait.

Coming back to our text, the sixth seal is the end of this world in its present form. These descriptions of a ruined universe wouldn't have sounded strange to John or his first audience. Not only was this de-creation (or un-creation) of the universe described in many Old Testament passages,[8] Jesus also mentioned phenomena in the sun, moon, and stars that would accompany his return (Mark 13:24–26; Luke 21:25–27).

The judgment will be comprehensive on the created order and upon humanity. As we have seen, one of John's favorite numbers is seven, the number of completion. It's probably no accident that John describes the de-creation of the world with seven descriptions: a terrible earthquake, a darkened sun, a bloody moon, falling stars, a vanishing sky, and every mountain and island taken away. This complete undoing of the created order prepares for the recreation of the entire cosmos (Rev. 21:1). But before that glorious renewal, this earth and its rebellious inhabitants must first be shaken (Heb. 12:26–27):

> *Then the kings of the earth and the great ones and the generals and the rich and the powerful, and everyone, slave and free, hid themselves in the caves and among the rocks of the mountains, calling to the mountains and rocks, "Fall on us and hide us from the face of him who is seated on the throne, and from the wrath of the Lamb, for the great day of their wrath has come, and who can stand?"* (Rev. 6:15–17)

Just as seven elements of creation face judgment, John lists seven categories of people: kings, great ones, generals, the rich, the powerful, slaves, and free. They beg for the mercy of death which is preferable to giving an account to the one seated on the throne.

Before the terror of this moment, John witnessed the sky vanish like a rolled-up scroll (Rev. 6:14). Imagine the sky as a scroll pressed down and stretched over the top of a table when suddenly it's torn down the middle, and each half recoils to the side. What, then, is revealed?

Perhaps it's the moment John spoke of in Chapter 1:

> *Behold, he is coming with the clouds, and every eye will see him, even those who pierced him, and all tribes of the earth will wail on account of him.* (Rev. 1:7)

On that day, the question is, "who can stand" before the face of the enthroned One and the wrath-filled Lamb? (Rev. 6:17).

The world's answer is often: "If there is a God and a judgment to come,

I can stand. I'm not as bad as some people. I'm a good parent and spouse. I've never killed anyone. There are horrible people in the world, and I'm not one of them." That is to say, "If there are sharks in the ocean, I'll be fine."

Such a response assumes we'll be assessed and evaluated against people like us. But that's not what the Bible tells us. The Lord won't evaluate us against each other but against our original design: did we mirror the One whose image we bear? How did we do with the command to *"Be holy, for I am holy"* (Lev. 11:45)?

With that in mind, the question comes before us again. On that day, who can stand? The Scriptures assure us that apart from some drastic, gracious intervention, no one can stand. Psalm 76:7 asks, *"Who can stand before you when once your anger is roused?"* The prophet Nahum asked, *"Who can stand before his indignation? Who can endure the heat of his anger?"* (Nah. 1:6). The psalmist asks, *"If you, O LORD, should mark iniquities, O Lord, who could stand?"* (Ps. 130:3).

To repeat, no one, apart from God's gracious intervention, can stand before his judgment. But thankfully, the psalmist continued: *"If you, O Lord, should mark iniquities, O Lord, who could stand? But with you there is forgiveness, that you may be feared"* (Ps. 130:3–4).

Christian assurance comes from the knowledge that they have already endured the day of judgment and are found innocent of all charges and fully obedient in all things.

How so? When Jesus died on the cross, he took to himself all of our guilt—past, present, and future—and the Lord poured his wrath out on him.

We hear the echoes of what happened at the cross in this sixth seal. An earthquake followed the crucifixion of Jesus (Matt. 27:51) while an earthquake follows the opening of the sixth seal. Likewise, the sun darkened during Jesus' crucifixion (Matt. 27:45) just as its light fades at the sixth seal. Before Jesus died, he lifted his voice in agony, having received no mercy from the Lord (Matt. 27:46). At the sixth seal, cries of terror come from those who find no mercy from the Lord. After Jesus died, though the sky remained intact, the curtain in the Temple tore from top to bottom (Matt. 27:51).[9]

Only Jesus could stand before the assessment of God. But, in love, he became sin to endure the sixth seal on behalf of his people (2 Cor. 5:21). Therefore, this vision is given not to scare the one who loves Jesus. Instead, it magnifies the wonders of his love and the surety we have before him. Consider these words of the Lord God through the filter of the sixth seal and the un-doing of the creation:

For the mountains may depart and the hills be removed, but my steadfast love shall not depart from you, and my covenant of peace shall not be removed," says the LORD, who has compassion on you. (Isa. 54:10)

Therefore Christian, don't fear. As we'll see in the next chapter, you'll stand on that day. But don't be silent about that day either. Love your neighbor by telling them about the coming judgment. Tell those heading toward the ocean of judgment that there are sharks. Tell them a day is coming when not all will stand after the judgment. Then tell them you'll stand because you've already faced judgment. Love God and love your neighbor. And when you speak, pray that the Lord will afflict them out of their comfortable rejection of Christ and into his merciful arms. Tell them.

Study Questions

Comfort the Afflicted:

1. "When Christ calls a man, he bids him come and die." In our "love is love" culture, in what ways has Christ called you to die to yourself, to abhor what is evil, and to show genuine love? How might this become even more challenging in the years and decades to come?
2. Of the two comforts offered by Christ to those who die for his name's sake, which one resonates most deeply with you? The white robe of victory and vindication or the promise of sovereign and holy wrath against sin? Why is God's wrath such an important part of his character, one that we must not attempt to soften or make more palatable?

Afflict the Comfortable:

1. The day of judgment will be comprehensive. The question then is "Who can stand?" How might we communicate the truth and seriousness of this coming day to our neighbors, family, and friends?
2. Look again at the echoes of the sixth seal on the cross at Christ's crucifixion. What is the significance of this? How does it stir up your heart to love God and your neighbor?

1. An excerpt from Tice's book *Honest Evangelism*, which includes this story, can be found at https://blog.truthforlife.org/honest-evangelism-loving-people-means-warning-people.
2. There was another altar in the Tabernacle/Temple, called the brazen altar of sacrifice, under which the priest would pour the blood of the animals (Lev. 4:7; 18). The altar in John's vision refers not to the altar of sacrifice, but to the altar of incense, as later passages (8:3–5; 9:13) will make clear.
3. Christopher Watkin notes "We commonly associate martyrdom with those who are killed for the faith, but that is only the most extreme form of witness. Martyrdom is not only dying for the truth—though in the first century as in many countries today, it not infrequently is—but a mode of being in the world that points away from itself to the glorious, finished work of Christ on the cross, his ascension to reign, and his soon return." Christopher Watkin, *Biblical Critical Theory: How the Bible's Unfolding Story Makes Sense of Modern Life and Culture* (Zondervan Academic, 2022), 538.
4. Dietrich Bonhoeffer, *The Cost of Discipleship* (London: SCM Press, 1948/2001), 44.
5. I am indebted to Tom Ascol for some of the insights in this paragraph. See Tom Ascol, "Love is Not Love," Founders Ministries (blog), at https://founders.org/2022/04/08/love-is-not-love/.
6. G.K. Beale, *The Book of Revelation: A Shorter Commentary* (Eerdmans, 2015), 135; Leon Morris, *Revelation* (Grand Rapids, MI: Eerdmans, 1984), 109. Perhaps these robes function, in part, like the white stone of acquittal in Rev. 2:17.
7. See G.K. Beale, *The Book of Revelation: A Shorter Commentary*, 137–140, for a more thorough presentation of this argument.
8. For example, Isa. 24:–6; Ezek. 32:6–8; Joel 3:15–16.
9. There is good reason to believe that the curtain in the Temple symbolized the night sky which kept people from "seeing" into heaven, which the Holy of Holies represented. See G.K. Beale, *The Temple and the Church's Mission* (InterVarsity Press, 2004), 34–36.

14

THOSE WHO STAND
REVELATION 7

Several years ago while visiting my parents, I opened up an old photo album and walked with them down memory lane. An old picture of me caught all of our attention. Judging by my clothes, I guessed it was from the mid-80s. At that time, everyone loved *Miami Vice*, starring Don Johnson and his side-kick, Tubbs. My outfit showed my attempt to bring a bit of Miami to the southern suburbs of Chicago; I wore a pastel-colored shirt underneath a white blazer, with sleeves rolled to the elbow. White linen pants, slip-on loafers, oversized sunglasses, and slicked-back hair rounded out my attempt to look the part of an undercover police officer from Miami.

As I looked at that picture, taken nearly forty years prior, I felt both embarrassed and amused. I asked my mother, "Did anyone in the family love me at this time? Didn't you see how ridiculous I looked? Why'd you let me go to school looking like this?" We laughed and reflected on how silly we are when trying to find joy, security, and meaning in empty things like clothing and image. Everyone had a great laugh.

Imagine seeing two photos that captured how we look in the present and—if possible—how we'll look in the future. But imagine the photos capture not how you see yourself but how the Lord sees you. We wouldn't laugh or be embarrassed if we could see those pictures. Instead, we'd find encouragement to press on until we see him face-to-face.

In Revelation 7, Jesus provides two pictures for our encouragement. One shows us sealed in the present, and the other reveals our future shelter.

Sealed in the Present

Remember, John records what he saw as he watched Jesus open a sealed scroll. In the last chapter, we looked at the fifth and sixth seals, which pictured God's people crying out for justice and the consequent undoing of the created order. When Jesus opened the sixth seal, the wailing lament was, *"On that great day of wrath... who can stand?"* (Rev. 6:17). Revelation 7 provides the answer:

> *After this I looked, and behold, a great multitude that no one could number, from every nation, from all tribes and peoples and languages, standing before the throne and before the Lamb, clothed in white robes, with palm branches in their hands, and crying out with a loud voice, "Salvation belongs to our God who sits on the throne, and to the Lamb!"* (Rev. 7:9–10)

Clearly, a significant number will stand on that day. Clad in white robes and holding palm branches, they sing of God's redemption. But even before that day comes, John describes them in the present:

> *After this I saw four angels standing at the four corners of the earth, holding back the four winds of the earth, that no wind might blow on earth or sea or against any tree. Then I saw another angel ascending from the rising of the sun, with the seal of the living God, and he called with a loud voice to the four angels who had been given power to harm earth and sea, saying, "Do not harm the earth or the sea or the trees, until we have sealed the servants of our God on their foreheads."* (Rev. 7:1–3)

The first thing to note is that what John describes here does not chronologically follow the sixth seal. Recall that the sixth seal showed the undoing of the created order. Now, John sees four angels holding back the world's destruction to seal those who will stand on that day of God's terrifying wrath. So it's best to see the first part of Chapter 7 (vv. 1–8) as a parenthesis, explaining how any will stand on that day. Put another way: what explains this great multitude standing before the throne of God in the future? God has placed his seal on them. Consider again v. 3: *"Do not harm the earth or the sea or the trees, until we have sealed the servants of our God on their foreheads."* (Rev. 7:3).

A few events from the Old Testament serve as a background for this seal of protection from judgment. The first and more familiar event is the Passover story found in Exodus. There, the Lord instructed the Israelites to put the blood of a lamb on the doorposts so that when he visited Egypt with the final plague, he would see the blood and pass over the house. Those people were, in a sense, sealed by the blood of a lamb.

The second event comes from the book of Ezekiel. At that time, Babylon was within just a few years from putting Jerusalem under siege, causing widespread destruction in the city and for God's people. Before the siege, the Lord visits Ezekiel in a vision in which he sees angels of destruction who've descended upon Jerusalem. The Lord sent the angels to slaughter the people for rebelling against him. But before the angels are set loose to destroy, they're instructed to mark the forehead of those who "sigh and groan" over all the idolatry and rebellion within the city (Ezek. 9:4). That is to say, "Put a mark on the foreheads of those who are faithful to me and grieved by the sins of the nation as well as their own." After this, the Lord instructed judgment to fall on the city except those marked as the Lord's treasured possession.

Ezekiel's vision of people with sealed foreheads is the likely background for John's vision of the same. There are angels of destruction present here, judgment is threatened, and a group of people are sealed. Only this time, judgment falls on the whole world, not just on Jerusalem. Two questions arise as we turn to John's vision. First, who are these people sealed on the forehead, and second, what does the seal symbolize?

We'll consider first the identity of those sealed. John records that the sealed number, 144,000, comes from the tribes of Israel:

> *And I heard the number of the sealed, 144,000, sealed from every tribe of the sons of Israel:*
> *12,000 from the tribe of Judah were sealed,*
> *12,000 from the tribe of Reuben,*
> *12,000 from the tribe of Gad,*
> *12,000 from the tribe of Asher,*
> *12,000 from the tribe of Naphtali,*
> *12,000 from the tribe of Manasseh,*
> *12,000 from the tribe of Simeon,*
> *12,000 from the tribe of Levi,*
> *12,000 from the tribe of Issachar,*
> *12,000 from the tribe of Zebulun,*
> *12,000 from the tribe of Joseph,*
> *12,000 from the tribe of Benjamin were sealed.* (Rev. 7:4–8)

At this point in our study, we should be comfortable knowing that John uses numbers symbolically. And we should also expect a symbolic use unless we have a reason to believe otherwise. We have no reason to treat 144,000 as anything other than symbolic. We've already encountered the number twelve when we looked at the twenty-four elders and suggested that they represent God's people from both the Old and New Testament eras. John describes the city of God as having twelve gates, which stand for the twelve tribes of Israel. He also describes twelve foundations, representing the twelve apostles of Jesus (Rev. 21:12–14). Twelve times twelve gives us 144.

Later, we'll encounter another symbolic number, 1,000, which points us to a large and complete number.[1] If we multiply 144 x 1,000, we arrive at 144,000—a large, complete number of people. Again, this is not a literal understanding of 144,000 people but a symbolic number representing the sum of all God's people.

John hears a voice informing us that the sealed come from the various tribes of Israel's patriarch, Jacob. This Jewish identity has led some to suggest that this is a limited group of ethnic Jews saved at the end of time.

But several reasons suggest this is not a description of one ethnic group.[2] First, we note that when John turns around to observe the 144,000 people, a great multitude from every nation fills his eyes:

> *After this I looked, and behold, a great multitude that no one could number, from every nation, from all tribes and peoples and languages, standing before the throne and before the Lamb, clothed in white robes, with palm branches in their hands, and crying out with a loud voice, "Salvation belongs to our God who sits on the throne, and to the Lamb!"* (Rev. 7:9–10)

This is not the first or the last time John hears one thing described, only to gaze at the subject and proceed to describe something altogether different. In Chapter 5, John heard about the Lion of the tribe of Judah, but when he turned to look at the Lion, he saw a Lamb (Rev. 5:6).

We need not decide between a Lion or a Lamb. Instead, we recognize they both have the same referent—Jesus Christ. Later in this book, John is told that he will see *"the Bride, the wife of the Lamb,"* but what he sees and describes is a city (Rev. 21:9–10). Again, we don't choose between a Bride and a city. They are both the same.

So here, John hears about sealed people, described as a complete number of God's Israel. But John sees an innumerable host of people from every nation, all tribes, peoples, and languages.[3] We need not choose between the 144,000 and the innumerable multitude. Nor between those described as Jewish and those described as coming from every nation. They are one and the same.

This is consistent with the teaching of the Scriptures, which posit that membership within the true Israel of God doesn't depend upon ethnicity, but upon faith. Paul addressed his multi-ethnic audience in Rome as the true Jews of God (Rom. 2:28–29) and those in Galatia as the "Israel of God" (Gal. 6:16). Those who place their trust in Jesus are "sons of Abraham" (Gal. 3:7).

Also in line with this theme, Jesus addressed the church in Philadelphia mentioning those attending "the synagogue of Satan, who say they are Jews but are not" (Rev. 3:9). Jesus indicates that true Jews are composed of those who, like Abraham, believe the promises, regardless of ethnicity.[4] All that to say, the 144,000 Jewish-described individuals are the same group of people John described as a multi-ethnic, great multitude none could number. This answers the first question: Who are the sealed people?

The second question pertains to what the seal represents. John tells us the seal was placed on the forehead of the 144,000. As the seal of Ezekiel's vision was symbolic, we should also expect the seal on the 144,000 to function similarly.[5] The Apostle Paul helps identify the seal on the forehead as a reference to the Holy Spirit, the mark of ownership by which the Lord seals us as his possession, safe from the coming destruction. Twice in the book of Ephesians, Paul points us in this direction:

> *In him you also, when you heard the word of truth, the gospel of your salvation, and believed in him, were sealed with the promised Holy Spirit, who is the guarantee of our inheritance until we acquire possession of it, to the praise of his glory. (Eph. 1:13–14)*

And again:

> *And do not grieve the Holy Spirit of God, by whom you were sealed for the day of redemption. (Eph. 4:30)*

Putting these pieces together, a picture emerges. This sealed multitude are those born again by the Holy Spirit. They bear God's mark of ownership, are sealed for redemption, and therefore will stand at the judgment. They are also the true Israel of God, consisting of a perfect number in which none has been lost (John 10:28–29) and from all the nations. When John attempted to count the vast multitude, their number exceeded the stars in the sky and the sand on the seashore (Gen. 22:17).

The only way to survive the judgment is to be sealed by the Holy Spirit. Remember Jesus' words: *"Truly, truly, I say to you, unless one is born again he cannot see the kingdom of God"* (John 3:3). You must be born again. There will be no bargaining with God on that great and terrifying day described in the sixth seal, opportunities to plead a case, or a jury to acquit you from the prosecutor's charges. Instead, you must bear the seal of God, or you will face eternal condemnation.

Is there a way to know if the Spirit has sealed us? That question is the grand takeaway from this section of Revelation.

Is there tangible proof that we can look for to answer the question? Thankfully, there is a God who loves us too much to let us swing in the winds of uncertainty on this matter.

The Apostle Paul tells us, *"No one can say 'Jesus is Lord' except in the Holy Spirit"* (1 Cor. 12:3. See also Matt. 16:17; John 15:26; Rom. 10:9). This is the question: Can I say, "Jesus is Lord"? Paul doesn't mean that the words "Jesus is Lord" can't be repeated or parroted by just anyone. Just repeating words says nothing about what is truly happening inside us.

Instead, Paul asserts that genuine, saving faith in Jesus traces its origin to the Holy Spirit's work in the Christian's heart. The question is not "Do I believe in Jesus?" The demons believe in Jesus, and they are heading for the wrath of the Lamb. Instead, "Do I love him, though imperfectly?" (1 John 1:10). Do you trust Jesus, though you stumble in many ways? (Jas. 3:2). Have you taken up your cross to follow him, though at times you still feel that inner tug toward rebellion? (Rom. 7:21–23). If you can answer yes to those things, there is one reason: the Holy Spirit has sealed you for the day of redemption. The Spirit is the Lord's pledge that what he has begun in you he will bring to completion on the day of Jesus Christ (Phil. 1:6). The Spirit is a "guarantee of our inheritance until we acquire possession of it" (Eph. 1:14). So our confession of faith is like an engagement ring given to us by the Lord, through which he vows that we are his treasured possession.

Can you say from the heart that Jesus is Lord? If so, then what you see in Revelation 7 is a photo of yourself as the Lord sees you today. You are a member of the Israel of God and marked out for redemption. You've been sealed in the present. But John shows us another picture of those marked by God's Spirit. The second picture reveals the future reality of being sheltered in his presence.

Sheltered in His Presence

Paul tells us that the seal of the Spirit is a guarantee of our inheritance. John was given a glimpse into that inheritance:

> *After this I looked, and behold, a great multitude that no one could number, from every nation, from all tribes and peoples and languages, standing before the throne and before the Lamb, clothed in white robes, with palm branches in their hands, and crying out with a loud voice, "Salvation belongs to our God who sits on the throne, and to the Lamb!" And all the angels were standing around the throne and around the elders and the four living creatures, and they fell on their faces before the throne and worshiped God, saying, "Amen! Blessing and glory and wisdom and thanksgiving and honor and power and might be to our God forever and ever! Amen." Then one of the elders addressed me, saying, "Who are these, clothed in white robes, and from where have they come?" I said to him, "Sir, you know." And he said to me, "These are the ones coming out of the great tribulation. They have washed their robes and made them white in the blood of the Lamb." (Rev. 7:9–14)*

John saw those who have come *"out of the great tribulation."* The tribulation mentioned here refers to the whole period between the ascension and return of Jesus.[6] Jesus spoke to the church in Smyrna, saying, *"I know your tribulation,"* and he even warned them of more severe problems to come (Rev. 2:9–10). Jesus promised all his followers that anyone following him would face tribulation (John 16:33). When Luke described the theme of Paul's preaching, he summarized his preaching with this sentence: *"Through many tribulations, we must enter the kingdom of God"* (Acts 14:22). And then, of course, John opened this letter, introducing himself as a partner with us in the tribulation (Rev. 1:9).

And now, in verses 15–17, we have a description of the inheritance kept in heaven for us:

> *Therefore they are before the throne of God, and serve him day and night in his temple; and he who sits on the throne will shelter them with his presence. They shall hunger no more, neither thirst anymore; the sun shall not strike them, nor any scorching heat. For the Lamb in the midst of the throne will be their shepherd, and he will guide them to springs of living water, and God will wipe away every tear from their eyes. (Rev. 7:15–17)*

The wonder and the glory of what we see here are not simply a description of our inheritance but God's! The Bible frequently speaks about the heritage God longs to acquire. For example, in the Old Testament, the Lord told his people he saved them to be *"his own inheritance"* (Deut. 4:21). Psalm 28:9 cries, *"Oh, save your people, and bless your heritage!"* Paul echoes this to the Ephesians, praying that his beloved people would have their eyes enlightened to the wonders of what God will inherit, namely, his people (Eph. 1:18).[7]

Can you imagine being so loved and so welcomed? So treasured? The one who spoke everything into existence and owns all the universe's resources looks on us through his son and says, "Here is my wealth. They are my inheritance."

John has shown us how God views us in the present, sealed for redemption, and how the Lord will shelter us with his presence in the future. Do you love Jesus? If so, it is because he has put a seal on you, which cost him the blood of his Son. And you will stand on that great day that is coming.

Study Questions

1. Who are those who are sealed? What is the seal? How does the Lord mark his people?
2. Is there a way to know that we've been sealed? What is your confidence as you reflect on this chapter?

---

1. See, for example, Deut. 7:9; Ps. 84:10; 105:8; Isa. 30:17; 2 Pet. 3:8. This will be essential when we come to Rev. 20:2.
2. Several anomalies in this listing of the tribes do not mirror any of the lists we find in the Old Testament. For example, Judah is listed first, though Reuben was the firstborn. Additionally, Dan and Ephraim are omitted. Joseph and Manasseh are listed, which is peculiar because Ephraim and Manasseh were the two sons of Joseph. So, we might have expected Joseph to be listed alone or Manasseh and Ephraim in his place. The irregularities mentioned suggest this list is symbolic. See Vern S. Poythress, *The Returning King: A Guide to the Book of Revelation* (P&R, 2000), 118.
3. I like what one author has said about this passage: "This is not a vanilla multitude. When we get to heaven we will be pleased to find a vast array of people that do not look like us. There are going to be millions of Africans in that great multitude and plenty of Brazilians and Chinese and Filipinos, and lots of Mexicans and Indians and Arabs, and there will be some white people too." He goes on to say our hearts are going to be thrilled to hear our favorite hymns sung in Swahili, French, Finnish, German, and Japanese. "Heaven will be diversity without the political correctness and multi-culturalism unified in one single purpose. Every heart, every head, every voice giving glory to God and to the Lamb." Kevin DeYoung, "A Great Multitude and a Great Hope," *The Gospel Coalition* (blog), https://www.thegospelcoalition.org/blogs/kevin-deyoung/a-great-multitude-and-a-great-hope/

4. For more evidence along these lines, see Leon Morris, *Revelation* (Grand Rapids, MI: Eerdmans, 1984), 114–115. For an overall examination of the identity of the 144,000, see Thomas R. Schreiner, *The Joy of Hearing: A Theology of the Book of Revelation* (Wheaton, IL: Crossway, 2021), 122–128.
5. This will come up again later when we examine the beast who insists upon having his mark placed upon either the forehead or wrist of his followers in Rev. 13:16–17.
6. G.K. Beale, *The Book of Revelation: A Shorter Commentary* (Eerdmans, 2015), 158; Vern S. Poythress, *The Returning King*, 119; Thomas R. Schreiner, *The Joy of Hearing*, 129.
7. See Andrew T. Lincoln, *Ephesians*, Word Biblical Commentary (Zondervan Academic, 2014), 59–60.

15

SILENCE IN HEAVEN, FIRE ON EARTH

REVELATION 8:1–5

During the American Revolutionary War, a Presbyterian pastor named James Caldwell fought for the Continental Army. An early supporter of American independence, Pastor Caldwell served at the First Presbyterian Church in Elizabethtown, New Jersey. Several of the  members of his church served as soldiers in the local militia, and Pastor Caldwell served as a military chaplain.

In June 1780, the British advanced on Pastor Caldwell and his fellow militiamen in what is known today as The Battle of Springfield. At the height of the battle, the American patriots faced a much larger British force and lacked needed supplies, especially wadding for their muskets. Wadding was a paper-like material that held the ball and powder together in rifles. Without wadding, the men could no longer engage in the battle.

Seeing the need for paper, Pastor Caldwell quickly ducked into his church and emerged from the sanctuary carrying as many hymnals as he could manage. Isaac Watts, the "Godfather of English Hymnody," published the hymnals in Caldwell's church. As Pastor Caldwell passed out the hymnals to the soldiers, he instructed them to tear out the pages and shouted, "Give 'em Watts, Boys! Give 'em Watts!"[1]

To be sure, it is a strange picture: employing hymns to engage in warfare. And yet John sets that very image before us in his vision. John witnessed the Lord bring justice and salvation to the world in response to his people's prayers. I need what this vision shows us, and I suspect you do too. Prayer is difficult, and one of the most challenging aspects of the Christian life. And if you're honest, you struggle in this area too.

But we are not alone. Many of the most well-known, honored saints also struggled to pray with enthusiasm, regularity, or Christ-centeredness. For example, consider this honest confession from John Bunyan, author of *The Pilgrim's Progress*:

> May I... speak my own experience, and from that tell you the difficulty of praying to God as I ought.... As for my heart, when I go to pray, I find it so reluctant to go to God, and when it is with him, so reluctant to stay with him, that many times I am forced in my prayers; first to beg God that he would take [my] heart, and set it on himself in Christ, and when it is there, that he would keep it there. In fact, many times I know not what to pray for, I am so blind, nor how to pray I am so ignorant.[2]

John Bunyan, the man about whom Charles Spurgeon said that if you pricked him, he would "bleed Scripture," confessed that he struggled to pray. And he penned that confession in jail, a place you might expect prayer to come easily. But even in prison, Mr. Bunyan struggled just like we all do.

Therefore, we need to see what John saw in this vision: the Lord not only delights in the prayers of his people, but he's also determined to respond to them. With those two truths, be encouraged to labor on in difficult and necessary prayer.

Before we look at the text itself, we are at another transition point in the Book of Revelation. I've suggested that John is like an artist who paints seven portraits of the time between the ascension and return of Jesus Christ. The first portrait, chapters 1 through 3, painted Jesus amid the lampstands. The second portrait, chapters 4 through 7, showed Jesus also in the throne room of God, opening the scroll with seven seals. John transitions to another picture of this period in the text before us.[3] This painting will reveal the blasting of seven trumpets that sound until the return of Jesus. The numerous portrayals of the same time period enhance our understanding of God's plan in the world as we await the return of the Lord Jesus. Much in the same way, we appreciate a sporting event through different camera angles.

But before John transitions into a new portrait—from the seven seals to the seven trumpets—the focus falls upon the integral role played by the prayers of God's people, which bring him pleasure.

Prayer Is Pleasing to God

> *When the Lamb opened the seventh seal, there was silence in heaven for about half an hour. Then I saw the seven angels who stand before God, and seven trumpets were given to them. And another angel came and stood at the altar with a golden censer, and he was given much incense to offer with the prayers of all the saints on the golden altar before the throne, and the smoke of the incense, with the prayers of the saints, rose before God from the hand of the angel.* (Rev. 8:1–4)

We'll return to the seventh seal and the silence in heaven in a moment. And our focus in the next chapter will be on the trumpets themselves. But for now, we'll consider the altar, the incense, and the desirability of our prayers before the Lord.

We've already encountered this altar; it's the location where the martyrs cried out to God for justice (Rev. 6:9–10). This heavenly altar served as inspiration for the earthly altar of incense in the temple. Before there was an 18x18-inch, three-foot-high altar built by Moses; this altar was in heaven. The altar of incense was, as the author of Hebrews tells us, "a copy and shadow of the heavenly things" (Heb. 8:5). In John's vision, we see the real deal, the true altar of incense. The earthly replica served to encourage the Lord's people. As the priest would light the incense, the smoke would ascend, and the people of God would have a visible picture of an invisible reality—the Lord delights in our prayer.

Think about how the altar communicates the heart of God toward us. First, the earthy and heavenly altars were made of gold, pointing to the value the Lord places on our prayer.[4]

Second, the incense itself had a sweet aroma. The Lord strictly commanded, upon pain of death, that none should alter the elements (Ex. 30:34–38). The incense, representing the prayers of his people, presented a sweet, "pleasing aroma" to the Lord. The sweetness communicates the Lord's pleasure in our petitions.

And then third, the incense altar's location speaks to our prayers' value and importance. Remember, the temple housed two altars. Located in the outer courtyard, the altar of bronze greeted the worshiper as they drew near to the Lord. At this altar, animals were slaughtered and offered as a sacrifice to the Lord. The placement of the bronze altar right at the worship area's entrance communicates the need for reconciliation with the Lord. There is no drawing near to God apart from a blood sacrifice. The bronze altar expressed distance between the Holy Lord, dwelling in the innermost room of the temple and the sinful worshiper stopped at the gate and made to confront his rebellion against God and man.

On the other hand, the golden altar of incense was the closest piece of furniture to the ark, where the unique presence of God dwelt. The gold, sweet smell, and the proximity of the incense altar all speak to God's heart for his people's prayer. The all-knowing, all-powerful, all-sufficient, all-sovereign Lord of the universe doesn't simply accept the prayers of his people. He desires and delights in them.

But how could this be? Remember what Bunyan said about his own prayers? He confessed he often drew near to the Lord reluctantly and found it difficult to remain focused. If we confess to the same weaknesses in prayer, how could what we offer the Lord be a delight to him? I'm not pleased with my prayers, let alone convinced—apart from persuasion—that the Lord delights in them. After all, when I consider my prayers (which often focus on my needs and the needs of my flock), I often find I have skipped over the whole first part of the Lord's prayer: Lord, make your name holy in my life, may your kingdom come, may your will be done on earth, as it is in heaven. Instead of beginning where Jesus instructs me to, my prayer often skips ahead to ask for daily bread and the forgiveness of my sin. When I consider my puny and self-centered prayers, I need the reminder that I'm not alone when I pray. And neither are you.

We have two helpers who take our feeble and sometimes silly words and make them into something so desirable that the Lord cannot say no to them. Our first helper is Jesus Christ.

When we offer a prayer, Jesus, who sits at the Father's right hand, intercedes for us. That means that no matter how silly, weak, frail, and doubt-filled my prayers may sound, when it issues from the heart, Jesus changes them to make them beautiful to his Father.

But we have another helper who makes our prayers desirable to the Lord. Like John Bunyan, the apostle Paul was brutally honest about his prayer life. Paul didn't always know what to pray for any more than we always do. But—and this is crucial—he tells us the *"Spirit himself intercedes for us with groanings too deep for words"* (Rom. 8:26).

I need this encouragement, and I bet you do too. Sometimes our hearts groan before the Lord when we're confronted with sin, our own and others.' In those times, we may not even know what to ask God. But the Spirit knows what to say at that very moment. When you feel weak, the Spirit speaks powerfully to the Lord, molding our prayers into petitions that please and satisfy him.

When I think of the way the Spirit speaks for us, something a friend wrote helps give me a picture. He said the Christian's prayers are like the icing bag used to decorate a cake. You have probably seen a baker glob icing into a piping bag as a chaotic unformed mess. But that's not the end of the process. Attached to the other end of the bag is a decorator tip. When the baker forces the icing through the tip, the mess gets shaped into intricate designs that make the cake beautiful.

In the same way, as I lift my cries to God, like so many globs of icing, they press through the Holy Spirit, who, like a decorator tip, forms my words into God's beautiful designs for all things.[5]

We need this assurance and encouragement when our doubting flesh tells us that our words go nowhere and are unheard. We have two intercessors. The Son and the Spirit present our words to the Father, who happily receives them. And the Lord will also purify the world in response to his people's petitions.

Prayer Prompts Purification

God's historical purposes are carried out, in part, according to his people's prayers, which is one of the most remarkable things we see in this vision. Remember, the martyrs under this same altar asked the Lord, *"How long before you will judge and avenge our blood?"* (Rev. 6:10). The Lord counseled them to be patient. In the passage before us, we have that same altar, and now angels take up the prayers of God's people and offer them to the Lord:

> *And another angel came and stood at the altar with a golden censer, and he was given much incense to offer with the prayers of all the saints on the golden altar before the throne, and the smoke of the incense, with the prayers of the saints, rose before God from the hand of the angel. Then the angel took the censer and filled it with fire from the altar and threw it on the earth, and there were peals of thunder, rumblings, flashes of lightning, and an earthquake.* (Rev. 8:3–5)

In response to the martyrs' requests, fire rains down upon the earth. We bump into a mystery here: God is sovereign over all history and simultaneously responds to his people's prayers. And we remain content, though we lack a full understanding of how the Lord makes both of these truths work together. Nevertheless, in his infinite wisdom and as a mark of the indescribable dignity bestowed upon his people, God has determined to carry out his sovereign will, often in response to our pleas.

What is this fire John saw cast upon the earth? Once again, we're helped by returning to the book of Ezekiel, who also saw fire cast upon the earth. The Lord told Ezekiel that Jerusalem would be overthrown and judged for refusing to repent of its idolatry.

First, however, the Lord instructed his angels to put a mark on the forehead of those who would be spared from the wrath to come. Then, once the angels marked his people, the Lord instructed a heavenly being to grab burning coals from before God's throne and cast them upon the city, a picture of the coming destruction (Ezek. Chps. 9–10).

John also saw a group of people, the 144,000, marked on the forehead, safe from the coming wrath. Now John sees, just as Ezekiel saw, an angel approach the altar to grab coals of fire, which were then cast upon the earth. Just as the fire thrown on the city of Jerusalem represented judgment, the fire cast down in John's vision represents the moment that the final judgment falls upon the earth.

Throughout the Scriptures, fire often represents judgment. For example, Isaiah describes the coming judgment saying:

> For behold, the LORD will come in fire, and his chariots like the whirlwind, to render his anger in fury, and his rebuke with flames of fire. For by fire will the LORD enter into judgment. (Isa. 66:15–16, Cf. Isa. 33:14; Mal. 3:2).

The New Testament picks up the theme of fire through Paul, who writes that when Jesus returns, he will be revealed:

> In flaming fire, inflicting vengeance on those who do not know God and on those who do not obey the gospel of our Lord Jesus. (2 Thess. 1:7–8)

Peter also tells us that:

> the heavens and the earth that now exist are stored up for fire, being kept until the day of judgment and destruction of the ungodly. (2 Pet. 3:7)

Fire represents the judgment of the Lord but so does the silence that accompanies the opening of the seventh and final seal: *"When the Lamb opened the seventh seal, there was silence in heaven for about half an hour"* (Rev. 8:1).

Consider how silence is associated with judgment in the Scriptures. Zephaniah warns, *"Be silent before the Lord God! For the day of the Lord is near"* (Zeph. 1:7). Zechariah also calls for silence in the context of judgment, saying, *"Be silent, all flesh, before the Lord, for he has roused himself from his holy dwelling"* (Zech. 2:13).

Putting the coming fire upon the earth and the silence in heaven together, we see a picture of the end. The final judgment will be so terrifying, awful, powerful, and thorough that those who survive it will stand in silent wonder. The four living creatures, the twenty-four elders, and the thousands upon thousands of angels cease from their audible, round-the-clock worship of God and fall silent. When the God of all power and limited patience finally unveils the fury of his wrath, even those safe in heaven can only stare in quiet solemnity.[6]

Jesus told his disciples that he had come to the earth to bring the fire John saw cast upon the earth. Consider these words from Luke's Gospel:

I came to cast fire on the earth, and would that it were already kindled! I have a baptism to be baptized with, and how great is my distress until it is accomplished! (Luke 12:49–50)

If someone asked you why Jesus came to the earth, this might not be your first answer: he came to cast fire upon it. But it's one of the sweetest promises he makes to those who have felt profound suffering.

The earth is full of evil, misery, and decay: human trafficking, the slaughter of children, oppression of the weak, authoritarian governments, unjust wars, slander, betrayals, deceit, addictions, mockery of the Savior in the universities, and the list goes on. And Jesus promises to cleanse the earth with fire.

Don't think of a fire that incinerates and therefore destroys. Instead, think of fire that cleanses something through the removal of impurities. Precious metals such as gold, silver, and more are purified through fire. Jesus says that he has come to set the world right again. He will address all wrongs and establish justice, righteousness, and truth. And how he longed for that moment, even as you and I do now![7] "Come, Lord Jesus" is this book's parting prayer of the Spirit and the Church (Rev. 22:17, 20). We groan, "Come and set the world right, Lord Jesus! Come to purify the earth!"

But before that fire comes, Jesus notes, another fire had to go first:

I came to cast fire on the earth, and would that it were already kindled! I have a baptism to be baptized with, and how great is my distress until it is accomplished! (Luke 12:49–53)

Jesus isn't referring to water baptism. At this point in his ministry, he had already been baptized in water by John. Instead, he refers to the cross on which he would pass through the flames of his Father's wrath.[8]

No wonder his soul was distressed! Before he could set the world on fire, making all things new, he first had to be baptized with the fire, which would save his people. Do you see the greatness of Jesus' love for you, which is so great that it endured the very fire of God in your place? Perhaps the audible worship in heaven ceased for six hours as the coals of God's righteous fury pelted Jesus on the cross. Maybe the four living creatures, the twenty-four elders, and countless angels endured six hours of horrified silence as they beheld the terrors falling on Jesus for you, me, and all who trust in him.

Even in this passage, where we see the great and terrible day coming, we see the indescribable love of God, who delights in our prayer and vows to purify the cosmos in response to them. So, therefore, continue to lift your requests to God. Plead with him to make his name holy in your life, that his kingdom would come, and that his will would be done on earth as it is in heaven. And continue to plead with those who don't know him. Tell them of the coming fire that will make all things new. Tell them also that the only way to be safe from that fire is to trust the one who has already passed through it.

Study Questions

1. What resonates with you about the difficulty of prayer? Let's begin by praying and asking the Lord to direct and keep our hearts as we focus on Him.
2. The all-knowing, all-powerful, all-sufficient, all-sovereign Lord of the universe doesn't simply accept the prayers of his people; he desires and delights in them. How can this be? How does this motivate you to continue in prayer?
3. If someone asks why Jesus came to this earth, your first response may not be, "To cast fire upon it." How does this promise comfort your soul?
4. Jesus passed through the fire of God's wrath on the cross so that you could draw near with confidence to the throne of grace. Let

that wash over you as you pray for a heart that responds in thankful joy.

---

1. For more on James Caldwell and the Battle of Springfield, see https://revolutionarywar.us/year-1780/battle-of-springfield/
2. This quote is from Bunyan's *I Will Pray with the Spirit*, accessible online at https://quod.lib.umich.edu/e/eebo/A30158.0001.001/1:2.2?rgn=div2;view=fulltext.
3. Rev. 8:1, 3–5 serves as a conclusion to the second portrait. Perhaps it would be best to say that portraits two and three overlap in 8:1–5. The seventh seal and the fire cast down upon the earth conclude the second description of this age. But in between the seventh seal and the judgment fire, seven angels with seven trumpets are introduced in 8:2. The narration breaks away from the angelic trumpeters in vv. 3–5, only to resume focus upon them in 8:6. John will employ this "overlap" technique again when transitioning from the fourth (Chs. 12–14) to the fifth portrait (Chs. 15–16).
4. Leon Morris, *Revelation* (Grand Rapids, MI: Eerdmans, 1984), 120.
5. Bryan Chapell, *Praying Backwards* (Grand Rapids, MI: Baker Books, 2005), 73.
6. For more on the silence accompanying judgment, see G.K. Beale, *The Book of Revelation: A Shorter Commentary* (Eerdmans, 2015), 164–165.
7. For an explanation of this passage in Luke and fire as a reference to the final judgment, see Leon Morris, *Luke* in Tyndale New Testament Commentaries (IVP, Downers Grove, 1988), 237; Robert Stein, *Luke* in The New American Commentary (B&H Publishing, Nashville 1992), 364–365.
8. The parallel statement in the Gospel of Mark reveals that the baptism Jesus refers to in Luke is described as the "cup" he must drink, which refers to the cup of God's wrath. See Mark 10:38 with Isa. 51:17, 22; Jer. 25:15.

PART 3

THE SEVEN TRUMPETS 8:6–11:19

16

SOUND JUDGMENT

REVELATION 8:6-12

When I was in seminary, I had the privilege of attending a chapel service at which an Englishman, and former police officer, told a story that occurred just outside of London. Late one night, a semi-truck had overturned on a highway, spilling its freight all over the road. The  truck had crashed because a thick fog had obscured a sharp turn on the street. Unfamiliar with the road, the truck driver sped headlong into a guardrail going full speed.

The police quickly got to the scene to attend to the driver and set up a roadblock to spare other drivers from the same terrible fate. The police wore yellow reflective vests and placed bright orange cones on the road to stop oncoming traffic from proceeding further. But sadly and tragically, many cars refused to stop. They wove around the cones, ignored the waving arms of the police, and several drivers barreled through the fog and into a terrible mix of crushed cars and injured drivers.

Now desperate to get the attention of the preoccupied drivers, with tear-filled eyes, the police officer grabbed the orange warning cones and slung them at the windshields of the distracted drivers, hoping this might save people's lives.

That scene is not unlike what John describes with the sounding of the seven trumpets, which, like the orange cones and roadblocks, warn of dangers ahead. The world, meanwhile, presses down the accelerator, trying to find peace, hope, meaning, and value apart from the Lord.

And like that police officer, with wet eyes and tears even, the Church picks up the cones and slings them at oncoming traffic, begging, "Turn from your madness! Danger lies ahead! This road leads to destruction, but another leads to life." The trumpets of God warn the world of his coming wrath, but they also signal the deliverance of his people.

Warnings of Wrath

As we come to the trumpets, remember that John is beginning a new portrait of the period between the ascension and return of Jesus. The seals and the trumpets conclude with what we call the end of the present world. Seal number six presented the complete undoing of the created order and the judgment of humanity.

The seventh trumpet will also show the wrath of God poured out again, and the judgment of the dead (Rev. 11:18). The same pattern will be repeated with the seven bowls later in the book. The seventh bowl describes the undoing of creation, the judgment of the wicked, and God's wrath fully unleashed (Rev. 16:17–21).

This repetition doesn't suggest three destructions of the present world or three separate judgments. Instead, John gives us three different descriptions of the same event. Transitioning from the seals to the trumpets, we're not entering a different time than the seals. Instead, the seals and trumpets coincide in timing but have a different focus.

The seals focus on what the Church should expect as she waits for the return of her Lord. In contrast, the trumpets focus on what a wayward world will experience in this period: great calamities, which serve as warnings of judgment.[1]

Two Old Testament events form a backdrop for the seven trumpets of Revelation. The first was the sending of plagues on Egypt when Pharaoh enslaved Israel. As we'll see, several trumpets release terrible things upon creation that strongly echo the plagues that caused havoc in Egypt.

The second Old Testament background comes from the book of Joshua, Chapter 6. There, seven priests armed with trumpets marched around the city of Jericho for six days. But on the seventh day, seven trumpets sounded, and the city fell. In the same way, when the seventh trumpet blows in Revelation, another city falls (Rev. 11:13).

Putting these two backgrounds together, these trumpets, which have sounded for the past 2,000 years, warn the wayward world of what is to come. They are the orange cones that the Lord slings at drivers heading for destruction.

If we take the first four trumpets together, we see God placing his hand upon the things people seek for their security but turn out to be lousy saviors. The first trumpet blows, and a plague descends upon the earth:

> Now the seven angels who had the seven trumpets prepared to blow them. The first angel blew his trumpet, and there followed hail and fire, mixed with blood, and these were thrown upon the earth. And a third of the earth was burned up, and a third of the trees were burned up, and all green grass was burned up. (Rev. 8:6–7)

The first trumpet falls upon the land, our food source. This trumpet reminds us of the seventh plague that fell upon the Egyptians in Exodus 9:23–24. Hail and fire fell upon Egypt, but John added the mixture of blood.

If we examine the hail and fire of Exodus, we see that they destroyed the food supply in Egypt. Moses tells us that the hail and fire destroyed any person or livestock working out in the field and every plant and fruit-bearing tree in Egypt (Ex. 9:25). Egypt's food chain was the target of the hail and fire.

Here, in Revelation, the scope of the destruction is not on Egypt alone but upon a third of the entire earth. And not just through one terrible storm but a storm that continuously rages until Jesus returns.

We should not force a literalism on this text which, to this point, John has not asked us to consider. The point of the hail and fire falling upon only a third of the earth communicates that the judgment is not total. These judgments are, at present, restrained in that only a third of the planet is affected.

Likewise, while John saw hail and fire falling to the earth to disrupt food supplies, that doesn't mean this is the only way the Lord brings warnings. Every natural disaster serves as a preview of the coming day of wrath. We can think of hurricanes, deadly tornadoes, tsunamis, and uncontrolled wildfires which disrupt food supplies. Each time a natural or manmade disaster brings about food shortages, it warns of a more extraordinary lack of sustenance.

Before we move to the second trumpet, we have an answer to the honest and often-asked question many non-Christian friends ask: "If God is all-powerful and all-good, why is the world the way it is? Why does he allow natural disasters? Viruses? Tsunamis and earthquakes? If God is, as you say, good and powerful, what explains these things?"

While it's not an exhaustive answer, what we learn in the first trumpet must factor into our response. We could say, "You are right this is not how things are supposed to be. God and people should live in harmony on earth, free of these disasters. That scenario once existed; your heart and mine long for its return. But until then, our Creator sends us previews of the undoing of all creation for re-creation. And unless you are in harmony with him through his Son, you will not survive what's coming."

The second trumpet turns from the land to the sea, reminding us of another Egyptian plague:

> *The second angel blew his trumpet, and something like a great mountain, burning with fire, was thrown into the sea, and a third of the sea became blood. A third of the living creatures in the sea died, and a third of the ships were destroyed.* (Rev. 8:8–9)

The first plague in Egypt turned the Nile River into blood and killed all the fish. So here in Revelation, the sea and the living creatures are partially affected. Moses' staff struck the Nile in the Egyptian plague, turning it into blood.

In John's vision, something like a great mountain burning with fire is thrown into the sea, turning it to blood. Once again, we don't look to our imaginations—picturing a meteor coming out of the sky—but rather to the Old Testament to ask if such an image has occurred there to inform our understanding here. An examination of the Old Testament shows us that mountains often represent nations that are the objects of God's wrath.[2] And more specifically, if we turn to the book of Jeremiah, he poetically describes Babylon, the great enemy of Israel, as a mountain that the Lord will burn with fire (Jer. 51:25) and later throw into the waters, where it will sink never to rise again (Jer. 51: 63–64).

Back to John's vision. It isn't the fall of literal Babylon pictured before his eyes. The Persians overthrew Babylon centuries before John's day. Instead, Babylon is code in Revelation for any empire that exalts itself against the Lord and his Anointed. In the Jewish mind, Babylon was the paradigm of wickedness, idolatry, immorality, and sheer cruelty.[3]

Babylon represents any government, people group, or legislation that is anti-Christ and, therefore, anti-Christian. Such things will face the fires of judgment and an eternal watery grave. The first trumpet warns through natural disasters of a coming judgment. The second trumpet warns every empire that exalts itself that the Lord will bring them low.

And Jesus has humbled many since he ascended to his throne. Every time the Lord humbles a self-exalting nation, we recall the promises of Psalm 2. As the nations rage and plot against the Lord and his anointed, David says, *"He who sits in the heavens laughs; the Lord holds them in derision."* And then he speaks terror to man-centered empires, saying, *"As for me, I have set my King on Zion, my holy hill... therefore... be wise, be warned.... Kiss the Son, lest he be angry, and you perish in the way, for his wrath is quickly kindled."*[4]

The first trumpet warns there will be natural disasters. The second warns that kingdoms will come and go until the coming of the eternal kingdom of Christ.

John heard a third trumpet blow a warning:

The third angel blew his trumpet, and a great star fell from heaven, blazing like a torch, and it fell on a third of the rivers and on the springs of water. The name of the star is Wormwood. A third of the waters became wormwood, and many people died from the water, because it had been made bitter. (Rev. 8:10–11)

The first trumpet affected the land, the second the sea, and the third turned toward the inland waterways. Freshwaters are made bitter. While this trumpet doesn't point us to an Egyptian plague, it seems to be an ironic reversal of something that occurred in the Old Testament.

When the people of Israel were traveling through the wilderness en route to the Promised Land, they came upon an area where the water was bitter and undrinkable. So the Lord instructed Moses to throw a log into the water. When he did, the water turned sweet or drinkable (Ex. 15:22–26). That event pictured the Lord's assurance to his people that he would bless and keep them if they entrusted themselves to his care. In an ironic reversal, where there is a refusal to trust the Lord, John sees drinkable water made bitter.

A great star falling from the heavens to spoil drinking water offers another reference to Babylon. The image comes from Isaiah 14:12–15. There, God described the Babylonian King as someone who desired to be like the Most High and has set his throne *"above the stars of God."* But the Lord promised the King of Babylon, the self-exalted star, that he would cast him down to the grave. In the words of Jesus, *"For everyone who exalts himself will be humbled"* (Luke 14:11).

The star is called Wormwood, which is a bitter herb. But the Old Testament also used wormwood as a symbol of the bitterness accompanying suffering (Jer. 9:15; 23:15). This trumpet points us to the type of bitterness that comes from seeking meaning, joy, value, and purpose in the things of this earth. We drink from the waters of this world—materialism, illicit relationships, sexual freedom, autonomy from God, living for the present, the redefinition of right and wrong—thinking that these give life. But in the end, they only poison us. This trumpet warns against the illusion of seeking joy in sin, as it only leads to destruction.

The fourth trumpet sounds, and again we return to Egypt:

> *The fourth angel blew his trumpet, and a third of the sun was struck, and a third of the moon, and a third of the stars, so that a third of their light might be darkened, and a third of the day might be kept from shining, and likewise a third of the night.* (Rev. 8:12)

The ninth Egyptian plague cast three days of darkness over all the land. Under this plague, no one could see each other except for the Israelites, who had light where they lived (Ex. 10:23). While literal darkness did fall on Egypt, the Old and New Testaments use the dark as a metaphor for spiritual blindness.

For example, the prophet Isaiah promised that when the Messiah arrives, it will be said:

> *The people who walked in darkness have seen a great light; those who dwelt in a land of deep darkness, on them has light shone.* (Isa. 9:2)[5]

The fourth trumpet pictures man-centered worldviews and spirituality. These attempt to navigate the world in a quest for meaning, purpose, dignity, value, and beauty, but they do so in the darkness because the light of the Gospel is absent. When we embrace the Gospel, Paul tells us that light shines in *"our hearts to give the light of the knowledge of the glory of God in the face of Jesus Christ"* (2 Cor. 4:6).

These are the first four trumpets, which have sounded across the globe for the past two thousand years, warning everyone of the disaster that awaits those unreconciled to the Lord through Jesus Christ. As we will see in the next chapter, these trumpets not only get worse (Trumpets 5 and 6 are positively spine-chilling), but they also don't work to bring people to repentance. Jumping ahead a bit, John reports at the end of the sixth trumpet:

> *The rest of mankind, who were not killed by these plagues, did not repent of the works of their hands nor give up worshiping demons and idols of gold and silver and bronze and stone and wood, which cannot see or hear or walk, nor did they repent of their murders or their sorceries or their sexual immorality or their thefts.* (Rev. 9:20–21)

No hurricane, tornado, food shortage, or collapse of an empire can break through the heart of rebellion against God. Without the Holy Spirit's enlightening work, the unbelieving mind is so dark, veiled, and blinded by *"the god of this world"* (2 Cor. 4:4) that no amount of trumpet blasting works.

We might expect that people would see how miserable they are apart from the Lord and make some changes. Perhaps we'd expect our fellow citizens to look at the consequences of the sexual revolution, the relativization of right and wrong, and how much Wormwood and bitterness fill the hearts of our countrymen and say, "We need to reevaluate. We must cry out to God for mercy!"

But, by and large, that's not what we see around us. Instead, people press down on the accelerator and weave around the cones, looking for political solutions to spiritual problems. No matter how loud they blast, the trumpets sound ineffectively. Just as the plagues of Egypt didn't soften the heart of Pharaoh, nor did the trumpet blasts around Jericho move its citizens to worship God, these plague-filled trumpets don't have the power to save.

But you and I have something in our possession that does. Paul tells us that he was *"not ashamed of the gospel, for it is the power of God for salvation to everyone who believes"* (Rom. 1:16). In one sense, that is where the story of this book is going. The trumpets alone don't work to change the hearts of unbelievers. But in Chapter 11, we'll hear the Church's voice crying out to the world, testifying to the life-giving power of Jesus Christ.

The Church warns people of the sounding trumpets and begs the world to turn from its madness. And then, and only then, at the end of that chapter, we are told that those who previously hated the Lord *"were terrified and gave glory to the God of heaven"* (Rev. 11:13).

My friend, do you see your high dignity and privilege as one who holds the Gospel treasure? The trumpets warn of the coming wrath of God and are sometimes made effective when the Church opens its mouth for Jesus.

But those same trumpets sound in the ears of Christ's people, not as warnings of wrath for them but audible promises from God of his determination to deliver them.

Promises of Deliverance

Through this vision of trumpets and plagues, John has placed us back in Egypt, where destruction fell all around the people of God. But he's also placed us in the Promised Land, marching around a city that will fall when the last trumpet blasts.

With that in mind, ask yourself: did the plagues or the trumpets cause concern for the people of God? The trumpets at Jericho didn't terrify the Israelites any more than they ought to frighten Christ's people today. As the Israelites marched around the city, they knew that with each passing day, they were closer to that final trumpet blast that would signal their inheritance was ready. In the same way, as the trumpets sound around us, we don't fear. Instead, our great warrior King tells us to *"straighten up and raise [our] heads, because [our] redemption is drawing near"* (Luke 21:28).

The trumpets were not a cause of concern for the Jews and neither were the plagues. All the plagues fell on the Egyptians but not the people of God. God spared his people from the plagues, and no arrangements had to be made to remain safe. That is, of course, except for one—the final plague. The Lord threatened the death of the firstborn of Egyptians and Jews alike. But God made a provision for his people—lamb's blood on the doorpost protected those inside from the Lord's wrath.

We are also the recipients of God's provision. If we know Christ as the one who loves us and has freed us from our sins by his blood, we have nothing to fear. We're covered by the blood of the lamb. The Lord will deliver his people.

Several years ago, a tornado ripped through a trailer park in Venus, Florida. One home destroyed belonged to Heather Town, the mother of a three-year-old little girl named AnnMarie.

Friends and family immediately went to the trailer park looking for Heather and her daughter when the tornado left the area, but they couldn't initially find them.

As the crew searched the area, someone heard the familiar sound of AnnMarie's crying. But debris muffled the sound of her voice, and they couldn't determine her location.

Finally, after several more minutes of searching, they found Heather's lifeless body two hundred feet from home, wrapped in barbed wire, and lying on top of a pile of rubble. Turning her over, they saw she held AnnMarie alive and well.

Paramedics arrived on the scene and determined that the only injuries suffered by the little girl were a few broken ribs from the crushing pressure of a mother's arms who would not let go of her child, even in death.[6]

Do you know that you are loved like that? Loved by a compassionate Christ, who, because of his consuming love for you, endured the hurricane of God's anger and was wrapped in the barbed wire of his wrath, to save you. If you don't know that love, he commands you to receive it. If you've experienced that love already, entrust yourself to it afresh until the seventh trumpet sounds, signaling that the day of your inheritance has come.

Study Questions

1. The first trumpet previews the scarcity of resources on the day of judgment. In what ways do we hear this trumpet blast today?
2. The second trumpet warns that kingdoms will come and go. In what ways do we hear this trumpet blast today?
3. The third trumpet warns those who think there is life and joy in sin. In what ways do we hear this trumpet blast today?
4. The fourth trumpet is a glimpse into the spiritual darkness of man-centered worldviews and spirituality. In what ways do we hear this trumpet blast today?
5. As we look at the first four trumpets which are powerless to save, do you see your high dignity and privilege as one who holds the treasure of the Gospel? The power of God for salvation! How does this empower your words and deeds in this world?

---

1. G.K. Beale, *The Book of Revelation: A Shorter Commentary* (Eerdmans, 2015), 174; Thomas R. Schreiner, *The Joy of Hearing: A Theology of the Book of Revelation* (Wheaton IL: Crossway, 2021), 88.
2. G.K. Beale, *The Book of Revelation: A Shorter Commentary*, 174–175.
3. N.T. Wright, *Revelation for Everyone* (Westminster John Knox Press, Louisville, 2011), 128. See also 1 Peter 5:13.
4. Selections from Psalm 2.
5. See also Acts 26:17–18 where Jesus describes the preaching of the gospel as turning *"from darkness to light and from the power of Satan to God."* See also G.K. Beale, *The Book of Revelation: A Shorter Commentary*, 176–177, for many more instances of darkness as a metaphor for judgment, spiritual stupor, and hard-heartedness.
6. https://www.huffpost.com/entry/heather-town-mom-dies-shielding-child-tornado_n_1631999

17

WAR AND PEACE

REVELATION 8:13–9:21

You may remember the Magic Eye 3D art craze of the 1990s. Even if that name doesn't ring a bell, seeing one of the pictures definitely would. Magic Eye 3D images are those two-dimensional pictures that look like a maze of squiggly lines or random images. But upon closer inspection, and usually with coaching from someone saying things like, "You have to cross your eyes a little" or "Try to look beyond the surface," another image would emerge.

Behind the surface of all those squiggly lines and repeated patterns appeared a previously undisclosed picture; sometimes a rocket ship, an elephant, the Statue of Liberty, and the list goes on. This art form intrigues us because we can always see the "revealed" images, but the picture remains concealed unless you train your eyes to see them.

You'll recall from an earlier study that John calls this book an apocalypse, which means to uncover, unveil, or reveal, hence the English title, the Book of Revelation. Trumpets five and six, our focus here, train our eyes to discern the nature of reality that would otherwise remain unseen.

If you are not following Jesus today, you need to see what John shows you about the war occurring in your soul. It's a very different picture than what you imagine. But, on the other hand, if you are a Christian, you need to see the power and love of Jesus for you, which saves you from this war and offers the peace of God that surpasses all understanding (Phil. 4:7).

John reveals an ongoing war on the battlefield of peoples' souls.

War

In our previous study, we examined the first four of seven trumpets. We noted that those trumpets affected creation, and they have been sounding for thousands of years and will continue until the blasting of the seventh. Trumpets five and six have also been blowing since the ascension of Christ and will continue until he returns. But the fifth and sixth trumpets no longer focus on warnings of judgment through physical catastrophes. These move into our souls, and they carry out their work in the minds of those who will not turn to Jesus.

These psychological and spiritual torments pictured here are much worse than the other warnings we've seen thus far. After the blast of the fourth trumpet, John sees an eagle flying overhead, announcing the greater severity of the last three trumpets to come:

> *Then I looked, and I heard an eagle crying with a loud voice as it flew directly overhead, "Woe, woe, woe to those who dwell on the earth, at the blasts of the other trumpets that the three angels are about to blow!"* (Rev. 8:13)

God sets apart the first four trumpets from the last three because they are far more severe than economic distress, natural disasters, falling empires, and spiritual ignorance.[1] The fifth trumpet shows us a demonic army, likened to locusts, which spiritually torment those who are outside of Jesus' care:

> *And the fifth angel blew his trumpet, and I saw a star fallen from heaven to earth, and he was given the key to the shaft of the bottomless pit. He opened the shaft of the bottomless pit, and from the shaft rose smoke like the smoke of a great furnace, and the sun and the air were darkened with the smoke from the shaft. Then from the smoke came locusts on the earth, and they were given power like the power of scorpions of the earth. They were told not to harm the grass of the earth or any green plant or any tree, but only those people who do not have the seal of God on their foreheads.* (Rev. 9:1–4)

The fifth trumpet sounds, and John sees a star fall from heaven, which opens the pit of hell with a key. A few clues from the Book of Revelation and the Gospel of Luke help us identify this star as Satan. Verse 11 says that this demonic locust army is ruled by a superior angel whose name matches what we know about Satan: *"They have as king over them the angel of the bottomless pit. His name in Hebrew is Abaddon, and in Greek he is called Apollyon"* (Rev. 9:11).

Both names mean "destroyer." While Jesus came into the world to give life to his people, Satan came only to steal, kill, and destroy (John 10:10). Another clue comes in Chapter 12, where John reports that he observed a war occurring in heaven that resulted in a great dragon thrown down from heaven, the ancient serpent who is called *"the devil and Satan"* along with his demonic army (12:9).

We've become accustomed to John's technique of recapitulation in this book. The casting of Satan from Heaven in Chapter 12 appears to be the same event pictured here. Finally, the Gospel of Luke records that Jesus sent out a group of disciples to preach the Gospel. They later returned to report that even the demons could not stop the Good News from going forth. Jesus responded by saying, *"I saw Satan fall like lightning from heaven"* (Luke 10:18). To the casual observer, all that happened with the sending out of the disciples was that a few men preached and healed people. But Jesus informs us that while the disciples preached the Gospel, Satan suffered a notable defeat and, like lightning, was cast down from heaven to the earth.[2]

Therefore, John likely sees Satan cast out of heaven here. Satan opened the gates of hell,[3] and John observed a demonic army of locusts:

> *Then from the smoke came locusts on the earth, and they were given power like the power of scorpions of the earth. They were told not to harm the grass of the earth or any green plant or any tree, but only those people who do not have the seal of God on their foreheads. They were allowed to torment them for five months, but not to kill them, and their torment was like the torment of a scorpion when it stings someone. And in those days people will seek death and will not find it. They will long to die, but death will flee from them.* (Rev. 9:3–6)

As with the first four trumpets, which each pointed to one of the plagues that fell on Egypt, the eighth plague—locusts—returns here (Ex. 10:12–20). But these are no ordinary locusts. They come from hell, and they don't eat grass, trees, or plants.

Instead, these locusts feast upon men and women. And like literal locusts, these demonic ones leave famine in their wake. They strip the souls of those who do not know Jesus of every tender blade of hope. Without Jesus, they have nowhere to take their guilt, no balm to ease their troubled consciences. There is no realistic hope that they will not stand before an angry Creator God when they die. Often, the locusts feed upon lives of quiet desperation, hoping that if there is a god, he/she/it will let them into paradise based upon their good deeds. But they do not have a substantiated hope.

These locusts consume blades of certainty about such matters before they can sprout. And they sting their victims like scorpions. This again points us to the identity of these hellish locusts. Scorpions, like serpents, were symbols of the demonic world in Jewish thought.[4] Consider again Jesus' words from Luke's gospel:

And he said to them, "I saw Satan fall like lightning from heaven. Behold, I have given you authority to tread on serpents and scorpions, and over all the power of the enemy, and nothing shall hurt you. (Luke 10:19).

Jesus assures his disciples that the serpents and scorpions—symbols of the demonic realm—shall not hurt his people. Likewise, these demonic locusts, which sting like scorpions, will not hurt those who have the seal of God on their foreheads (Rev. 9:4. cf. 1 John 5:18). We'll return to those who are sealed on the forehead, but for now, John continues his description of this hellish band:

In appearance the locusts were like horses prepared for battle: on their heads were what looked like crowns of gold; their faces were like human faces, their hair like women's hair, and their teeth like lions' teeth; they had breastplates like breastplates of iron, and the noise of their wings was like the noise of many chariots with horses rushing into battle. They have tails and stings like scorpions, and their power to hurt people for five months is in their tails. (Rev. 9:7–10)

Returning to the Old Testament for inspiration, John utilizes the words of the prophet Joel, who also described a locust plague using military imagery (Joel 2:1–11). John piles metaphor upon metaphor, straining to describe these demons in terms we can recognize. The golden crowns may point to their authority over the rebellious, the human face to their cunning ways. A woman's hair may suggest their ability to seduce, breastplates of iron, and the noise of their wings—like the noise of many chariots—to their invulnerability. Their teeth, like a lion, point to the end for which they torment their victims. These locust-like demons are permitted to afflict the souls of men for five months, which is the length of the life cycle of the locust.

Perhaps the idea here is that these demons give the totality of their existence to the torment of men and women. Like Apollyon—the devil—they prowl to and fro within the souls of men, seeking to feast upon any sign of eternal hope.

The fifth trumpet gives us a pictorial description of the inner state of those alienated from God. The Bible tells us that apart from Jesus Christ, we live under the power of the evil one (1 John 5:19). The crowns atop the locusts' heads may point to that authority.

Apart from Jesus, we are estranged from God, and therefore we have no true hope (Eph. 2:12). Because, apart from the protection of Jesus, demonic locusts are allowed to chew back and destroy any signs of valid optimism regarding the future. Apart from Jesus Christ, everyone lives out a lifelong slavery to the fear of death (Heb. 2:14–15). People may distract themselves with family, careers, and sports, but under the surface, John shows us scorpion stings torment them. The Christian can say, "*O death, where is your victory? O death, where is your sting?*" (1 Cor. 15:55) but those who don't know Jesus have their souls tormented and repeatedly punctured with fear and uncertainty about what happens after death: "*Woe,*" cried the eagle flying overhead to those who endure such spiritual torment."

But a second, and even greater woe comes with the blasting of the sixth trumpet:

> *Then the sixth angel blew his trumpet, and I heard a voice from the four horns of the golden altar before God, saying to the sixth angel who had the trumpet, "Release the four angels who are bound at the great river Euphrates." So the four angels, who had been prepared for the hour, the day, the month, and the year, were released to kill a third of mankind. The number of mounted troops was twice ten thousand times ten thousand; I heard their number* (Rev. 9:13–16)

These four angels are probably demonic in origin, as the Bible doesn't describe good angels as bound, or breathing out fire, sulfur, and smoke (Rev. 9:17).[5] The mention of an enormous army crossing over the Euphrates River has led some well-meaning Christians to identify this trumpet with a future, literal human army coming from Russia or China that will enter the Holy Land at the end of time.

I don't think that suggestion captures John's meaning. Instead, for John's audience, the Euphrates River was a symbolic border beyond which evil resided. The terrible Assyrians came from beyond the Euphrates, and they destroyed the northern kingdom of Israel. So did the Babylonians, who later exiled the southern kingdom of Judah. They were followed by the Persians, who also dwelt beyond the Euphrates.

Even in John's day, the Euphrates River was the easternmost border of the Roman Empire, beyond which resided the dreaded Parthians, who repeatedly created problems for Rome. The Euphrates symbolizes the boundary between peace and safety and war and uncertainty.

John continues to symbolize these demonic entities as lion-headed horses that exhale filth from their mouths. Notice that John directs us twice to focus on what comes from the mouths of the horses. This suggests that they execute their work through the power of speech:

> *And this is how I saw the horses in my vision and those who rode them: they wore breastplates the color of fire and of sapphire and of sulfur, and the heads of the horses were like lions' heads, and fire and smoke and sulfur came out of their mouths. By these three plagues a third of mankind was killed, by the fire and smoke and sulfur coming out of their mouths. For the power of the horses is in their mouths and in their tails, for their tails are like serpents with heads, and by means of them they wound.* (Rev. 9:17–19)

If the fifth trumpet represents the spiritual torment of those outside of Christ, the sixth trumpet pictures the seductive teaching whispered into the ears of non-Christians. John will sometimes place items in the mouths of individuals to symbolize speech. For example, when John saw the vision of Jesus in the first chapter, he described a two-edged sword protruding from Christ's mouth.

The sword likely represents the condemnation he will speak over his enemies. In another vision (Rev. 12:15), John sees a dragon chasing after a woman in the desert, pouring water like a river out of its mouth, and trying to drown the woman. We'll see that the river coming from the mouth of the dragon represents false teaching by which Satan attempts to destroy the bride of Christ.

Here we find another instance of items protruding from the mouths of these beasts—fire, smoke, and sulfur—pointing us to their words, which they use not only to seduce people away from Jesus but also, their words lead to premature death: *"By these three plagues a third of mankind was killed, by the fire and smoke and sulfur coming out of their mouths."* (Rev. 9:18)

Through these entities' deceptive and seductive influence, countless wars of conquest have come and gone, leaving scores of innocent dead behind. Through the poisonous influence of this demonic army, many feel hopeless, so they turn to the bottle or pills, and their lives are swept away. In addition, we've seen the explosive growth of Islamic jihadists, who have been duped into believing they can serve God through terror. And most recently of all, we've watched in stunned horror over the last several years as children take up weapons and tear down the lives of their peers. While many contributing factors lead to these horrific actions, focusing on the visible contributors alone when looking for the cause of these atrocities misses what lies behind them all. *"For the power of the horses is in their mouths"*—fire, smoke, and sulfur—and *"by these three plagues a third of mankind was killed."*

The sixth trumpet represents what the rest of the Scriptures spell out in different words:

> *For we do not wrestle against flesh and blood, but against the rulers, against the authorities, against the cosmic powers over this present darkness, against the spiritual forces of evil in the heavenly places.* (Eph. 6:12)

If you read this today and you're not a follower of Jesus, and if you are anything like I was before I trusted Jesus, you probably think the ability to accept or reject him is within your power. Or you may think that there are intellectual reasons that keep you from becoming a Christian. "Where is the evidence for God? If God is good and powerful, why is there so much suffering?"

These are good questions, and they deserve good responses. But your unbelief does not come as a result of pure intellectual objections. Instead, this passage shows you in picture form what the apostle Paul describes elsewhere: *"The god of this world has blinded the minds of unbelievers, to keep them from seeing the light of the gospel"* (2 Cor. 4:4).

Fire, smoke, and sulfur lie behind every objection to trusting Jesus and undergird every intention of taking him seriously later on. The god of this world creates a veil over your heart, leaving you in the dark and blinding you from the light of Christ. But there is still hope for you. Christ can remove that veil. Paul says, *"When one turns to the Lord, the veil is removed"* (2 Cor. 3:16). And in so doing, the war will cease, and in its place, there will be a peace that passes all understanding.

Peace

We cannot leave this section without observing that some don't get spiritually tormented by locusts or convinced that there is no hope by the sulfur-spewing armies. We've met them already in the book of Revelation, and they will appear over and over again:

> *Then from the smoke came locusts on the earth, and they were given power like the power of scorpions of the earth. They were told not to harm the grass of the earth or any green plant or any tree, but only those people who do not have the seal of God on their foreheads.* (Rev. 9:3–4)

We met this group of those who bear the seal of God on their foreheads back in Chapter 7. We discovered that the seal represented the Holy Spirit of God, which is God's mark of ownership on someone. Those who have been born again by the Spirit of God, and therefore trust in Jesus Christ, don't get destroyed by the devouring locusts. In another allusion to the plagues of Exodus, this plague of demonic locusts cannot torment those whom God protects.

But that is not to say that we are no longer of interest to the demonic hoard. On the contrary, Peter warns us to be *"sober-minded; be watchful. [Our] adversary the devil prowls around like a roaring lion, seeking someone to devour"* (1 Pet. 5:8).

Also, the presence of the Holy Spirit does not mean that Christians will never face times of deep discouragement, instances of weak faith, depression, and even what can feel like hopelessness. But, the seal on our foreheads, which is the Spirit of God, who has renewed our minds, enables us to "resist [the Devil], firm in [our] faith" (1 Pet. 5:9).

John Bunyan left us a picture of what that looks like in *The Pilgrim's Progress*. Christian, the story's main character, travels from the City of Destruction to the Celestial City, but he gets stopped by a foul creature named Apollyon, the same fallen angel John saw. Apollyon tries to stop Christian from moving forward, and he does so by way of accusation. He tells Christian that he knows the king he serves and what that king demands of his followers. He also told Christian that he knew how he had failed to serve his king.

Christian wanted to know how he had failed his king. Apollyon, the accuser of the brethren (Rev. 12:10), reminds Christian that he almost drowned in the swamp of discouragement and how he tried to get rid of his burden in the wrong way. Additionally, Apollyon reminded Christian that he'd once fallen asleep on his journey. And with one last accusation, Apollyon noted that when Christian could record any good he had done for his king, it was done with "vainglory." That is to say, Christian was full of self-pride.

All of these things that Apollyon brought before Christian were true. Christian stumbled in many ways along the journey. He was quickly overwhelmed, he thought about turning away from the path, and selfish motives drove him at times. Apollyon tried to torment Christian's spirit and seduce him to lose faith.

But Christian responds, "All this is true, and much more which thou hast left out," but "the Prince whom I serve and honor is merciful and ready to forgive." After a few more words between the two, Christian took his sword and plunged it deep into the body of Apollyon, saying, "We are more than conquerors through him who loved us."

And with that, Apollyon stretched out his dragon wings, which sped him away, and Christian saw him no more.

My friend, Jesus promised you that you would have trouble in this world. Apollyon will, at times, breathe accurate accusations against you. But, to those sealed on the forehead, Jesus says, *"Take heart; I have overcome the world."* Resist the devil, and he will flee from you. For greater is he who is in you than he who is in the world.

Study Questions

1. The fifth trumpet gives a depiction of the inner state and spiritual turmoil of those outside of Christ. In what ways do you see this trumpet in the lives of unbelievers around you today?
2. The sixth trumpet shows us what Ephesians 6:12 teaches. Read and reflect on that passage and the implications for your life. How does this shape your response to difficult circumstances or events in your life?
3. We are told that when one turns to the Lord, the veil is removed, the war will cease, and there will be peace that passes all understanding. How have you experienced this reality? How might this perspective change your evangelism?
4. Apollyon will breathe accurate accusations against you, and you will have trouble in this world, Jesus has promised as much. But, he promises something else as well. Meditate on, and pray with thanksgiving, the truth that we can take heart! The one in you is greater than he who is in the world.

1. When the Jews wanted to emphasize something, they would repeat the word twice, as in *"Truly, truly I say to you."* When they desired to communicate totality, they would repeat a word three times as both the seraphim of Isaiah's day (Isa. 6:3) and the living creatures of John's (Rev. 4:8) sang, *"Holy, holy, holy."* The eagle's thrice-spoken woe calls attention to the totality of the anguish of those who experience the last three trumpets. For the Jewish use of repetition to express superlatives or totality, see J. Alec Motyer, *The Prophecy of Isaiah* (Leicester, UK: InterVarsity, 1999), 76–77.
2. For more on this passage, see Leon Morris, *Luke,* Tyndale New Testament Commentaries (Downers Grove: IL, IVP, 1998), 203–204.
3. Revelation 1:18 informs us that Jesus holds the keys of Death and Hades, reminding the reader here that Jesus is sovereign over the entirety of history, even the actions of Satan.
4. As we will discover in the sixth trumpet, the tails of the horses are likened to serpents (Rev. 9:19). For an examination of the symbolic associations of serpents and scorpions to demonic entities in Judaism, see G.K. Beale, *The Book of Revelation: A Commentary on the Greek Text* (Grand Rapids: MI, Eerdmans, 2013), 515–516.
5. John suggests that after the four angels are released, they morph into many mounted riders. On the probable demonic nature of these four angels, see G.K. Beale, *The Book of Revelation: A Commentary on the Greek Text,* 14; Thomas R. Schreiner, *The Joy of Hearing: A Theology of the Book of Revelation* (Wheaton: IL, Crossway, 2021), 91.

18

THE CONQUEROR AND THE COMMISSIONED

REVELATION 10

Not long ago, I had the privilege of standing in the pulpit of a pastor I deeply admire. It once belonged to Fred Shuttlesworth, former pastor of Bethel Baptist Church in Birmingham, Alabama. During the 1950s and 1960s, Birmingham was considered the most segregated city in the United States. And if you were an African American, it was one of the most dangerous places to live. Between 1947 and 1965, over fifty explosions targeted black-owned homes, businesses, and churches earning the city the sad nickname "Bombingham."

Fred Shuttlesworth stood at the center of the cause for Civil Rights in Birmingham. This courageous pastor underwent terrible threats and physical beatings for his fellow man. People bombed his church and parsonage three different times.

Once when attempting to enroll his children in an all-white school, an angry mob of Klansmen pulled Fred from his car and beat him with brass knuckles and chains. They stabbed his wife, Ruby, in the hip during the same incident. On another occasion, Fred's vehicle was surrounded by an angry mob, who rocked his car, threatening, "We're gonna kill you!" With this warning ringing in his ears, Fred got out of his car, walked up to those threatening him, and said, "If you're gonna kill me, kill me. But you can't intimidate me."[1]

What explains such courage? What enables someone to stand up to such threats saying, "You can kill me, but you can't intimate me?" Fred regularly told his congregation and any who asked him two things about the source of his courage. First, he knew his cause was just, and second, his life was in the hands of a mighty Savior. Therefore, no one could intimidate him.

Every Christian can have such courage. Our mighty Jesus holds all of our lives in his hands, and he gives us all a just cause. What difference would it make in your life if you built it on the two truths the strong Savior calls you to live publicly for him? You'd be bold and courageous, and no one could intimidate you. Isn't that the voice you want to have for Jesus? I trust it is. This chapter helps us because it displays a conquering king who commissions his people to announce his victory.

Conquering King

Before we jump into the text, recall that in the previous two chapters, John described the trumpets of warning which have sounded since the ascension of Jesus to his throne. Trumpets one through four deal with calamities that occur on earth: famines, falling empires, and spiritual ignorance. Trumpets five and six deal with the internal, spiritual torment and the powerful deception that characterizes those who don't know the peace of Christ.

Turning to our chapter, we might expect to find the seventh trumpet here. But that's not what we see. Instead, there's a break between trumpets six and seven, just as there was a break between seals six and seven.

What's the purpose of the break? The gap functions as it did between seals six and seven. Between the sixth and seventh seals, we saw a picture of those spared from the wrath of God poured out in the seventh seal. Those spared bore the seal of God on their foreheads (Rev. 7:1–17). So similarly, before the seventh and final trumpet sounds, God makes a break in the narrative to focus on the church.

The interval between the sixth and seventh seals answered the question: Who will stand on the day of God's wrath? The break between trumpets six and seven answers the question: What is the church's role in this time period?[2] Chapters 10 and 11 provide the answer.

Our role is first to hold fast to our conquering king Jesus Christ, who sends an angel with a scroll to John:

> *Then I saw another mighty angel coming down from heaven, wrapped in a cloud, with a rainbow over his head, and his face was like the sun, and his legs like pillars of fire. He had a little scroll open in his hand. And he set his right foot on the sea, and his left foot on the land, and called out with a loud*

voice, like a lion roaring. When he called out, the seven thunders sounded. (Rev. 10:1–3)

Think back to chapters 4 and 5, where John was transported to heaven and saw the Lord of Glory seated on a throne. In his hand, the Lord held a scroll sealed with seven seals. Then a mighty angel cried out, *"Who is worthy to open the scroll and break its seals?"* (Rev. 5:2). As we found, the scroll represents God's plan for the salvation of his people and the judgment of the wicked. From the earliest days of creation God designed to have people, his image bearers, ruling over creation.

In thought, word, and deed, man should function like a little mirror, reflecting the very image of God to the observer. In response to the angel's question—who is worthy to open the scroll?—none were found, for all have sinned and fallen short of the glory of the Lord.

John began to weep in despair until an elder said to him, *"Weep no more... the Lion of the tribe of Judah... has conquered, so that he can open the scroll and its seven seals"* (Rev. 5:5). Jesus alone was worthy to open the seals. And as the executor of God's plan, Jesus reigns with all authority in heaven and earth.

In the following chapters, Jesus unsealed the scroll, revealing the nature of the period between his ascension and return. As we come to Chapter 10, John encounters another mighty angel holding a little scroll. Before we consider the scroll, let's consider the angel John saw.

The angel reflects the conquering king who sends him. The angel so closely resembles the Lord that some suggest that this angel is Christ himself.[3] It's better to understand that this angel is just that... an angel. He comes reflecting the radiance and image of his maker. Like Moses in the Old Testament, whose appearance changed when he came into the immediate presence of God (Ex. 34:29–35), so too, this angel, descending from heaven's throne room, shines in such a way that we see his master and ours —Jesus Christ.[4]

The angel reflects the sovereignty of Jesus as we look at his feet: *"He had a little scroll open in his hand. And he set his right foot on the sea, and his left foot on the land"* (Rev. 10:2).

There are two important details to note here. The first is that when the Bible describes someone's foot on top of something, it means they have authority over it. So, for example, when Joshua conquered enemy kings, he had them brought before him. Once there, he ordered his generals to place their feet on the necks of the enemy kings while Joshua proclaimed that the Lord had subdued his enemies (Josh. 10:24–26). Additionally, Psalm 8:6

reminds us of the original state of creation when the Lord gave man dominion over the earth, putting *"all things under his feet."* This angel gives us a picture of the one who has all authority in heaven and on earth. All things on the earth and the sea are now under his feet.

This will be important for us later as John will observe two terrible beasts, one rising out of the sea and another rising out of the land, who both wage war on the Church (Rev. 13:1, 11). That is to say, in this world, we will suffer. There is a devil. Some wicked men and women will malign and mock you for your faith. To say that Christ has all authority over heaven and earth doesn't mean that we shouldn't suffer for his name's sake.

Jesus reminds us repeatedly that servants are not above their master: *"If they persecuted me, they will also persecute you"* (John 15:20). Jesus promises us that when we align ourselves with him, the world will hate us (John 15:18–19). But the authority of Jesus means that both the beast rising of the sea and the beast that rises out of the land are still under the feet of your master—Jesus Christ. To summarize Martin Luther: There is a devil, but he's God's devil. The devil is on a leash and can only do what will serve the purposes of his master.

We will only sometimes understand how Jesus uses our suffering for our good and his glory. But he wants us to know and hold fast to the glorious assurance that whatever comes our way comes first through hands nailed to a tree for you. Jesus' hands have the blueprints over all history, from the macro-events of empires rising and falling to the micro-events which make up our sometimes mundane lives. The King over all kings (Rev. 1:5), calls you his friend. Even now, he stands over us with feet on land and sea, with all authority in heaven and on earth. This should encourage us.

Another image of encouragement emerges as we consider the cloud that envelopes the angel and his legs like pillars of fire. To appreciate these images, recall that the six trumpets echoed the plagues which fell upon Egypt. Observing the angel, we are again transported back to the Exodus event. Notice a cloud wraps his body, and his legs are described as pillars of fire, reminding us of how the Lord led Israel through the wilderness—a pillar of cloud by day and a pillar of fire by night. Through the cloud and fire, God not only showed his presence with his people but also that he would accompany them to the Promised Land.

We are assured of the very same truth here. This angel represents Christ, who also promises to be with us and lead us home. Here we touch on a mystery that is hard to comprehend but also thrilling to consider. While the Church has confessed for two thousand years that Jesus bodily ascended to the right hand of God the Father, she has also confessed that this same Jesus promised never to leave or forsake her. His parting words to the disciples were a promise of his ongoing presence: *"Behold, I am with you always, to the end of the age"* (Matt. 28:20). The opening vision of Revelation showed Jesus standing among the lampstands (Rev. 1:12–13), which represent the Church of all ages. The book of Hebrews tells us that when the Church gathers for worship, Christ proclaims his Father's name in her midst (Heb. 2:12). He also leads our singing: *"In the midst of the congregation I will sing your praise"* (Heb 2:12).[5]

What a remarkable assurance to us! When we gather in the name of Jesus, we also assemble in the presence of Jesus. John's vision of this angel places the church, like the Exodus generation, in the wilderness, making its way to the Promised Land. And like the Exodus generation, we don't travel alone. Christ, the mighty king, meets with us, prays with and for us, and he sings and eats with us. And remarkably, he speaks with us.[6]

Maybe today you hear his voice asking you what frightens you. Are you worried about the future? He says, "I hold the scroll in my hands. And my feet are on the earth and sea. Nothing happens apart from my will." Are you trusting in Jesus and yet worried that there is some sin that he's not forgiven? He says, "I am the Lamb John saw slain for you." Are you concerned about being ridiculed for your faith? Mocked and maligned for Jesus? Jesus speaks to us, saying, "The Lord is [your] helper... what can man do to [you]?" (Heb. 13:6). Mock you? Revile you? Imprison you? Kill you? They may do all of those things to you. But don't let them intimidate you! Because in all these things, we are *"more than conquerors through him who loved us"* (Rom. 8:37).

We need that assurance because he commissions us to carry his victory into the world through our public witness.

Commissioned Church

In the next chapter, we will see more clearly our commission, but we can also draw on John's experience. Jesus commissions all his followers to testify to his victory in a world that refuses to listen to the warnings around them. Remember, the book's flow has been interrupted between the first six trumpets and the final one, which will mark the judgment. For thousands of years, the trumpets have blasted repeatedly, giving humanity a snapshot of the coming day of wrath (Rev. 6:16–17; 11:18; 14:19; 15:1; 16:19; 19:15). But they don't get through to people. They cannot hear what the trumpets signal. John reports:

> *The rest of mankind, who were not killed by these plagues, did not repent of the works of their hands nor give up worshiping demons and idols of gold and silver and bronze and stone and wood, which cannot see or hear or walk, nor did they repent of their murders or their sorceries or their sexual immorality or their thefts.* (Rev. 9:20–21)

Just as the plagues hardened Pharaoh's heart instead of moving him to repentance, the trumpets serve only to make men and women dig in their heels against the Lord. They ignore the trumpet's warnings. The ineffectiveness of the alarms may be behind the announcement of the seven thunders, which John heard but was forbidden from sharing:

> *[the angel] called out with a loud voice, like a lion roaring. When he called out, the seven thunders sounded. And when the seven thunders had sounded, I was about to write, but I heard a voice from heaven saying, "Seal up what the seven thunders have said, and do not write it down."* (Rev. 10:3–4).

No one but John, the angel, and the assembly in heaven knows for sure what these seven thunders communicated. Thunder is often associated with judgment, and we have encountered seven seals and seven trumpets, each series growing in severity. The seven seals affected a quarter of the earth (Rev. 6:8), and the trumpets affected a third. The seven thunders may have been another series of warnings that would affect half of the planet. But it is not to be. Bauckham notes, "It's not that God's patience has run out, but that such judgments do not produce repentance."[7] So the seven thunders are withdrawn, and John isn't allowed to disclose their content. The angel then warns that only the seventh trumpet remains to be blown. And when it sounds, there will be no more warnings, only the revelation of Christ:

> *And the angel whom I saw standing on the sea and on the land raised his right hand to heaven and swore by him who lives forever and ever, who created heaven and what is in it, the earth and what is in it, and the sea and what is in it, that there would be no more delay, but that in the days of the trumpet call to be sounded by the seventh angel, the mystery of God would be fulfilled, just as he announced to his servants the prophets.* (Rev. 10:5–7)

Paul tells us that the mystery of God has been made known to us, namely that God would carry out his plan of redemption through his son, who would unite all things in heaven and earth (Eph. 1:9–10). On that day, that mystery, already disclosed to the church, will be revealed before all men and women.

This brings us back to the church's role as it awaits the final trumpet. If the warnings don't work to bring about repentance, what hope does humanity have? Unfortunately, falling empires, food shortages, wars, economic distress, and spiritual misery don't have the power to bring repentance. But you and I possess something that does—the Gospel:

> *Then the voice that I had heard from heaven spoke to me again, saying, "Go, take the scroll that is open in the hand of the angel who is standing on the sea and on the land." So I went to the angel and told him to give me the little scroll. And he said to me, "Take and eat it; it will make your stomach bitter, but in your mouth it will be sweet as honey." And I took the little scroll from the hand of the angel and ate it. It was sweet as honey in my mouth, but when I had eaten it my stomach was made bitter. And I was told, "You must again prophesy about many peoples and nations and languages and kings."* (Rev. 10:8–11)

This scroll handed to John is the same one Jesus opened in Chapter 5. That scroll represented God's plan for the salvation of his people and the judgment of those who refuse to repent.

The angel instructed John to eat the scroll, symbolizing that he had internalized its message. In John's mouth, the message tasted sweet, representing the glorious, heart-stirring assurances of Jesus' indescribable love and kindness to his own. But the scroll soured in his stomach because many will reject the message. Like Jesus, who wept over Jerusalem, John's heart broke when men and women refused the offer of Christ's mercy. Even so, the Gospel you know and cherish is the power of salvation for all who believe.

Will you trust Jesus to show you the potency of his message? Will you put yourself in the way of a desperate sinner this week who cannot and will not hear the blasting trumpet warnings? Have you forgotten how powerful the Gospel is in the mouth of those who trust that Jesus uses ordinary people just like you and me? Can you trust him?

Someone once asked me what gave me the confidence to get into the pulpit weekly, year after year. I asked if they'd ever seen the movie *The Lion King*. I reminded them of a scene where Simba, as a tiny little cub, was cornered by hyenas who chased him down to kill him. Terrified and facing certain death, Simba draws air into his little lungs and tries his best to produce a terrifying roar, but only a pitiful yap comes from his mouth. The hyenas laugh at Simba and move in for the kill. Once again, Simba takes a deep breath and opens his mouth. But this time, we don't hear a yap from a lion cub but the mighty roar of an adult lion. Behind Simba stood his powerful father, bearing his teeth at the hyenas. The audience saw the mouth of Simba moving, but they heard his father's voice.

We are little lion cubs capable of pitiful yapping whenever we invite people to know Jesus on our own. But the world may hear his voice when we yield ourselves to the conquering king, who has commissioned us to open our mouths for him. And we pray that it would be his voice they hear.

You serve a mighty savior. Our cause is just. Let no one intimidate you.

Study Questions

1. Do you feel bold and courageous for Christ? If the answer is no, think of a few ways your life may look different if you were. If your answer is yes, write down how Christ's victory has made you bold.
2. The first role of the church, as seen in this break between trumpets six and seven, is to hold fast to the conquering King. How does the image of the sovereignty of the Lord, as represented in the angel's foot placement, embolden us?
3. Consider the meaning of the cloud that envelopes the angel's legs like pillars of fire, compared to the meaning of the Lord as a pillar of smoke and fire in the wilderness. If Christ is truly seated at the right hand of the Father, and is here with us today, how should this inform our hearts, minds, and lives? What are we so afraid of?
4. If the warnings of the trumpets do not bring repentance, what hope does the world have? This brings us to the second role of the church—we have in our possession that which brings about repentance, the Gospel! How will you trust the potency of Jesus' message this week in the lives of an unbelieving world?
5. Pray. When we yield ourselves to the conquering king, who has commissioned us to open our mouths for him, then the world has hope. And we pray that it would be his voice they hear. You serve a powerful savior. Our cause is just. Let no one intimidate you.

1. Pastor Shuttlesworth's pulpit is housed in the Birmingham Civil Rights Institute in Birmingham, Alabama. Some of the details related above can be found in Greg Thompson, "An Experiment in Love: Martin Luther King Jr. and the Re-imagining of American Democracy" (PhD diss., University of Virginia, 2015), https://libraetd.lib.virginia.edu/public_view/5425k998h and Taylor Branch, *Parting the Waters: America in the King Years 1954–63* (Simon and Schuster, 1989).
2. William Hendriksen, *More than Conquerors* (Baker Books, 1998), 125; Vern S. Poythress, *The Returning King: A Guide to the Book of Revelation* (P&R, 2000), 125.
3. After all, the angel is wrapped in a cloud, which reminds us of the opening chapter of Revelation, where we're promised that Jesus *"is coming with the clouds"* (Rev. 1:7). The rainbow over the angel's head points to the rainbow surrounding the throne of God in Rev. 4:3. His face shone like the sun as did Christ's in John's opening vision (Rev. 1:16). The legs of fire remind us of Jesus' feet which were *"like burnished bronze"* (Rev. 1:15). The now-opened scroll in the angel's hand is easily linked to the scroll that Jesus opened in Chapter 5. And the angel's lion-like voice connects back to the Lion of the tribe of Judah in the heavenly throne scene (Rev. 5:5), in addition to several Old Testament descriptions of God's voice roaring out like a lion (Joel 3:16; Amos 1:2). For an extended argument identifying this angel with the Old Testament *"angel of the Lord"* or Christ himself, see G.K. Beale, *The Book of Revelation: A Shorter Commentary* (Eerdmans, 2015), 200–201.
4. Lending support to this view is the five-link transition of communication which Chapter 1:1–2 prepared us to expect: *"The revelation of Jesus Christ, which God gave him to show to his servants... He made it known by sending his angel to his servant John, who bore witness to the word of God and to the testimony of Jesus Christ, even to all that he saw"* (Rev. 1:1–2). In Chapter 5, God gave the scroll to the Son. In Chapter 10, an angel has the same scroll, which we understand as having been delivered to him by Jesus. The angel gives the scroll to John, who then shares the revelation with the servants of Jesus.
5. Calvin writes of this verse, "And it is a truth, which may serve as a most powerful stimulant, and may lead us most fervently to praise God, when we hear that Christ leads our songs, and is the chief composer of our hymns." See John Calvin, *Commentary on the Epistle of Paul the Apostle to the Hebrews* (Calvin's Commentaries; trans. John Owen; Edinburgh: Calvin Translation Society, 1853; repr. Baker Books, 1999), 66–67.
6. See Rom. 10:14 along with the ESV footnote, which I think is the better rendering of Paul's words, which would read, *"How then will they call on him in whom they have not believed? And how are they to believe in him* whom they have never heard" (emphasis mine). John Murray, commenting on this passage, states, "A striking feature of this clause is that Christ is represented as being heard in the gospel when proclaimed by sent messengers. The implication is that Christ speaks in the gospel proclamation." See John Murray, *The Epistle to the Romans: The English Text with Introduction, Exposition and Notes* (Wheaton, IL: Eerdmans, 1997), 58.
7. Richard Bauckham, *The Theology of the Book of Revelation* (Cambridge University Press, 2012), 82.

19

FIRE AND RAIN

REVELATION 11:1-14

A few years after the September 11th terrorist attacks, the United States Navy built a ship in response. They named the ship the USS New York, titled after the state once home to the Twin Towers. Several details about the ship harken back to that terrible September day. Parts of the vessel were constructed using seven and a half tons of recycled steel recovered from Ground Zero.

Inside the boat, dozens of artifacts from that day fill glass display cases and hang on walls. In one section, you can see the helmet of a firefighter who didn't make it home. A police officer uniform hangs under a spotlight, with a badge still pinned on the chest. Charred street signs, baseball caps, and pictures of numerous people lost that day dot the walls. Every one of those items reminds those on board of what happened on September 11th, 2001.

Imagine how people might view the same boat but with different responses. A sailor aboard the USS New York might look at those reminders and feel immediate grief. The artifacts bring to mind the thousands of Americans who lost their lives—the husbands, wives, siblings, friends, and co-workers who went to work that morning but never came home.

To the casual observer, the USS New York might look like a floating museum commemorating a day of vulnerability, weakness, and defeat.

Consider now that same boat from the perspective of a Somalian pirate. One of the first missions of the USS New York was to patrol the Persian Gulf, plagued at the time by Somalians who wreaked havoc in the region. Imagine you're one of those pirates and coming over the horizon, you see three vessels. On one side is the USS Abraham Lincoln, a nuclear-powered aircraft carrier. On the other side is the USS Porter, a guided missile destroyer. And tucked between those two boats is the USS New York, transporting not a museum for the dead but four hundred United States Marines looking forward to meeting you. What a difference it would make if you were to see that boat through the eyes of the hunted pirate.

What John describes in this chapter is a way of viewing the Church that should make us bold to live for Jesus. For John's audience, they must have felt like they were standing against the whole world when they refused to alter their witness for Jesus. They faced both internal and external temptations to compromise. The call to hold fast to what they received in the beginning (Heb. 10:23), must have felt like an impossible command. Perhaps they felt weak and ill-equipped. They needed to see themselves from the Lord's perspective, which this chapter presents.

We also benefit from this chapter because we are shown not in weakness but in strength. It shows us afflicted and persecuted as we carry out our task but, we aren't driven to despair. Let's consider first how the Lord protects his Church as she waits for Jesus to return.

Protected People

Before we look at the text itself, recall that we're still in an interlude between the sixth and seventh trumpets. Six trumpets have been sounding for the last 2,000 years and will continue to do so until the seventh and final trumpet sounds, signaling the return of Jesus (1 Thess. 4:16). Remember the narrative broke between seals six and seven, answering the question of who will stand on the day of God's wrath. John heard the answer counted out as the true Israel of God (Rev. 7:1–8), which consists of an innumerable number of people from every nation (Rev. 7:9–17). In short, those who belong to the Lion of the tribe of Judah will be spared from the wrath of the Lamb (Rev. 6:16).

The interlude between trumpets six and seven serves a similar purpose. Who will be spared at the seventh trumpet, which signals not only the return of Jesus but also the release of God's wrath?[1] Once again, we're directed to the same people—the Church of Christ. But John piles up three different images to describe the church. The first two images he uses to describe the Church are a temple and a city:

> Then I was given a measuring rod like a staff, and I was told, "Rise and measure the temple of God and the altar and those who worship there, but do not measure the court outside the temple; leave that out, for it is given over to the nations, and they will trample the holy city for forty-two months. (Rev. 11:1–2)

Some well-meaning Christians teach this passage points toward a future rebuilding of the temple in Jerusalem. After all, aren't we just taking the Bible for what it says? It says John measured a temple in Jerusalem. What else is there to say?

That's a fair question, but we want to remember the type of book John writes. Revelation is an apocalypse, a genre known for communicating eternal truth through symbols. We've already encountered numerous symbols and plenty more lie ahead of us. We should also note that the New Testament never promises the rebuilding of the physical temple in Jerusalem.

Instead, Jesus foretold the destruction of the Temple, not its rebuilding (Matt. 24:2). But he also said that in place of the brick and mortar temple—which was coming down—Jesus would raise another, better temple in its place, one not made with human hands (John 2:19. Cf. Matt 26:61; 27:40; Mark 14:58). And that better temple, is repeatedly said to be the church. Writing to Christians in Corinth, Paul said, *"Do you not know that you are God's temple and that God's Spirit dwells in you?"* (1 Cor. 3:16). Later in the same letter, he includes himself, saying, *"For we are the temple of the living God"* (2 Cor. 6:16. cf. 1 Cor. 3:17; 6:19; Eph. 2:2). Peter also describes the Church as living stones, built upon Jesus Christ, *"being built up as a spiritual house, to be a holy priesthood"* (1 Pet. 2:4–5. Cf. Heb. 3:6).

The New Testament consistently presents the Church of all ages and across all cultures as the temple of God. Turning to Revelation, we've already seen the Church likened to seven lampstands, which were pieces of temple furniture. When John saw Jesus standing among the seven lampstands, he witnessed his abiding presence in the temple of God—his church.[2] In a book of symbolism, we shouldn't be surprised that John would see Christians as a temple. But we are not only the temple; we're also the holy city:

> *But do not measure the court outside the temple; leave that out, for it is given over to the nations, and they will trample the holy city for forty-two months.* (Rev. 11:2)[3]

Later in this book, John gets invited to see *"the Bride, the wife of the Lamb,"* which is the church. But he'll describe a beautiful city coming down from heaven. Recall that one of the promises Jesus made to the Philadelphian church weds both temple and city images together:

> To the one who conquers, I will make him a pillar in the temple of my God.... And I will write on him... the name of the city of my God, the New Jerusalem. (Rev. 3:12)

Putting this together, John sees the church of this age described as a temple and a holy city. What do we make of the command to measure the temple? It means to establish and protect it.[4] The backdrop for this is another prophet, Ezekiel, who also saw a temple that was measured (Ezek. 40–48). Ezekiel took a visionary tour of the temple and repeatedly heard detailed measurements of every room, doorway, and piece of furniture. This process goes on for several chapters communicating to the reader that the Lord will build his temple, and his presence will protect it down to the square inch.

Again, we see a pictorial representation of truths familiar to us all: *"I will build my church, and the gates of hell shall not prevail against it"* (Matt. 16:18). Ezekiel looked forward to the day the Lord would build his temple. John sees he has done so, using his Son as the cornerstone (Eph. 2:20; 1 Pet. 2:6–7). Jesus' parting promise to the disciples was, *"Behold, I am with you always, to the end of the age"* (Matt. 28:20). Through the measuring of the temple, John sees Jesus keeping his promise; his protective presence dwells among his people. That assurance of spiritual protection buoys us and keeps us engaged in the Lord's work, to be a prophetic people.

Prophetic People

That is to say, Jesus commissions us to tell others the glorious truth of the gospel. But in telling the glorious things, we must also warn others about the terrible things that await those who refuse to turn to Jesus. Another image emerges here as the temple and city fade away. He introduces two witnesses who also represent the church: *"And I will grant authority to my* two witnesses, and they will prophesy for 1,260 days, clothed in sackcloth" (Rev. 11:3-4).

Why does John picture the Church as two witnesses? We can point to a few reasons. First, in Judaism, two people were the required number of witnesses to establish a charge in a court of law (Num. 35:30). In the same way, as the Church gives testimony to the threats and assurances found in Scripture, the charges against the world are established. A second reason for the two witnesses may be a comparison of the church's testimony to the ministries of Moses and Elijah. We read that these witnesses pour fire from their mouths and can stop the rains:

> *And if anyone would harm them, fire pours from their mouth and consumes their foes. If anyone would harm them, this is how he is doomed to be killed. They have the power to shut the sky, that no rain may fall during the days of their prophesying.* (Rev. 11:5-6)

This seems to be an allusion to Elijah, who stood up to the mighty King Ahab and demonstrated God's power by praying for the rains to stop, which they did for three and a half years as a judgment against Israel (1 Kgs. 17:1). Elijah also called down fire from heaven to consume soldiers sent to arrest him (2 Kgs. 1:10). But Moses also comes to mind when John tells us, *"and they have power over the waters to turn them into blood and to strike the earth with every kind of plague as often as they desire"* (Rev. 11:6).

You'll recall that the Lord, through Moses, threatened Pharaoh with plagues of judgment if he did not repent. And when he did not, plagues affecting the waters fell upon Egypt, as John describes.

What are we to make of this image of fire pouring from our mouths and the calling of plagues to fall upon the earth? Two things strike me; one sobering, and the other encouraging. The Lord will use the words of the Church against the unrepentant at the judgment.[5] The Lord told Jeremiah, *"I am making my words in your mouth fire and this people wood, and it will consume them"* (Jer. 5:14). When we warn others of the wrath to come (fire in our mouths) and point to the trumpet warnings (likened to plagues), evidence mounts up against the unrepentant.

It's a sobering reminder that what we say about eternal things matters.[6] We should never try to minimize or avoid what we perceive as harsh, hard truths in the Scriptures. When we blunt the clear warnings of this book, we create a situation where those listening wonder why they need Jesus. Speak the truth with love. Testify to what you've learned in this book. Plead with people to turn from the coming wrath.

On the other hand, be encouraged because the Lord sees power coming from our mouths when we share the Gospel. Sometimes after I preach a sermon or share the Gospel one-on-one, I look at the results and think, "How pitiful!" You and I both need reminders of heaven's perspective of the Gospel so we stop thinking that its power comes from our skill sets.

The power of the Gospel is the Gospel itself. The Gospel makes the Church potent in the world. Not money. Not political influence. Nor marketing gimmicks. The potency of the Church is found in the "Spirit-empowered, Father-protected proclamation of Jesus Christ and him crucified."[7]

How long will this be the task of the church? John tells us it will last forty-two months or, put another way, 1,260 days:

> but do not measure the court outside the temple; leave that out, for it is given over to the nations, and they will trample the holy city for forty-two months. And I will grant authority to my two witnesses, and they will prophesy for 1,260 days, clothed in sackcloth. (Rev. 11:2–3)

We've learned that Revelation uses numbers symbolically to communicate eternal truths. The forty-two-month period, the same as 1,260 days, should likewise be viewed as a symbol. The Scriptures associate the number 42 with periods of intense trial and protection.[8] Consider that Israel traveled for two years in the wilderness before they rebelled. That rebellion added another 40 years to the trip, resulting in 42 years in the wilderness. Also, the book of Numbers tells us that the Israelites stopped and made camp 42 times throughout the wilderness journey (Num. 33:5ff).

Also, when Elijah prayed that the Lord would stop the rains from falling, the rains ceased for three and a half years or 42 months. So, John isn't using these numbers to tell us how long this period will last, but what the time will be like—a time of testing and trials.[9] John's already placed the Church in the wilderness with the angel clothed with a cloud and legs like pillars of fire. With this forty-two-month period, he sets us there again.[10]

It's easy to get overwhelmed with some of these details so let's summarize what John shows us. You're already familiar with the truth behind John's image; he dresses the truth in different clothing. So here is the truth—in this world, you will have trouble. You will be hated if you are a faithful witness to your calling. John tells us in his gospel that the light has come into the world, but the world loves darkness. The world hates the light because the light exposes them (John 1:19–20). And some of us, for the first time in our lives, are on the receiving end of the hatred and reviling for

Christ that Christians in other ages and places have known for a long time. But Jesus says to us, I have told you these things ahead of time so that when they occur, you would believe. John shows us that to publicly live for Christ may come with a profound cost. Right before the seventh trumpet sounds, the Church will suffer to such a degree that it will appear to be destroyed forever:

> *And when they have finished their testimony, the beast that rises from the bottomless pit will make war on them and conquer them and kill them, and their dead bodies will lie in the street of the great city that symbolically is called Sodom and Egypt, where their Lord was crucified. For three and a half days some from the peoples and tribes and languages and nations will gaze at their dead bodies and refuse to let them be placed in a tomb, and those who dwell on the earth will rejoice over them and make merry and exchange presents, because these two prophets had been a torment to those who dwell on the earth. But after the three and a half days a breath of life from God entered them, and they stood up on their feet, and great fear fell on those who saw them. Then they heard a loud voice from heaven saying to them, "Come up here!" And they went up to heaven in a cloud, and their enemies watched them.* (Rev. 11:7–12)

John introduces the beast that rises from the sea to snuff out the church's witness. John's language *"when they had finished their testimony"* indicates that a day is coming when the Gospel will be offered one last time through a faithful witness' mouth, only to be then clamped shut by this beast. As we'll discover later, the beast represents an evil king or kingdom committed to the destruction of God's people. And he'll succeed, at least for a time.

In some way, the church's warnings of judgment and offer of refuge in Jesus will go silent. And those who helped silence the Church will rejoice, give gifts, and make merry because those pesky Christians with their outdated sexual ethics, sermons against materialism, and insistence upon a day of reckoning no longer torment their consciences (Rev. 11:10).

The celebration will be short-lived. In contrast to the long period of forty-two months, only three and half days will pass, and the Lord will breathe life back into the lifeless bodies of his people, emptying their graves and bringing them body and soul to be with the Lord forever.

Notice that God calls us to mirror the path his beloved Son walked. The trajectory of the church's story matches the Savior's. He was the temple trampled upon by the Gentiles. He opened his mouth, offering pardon to sinners and fire and plagues to those who refused. He was killed for his testimony but raised three days later and caught up in the clouds. John is showing us how our Father sees the story of the church. We walk the same path to glory that the Savior did. The cross comes before the crown. But the crown does come, and that's important for us to keep before our minds!

Terrible things await the church; that is true! Jesus shows us here that the Church heads toward crucifixion. But we dare not adopt a victim mentality or gather in our churches to lament the culture and lick our wounds. Nor do we look to politicians to fix the world.

Jesus has already walked the path to the cross before us, and he'll walk this path with us. So, don't be afraid, don't retreat, and by all means, let us not pity ourselves. We're on the winning side. We speak for a King who cannot lose and take the Gospel into a dying world that cannot win.

So, if you've gone silent with the Gospel or retreated from the battle, go back to the front, open your mouth, and let the Lord fill it with the fire of his word. Some may trample you, others will hate you, and some will revile and curse you. But some may listen. Even at that final hour when the Church has been silenced and seems all hope lost for the world, some who participated in the silencing of the Church will repent:

> *And at that hour there was a great earthquake, and a tenth of the city fell. Seven thousand people were killed in the earthquake, and the rest were terrified and gave glory to the God of heaven.* (Rev. 11:13)

Just as the centurion who witnessed Jesus' death was moved to say, *"Truly this was the Son of God!"* (Matt. 27:54), it seems that some who will watch the Church get put down but then vindicated by God will be moved to repentance.[11] It reminds us never to underestimate what God can do with those who entrust themselves to Jesus.

When I think about how we underestimate what the Lord intends to do with his church, I'm reminded of a story that Dr. Peter Lillback, President of Westminster Seminary, shared with me. Once while visiting Korea, he was invited to attend a breakfast honoring seminary presidents. Six Korean men, each the head of a seminary in Korea, attended the event with Dr. Lillback. As they introduced themselves around the table, one president reported that they had 5,000 students enrolled that year in pastoral training. Dr. Lillback was stunned!

Even in the best of times, Westminster has no more than 700 students. Another man got up and reported 3,000 students. Then another spoke of

4,000 students. And another still said that 8,000 men and women were training that year for the ministry.

Now it was Dr. Lillback's turn to introduce himself. Feeling like a lightweight, he opened his introduction by saying, "I'm so embarrassed. I'm the president of Westminster Seminary in Philadelphia. We barely have 700 students in a good year and are always struggling to pay our bills. I feel like a lightweight sitting at this table." The other men at the table smiled and started laughing. Dr. Lillback assumed they were laughing at the pitiful numbers he'd just reported. But then one of the men said to him, "We aren't laughing because of the size of your seminary. We are laughing because you feel unused. You see, all the men at this table graduated from Westminster Seminary in Philadelphia!" Dr. Lillback told me that he has stopped underestimating what God can do with the smallest acts of faith.

Put yourself at the crossroads between this dying world and the world that is coming, and let the Lord speak through you. Don't underestimate the Lord.

Study Questions

1. What do we make of the command to measure the temple? What promise do we see Jesus keeping in this command?
2. What two things do we see from the image of fire pouring from the mouths of the two witnesses?
3. How does setting your mind on heaven's perspective of the Gospel change your witness?
4. Reflect on the summarization of this passage—the promise that you will have trouble in this world, be hated for your witness and testimony, and even for a time perhaps appear to have been destroyed. How does this mirror the same path our Savior walked? Why does this matter?
5. Terrible things await Christ's Church, that is true, but take heart! We are on the winning side! Spend some time today praying the Lord will keep your mind and heart on the crown because, after the cross, there is a crown! May we never underestimate what the Lord is doing.

---

1. After the seventh trumpet in 11:15, the elders sing that with its sounding, the wrath of God and the judgment of people has come (Rev. 11:18).
2. See also Jesus' promise to the one who conquers: *"I will make him a pillar in the temple of my God"* (Rev. 3:12).

3. The meaning behind the command not to measure the temple's outer court is tough to determine. The interested reader should consult the major commentaries for argumentation. Three suggestions dominate the discussion. Some argue the outer court represents nominal Christians who will not be protected on the day of wrath. Others suggest that the trampling of the gentiles on the outer courts, which John doesn't measure, points to the physical vulnerability of Christians in this age who are nevertheless spiritually protected from all lasting harm. Others think John is simply dividing all humanity into Christians and Gentiles (Eph. 4:17, 1 Thess. 4:5). I lean toward the third option.
4. See G.K. Beale, *The Book of Revelation: A Shorter Commentary* (Eerdmans, 2015), 215.
5. See Beale, 223
6. "The witness of the saints on earth against their adversaries is recorded in heaven as a testimony from which they are unable to escape." Simon Kistemaker, *Revelation*, New Testament Commentary (Baker, 2001), 330.
7. James M. Hamilton Jr., *Revelation: The Spirit Speaks to the Churches* (Wheaton, IL: Crossway, 2012), 239.
8. See G.K. Beale, 218; Leon Morris, *Revelation* (Grand Rapids, MI: Eerdmans, 1984), 147.
9. Kistemaker writes: "The trampling of the holy city [for forty-two months] refers to a period of persecution that Christians suffer throughout the ages." Simon Kistemaker, 327.
10. Some question revolves around why John tells us that the city is trampled for forty-two months but that the Church will prophesy for 1,260 days. One suggestion is that the holy city is pictured under siege, and sieges were measured in months. The witness of the church, however, is to continue its testimony day after day. See William Hendriksen, *More than Conquerors* (Baker Books, 1998), 129.
11. This is a difficult passage giving rise to strong opinions leading in two different directions. Are those who will *"give glory to the God of heaven"* simply acknowledging what is true, or are they genuinely repenting? Commentators are generally split on the issue. Some argue that those giving glory to God recognize God's rule in Christ (see Phil. 2:10–11), but it comes too late. Primary among the reasons for this position is the lack of any indication elsewhere in Revelation that suggests conversions to Christ after the church's witness has ceased. At the same time, others argue that giving glory to God throughout Revelation refers to the proper response to God of true worship. For this reason, I lean toward the second option.

20

THE UNENDING JUBILEE
REVELATION 11:15-19

If you were a Jewish person living in the days of the Old Testament, you would have observed an annual event called the Day of Atonement. On that unforgettable day of the year, the High Priest would enter the innermost room of the temple, which housed the ark of the covenant.

Every other day of the year, that room was off-limits. But on the Day of Atonement, one priest could enter into the special presence of God. This yearly event remains well-known among most Christians.

On the other hand, the Year of Jubilee feels less familiar. Here's how it started. On the Day of Atonement, every fiftieth year, the Priest would carry out all the normal activities of that day. But when he emerged from the temple, a loud trumpet would blast, signaling that life in Israel was about to change. All those who sold themselves into slavery were set free. All property sold to pay off debts reverted to the original owner. The Lord permitted no planting or harvesting the entire year.

The Year of Jubilee announced a fresh start for the people of God and creation. The Jubilee year proclaimed good news to the poor, and liberty to those held captive. So you can imagine the anticipation that must have filled the hearts of those present who looked forward to the sound of that trumpet signaling the start of the Year of Jubilee (Lev. 25:8–22).

With that in mind, we can see what that Year of Jubilee pointed toward. The High Priest's entrance into the temple's innermost room pictured Christ ascending to the throne room in heaven. And the High Priest's emergence from the temple, accompanied by the blast of trumpets, depicted Christ's return. The Bible informs us that trumpets will announce the return of the Lord Jesus Christ (Matt. 24:31; 1 Thess. 4:16; 1 Cor. 15:52).

As we arrive at the seventh trumpet of Revelation, this trumpet accompanies his emerging from the temple in heaven to announce that the true Jubilee has come. But the Jubilee Jesus brings won't last a mere calendar year. Instead, he will usher in the eternal canceling of debt, freedom from slavery, and restoration of the land that he has promised and for which our hearts long.

It all begins with the sounding of the seventh trumpet.

This section marks the conclusion of the third of seven portraits John paints of this time between the ascension of Jesus into heaven and his return to the earth. Six trumpets have sounded for thousands of years and will continue to blast until the seventh blows. The seventh trumpet then gives a picture of what will be. It's a glimpse of the return of Christ and a peek at our response to it.

We see ourselves as embodied in the twenty-four elders first introduced in Chapter 4. We suggested that these elders represent all the redeemed people of God from both the Old and New Testament eras. It's instructive to listen to what these elders say about the future because their words will be yours when the unending Jubilee begins.

That's important to consider because some of our future words may catch us off-guard in the present. On that day, we will praise the Lord for his wrath. We'll consider that challenging idea and then examine how we will also praise him for the restoration he will bring.

Praise for Wrath

Remember, John uses the familiar story of Joshua and the battle of Jericho as a background for the seven trumpets. That Old Testament story records that seven priests, armed with trumpets, circled the city of Jericho once a day for six days (Josh. 6:1–27). Trailing the priests, another group of men carried the Ark of the Covenant, the symbol of God's presence. The trumpets blasted each day and signaled a forthcoming judgment. But the Lord instructed the people to remain silent—no shouting, no whispering, not a word. Just trumpets.

On the seventh day, however, when the priests blew their trumpets again, Israel was instructed to shout with a "great shout," and the Lord would destroy the city. And so, on the seventh day, when the seven trumpets sounded, Israel shouted with a great shout, and the city of Jericho fell. Notice how John picks up on that story here. Seven trumpets have sounded. Loud voices[1] are heard from heaven (v. 15) announcing the full arrival of the kingdom of God:

> *Then the seventh angel blew his trumpet, and there were loud voices in heaven, saying, "The kingdom of the world has become the kingdom of our Lord and of his Christ, and he shall reign forever and ever."* (Rev. 11:15)

There is shouting in heaven because the Lord has answered the church's prayer, *"Your kingdom come, your will be done, on earth as it is in heaven"* (Matt. 6:10). The Kingdom of God has come to the earth. More accurately, we should say the Kingdom of God has come in its fullness. When we speak of God's kingdom coming, we are not suggesting that God does not already reign as king over the world. As we have seen, all things already sit under the feet of Jesus (Rev. 10:2).

Nor should we think that the coming of the Kingdom of God is a purely future event. Jesus opened his ministry with the promise that *"The time is fulfilled, and the kingdom of God is at hand; repent and believe the gospel"* (Mark 1:15). Instead, we recognize that we live in what theologians call the already-not-yet period. The Kingdom of God—the manifestation of his righteous rule over creation—has already come with the life, death, and resurrection of Jesus Christ. But we look forward to the time when no one opposes God's rule.[2] The seventh trumpet celebrates the arrival of the "not yet" of the kingdom.

Going back to the battle of Jericho where trumpets blasted, people shouted, and the city of Jericho fell, so also after John hears the trumpets and shouting, the city of the world falls:

> *We give thanks to you, Lord God Almighty,*
> *who is and who was,*
> *for you have taken your great power*
> *and begun to reign.*
> *The nations raged,*
> *but your wrath came,*
> *and the time for the dead to be judged,*
> *and for rewarding your servants, the prophets and saints,*
> *and those who fear your name,*
> *both small and great,*

and for destroying the destroyers of the earth.
(Rev. 11:17–18)

Notice two things. First, we know this speaks of the future because God's name changes. Three times previous to this text, the Lord is described as the one who is and who was and who is to come (Rev. 1:4, 8, 4:8). But now the Lord is defined as the one *"who is and who was"* but without reference to his coming. This omission suggests that the Lord has come as promised. And when he arrives, he brings his wrath with him:

The nations raged,
but your wrath came,
and the time for the dead to be judged,
and for rewarding your servants, the prophets and saints,
and those who fear your name,
both small and great,
and for destroying the destroyers of the earth.
(Rev. 11:18)

Let's not forget that all God's people will sing these words praising God for his wrath against all peoples, governments, and cultures that oppose the Lord and his Christ. This presents a difficulty that will only become increasingly so as we move forward toward descriptions of the coming judgment. Coming are images of people forced to drink the wine of God's anger and tormented for eternity (Rev. 14:10). John will see Jesus coming with a sword in his mouth—robes dripping with the blood of his enemies—ready to strike down those who refuse his rule (Rev. 19: 11–15). And, of course, there's the familiar and soul-chilling description of the lake of fire, a place of weeping and gnashing of teeth (Rev. 20: 14–15).

We are startled by these descriptions because they are so irregular. Since we're so accustomed to the mercy and patience of God, when his justice comes, it seems like an overreaction.[3] Think of the story of Uzzah from the Old Testament (2 Sam. 6:5–7). Uzzah and several men were transporting the ark of the covenant on a cart pulled by oxen. When an ox stumbled, the ark started to tip over, and Uzzah reached out to stabilize it. The Lord was angry with Uzzah. No one was allowed to look at the ark, let alone touch it.[4] The Lord killed Uzzah on the spot. And we respond, "Poor Uzzah!"

Or we can think of the sons of Aaron, Nadab, and Abihu (Lev. 10:1–2). They were priests in the Old Testament who tried to bring some innovation to the worship of God. We read they offered "unauthorized fire" (lit. strange fire) during a worship service. We don't know precisely what that means; perhaps they were creatively experimenting with the liturgy. But God responded swiftly and violently. Fire came down from the Lord and consumed the priests. We read that story and say, "That seems extreme!"

And if it's tempting to think this is an Old Testament phenomenon, remember Ananias and Sapphira of the New Testament (Acts 5:1–11). This married couple lied to the disciples, and they were killed by the Lord. They misrepresented the sale of a piece of property they sold. Because they didn't want to give a full portion to the church, they lied about its value to minimize their offering. Both were caught in their lies, and they fell dead in the disciples' presence. Our response? "That seems severe. Have we all not lied?"

We're astonished when we read of such events. But we must be clear that those rare events—Uzzah, Aarron's sons, and Ananias and Sapphira—do not portray emotional outbursts from a cranky God. Nor do they reveal to us a nasty and unpleasant side of the Lord. Instead, they depict rare intrusions of his holy justice. The Lord's ordinary course of treatment of humanity remains merciful, patient, and long-suffering. But that does not mean his present demeanor is owed to any, nor should it be presumed upon. But often, we do it anyway. Jesus' audience had the same problem. Once while speaking to the crowds, Jesus brought up a tragedy familiar to his audience. The incident involved a tower that fell and killed eighteen people. The people presumed that those eighteen men must have done something terrible to have that tower fall on them and kill them. But Jesus pulled the carpet out from beneath them when he asked:

> *Do you think that they were worse offenders than all the others who lived in Jerusalem? No, I tell you; but unless you repent, you will all likewise perish.* (Luke 13:4–5)

Jesus showed them that they were asking the wrong question. It's as if he said, "The question that plagues you shouldn't be, 'Why did that tower fall on those men?' But rather, you should ask, 'Why don't towers fall on every one of us every day?'" Therefore, we shouldn't be asking, why did God strike down poor Uzzah for touching the ark? But instead, why doesn't he strike down everyone who profanes the name of God? The answer points to his mercy, patience, and long-suffering which should lead us to repentance (Rom. 2:4).

R.C. Sproul taught thousands of seminary students over several decades and noted that countless students asked him why God doesn't save everyone. But only once did a student come to him and say, "There's something I just can't figure out. Why did God redeem me?"[5]

That question should fill us with astonished wonder! Instead of asking, "How can anyone worship God on that day of wrath?" On that day, our question will be, "Why was I shown such mercy? Why did the Lamb die for me? Who am I, a broken sinner, that I should be rewarded with an inheritance from God?" Those questions need not wait for the future. Instead, work them into your soul today.

Though it may sound unbiblical, I counsel you to rest in the wrath. I'll tell you why I say that. Each of us has been deeply wronged and sinned against in this world. Some of us have been hurt so profoundly that words cannot capture the emotional pain we feel. And as hard as we have tried, justice alludes us on this side of heaven. In those times, rest in the wrath of God. In verse 18, we see God addressing every wrong: *"The nations raged, but your wrath came."* At the end of the same verse, we're promised that he will *"[destroy] the destroyers of the earth."* The punishment will fit the crime. Every sin will be dealt with either on the cross or in God's anger.

Therefore, we neither seek revenge nor do we despair. Instead, we rest in the care of our Father, who will carry out his perfect justice, and we will praise him for it.

It isn't just the wrath of God that elicits praise in this passage but also the restoration that the return of Jesus will bring.

Praise for Restoration

Following the seventh trumpet, John saw the most sacred object in Israel:

> *Then God's temple in heaven was opened, and the ark of his covenant was seen within his temple. There were flashes of lightning, rumblings, peals of thunder, an earthquake, and heavy hail.* (Rev. 11:19)

Why does this vision end with John seeing the Ark of the Covenant? I believe the ark appears for two reasons. First, this series of seven trumpets ending with a city falling echoes the fall of the city of Jericho. And just like in Jericho, where the ark of the covenant followed the blowing of the seven trumpets, the ark also makes its appearance here.

The second reason goes back to the ritual on the first day of the Year of Jubilee. Remember, when the High Priest emerged from the temple, trumpets blasted, he announced freedom had come, debts were canceled, and the land was given rest. And for all the good news, there remained a problem: behind the back of the priest, obscured by heavy curtains and darkness, sat the Ark of the Covenant. The Ark represented the intimate presence of our God and it had to be separated from the people because of their sin.

When Jesus Christ died on the cross, however, the curtain in the temple tore from top to bottom (Mark 15:38). This ripping symbolized that the way into the glorious presence of God was now open.

When the faithful High Priest emerges from the temple of heaven, the seventh trumpet will sound, he will proclaim freedom, and the land will be renewed. All vestiges of remaining sin within us will be fully and finally removed. And it won't be a gold-covered wooden box on poles that will fill our hearts with the greatest joys. Instead, we'll see the one who is the sum total of all bliss, love, mercy, and kindness. We will see our Savior! And he will say, "Enter into the joy of your master," for the unending Jubilee has begun.

Study Questions

1. Do you see yourself as having become accustomed to the mercy and patience of God? How does your heart respond to the glimpses of his wrath and judgment in Scripture?
2. Consider your posture towards the Lord's just wrath. Do you find yourself wondering what those poor people did? Or why would the Lord do such a thing? Or are you astonished that he hasn't done it to you? If our hearts find themselves in the former two, how might we realign them to better consider the mercy, patience, and wrath of the Lord?
3. The wrath of God allows us to never need to seek revenge and keeps us from despair. Take some time to journal your thoughts, praise, and repentance in light of God's wrath.
4. How does this promised restoration of God dwelling with his people, as seen by the image of the Ark of the Covenant, change how we live today? What thoughts, feelings, and excitement stirs in you when you read of the torn curtain and the beginning of the unending jubilee?

---

1. In contrast to the silence that accompanied the opening of the seventh seal.
2. For an excellent contemporary treatment of the Kingdom of God, see Thomas R. Schreiner, *New Testament Theology: Magnifying God in Christ* (Grand Rapids, MI: Baker Academic, 2008).

3. I am indebted to the late Dr. Sproul for several of the insights of this paragraph, which are detailed in R.C. Sproul, *The Holiness of God* (Carol Stream, IL: Tyndale House, 1985 repr. 1998). See especially pp. 97–130.
4. For an examination of the problems surrounding the Uzzah incident, see R.C. Sproul, *The Holiness of God*, 102–108.
5. R.C. Sproul, *The Holiness of God*, 124.

PART 4

THE WOMAN, DRAGON, AND TWO BEASTS 12:1–15:4

21

SILENT NIGHT, FRIGHTFUL SIGHT
REVELATION 12

When I was in high school, my brother had a terrible car accident. We found out about it by a phone call from the hospital. They told us that he'd struck a deer, an ambulance arrived, and he'd been delivered—alive—to the local hospital. That's all we knew: terrible accident, driver alive.

Not knowing what to expect, we made our way to the hospital. I still remember walking into his room and nearly losing my breath at what I saw. My brother had a black eye, a tube down his throat, and several up his nose. Small spots of dried blood speckled his face and arms. And his whole torso was bandage-wrapped. At that moment, I knew one thing for sure: my brother was dying. Looking at him brought a sudden wave of sadness, pity, and hopelessness.

Thankfully, not long after we'd arrived, so did the attending physician. After checking my brother's chart and the various machines attached to him, the doctor said, "He's going to be just fine." He explained that my brother looked banged up, but there was nothing to worry about. He was treated for a minor sternum fracture and discharged a few days later.

In the thirty years since that terrible day, hospitals now better prepare visitors before seeing the patient. Had that accident occurred today, a staff member would first greet us and tell us what we should expect before entering the room. "He has tubes in his nose. His midsection is wrapped. He's got a black eye. But he's going to be fine. It looks far worse than it is."

And what a difference that would have made. Not only would we be prepared for what we'd see, but we'd also not lose hope. Despite what our untrained eyes might lead us to conclude, we'd reassure ourselves and trust the doctors and nurses that my brother would be fine.

This chapter and those that follow function much like a staff member who comes to us saying, "This is what you should expect. In this world, you'll have trouble. If you follow Jesus, you'll be hated, and a terrifying, malicious entity seeking your eternal destruction pursues you. But take heart! Jesus has overcome the world. Jesus has conquered the enemy. And if you abide in him, you will be more than conquerors through him."

An incomplete picture of my brother's situation led me to a hopeless conclusion about his future. Likewise, trying to follow Jesus with untrained eyes might lead us to the same desperate assumptions. However, the vision before us pulls back the veil to give us the truth, which enables us to take heart and press on, especially when things look bad. We can do so because, in Jesus, we have a powerful King, Priest, and Prophet.

Powerful King

Chapter 12 begins the fourth of seven portraits John paints of the time between the ascension and return of Jesus Christ. The first portrait painted Jesus as the one who walks among the lampstands of the churches (Chps. 1–3). The second portrait ushered us into the throne room of God, where the ascended Jesus opened the scroll with seven seals, the last ending with judgment (Chps. 4–7). Portrait three, the Seven Trumpets of Warning, also finished with the final trumpet ushering in the final judgment.

The picture before us now gives us another angle of the same time period (Chps. 12–14). This section begins with Christmas morning, and like the seals and the trumpets, the fourth portrait will conclude with the final judgment (Rev. 14:14–20). But before we reencounter the judgment scene, we first go back to the first Christmas morning when a mighty King arrived:

> *And a great sign appeared in heaven: a woman clothed with the sun, with the moon under her feet, and on her head a crown of twelve stars. She was pregnant and was crying out in birth pains and the agony of giving birth.* (Rev. 12:1–2)

Three main characters play out a symbolic drama portraying the nature of the time between the ascension and return of Christ. We first meet a pregnant woman clothed with the sun, standing on the moon, and wearing a crown of twelve stars. While some, particularly Roman Catholic theologians, place Mary, the mother of Jesus, here, I don't think this best fits the details.

We'll see later that a dragon chases this woman into the wilderness, and she gives birth to many more children. While Mary did have other children after Jesus (Matt. 12:46; 13:55; Mark 6:3), being chased through the wilderness by a dragon doesn't fit what we know of Mary's later life.

Instead, examining the details shows us we're looking at a symbolic picture of the Old Testament people of God. The sun, which clothes her, the moon under her feet, and the crown of twelve stars take us back to Joseph's dream in the book of Genesis (Gen. 37:9–11). In that dream, he saw the Sun, which represented his father, Jacob. And the moon represented his mother, Rachel. The eleven stars, each picturing his brothers, all bowed down to him. Here, John uses a familiar description of not one individual but the entire Old Testament community of faith.[1]

Additionally, the Bible often poetically describes Israel as a pregnant woman who would give birth to the One who would conquer evil (Isa. 26:17–27:1; 51:2–11; 66:7–10). But it didn't come easy for her; a treacherous beast had opposed her from the beginning:

And another sign appeared in heaven: behold, a great red dragon, with seven heads and ten horns, and on his heads seven diadems. His tail swept down a third of the stars of heaven and cast them to the earth. And the dragon stood before the woman who was about to give birth, so that when she bore her child he might devour it. (Rev. 12:3–4)

Later in this chapter, John tells us the dragon goes by the familiar name of Satan, or the devil (Rev. 12:9). John saw Satan portrayed with seven heads and ten horns, and on his heads, seven diadems. Seven and ten represent numbers of completion or fullness. Horns in the Bible represent strength. The seven heads with ten horns point to the totality of Satan's power to deceive and destroy.[2] The seven crowns atop his heads "represent the devil's false claims of sovereign, universal authority, which is in opposition to the true 'King of kings and Lord of lords.'"[3] John refers to the dragon as both the devil and Satan. He also describes him as *"that ancient serpent... the deceiver of the whole world,"* which connects to the story of the Garden of Eden.

There, through deceit and trickery, Satan brought pain and misery into the world. And there Satan was promised that the Lord would send one who would crush the head of the serpent (Gen. 3:15). Since that time, Satan has tried to thwart the plan of God. Through Pharaoh, Satan tried to kill all the male infants of the Jews while in Egypt. God spared Moses. Later, through Saul, Satan tried to kill King David, from whom the Messiah would come. God spared David. When Israel was in exile, Satan tried to kill the Jews through an evil man named Haman. But through Queen Esther, God spared his people.

What are we to make of the statement that the dragon's tail swept down a third of the stars of heaven to the earth (Rev. 12:4)? This verse has given rise to speculation about a pre-creation war in heaven in which a third of the angels joined forces with the Devil. But a closer examination shows this is an allusion to a verse in the book of Daniel, describing a terrible King who would arise and persecute the people of God. This king would throw stars *"down to the ground and trample on them"* (Dan. 8:10).

That terrible prediction came true when the Greek general Antiochus Epiphanes entered Jerusalem and slaughtered thousands of Jews, trampling them to the ground.[4] Satan has a long history of trying every means possible to keep the promise of his demise, made in the Garden, from coming true. And God has been just as committed to ensuring his plan to exalt his Son and redeem his people would occur.

Now John brings us to Christmas morning and shows us what no Christmas cards ever capture. Here we find no shepherds, sheep, baby lambs, or cattle lowing around a baby in a manger.[5] Instead, John's silent night included a frightful sight: a baby-eating dragon who desperately tried to end God's plan to exalt his Son and redeem his people:

> *And the dragon stood before the woman who was about to give birth, so that when she bore her child he might devour it. She gave birth to a male child, one who is to rule all the nations with a rod of iron, but her child was caught up to God and to his throne, and the woman fled into the wilderness, where she has a place prepared by God, in which she is to be nourished for 1,260 days.* (Rev. 12:4–6)

The child born to the woman is, of course, Jesus Christ.[6] Satan tried to destroy him. First, he tried to kill him through Herod, who slaughtered all the male children in the region like Pharaoh before him (Matt. 2:16). God spared his Son. Later, Satan tried to destroy him through temptation in the wilderness (Matt. 4:1–11). If Satan could get the Son of God to sin, he'd be disqualified as the redeemer. God spared his Son. Finally, Satan entered Judas (Luke 22:3; John 13:2), who betrayed Jesus, handing him over to be crucified. But this time, God did not spare his Son. On the cross, the dragon consumed the child. But he swallowed poison. You know how the story goes. Satan's victory was short-lived.

With remarkable brevity, John collapses everything from Christmas morning to the ascension of Jesus in one sentence, followed by events recorded in the book of Acts:

> *She gave birth to a male child, one who is to rule all the nations with a rod of iron, but her child was caught up to God and to his throne, and the woman fled into the wilderness, where she has a place prepared by God, in which she is to be nourished for 1,260 days.* (Rev. 12:5–6)

In a moment, we'll return to examine the woman's flight into the desert, but for now, let's remember that we know what happened when Jesus ascended to God and his throne. John saw Jesus take a scroll from his Father, representing the plan of salvation and judgment, and begin to rule over all nations, peoples, kings, beasts, dragons, traffic lights, tumors, weddings, and funerals. All authority in heaven and on earth belongs to Jesus (Matt. 28:18).

Reflect on the difference this truth makes in your life—knowing that an all-powerful King who loves you, right now reigns over life's macro and micro details. It changes our perspective.

Consider these words once penned by Fredrick Langbridge: Two men look out through the same bars: One sees the mud, and one the stars.[7] What a difference hope makes!

It contrasts a worldview that says we live, and we die, then we're stuffed in a coffin only to return to the dirt versus the worldview that knows all things are overseen by One who loves me. And he calls me friend, his bride, his beloved. That One has promised to astound us when we see him face to face. Then we'll know in full that he truly worked all things together for our good. With this in our possession, we steward it now and pass it along to a hopeless generation.

John sees another reason for our hope. Jesus ascended not only as a powerful King but also as a pardoning Priest.

Pardoning Priest

> Now war arose in heaven, Michael and his angels fighting against the dragon. And the dragon and his angels fought back, but he was defeated, and there was no longer any place for them in heaven. And the great dragon was thrown down, that ancient serpent, who is called the devil and Satan, the deceiver of the whole world—he was thrown down to the earth, and his angels were thrown down with him. And I heard a loud voice in heaven, saying, "Now the salvation and the power and the kingdom of our God and the authority of his Christ have come, for the accuser of our brothers has been thrown down, who accuses them day and night before our God. And they have conquered him by the blood of the Lamb and by the word of their testimony, for they loved not their lives even unto death. Therefore, rejoice, O heavens and you who dwell in them! But woe to you, O earth and sea, for the devil has come down to you in great wrath, because he knows that his time is short!" (Rev. 12:7–12)

To appreciate what John sees here, we need to remember that before the ascension of Jesus, Satan had access to the throne room of God, where he would accuse both God and man of inconsistencies. For example, the book of Job presents Satan before God's throne charging Job with a shallow faith and, by implication, that God is not worthy of man's trust in suffering (Job 1:6–12). In the book of Zechariah, the prophet sees Satan standing next to Joshua the priest, accusing him of sin (Zech. 3:1). And, until Christ ascended to the Father, it may have appeared that Satan had a good case. After all, the book of Hebrews tells us that the blood of bulls and goats cannot take away sin (Heb. 10:4). So how could the Lord let Moses, David, Isaiah, and Jeremiah into his presence? He might say to God, "I thought you were holy and could not abide with sin?"

But when Jesus ascended to his Father's right hand, Satan was expelled from the courtroom above. So looking back at this war in heaven, we shouldn't confuse this with some pre-creation conflict between God and Satan or between good angels and bad. Instead, this war and the consequent casting down of Satan is one more picture of the neutering of Satan's accusatory privileges. Jesus spoke of this event once when his disciples returned from preaching the Gospel and casting out demons, saying, *"I saw Satan fall like lightning from heaven"* (Luke 10:18). In anticipation of his death, resurrection, and ascension to God, John records Jesus saying, *"Now the ruler of this world will be cast out"* (John 12:31).[8] We look forward to the day when Satan will forever be cast out of creation and into the presence of God's wrath (Rev. 20:10). Until then, Jesus assures us that the accuser of the brethren has been forever removed from heaven's courtroom.

Two immediate consequences of Satan's expulsion from heaven shape our understanding. First, we are assured that those who belong to Jesus have nothing to fear about the coming judgment day. No charge made against you will carry any weight. As Paul writes:

> *Who shall bring any charge against God's elect? It is God who justifies. Who is to condemn? Christ Jesus is the one who died—more than that, who was raised—who is at the right hand of God, who indeed is interceding for us.* (Rom. 8:33–34)

Satan, who could accurately charge you with inconsistencies and rebellion, will have no audience with the Lord on that day. But the one who died for your inconsistencies and rebellion, and always has the ear of his Father, will perhaps show us his hands, feet, and side, all bearing the marks of his love for us.

And second, we must take this vision's warning seriously. Satan has been cast down from heaven and pursues the church. After the ascension of Jesus, a chase through the wilderness begins:

> *...and the woman fled into the wilderness, where she has a place prepared by God, in which she is to be nourished for 1,260 days... And when the dragon saw that he had been thrown down to the earth, he pursued the woman who had given birth to the male child. But the woman was given the two wings of the great eagle so that she might fly from the serpent into the wilderness, to the place where she is to be nourished for a time, and times, and half a time. The serpent poured water like a river out of his mouth after the woman, to sweep her away with a flood. But the earth came to the help of the woman, and the earth opened its mouth and swallowed the river that the dragon had poured from his mouth.* (Rev. 12:6, 13–16)

We've already looked at the number 1,260 days when we studied the two witnesses commissioned to preach the gospel for the same amount of time.[9] There we saw that 1,260 days, the same as 42 months, and three and a half years, is a symbolic number representing a period of testing and trial.[10]

The whole time between the ascension and return of Christ will be a wilderness-like trek through this world until we reach the Promised Land. And until the Church arrives, a dragon known for accusation will pursue her. We've already noted that when the Book of Revelation puts items in someone's mouth, it does so to symbolize speech.[11]

Here, the dragon opens his mouth and unleashes a river designed to drown the woman. What is this water? How does Satan try to tear down the church? Through false teachers, persecution, dead orthodoxy, and the temptation to compromise—all the issues that the seven churches faced which we studied earlier.

But sometimes, he comes after us in our hearts, living up to his name—the accuser. Even though Satan can no longer accuse us before God, he still wields this weapon to keep us in shame, guilt, and lies. After all, Peter warns us to remain sober and watchful because our *"adversary the devil prowls around like a roaring lion, seeking someone to devour"* (1 Pet. 5:8).

It's important to know that Satan will try to devour you through accusation. But it's equally essential to be equipped to tell the difference between Satan's accusations and the work of the Holy Spirit.

Let me explain with a story. In seminary, one of the classes taught future pastors how to prepare and preach a sermon. Each student preached before peers, and a professor gave valuable feedback. My professor would follow every sermon with two questions for the entire class: "What went well? And what could have gone better?" I took numerous preaching courses, and those two questions were always what followed each sermon—all except one. One student stood in the pulpit and for thirty minutes told us how sinful we were. He charged the class with prayerlessness. He accused us of a lack of boldness in evangelism. We didn't prioritize family worship in our homes.

He explained that we didn't treasure Christ above all things. He continued until he finally closed, offered a short prayer, and sat down. Relieved it was all over, the class expected to hear the usual: "What went well? What could have gone better?"

But the professor didn't offer the usual response. Instead, he walked over to the student and gently said to him, "Brother, Satan is the accuser of the brethren. Not you." And with that, he dismissed the class.

That seminary student didn't utter a false word. We didn't pray, evangelize, or love Christ as we ought. True, and terribly so.

But his message remained incomplete. The preacher extended no hope to the broken and weary among us. No promise of God's help was assured. No reassurance that Christ saw us through anything but our failures.

That's the way Satan operates. He offers no hope, promise of God's help, or Christ's love. And we must recognize the difference between the accusations of Satan and the conviction of sin the Spirit elicits. Both Satan and the Spirit will point their fingers at sin. Satan will remind you of gossip, as will the Spirit. Satan will highlight your neglect of the needy, just like the Spirit does. Satan will tell you that you should live a holy life, and so will the Spirit.

But here is the difference: having exposed sin, Satan will either convince you there's no hope for you or that you must try harder to please God. However, the Spirit will also point to your sin, but then he will take you to the Savior, whoever lives above, to intercede for you. Satan wants to leave you in despair; the Spirit wants to drive you into the arms of the heavenly Priest who desires to shower you with his grace.

Prophetic Presence

This is how God nourishes his Church in her calling to run ahead of a water-vomiting dragon who tries to drown her assurance, joy, and witness to Christ. But John saw the Lord nourish and sustain the woman dwelling in the wilderness:

> *But the woman was given the two wings of the great eagle so that she might fly from the serpent into the wilderness, to the place where she is to be nourished for a time, and times, and half a time.* (Rev. 12:14)

The flight through the wilderness on eagles' wings recalls the very language the Lord used to portray Israel's deliverance from Egypt: *"You yourselves have seen what I did to the Egyptians, and how I bore you on eagles' wings and brought you to myself"* (Ex. 19:4). In the same way, the Christian can say, "I've been freed from slavery! And I am confident that what God has begun in me, he will bring to completion on the day of Jesus Christ" (Phil. 1:6).

This wilderness sustenance again recalls the Exodus generation that the Lord fed through the sending of manna, that bread-like substance that came down from heaven (Ex. 16). What manna has he given the church? He's given us the One that the manna pointed toward. He gives us Jesus, who said, *"I am the bread that came down from heaven"* (John 6:41). He nourishes us through the One who promised never to leave or forsake his church. Christ stands among the lampstands today. He sings with us. He eats with us, and he speaks to us when the Gospel is proclaimed. And if we listen and cling to Jesus, the watery flood of Satan's lies will not consume us: *"But the earth came to the help of the woman, and the earth opened its mouth and swallowed the river that the dragon had poured from his mouth"* (Rev. 12:16).

Several years ago, a group of Bible translators with a Christian organization were attacked in the Middle East.[12] One day as the translators went about translating the Bible in the local language, several men, presumably Al Qaeda, stormed the office and emptied their machine guns into the bodies of the translators and their computer equipment. When the terrorists ran out of bullets, they used the butt of their guns to bludgeon several people. The lead translator survived.

In the aftermath, he sent out an email to his supporters back home. What do you think he wrote? Perhaps he decided that God had closed a door in the Middle East so he was coming back home? That would be reasonable.

Remarkably, that's not what he wrote. Instead, he asked the people back home to pray for the families of those murdered and the murderers themselves. He then gave notice that the terrorists missed one computer, and that hard drive still contained all the work the translators had done. They were already at work assembling a new team.

How do you explain that? In the words of Martin Luther: "The prince of darkness grim, we tremble not for him; his rage we can endure, for lo! his doom is sure; one little word shall fell him."[13] What is that little word? That word is Jesus Christ, the Prophet, Priest, and King of the church, and he must win the battle.

Study Questions

1. Can you identify two immediate consequences of Satan's expulsion from heaven? And how do these consequences impact your life today?
2. It can be difficult to tell whether sin is being pointed out by Satan or the Spirit. Why is it crucial to differentiate between the two?
3. In Martin Luther's commentary on Galatians, he imagines a dialogue with Satan as he charges a Christian with sin. Reflect on how Luther suggests we respond to Satan's attack: "As often as you object that I am a sinner, so often you remind me of the benefit of Christ my Redeemer, on whose shoulders, and not on

mine, lie all my sins. So when you say I am a sinner, you do not terrify me but comfort me immeasurably."

---

1. Perhaps viewing the woman as a symbol of the faithful community, existing both before and after the coming of Christ, is more precise. While she is described with Old Testament symbols, after the birth of Christ, "the rest of her offspring" (v. 17), also pursued by the dragon, points to those who've placed their trust in Jesus.
2. G.K. Beale, *The Book of Revelation: A Shorter Commentary* (Eerdmans, 2015), 246.
3. Ibid., 246.
4. Daniel 12:3 likens the wise to the stars which shine bright in the skies. The Daniel allusion, along with the twelve stars of the woman's crown representing the covenant people of God, favor seeing the stars cast down by the serpent's tail as the persecuted people of God.
5. Some scholars suggest that John is tapping into a local myth that told the story of Apollo's birth. The legend tells of Zeus, Apollo's father, who impregnates Leto. Python, a great dragon, threatens to kill the child at birth, causing Leto to flee to a hiding place provided by the sea god Poseidon. Apollo, Leto's son, is safely born and later pursues the dragon and slays him. To examine one scholar's suggestion that John is deliberately echoing this myth, see Jerram Barrs, *Echoes of Eden: Reflections on Christianity, Literature, and the Arts* (Wheaton, IL: Crossway, 2013), 79–84. For a rejection of this thesis, see Leon Morris, *Revelation* (Grand Rapids, MI: Eerdmans, 1984), 155–156 and Simon Kistemaker, *Revelation*, New Testament Commentary (Grand Rapids, MI: 2001), 353–354.
6. The description of Jesus as the one who was to rule all the nations with a rod of iron alludes to the prophetic words of Psalm 2, which speak of the Messiah. See also Rev. 2:27.
7. Quoted in Alister McGrath, *"I Believe": Exploring the Apostles' Creed* (Downers Grove, IL: IVP Books, 1998), 81–82.
8. John 12:31. D. A. Carson writes, "When Jesus was glorified, 'lifted up' to heaven by means of the cross, enthroned, then too was Satan dethroned." D. A. Carson, *The Gospel According to John* (Grand Rapids, MI: Eerdmans, 1991), 443.
9. See my chapter on Revelation 11:1–14.
10. Additionally, the *"time, and times, and half a time"* of verse 14 should be regarded as another way of measuring 1,260 days, forty-two months, and three and a half years. "Time" would equal one year; "times" would be two years, and "half a time" six months. For more on this, see G.K. Beale, *The Book of Revelation: A Shorter Commentary*, 218, and Leon Morris, *Revelation*, 147.
11. See my chapter on Revelation 8:13–9:21.
12. https://www.christianpost.com/news/4-wycliffe-bible-translators-brutally-murdered-by-radicals-sacrificed-bodies-to-save-lead-translator.html
13. Martin Luther, "A Mighty Fortress is Our God" (1529).

22

THE BEAST FROM THE SEA

REVELATION 13:1-10

A moving story from World War II comes from the Battle of Wake Island, one of the most isolated places in the entire world. Since it's in the middle of the Pacific Ocean, Japan and the United States coveted this tiny island because it had an airstrip for planes to land and refuel.

Hours after the attack on Pearl Harbor, Japanese troops invaded Wake Island and began a two-week assault on the United States Marines stationed there. Eventually, the Marines surrendered and were immediately punished. The Japanese soldiers doled out daily beatings, round-the-clock interrogations, random executions, and meager food rations to the captive Americans.

But then, one day, and without any warning, there was a dramatic change in the treatment of the prisoners. The daily beatings stopped, food rations increased, and the Japanese soldiers greeted prisoners with a smile. And even more strange, the Japanese invited several Americans to a banquet that included the finest food, music, and champagne. Once the Americans were seated at the table, each Japanese soldier stood from their chair, glass in hand, and offered a toast to the "everlasting friendship between America and Japan." After the last toast, the Japanese smiled and awaited the American response.

What explained the sudden change from cruelty to kindness, from famine conditions to a feast? The Marines knew something had happened. And what they suspected turned out to be true. The war had changed. Japan could no longer win the war or hold the island, and the captors knew it. Realizing the change in circumstances, the American response to the lavish meal came from a haggard, skeletal-looking Marine named Major Luther Brown. Standing up from his chair, he promised his captors, "If you behave yourselves, you'll get fair treatment."[1]

What a moment that must have been! An unshaven, unkempt, emaciated prisoner stood before a well-fed, well-dressed, and well-armed Japanese army, promising mercy to the obedient. He could do that confidently because he knew he stood on the winning side.

To everyone at that banquet, it must have appeared that the Americans would lose. But looks were deceiving. An American flag flies over Wake Island today and has done so since 1945.

Jesus promised the Church victory and we are conquerors, whether we feel like it or not. When Major Luther Brown realized the war had turned, it shaped how he lived in the present. Though tattered clothes hung off his skeletal frame, bravery and assurance flowed from his heart. Chapter 13 should fill the Church with the courage to press on. Again, Christ and his Church will win the battle. And that truth must shape how we live until we see our Savior face to face.

What John sees here should shore up our courage and shape our behavior. For he sees a defeated beast coming after the church, and he hears the Lord's desire for how we are to respond.

The Defeat of the Beast

In the last chapter, we met a dragon, a pregnant woman, and a child caught up to heaven. The dragon represents Satan. The pregnant woman pictures the Old and New Testament community of faith, which gave birth to a child: Jesus Christ. After trying and failing to destroy the child, the dragon pursued the woman through the wilderness, where the Lord nourished her. At the end of Chapter 12, the dragon stood by the seaside. And now John sees why. From the sea, a frequent image of chaos and surging evil in Judaism,[2] the dragon calls forth a helper:

> And I saw a beast rising out of the sea, with ten horns and seven heads, with ten diadems on its horns and blasphemous names on its heads. And the beast that I saw was like a leopard; its feet were like a bear's, and its mouth was

like a lion's mouth. And to it the dragon gave his power and his throne and great authority. (Rev. 13:1–2)

There are two things the original audience of this text would have picked up on. First, the beast, in many ways, mirrors the dragon. And second, a beast coming out of the sea sounds like something from the book of Daniel.

Let's first consider how the beast's description echoes the description of the dragon. Both the dragon and the beast have seven heads. Both have ten horns. The dragon has crowns on his heads; the beast has crowns on his horns. These similarities aren't just interesting; they point to something more sinister.

This vision introduces a parody or counterfeit of the Trinity.[3] John will eventually see three entities: a dragon, a beast from the sea, and a beast from the land. The beast from the sea appears remarkably similar to the dragon. This mimics what we know of the Father and the Son. Writing of Jesus, Paul says, *"He is the image of the invisible God, the firstborn over all creation"* (Col. 1:15).

We note, too, that while the dragon has crowns on his head, the beast wears crowns on his horns. This suggests the dragon has all authority and mandates his will through the beast,[4] much in the same way that the Father initiates the plan of redemption and carries it out through his Son (Isa. 52:13–53:12). Likewise, a counterfeit of the Holy Spirit appears on the scene. After John sees a beast coming out of the sea, another beast will come up from the earth. Like the Holy Spirit in the book of Acts, this second beast works miraculous signs (Rev. 13:13). The second beast promotes the worship of the first beast (Rev. 13:12), just as the Holy Spirit promotes the worship of the Son (John 16:14). The second beast comes to deceive people —a mockery of the Holy Spirit who comes to guide us in all truth.

The dragon and the two beasts form a counterfeit trinity that labor to destroy those who follow the true and living God, the blessed Three in One.

In addition to looking like the dragon, the beast coming out of the sea would have reminded John's audience of the four beasts that Daniel saw, which also came out of the sea (Dan. 7:1–8, 17–27). While living in exile, like the rest of the Jews, Daniel wondered how and when God would keep his promise to bring the Messiah who would rule over all the nations.

The answer came to Daniel as a vision: four beasts rising out of the sea. A lion manifested as the first beast, followed by a bear. After the bear, came a leopard, on whose tail an exceedingly strong beast with iron teeth followed. As Daniel considered these four beasts, another scene unfolded before him. He saw God Almighty, seated upon his throne, and approached by a cryptic figure described as *"one like a son of man"* (Dan. 7:13), to whom the Lord gave an everlasting kingdom.

Overwhelmed by the vision, Daniel asked about its meaning. He learned that each beast represented a kingdom or an empire. Each would overthrow the other until "one like a son of man" would be presented before the Lord and given all dominion.

Generally, commentators[5] suggest that the four beasts represent Babylon, Persia, Greece, and Rome. Babylon fell to the Persians, who later lost to the Greeks, who would succumb to the fourth beast: Rome. Each of Daniel's four beasts represented a man-centered kingdom, which also caused great suffering to fall upon God's people. And just as Daniel's dream revealed, during the time of the fourth beast one, like a Son of Man, Jesus' favorite title of self-identification, received an everlasting kingdom.[6]

With Daniel's four-beast background in mind, we identify John's beast from the sea as a man-centered kingdom that resists the reign of God and persecutes his people. For John and his audience, the beast from the sea represented Rome. The beast's ten horns and seven heads aptly symbolized Rome's oppressive power and widespread influence. The blasphemous names on the beast's heads undoubtedly allude to the emperors of Rome who asserted divine status.

The first century witnessed a time of great military and economic prosperity for Rome. And so, the assertion of the emperor's divine status seemed reasonable:

> *And they worshiped the dragon, for he had given his authority to the beast, and they worshiped the beast, saying, "Who is like the beast, and who can fight against it?"* (Rev. 13:4)

Once again, we find a caricature in these wonder-filled words of admiration for the state. The praise offered to the government eerily echoes words used in the Scriptures for the Lord:

> *Who is like you, O LORD, among the gods? Who is like you, majestic in holiness, awesome in glorious deeds, doing wonders?* (Ex. 15:11).

While, on the one hand, this beast from the sea would have been associated with Rome in the first century, further descriptions of the beast suggest the beast represents more than one empire. Remember, Daniel saw a lion, a bear, a leopard, and a beast of incomparable ferocity. Each represented a kingdom. When John describes the beast he saw, he does so by combining all of those images into one:

> ...*the beast that I saw was like a leopard; its feet were like a bear's, and its mouth was like a lion's mouth. And to it the dragon gave his power and his throne and great authority.* (Rev. 13:2)

This composite picture, with the piling of various animal descriptions into one beast, suggests that more than one empire is in mind here.[7] After all, the Roman Empire fell in the fifth century. This beast, on the other hand, will live much longer:

> *And the beast was given a mouth uttering haughty and blasphemous words, and it was allowed to exercise authority for forty-two months.* (Rev. 13:5)

We've already observed that this period of forty-two months symbolizes the entire period between the ascension and return of Jesus. In other words, while the Church awaits its Savior's return, the threat or practice of persecution from the state will remain. For John, threats and harm came from the Romans. For Christians, like those who died in the Armenian genocide, terror came from the Ottoman Empire. For our brethren in North Korea, the Kim family are beasts. For Christians in China, the Communist government wars against them. The beast represents any and every empire that exalts itself, tramples on the law of God, and persecutes his people. Every nation, including where you live, can turn beastly toward the Church at any time.

But we should notice something of tremendous encouragement. The beast cannot win. In a real sense, it has already lost. Look at his head:

> *One of its heads seemed to have a mortal wound, but its mortal wound was healed, and the whole earth marveled as they followed the beast.* (Rev. 13:3)

How should we understand the wound on the head of the beast that appears lethal but doesn't end its life?[8] If we remember that the beast mirrors the image of the dragon, we know what the wound points to. Recall the first Gospel announcement made back in the book of Genesis. There, the Lord promised that a redeemer would come who would crush the head of the serpent (Gen. 3:15). With the death and resurrection of Jesus Christ, he crushed Satan's head.

The hill upon which Jesus was crucified was called Golgotha, an Aramaic word for "skull."[9] The name of the hill represents more than an interesting topographic detail. Instead, as we consider the Lord crushed upon a skull hill, another crushing occurred. When the cross fell into place atop skull-hill, a dagger plunged deep into the serpent's head.

Satan has been neutered of his power. The coming of Christ into this world to live, die, and be raised to his Father's right hand inaugurated a kingdom that cannot fail. Christ has been given all authority over heaven and earth, which means every earthly kingdom that rejects the rule of God and tramples on his people will not survive the judgment (Ps. 2:10–12). Only one kingdom will rule in the new heavens and earth, the Kingdom of our Lord and of his Christ (Rev. 11:15).

Satan has received a death blow, but he lingers on for a time. And the beast, made in his image, likewise lingers on for a time. But its days are numbered. The well-used illustration of the defeat of Satan likens his loss to D-Day in World War II. When the Allied troops crossed the beaches of Normandy, they broke the back of Nazi oppression. D-Day commenced the beginning of the end of Hitler's dreams. And yet, there remained pockets of German resistance for another eleven months, until finally, VE-Day came, when the last of the German forces surrendered.

As Christians, we live after the heavenly D-Day, which broke the back of Satan's plans. And as we press toward the great VE-Day to come, we will encounter pockets of resistance from the unholy trinity.

The mortal wound on the head of the beast would have filled our first-century brothers and sisters with a defiant assurance that Rome could not win. Even if Rome pressured them, mocked them, and trampled their bodies into the dirt, they knew that "the body they may kill: God's truth abideth still. His Kingdom is forever."[10]

The Desire of the Lord

How would the Lord have us live in light of what he shows us here? Remember, the book of Revelation trains our eyes to see the world as it truly is. This vision reveals the one who governs governors. Even when beasts arise against his people, the Lord reigns. Notice that everything the dragon and the beast do, they do under the permission of the Lord.

Verse 5 tells us that the Lord permits the beast to exercise authority only for a set period: "Only God, not the devil, sets times and seasons. The devil would never limit his work against God's Kingdom."[11] Verse 7 tells us the Lord allows the beast to war against the saints. Verse 8 tells us that the

Lord has sovereignty over those who will worship the beast and those who will not. Even before the world's creation, God set his affection on his people, writing their names in the Book of Life (Eph. 1:3–6; 2 Thess. 2:13; 1 Pet. 1:1).

Returning to Chapter 6 of Revelation, we recall Christ breaking the seals and releasing the four horses that trample on his people. The opening page of John's Revelation reveals that Jesus Christ is the *"ruler of kings on earth"* (Rev. 1:5). Indeed, this would have greatly motivated the early church. Beyond the beast, they would have set their hearts upon the one who has the beast on a leash. It doesn't mean they would have liked what they endured for the name of Christ or even understood it. But they knew he loved them. And they knew that his plan was going forward for them without a hitch.

So we too must look past the one sitting in the Oval Office. Whether you like the individual there or not, they are there under the placement of God. At the end of the day, we are not governed by the results of the voting booth. Christ rules over all kings. Therefore, we should challenge ourselves, "How would the Lord have me live before a watching world? When I serve a person I disagree with, do I honor him or her as Scripture instructs me to do? (Rom. 13:7) Do I pray for that person? (1 Tim. 2:2) When I speak about those in authority, do I sound like the non-Christians in my political party? Or do they see the Spirit's work within me?"

Every Christian I know has prayed a prayer asking the Lord to use them for his glory. The Lord may seek to answer that prayer in your life and mine as we embody the ethics of a kingdom not of this world.

We also want to avoid the conclusion that all governmental bodies are evil and consistently beastly. Paul tells us that the Lord created the institution of human government: *"There is no authority except from God, and those that exist have been instituted by God"* (Rom. 13:1). God instituted human government for the establishment and maintenance of law and order. Satan did not create government; he often perverts it from its divine purpose. With that in mind, Christians should not refrain from engaging in politics or pursuing careers in government. Here we might recall the Lord's words to his people living in Babylon:

> *Build houses and live in them; plant gardens and eat their produce. Take wives and have sons and daughters; take wives for your sons, and give your daughters in marriage, that they may bear sons and daughters; multiply there, and do not decrease. But seek the welfare of the city where I have sent*

you into exile, and pray to the LORD on its behalf, for in its welfare you will find your welfare. (Jer. 29:5–7)

Like Jeremiah's audience, we also live in exile (1 Pet. 1:1) and should strive for the betterment of our homeland. We can't do this if we raise our kids believing that only preachers and missionaries truly serve the Lord.

Instead, we want to raise an army of Christians who penetrate the public square. We want to raise judges and lawyers whose concepts of justice, the protection of the weak, mercy toward the foreigner, and impartiality mirror God's laws. We can raise children who enter public schools to teach. We can raise politicians known not for soundbites or toeing the party line, but for integrity, honor, character, doing justice, loving kindness, and walking humbly before God (Mic. 6:8).

But even so, we must also recognize the limits of even the best of governments. We must not put our trust in a political party. Getting your favorite candidate in the Oval Office will not advance the kingdom of God one bit.

Additionally, history has shown that the Church thrives in times of persecution, not prosperity. The church in China and North Korea thrives today under godless communists. The church in Afghanistan grows today under Islamic oppression, just as the church in India, thrives under Hindu officials. Tertullian, a second-century church father, said, "the blood of the martyrs is the seed of the church," and "the more you kill, the more we are."[12] While we can seek the good of our fellow man through politics, our hope for them and ourselves must always remain Jesus.

For, at any time, the country in which Christians live may become beastly. And when it does, Christians must resist:

If anyone has an ear, let him hear:
If anyone is to be taken captive,
to captivity he goes;
if anyone is to be slain with the sword,
with the sword must he be slain.
Here is a call for the endurance and faith of the saints.
(Rev. 13:9–10)

Faithfulness to Christ will sometimes mean putting us at odds who those in authority over us and even those who share our political preferences. Following Jesus means we cannot accept the redefinition of marriage on the one hand, nor the neglect and protection of the weak on the other. If Jesus shapes our ethics and not political party platforms, we will not accept the mistreatment of foreigners nor the celebration of deviant sexual lifestyles.

To live for Jesus may mean you will be rejected by those in authority and even those who share your political preferences but not your allegiance to Jesus. In those times, Jesus reminds us that following him invites the hatred of the world, made up of political liberals and conservatives. But we remain bold! Jesus has overcome the world. He has defeated the beast. And we should follow him wherever he leads us.

A friend of mine recently shared a story about a trip he took spelunking, which is another word for cave exploring. Along with a group of students from his church, he showed up at the mouth of a cave, where they were met by an expert spelunker who would guide their adventure. But before they entered, the guide warned them that it would be a challenging venture. The exploration would take several hours and all of their physical energy.

He described the rigorous and painful elements of the trip which tempts most climbers to turn back. Even so, the guide offered numerous assurances that if one endured to the end, they would witness a stunning wonder that would make the difficult journey worth the effort.

The cave lived up to the guide's challenging descriptions. Some of the narrow passages required the help of another hiker to grab your arm or leg to pull you through. At other times, low tunnels required the use of fingertips and toes to inch one's way to the other side. Several people got hurt on the expedition. One girl twisted her ankle, another hit her head on a rock opening a fountain of blood on her face, and everyone had scrapes up and down their legs and forearms.

Finally, after several hours, they arrived at the end of the cave. The guide instructed everyone to put their backs against a wall and to look in front of them. Then, with everyone in place, the guide said, "This is the moment you've been waiting for." He then flipped a switch which turned on lights illuminating an enormous, cavernous space. Stalactites of radiant blue, purple, and orange hung from the ceiling. Below, a crystal-clear pool of icy water housed sparkling stalagmites growing from the floor. Among the awe-inspiring sight, in the middle of the water, sat a large throne-shaped stone formation, covered with such shades of pink, yellow, and gold. It made the audience think they'd never truly seen those colors before.

After a few moments, the guide with a lamp in his hand, illuminating the girl with the twisted ankle, another with a bandage on her head, and the whole crew with mud and muck on their clothes, asked, "Well? Was it worth it?" And without exception, all those beaten and bruised travelers said, "Yes! And I'd do it all over again!"

My friend, those responses came from people like you, people looking at a hole in the ground with a flashlight. How much more will our pilgrimage through the wilderness be worth it when we see the Savior, the light of heaven? On that day, if he should ask us, "Well? Was it worth it?" For all eternity, we will say, "Yes! And I'd do it all over again. Just to see you." Until then, be strong and courageous. Don't give up.

Study Questions

1. How does the imagery of the beast's mortal wound shore up your courage and shape your behavior?
2. Notice that everything the dragon and the beast do, they carry out under the permission of the Lord. How does this truth sit with you? Does it give you comfort? Or are you uncomfortable with it?
3. In what ways does Christ call you to seek the welfare of this land while living here in exile?
4. Jesus promises trouble in this world for those who follow Him. He comforts us in this—he has overcome the world! Ask the Lord to shape and strengthen you with this truth.

---

1. https://www.warhistoryonline.com/world-war-ii/battle-of-wake-island-japanese-atrocities.html?chrome=1
2. Thomas R. Schreiner, *The Joy of Hearing: A Theology of the Book of Revelation* (Wheaton, IL: Crossway, 2021), 34.
3. For an extensive examination of the theme of counterfeiting in Revelation, see Vern S. Poythress, *The Returning King: A Guide to the Book of Revelation* (P&R, 2000), 16–22.
4. G.K. Beale, *The Book of Revelation: A Shorter Commentary* (Eerdmans, 2015), 267.
5. For example, Edward J. Young, *The Prophecy of Daniel: A Commentary* (Grand Rapids, MI: 1980), 143–147.
6. Chapters 4 and 5 of Revelation give us another angle of the same event Daniel saw. Daniel saw *"one like a son of man"* approach the Ancient of Days. John saw a lamb do the same.
7. G.K. Beale, *The Book of Revelation: A Shorter Commentary*, 268; William Hendriksen, *More than Conquerors* (Grand Rapids, MI: Baker Books, 1998), 146; Dennis E. Johnson, *Triumph of the Lamb: A Commentary on Revelation* (Phillipsburg, NJ: P&R, 2001), 188–189.
8. Some commentators think John is alluding to a well-known legend surrounding the suicide of the emperor Nero in 68 AD. After his death, rumors suggested that Nero hadn't died but escaped enemies in Rome. As a result, some legends anticipated that

Nero would return to Rome to reclaim his throne. For problems with this view, see G.K. Beale, *The Book of Revelation: A Shorter Commentary*, 270–271; Vern S. Poythress, *The Returning King: A Guide to the Book of Revelation*, 142.
9. Matthew 27:33; Mark 15:22; John 19:17. Calvary is the Latin term which also means "skull."
10. Martin Luther, "A Mighty Fortress is Our God" (1529).
11. G.K. Beale, *The Book of Revelation: A Shorter Commentary*, 273.
12. https://www.tertullian.org/works/apologeticum.htm

23

THE BEAST FROM THE EARTH
REVELATION 13:11-18

The founding president of the seminary I attended was Dr. Robert Rayburn. While there, I heard a story about Dr. Rayburn involving severe temptation. In its earliest days, the school struggled financially. With fewer than a dozen tuition-paying students and half as many professors, finances were in short supply

But one day, a man who was an heir to a fortune sent a letter to Dr. Rayburn's office with the promise of a significant financial gift. The man had heard Dr. Rayburn preach at a local church and decided to help fund the seminary. But he informed Dr. Rayburn that the donation came with a condition.

After explaining that he was involved in a well-educated and highly-cultured circle of friends, the man told Dr. Rayburn that the frequent references to the wrath of God, the cross, and the bloody death of Jesus were off-putting to his sophisticated acquaintances. He explained that while he'd love to invite his friends to the church and to visit the seminary, he felt uncomfortable doing so because of the repeated mention of these things.

Seeking a compromise with Dr. Rayburn, the donor requested that a particular hymn, one that mentioned the blood of Jesus, be struck from the hymnals of the seminary chapel. The letter ended with his offer of a financial gift if Dr. Rayburn would comply with his request.

We have to appreciate the temptation Dr. Rayburn must have faced. With this one financial gift, many of his problems would disappear. He could pay his faculty. He could connect with wealthy donors who could fund other projects. He could move out of fundraising mode and back into teaching and preaching, which he loved more than any other activity. And what preacher doesn't want more people to come to church? The temptation must have been intense.

The man who wrote the letter asked for an answer from Dr. Rayburn. Today, if you visit the seminary and attend a chapel service, you will hear Dr. Rayburn's response: seminarians and professors singing, "There is a fountain filled with blood, drawn from Immanuel's veins; and sinners, plunged beneath that flood, lose all their guilty stains."[1]

Similar temptations will find us. As we live publicly for Jesus, some will ask about our faith. And when requested, we can be tempted to soften what we perceive as some of the Bible's difficult truths. Or we can be tempted to be silent on issues where the Scriptures are not silent. For me, sometimes these temptations come because I don't want to push people away. Even Christians struggle to embrace some of the uncomfortable truths in the Bible. So, I reason, "I'll change the subject so they won't walk away." And other times, the temptations to soften, adapt, or ignore the things of God when talking about my faith come because I can be a coward. Like anyone else, I don't want to be disliked or rejected.

External pressures also invite us toward compromise. John shows us a beast of deception laboring against the church's commitment to Jesus. But this vision encourages bravery and boldness before the beastly attempts to get us to soften, adapt, or abandon our trust in Jesus. But Jesus will destroy this beast (Rev. 20:10). Jesus wins. Therefore, don't be deceived by the lies you will hear, and don't be afraid. Instead, with patient endurance, cling to Jesus no matter the cost.

This vision shows us a beast of deception and calls us to discern the beast's true nature.

The Beast of Deception

Before we look at the text, recall that John saw a dragon, representing Satan, chasing a woman in the wilderness, representing the church, in an attempt to destroy her. The dragon enlists the help of an ally—the beast from the sea. This beast represents man-centered, self-exalting empires or governments that resist the rule of Christ and persecute his people. Here John sees another beast, this time coming from the earth:

> *Then I saw another beast rising out of the earth. It had two horns like a lamb and it spoke like a dragon. It exercises all the authority of the first beast in its*

presence, and makes the earth and its inhabitants worship the first beast, whose mortal wound was healed. (Rev. 13:11–12)

As we have previously mentioned, the first beast depicted in John's writings symbolizes the state, specifically Rome during his time. On the other hand, the second beast represents the propaganda mechanism that influences people to comply with the government's directives.

Put another way, the second beast represents those who encourage and enforce obedience to and the adoration of the government. In John's day, the beast of the land represented the local elites, the religious and political officials that enforced imperial worship upon the citizens.

You'll recall from our earlier studies that at this time in Roman history, those in authority expected every citizen to participate in various celebrations and festivals honoring the pantheon of gods and the emperor himself. By the end of the first century, every city that John wrote to had a temple built to Caesar where the faithful adored his image.[2]

In these cities, local town councils mandated all citizens offer sacrifices to both the emperor and Roman gods at festivals and feasts thrown in their honor. By the end of the first century, many local officials forbade people from buying or selling at the local market unless citizens made the required sacrifices.[3]

We also know temples often housed images of the emperor, where local priests performed sleight-of-hand magic tricks[4] like the use of lighting, sounds, and ventriloquism to create the illusion that the images moved about, cried, breathed, and spoke. That may be what John alludes to in verses 13–15:

> *It performs great signs, even making fire come down from heaven to earth in front of people, and by the signs that it is allowed to work in the presence of the beast it deceives those who dwell on earth, telling them to make an image for the beast that was wounded by the sword and yet lived. And it was allowed to give breath to the image of the beast, so that the image of the beast might even speak and might cause those who would not worship the image of the beast to be slain.* (Rev. 13:13–15)

In John's day, the beast from the land represented those who persuaded the masses to get in line with the government. Today, the beast still lives on in the form of media, journalism, university lecterns, civic authorities, and other parents on the bleachers at the tee-ball game.

A chorus of voices surrounds us calling us to move beyond the antiquated thinking of the Bible: "Only the uneducated believe the theory of creation over the science of evolution. Only the narrow-minded believe that Jesus is the only way to heaven. Only the arrogant and judgmental would speak to someone else about sin or judgment. Only those filled with hate and phobias oppose same-sex marriage."

It's all around us. Some in John's audience lost their lives because they would not worship the state (Rev. 2:13). Others were imprisoned (Rev. 2:10). All of them were mocked and reviled for their faith. Most Christians in China, North Korea, India, and Afghanistan, worship Jesus today under the genuine threat of death.

And while not facing death for our faith at this time, the beast will sometimes punish you for public trust in Jesus. Publicly following Jesus will keep you out of some state university teaching positions. Refusing to partake in and celebrate the newest wave of the sexual revolution will earn you titles of disrespect.

You may not lose your life for Jesus, but you may lose your reputation, business, acceptance in certain social circles, and job opportunities. You may not get killed, but you may get "canceled." And when it becomes costly to follow Jesus, we should not strike back at the beast using its weapons but continue boldly living for Jesus.

We're told the beast sets apart those who follow him with a distinguishing mark on the forehead or the wrist:

> *Also it causes all, both small and great, both rich and poor, both free and slave, to be marked on the right hand or the forehead, so that no one can buy or sell unless he has the mark, that is, the name of the beast or the number of its name.* (Rev. 13:16–17)

What is this mark the propaganda machine places on its followers? Understanding the Old Testament background helps us. In the book of Deuteronomy, the Lord instructs his people to be shaped both in thought and deed by his commands. Sometimes we call this blending orthodoxy (right thoughts and beliefs) with orthopraxy (right actions).

To that end, the Lord instructed the Jewish people to bind his Law to their hands and foreheads (Deut. 6:8, cf. Ex. 13:9,16). The forehead represents one's ideological commitments or worldview. The wrist or hand represents the practical outworking of what you believe. Most understood this instruction as figurative language, though some took it literally and tied boxes containing pieces of the Law to their heads and hands.

That background of figurative language relating to marks on the forehead and hand discourages looking for literal brandings in the form of barcodes, microchips, or UPC codes.[5] John observed a present reality in picture form, not a future technology branding non-Christians as beast-followers. If we've not been born again by the Spirit, our forehead bears the mark of the beast (Rom. 12:2). The Spirit's renewal of the mind removes the man-centered, Christ-rejecting, and worldly thinking common to all people.

Those who denied Christ's claim over them in John's day already had the mark of the beast on their foreheads, just as those who refuse Christ today do. In the same way, for those who don't live by the Spirit of God, endeavoring to love God and man, their wrists also bear the beast's mark. The beast's mark on the wrist stands for the *"the passions of our flesh"* and *"carrying out the desires of the body"* (Eph. 2:3). Those who bear the beast's marks are those who follow the "course of this world" and remain dead in sin (Eph. 2:2).

Turning to Jesus remains the only solution. Only he can remove the mark of beastly thinking and behavior (2 Cor. 3:14, 16).

But Christian, your forehead also bears a mark. In Chapter 7, we read about the servants of God spared from his wrath because they carried God's mark on their forehead (Rev. 7:3). In Chapter 9, the locust-like demons could not harm those sealed on the forehead with God's seal (Rev. 9:4). In Chapter 14, John saw 144,000 people—whom we've already met in Chapter 7—with the name of God on their foreheads (Rev. 14:1).

Remember that these three characters—the dragon, the beast from the sea, and the beast from the earth—form a counterfeit trinity. The dragon made the beast from the sea in his own image, counterfeiting the relationship between the Father and the Son, who mirrors the image of the Father. The dragon also uses the beast of the sea to do his bidding, much like how the Father carries out his plan of salvation and judgment through his Son.

Now we see the Holy Spirit mocked and mimicked through the beast from the earth. In the same way that the Holy Spirit worked miraculous signs in the book of Acts, the beast from the earth uses pseudo-magic tricks to wow the masses.

And just as the Holy Spirit promotes the worship of the Son of God, the beast from the earth encourages the worship of the beast from the sea. Finally, just as the Holy Spirit renews our minds, leads us in all truth, and seals our foreheads as a mark of ownership. So also, the beast from the earth shapes the minds of its followers, leads them with all deception, and seals their foreheads with its mark of ownership.

No one is exempt from a mark on the forehead: *"Also it causes all, both small and great, both rich and poor, both free and slave, to be marked on the right hand or the forehead"* (Rev. 13:16). Every person John saw in these visions bore a mark on their forehead—either the mark of the beast or the seal of God. Either we serve Jesus, or we follow the way of the beast that is heading for damnation. In the words of one author: "We would like to think that there is some sort of middle ground, a way of neutrality for nice but unconvinced people. But there just isn't."[6]

The Bible differentiates between those who are children of wrath (Eph. 2:3) and those who are children of God (John 1:12). Either you trust and serve Jesus, or you trust and serve the beastly way of the world, which has no love for Christ, no pursuit of living for him, and consequently, no hope of escaping judgment.

The beast from the earth seeks to influence the Church not only through external pressure but also by working from within: *"Then I saw another beast rising out of the earth. It had two horns like a lamb and it spoke like a dragon."* (Rev. 13:11).

A close examination of the beast reveals a promotion of state appeasement through compromise coming from within the Church itself. Sometimes this beast stands in church pulpits. A number of clues point us in this direction.[7]

First, elsewhere the title "the false prophet" describes the beast of the earth (Rev. 16:13; 19:20; 20:10). In the Old Testament, the designation of false prophet refers to someone within the covenant community who teaches false doctrine.

Therefore, the description of the beast as a false prophet suggests it has influence from within the church community. The second clue comes in the beast's appearance, which matches what Jesus tells us to look for in false teachers. Jesus said, *"Beware of false prophets, who come to you in sheep's clothing but inwardly are ravenous wolves"* (Matt. 7:15). This description matches the description of the beast of the earth. On the outside, false prophets look like a lamb. But inwardly, they are wolves and speak for the dragon.

We know that John's audience dealt with false teachers in the churches (Rev. 2:14–15, 20). Some from within the flock promoted participation in the feasts to the emperor, while others, we think, encouraged people not to be so prudish when it came to sexuality. They didn't stand in the pulpit wearing red jumpsuits saying, "Thus sayeth the dragon." Instead, I'm sure they offered what sounded like reasonable, sophisticated arguments for why a little give and take with doctrine and practice made sense. We can imagine them saying, "We don't want to stick out in the community. Go to the feasts for the gods. Burn a little incense for the emperor. Jesus knows what's in your hearts." Or perhaps they said, "We all know those feasts end with all kinds of sexual promiscuity.

But if someone asks what you think about it, don't push them away. Don't say those who practice such things will not inherit the kingdom of God. We don't want to be judgmental. Remember, Jesus said to take the log out of our eye before looking for specks in others," and so on. It sounds persuasive and kind. The beast looks like a lamb. Something a child could pet. But its words are those of the dragon.

This deception will remain in the Church until Jesus returns. Therefore, we need to exercise wisdom and discernment whenever we listen to those who speak in the name of Jesus. Back in seminary, the professors introduced something called the "Synagogue Test" that may be helpful for you.[8]

The basic idea of the Synagogue Test is this—if a Christian minister preaches a sermon that would be acceptable to the members of a Jewish synagogue or a Unitarian congregation, there is something terribly wrong with it. So, for example, if the thrust of a sermon is "Do not steal. Be faithful to your spouse. Be kind to others." Would any Jewish congregants be upset with that message? What about a Unitarian? Probably not.

And, of course, those are all good things; we ought not to steal or be unfaithful to our spouses or terrible toward others. But if that's where the message ends, you have not heard the Gospel. A Gospel presentation sets before the audience "the all-pervading presence of a saving and sanctifying Christ. Jesus Christ must be at the heart of every sermon" if it will pass the Synagogue Test.[9]

Whenever we listen to a preacher, Sunday school teacher, or anyone who speaks on behalf of Jesus, we must apply the Synagogue Test. We should ask ourselves: "Do I need Jesus for this teaching? Is the grace of God ignored in this message? Does the teacher imply that God will love me more if I do this? Or that I can do this on my own without Jesus? Does this person speak against things clearly outlined in Holy Scripture?"

I run my work through the Synagogue Test whenever I teach or preach. I ask myself, "Will the audience walk away trying harder to please God? Or will they find God's pleasure unchangeably resides over them in Jesus? Will my audience respond to my teaching, thinking they can tough out the path to heaven on their own? Or will they be left praying, "Jesus, I'm clinging to you to keep me on the way." To the Jewish person, such a message is blasphemous nonsense. To the Unitarian, it's closed-minded, unsophisticated, and the stench of death. But to those who love Jesus, the presence of a saving and sanctifying Christ carries the fragrance of life.

From the church's earliest days, false prophets found places in church pulpits and will continue to do so until the Lord returns. Therefore, John tells us we need to be wise and discern actual Gospel teaching from its counterfeit. And to observe the true nature of the beast.

The Beast's True Nature

Let's look at one of the most controversial parts of Revelation, and then we'll consider how to put all this information together:

> *This calls for wisdom: let the one who has understanding calculate the number of the beast, for it is the number of a man, and his number is 666.* (Rev. 13:18)

What do we make of this number 666? Some have suggested that John provides a numeric code concealing a secret name for the beast. They appeal to an old practice called "gematria." Gematria assigned numeric values to letters of the alphabet.

So the letter A might equal 1, B equals 2, C equals 3, and so on. While gematria included other complexities, this provides enough information for the purposes here. Some have suggested that John invites us to crack a code. Those who are clever enough can use gematria to solve the riddle of 666 and reveal the individual behind the number.

Over time many candidates have been set forth with this technique: Caesar Nero, Titus, Domitian, Balaam, Mohammed, Martin Luther, Kaiser Wilhelm, the Nicolaitans, and even Ronald Reagan (Ronald Wilson Reagan has six letters in each of his names, hence 666). Even poor Billy Graham, whose name, when spelled using William Graham, comes out to 666!

One commentator even suggests, tongue in cheek, that 666 refers to Barney, the children's television figure since the words "cute purple dinosaur" results in 666.[10] You can see the problem with this approach. As one commentator notes, "We cannot infer much from the fact that a key fits the lock if it is a lock in which almost any key will turn."[11] That leaves us where we started, scratching our heads, not knowing to whom 666 refers.

A better approach treats this number symbolically as John uses other numbers throughout the book. Symbolic numbers represent the church: seven lampstands, twenty-four elders, two witnesses, and 144,000 people. Symbolic numbers represent the time between the ascension and return of Jesus: 42 months, 1,260 days, and 3½ years.

So approaching this number not as a hidden code but as a symbol keeps us consistent with the author. With that in mind, remember two things we have learned thus far in this book. First, John favors the number seven: the number of completion, totality, and perfection (seven churches, the seven eyes of Jesus, seven seals, the seven spirits of God, and so on).

The number 6 would be the number of falling short or incompletion. Six also stands as the number of mankind, created on the sixth day of creation. Remember, too, that the dragon and the two beasts counterfeit the real Trinity, the being of absolute perfection, or 777. But the dragon and the two beasts, eternally fall short of the triune God. 666 represents the inadequate and temporal empire of Satan and those (unknowingly) in league with him.

This number represents God's verdict upon the foolish unholy alliance that wars against the Lord and his church. The dragon and his servants will not and cannot win. Until the return of Christ, this parody of the Trinity may appear to have all the power and authority. And this clownish trinity will often use its reign to stomp the Church into the ground.

But in the end, their power and authority will end when Christ throws the dragon, the beast, and the false prophet into a lake of fire. So what's the point of 666? It reminds us that the satanically-inspired, man-centered, Christ-denying kingdoms of this world will be short-lived and eternally fall short. Christ and his kingdom will win the battle.

There is a story about the Italian conductor Arturo Toscanini, who led one of the finest performances of Beethoven's Ninth Symphony ever heard. One night, before a packed orchestral hall, a ten-minute standing ovation followed what Toscanini considered the finest performance of his life. Filled with emotion, Toscanini turned to the orchestra and said, "Who are you? You are nothing. Who am I? I am nothing. But Beethoven. Beethoven is everything! Everything! Everything!"

My friend, until we see Jesus, the threatening trio of Satan, tyrants, and false prophets oppose the church. But when held up against the glory, power, and assurances of our Lord, they are but nothing. Christ is everything! Everything! Everything! Cling to him. Don't give up, and don't give in. No matter what the cost.

Study Questions

1. Think about Dr. Rayburn's temptation to compromise. Have you faced similar situations? In what way may Jesus be calling you to boldness, and to stop softening the hard truths of Scripture?
2. When following Jesus comes with a social cost, what do you cling to for hope and boldness? In what ways have you experienced the cost of loving Christ?
3. How is this teaching of the mark of the beast different than what you've previously been taught? What does it mean that everyone is marked? How does the truth that there is no neutrality toward Christ shape your witness?
4. The point of 666 may be very different than we previously thought, but it serves to show us that the unholy alliance that wars against the Lord and His Church will not and cannot win. How does this inform our lives, choices, and responses?

---

1. William Cowper, "There is a Fountain Filled with Blood" (1771). I confirmed the details of this story with Dr. Rayburn's son, Robert S. Rayburn, via phone on September 15, 2022.
2. G.K. Beale, *The Book of Revelation: A Commentary on the Greek Text* (Eerdmans, 2013), 710.
3. N.T. Wright, *Revelation for Everyone* (Louisville, IL: Westminster John Knox Press, 2011), 121. This practice seems to be alluded to in v. 17.
4. For a survey of this topic, see David E. Aune, *Revelation 6–16*, Word Biblical Commentary (Nashville, IL: Thomas Nelson, 1997), 762–765; N.T. Wright, *Revelation for Everyone*, 120–121.
5. The marks here are no more literal or physical than the seal on the foreheads of God's people in Rev. 7:2–3 and 9:4 or the name of God written on the foreheads of those in 3:12 and 14:1.
6. Nancy Guthrie, *Blessed: Experiencing the Promise of the Book of Revelation* (Wheaton, IL: Crossway, 2022), 158.
7. For further reasons pointing to the beast's presence within the faith community, see G.K. Beale, *The Book of Revelation: A Commentary on the Greek Text*, 709–710.
8. The "synagogue test" comes from Jay Adams' book on preaching. See Jay E. Adams, *Preaching with Purpose: The Urgent Task of Homiletics* (Grand Rapids, MI: Zondervan, 1982), 147.
9. Ibid., 147.
10. Craig S. Keener, *Revelation*, NIV Application Commentary (Grand Rapids, MI: Zondervan, 1999), 359.
11. G. Salmon, quoted in G.K. Beale, *The Book of Revelation: A Commentary on the Greek Text*, 721. Of the most plausible suggestions for identifying a particular person through gematria is that of Caesar Nero. But even the best arguments for Nero are fraught with problems. See G.K. Beale, *The Book of Revelation: A Commentary on the Greek Text*, 718–728.

24

THE LAMB'S ARMY
REVELATION 14:1-5

The New Testament scholar John Stott used to share about a bus trip he took through Israel that gave him insight into shepherds and sheep. While the bus traveled through the rural areas of Judea, the tour guide directed the tourists' attention to the flocks and the shepherds that attended them.

One of the details he shared highlighted the difference between shepherds in Israel versus shepherds in other parts of the world. In other regions of the world, shepherds drive sheep forward from behind. In Israel, however, shepherds lead sheep from the front of the herd, while the animals listen to the shepherd's voice and follow. Just as the tour guide shared that piece of trivia, a tourist raised his hand and pointed out the window saying, "What about that guy?" Everyone looked out the windows and saw a man driving a flock of sheep forward with a menacing stick.

Was the tour guide wrong? He asked the driver to stop the bus so he could speak with the man they saw in the field. After a few moments, he returned, his face beaming. He announced, "I've just spoken to the man. Ladies and gentlemen, he is not the shepherd. He is, in fact, the butcher!"[1]

As the Good Shepherd, Jesus Christ leads us not to slaughter but to safety. "Follow me" remains one of the most persistent commands that the Good Shepherd gives the sheep (Matt: 4:19; 8:22; 9:9, 10–38; 17:24; 19:21). You might even say that the best description of a Christian is not "someone who believes in Jesus" but rather "someone who follows Jesus." Jesus said:

> *I am the good shepherd. I know my own and my own know me.... My sheep hear my voice, and I know them, and they follow me.* (John 10:14, 27)

This chapter shows us the reward for those who follow the Lamb. And what a contrast this vision presents to what has proceeded! In the previous two chapters, we witnessed a dragon terrorizing a woman trying to escape in the wilderness. The dragon had two companions, one from the sea and the other from the earth, who assisted in the attack. The woman represents the Church. The dragon and its allies portray Satan and his use of the powerful state and its propagandists to squelch the Church's witness. God answers the dragon's mad raging against Christ's kingdom and his bride with the vision before us.

One of David's psalms records the Lord's response to the nations who oppose the Davidic King (Ps. 2). The nations are said to rage against the Lord and against his Anointed, or Messiah. The Lord responds to the raging nations first with laughter, and then with an assurance, *"As for me, I have set my King on Zion, my holy hill"* (Ps. 2:6).

John sees the Lord's King set on Zion. But the King has an army, comprised of those who followed him, no matter the cost. As we examine this snapshot of the future, may it encourage us to press on toward heaven. Chapter 14 will conclude John's fourth portrait of the time between the ascension and return of Christ. The chapter ends with a terrifying description of the penalty inflicted upon those who refuse to submit to Jesus. But the chapter opens with the reward that awaits those who call on him as their loving Lord.[2] The Bible openly presents the challenges we'll encounter if we follow the Lamb. But the Lord encourages us by setting glories so stunning and magnificent before his people that render those present sufferings inconsequential.

This vision reveals the full deliverance of those fully loved by the Lord.

Delivered

The first word of encouragement for the Christian is the location where John sees the Lamb and 144,000:

> *Then I looked, and behold, on Mount Zion stood the Lamb, and with him 144,000 who had his name and his Father's name written on their foreheads.* (Rev. 14:1)

The Bible uses Zion in a number of ways. Sometimes Zion refers to

God's unique presence in the Temple of Jerusalem. At other times, Zion substitutes as a name for God's people. But more often than not, Zion refers to the city that God will establish and rule over at the end of history.³ That end-time Zion, or what we might call heaven, appears before John's eyes.⁴ The 144,000 people with Jesus, reemerge onto the scene after their introduction in Chapter 7. Their return here should thrill our hearts.

And here's why. Remember the situation when we first examined this group of people? Jesus opened the seals of the scroll, unleashing judgment upon humanity. John saw that dreadful day come upon the world. It came with such ferocity and terror that people cried out to the mountains and rocks:

> *Fall on us and hide us from the face of him who is seated on the throne, and from the wrath of the Lamb, for the great day of their wrath has come, and who can stand?"* (Rev. 6:16–17)

John then heard the answer to the question: the 144,000 sealed on the forehead by God. John overhears the Lord counting off 12,0000 from one tribe of Israel to the next until the number reaches 144,000. That number, like all numbers in this book, is a symbol. It doesn't point to a literal 144,000 ethnic Jews but to the whole number of God's people, the true Israel of God. Not according to the flesh, but by faith.

Recall that while John heard the number 144,000, when he looked to see the 144,000, an innumerable host of people that no one could count, from every nation, tribe, people, and language filled his sights (Rev. 7:9). So catch the beauty of what we now have before us. When we first met the 144,000 people, the descriptions of the group suggest they are an army.⁵

If you go back to Chapter 7, listing the tribes that make up the 144,000, it echoes some of the lists we find in the book of Numbers. Before Israel engaged in a holy war, the men of fighting age were counted from each tribe and numbered to determine military strength. Additionally, the Law of God forbade men from sexual relations while engaged in warfare (Deut. 23:9–10; 1 Sam. 21:4–5). This explains the otherwise strange description of the 144,000 as celibate men:

> *It is these who have not defiled themselves with women, for they are virgins.*
> *It is these who follow the Lamb wherever he goes.* (Rev. 14:4).

This description doesn't mean that only the celibate will enter the heavenly Zion. That would contradict the high value Scripture places on marriage and children as gifts from the Lord. Instead, John used military terms to describe a people who fought for the Lord. They fought against the dragon, the beast from the sea, and the beast from the earth. In the end, they did not give in or give themselves over to the lies of the false trinity.

Instead, they waged war against their sin, doubt, and fears. They continued to cling to Jesus for life and now stand with him in victory. The first time we saw the 144,000, God sealed them mid-battle. This time we see the same group of people, and not one has been lost. Chapter 7 makes a promise; Chapter 14 reveals the fulfillment. This vision of the delivered army standing with their King strengths the soldier to continue in the fight. I know I need the reminder that the Lord never fails to keep his promises. Sometimes I feel weary and ready to give up. When I assess myself as a soldier in the Lord's army, I feel puny, prone to wander, and easily distracted. When my sights are on myself, I get discouraged. But when the Lord sets my eyes on his promises to never leave, lose, or forsake me, I can fight on. One of the Lord's promises that I often need in the weary parts of my soul comes from John's gospel:

> *All that the Father gives me will come to me, and whoever comes to me I will never cast out. For I have come down from heaven, not to do my own will but the will of him who sent me. And this is the will of him who sent me, that I should lose nothing of all that he has given me, but raise it up on the last day. For this is the will of my Father, that everyone who looks on the Son and believes in him should have eternal life, and I will raise him up on the last day.* (John 6:37–40)

Jesus gives a mission statement: he will never lose one given to him by the Father.

We may object. Don't we all know people who begin with Jesus but later walk away?

Sadly, I know many just like this. In the parable of the sower, Jesus explained that people respond to him in different ways, and not all of these responses end in salvation (Mark 4:1–20). On hearing the command to follow him, some immediately reject the message. Others throw their lot in with Jesus for a time, but then trouble comes along, and they walk away. Still others believe in him but remain more in love with the world's offering and their faith becomes worthless.

But in some people, the message goes deep into the soul, and they live out the rest of their days producing the fruit of repentant trust in Jesus. Indeed, some begin with Jesus and fall away. But those who have been born again by the Holy Spirit—the 144,000 sealed by God—will not and cannot fall away.

My tired soul finds strength in Jesus' assurance to those who love him. Do you love Jesus? Not perfectly and without stumbling along the way. But does love for Jesus describe the general pattern of your life? Do you actively strive to turn from sin and seek Jesus' guidance for the way you should live? Does God's affirmation of you mean more than the world's?

Your answer can be explained with one truth if you answer yes to these questions: the Father gifted you to his Son. You stand among the 144,000 sealed by God in this world, and you will stand delivered in the one to come. For my soul, no words of Scripture exceed the sweetness of these—"I will not lose one"—when I feel the weakness of my faith. Thankfully, salvation depends not on the quantity of our faith but by faith's object: the Lamb who will stand on Mount Zion and will deliver all of his warriors safely to their inheritance. Treasure this glorious assurance!

In the meantime, be sustained during the battle by the love of God for you as found in Jesus Christ.

Loved

John not only saw the Lamb and the 144,000, but he also heard this great company of people singing:

> *And I heard a voice from heaven like the roar of many waters and like the sound of loud thunder. The voice I heard was like the sound of harpists playing on their harps, and they were singing a new song before the throne and before the four living creatures and before the elders. No one could learn that song except the 144,000 who had been redeemed from the earth.* (Rev. 14:2–3)

John notes that only the 144,000 know the lyrical content of the song he heard. The purpose of the secrecy may symbolize the astonishing truth that only those who have experienced the power of salvation can truly testify to its majesty. Only those who have realized the extent of their sins and have received God's grace can truly appreciate and give thanks for His love.

I understand that's a counter-cultural statement. If they believe in god, many non-Christians will say that they believe in a god of love.[6] But, more often than not, when asked probing questions about this god, the answers offered present not love, but mere sentimentality. They imagine a wrathless god, in a universe with no hell, no judgment, no eternal punishment. And if asked if this god of love had to do anything to receive them—like being nailed to a cross, wearing a crown of thorns, or buried in the ground—they often scoff at such things. None of that is necessary.

While it's true that "God is love" (1 John 4:8, 16) and that he has a general love for all humanity (Matt. 5:45), God reserves a costly and non-sentimental kind of love for those united to his Son.[7] It's a love that cost him tremendously to rescue you.

Some time ago, I read a story by Mindy Belz, the senior editor of *World Magazine*.[8] The story involved Islamic tribes in Sudan who kidnapped Christian children, demanding a ransom for their return. Mindy interviewed several parents who paid a ransom to redeem their children. Some spent hundreds of thousands of dollars to save their children. Others had to give the militants every piece of livestock they owned, leaving them with nothing.

But during the interviews, one man avoided her. So Mindy approached him and said, "Did they also kidnap your child?" "Yes," he answered. "Were you able to redeem him?" Again, he answered yes. "What did you have to pay?" she asked. Hanging his head in embarrassment, the father said, "$750." The man felt ashamed and embarrassed that the kidnappers had so undervalued his son. Defined by our culture, the love of God remains grossly undervalued. What did it cost the true and living God to secure heaven for you? His Son.

God says, "I redeemed you with the King of Glory. I so loved the world that I gave to it, the One in whom is all of my delight. So that you might be called, my people, friends, the pearl of great price." But also, John tells us that the love of God has made us firstfruits for him and the Lamb:

> It is these who have not defiled themselves with women, for they are virgins. It is these who follow the Lamb wherever he goes. These have been redeemed from mankind as firstfruits for God and the Lamb, and in their mouth no lie was found, for they are blameless. (Rev. 14:4–5)

In the Old Testament, the firstfruits were the early crops that preceded the more extensive and later harvests to come. God commanded the Jews to set this first crop aside as sacred (Ex. 23:19; Lev. 23:10–11; Deut. 26:10). This command had two purposes. First, it was a public confession of faith. Giving the Lord the first fruits expressed trust that more produce would soon follow. Labeling his people as first fruits points to God's plan to redeem and renew more than just humanity. The promise of eternal life lived in resurrected bodies constitutes only part of the Lord's plan of a greater, cosmos-wide re-creation to come.[9] The entirety of the universe will be renewed, and until it comes, it groans like a woman in childbirth, longing for the labor to be over (Rom. 8:20–23).

The firstfruits' second purpose provided worshippers a gift to offer to the Lord.[10] The fruit gifts acknowledge that while everything belonged to the Lord, these offerings explicitly belonged to the Lord. While the rest of the harvest could be used for everyday purposes, the firstfruits belonged to God and, therefore, remained holy and sacred to him.

Do you hear the love of God poured out for you in this description? The Lord promises to restore and renew humanity as part of a fuller, cosmos-wide restoration of the entire universe. The recreations he started in you at your re-birth by his Spirit, he will bring to completion at the resurrection. But more will follow. We are firstfruits. But also, God has gifted us to himself. We've been *"redeemed from mankind as firstfruits for God and the Lamb"* (Rev. 14:4).

Can you imagine being so loved by God? Can you look in the mirror and see one the Lord has given himself as a gift for all eternity? No wonder John tells us that only those redeemed by that type of love will eternally sing about it.

But there's no need to wait until that day. I heard a pastor talk about a strange situation he sometimes encounters at his church. As a result of the church's size and popularity sometimes one room hosts a funeral service while an adjacent room holds a wedding ceremony at the very same time. And in moments of silence in one or either of the ceremonies, you can hear what's going on in the other room.

That image of attending one event while overhearing another pictures the faith posture Jesus calls us to adopt. Sometimes the ugliness of my sin or the sin of others makes me feel like I'm attending a funeral with no end in sight. Maybe you know how this feels too. In those times, Jesus calls us to press our ears to the wall to hear the wedding on the other side. In the other room, songs of triumph and loud shouts of full delivery fill the air. One day, you will pass from this room to the other. You will not only be at the wedding, but you will also be the bride. Until then, follow the Shepherd, who always leads his sheep to safety.

Study Questions

1. There is a sharp contrast between the 144,000 we saw in Chapter 7 and the same group in Chapter 14. How does the contrast comfort you?
2. Meditate on this promise of Jesus: "I will not lose one." How does this change your response to your suffering and circumstances?
3. Do you see yourself as a gift that the Lord gives to himself for all eternity? Revisit the section on first fruits and commit that truth to your heart and mind.
4. Pray for the Spirit to quiet your anxieties and to help you entrust your heart, life, circumstances, work, and family to the Lord. Follow the Good Shepherd who promises to lead His people safely home.

---

1. John Stott, *The Contemporary Christian: Applying God's Word to Today's World* (Inter-Varsity Press, 1992), 284–285.
2. See G.K. Beale, *The Book of Revelation: A Shorter Commentary* (Eerdmans, 2015), 290; William Hendriksen, *More than Conquerors* (Baker Books, 1998), 151.
3. See G.K. Beale, *The Book of Revelation: A Shorter Commentary*, 291.
4. Leon Morris, *Revelation* (Eerdmans, 1984), 175. Heaven is further suggested by the presence of the throne, the four living creatures, and the twenty-four elders John saw here (v. 3) and in the heavenly throne room scene of Chapter 4. See also Heb. 12:22, which speaks of Mount Zion as the city of the living God and the heavenly Jerusalem.
5. Richard Bauckham, *The Theology of the Book of Revelation* (Cambridge University Press, 2012), 77.
6. See Tim Keller's excellent treatment of this issue in Tim Keller, "Preaching Hell in a Tolerant Age," *Christianity Today* (Online), https://www.christianitytoday.com/pastors/1997/fall/tim-keller-preaching-hell-tolerant-age.html.
7. For a good treatment of God's common and redemptive love, see D.A. Carson, *The Difficult Doctrine of the Love of God* (Wheaton, IL: Crossway, 1999).
8. Mindy Belz, *They Say We Are Infidels: On the Run from ISIS with Persecuted Christians in the Middle East* (Carol Stream IL: Tyndale House, 2016), 123–124.
9. See here Jas. 1:18, which describes Christians as "firstfruits of his creatures"(literally "firstfruits among that which is created [anew]"). See G.K. Beale, *The Book of Revelation: A Shorter Commentary*, 296; Michael D. Williams, *Far as the Curse is Found: The Covenant Story of Redemption* (P&R, Phillipsburg, New Jersey,k 2005), 275–276.
10. Leon Morris, *Revelation*, 177–178.

25

THE ETERNAL GOSPEL

REVELATION 14:6–13

I'll never forget the television images showing the devastating results of the Indian Ocean Tsunami of 2004. An underwater earthquake created waves upwards to 100 feet tall, which slammed through many island countries taking an estimated 227,000 lives. Sri Lanka experienced horrendous levels of loss, particularly in Hambantota, a small fishing town described by many as "swept off the map" by the tsunami.[1]

A thirty-foot wall of water crashed through this coastal village leveling homes, schools filled with children, and the entire fleet of fishing boats. But in the middle of the devastated town, one structure remained unfazed: a large, sturdy statue of Buddha, with eyes closed and a smile on its face. The stone-faced Buddah revealed no signs of trauma, though chaos and suffering encircled him. A reporter asked a villager if the unmoved Buddha brought her a sense of stability in the middle of such chaos.

To the reporter's surprise, the woman responded, "What kind of god would save himself and not save his people?" Though this dear woman cried out for deliverance, the hand-made god could neither hear nor see to deliver his follower.

The Gospel tells a different kind of story, about a different kind of God.

The true and living God did not remain aloof to the pain and suffering of his people. Nor is the Lord impervious to suffering and agony. Instead, the Son of God left a world immune from pain and suffering to enter a world of flesh and blood, wars and tears, life, and death. But Jesus' experience of pain and suffering far surpassed those common to us all. In addition to rejection, hunger, loneliness, and betrayal by friends and family, he bore the wrath and fury of the Lord (Rom. 2:8).

That woman asked what kind of god would save himself and not his people. I hope she has since found the One who came *"not to be served but to serve, and to give his life as a ransom for many"* (Matt. 20:28).

But Jesus also warns that a dreadful consequence will find those who refuse his gracious offer of pardon and acceptance. Through the Apostle Paul, Jesus cautions the world that when he returns, he will inflict *"vengeance on those who do not know God and on those who do not obey the gospel of our Lord Jesus"* (2 Thess. 1:7–8).

Soul-chilling words, to be sure. In this part of John's vision, he sees the beginning of that terrible judgment that will find those who die in rebellion against the Lord. One cannot overstate how different the eternal destiny of those who believe in Jesus is from that of those who reject his care. Every human will spend eternity in the presence of God. But not all will experience the Lord in the same way. Revelation 14 provides a limited glimpse of the eternal sorrows awaiting those who refuse to follow Jesus.

But why do we need such a vision? I believe God gives us this vision for two reasons. First, it encourages his people to press on in faith. Verse 12 provides the big takeaway from this section: *"Here is a call for the endurance of the saints, those who keep the commandment of God and their faith in Jesus"* (Rev. 14:12).[2]

John's audience suffered under the strong arm of Rome, which punished and persecuted them for their public faith in Jesus. This vision shows the short-lived triumph of evil and, consequently, shores up the faith of those suffering for Jesus then and now. Sometimes it can feel like God hides himself in times of trouble and allows the wicked to crush the weak without consequence (Ps. 10:1, 4–11). This vision reminds us that God will not overlook a single crime committed against his people or his holy name. Therefore, we press on in faith.

In addition to encouragement, this vision helps shape the content of our Gospel testimony. In courtrooms around our country, witnesses receive the charge to tell the truth, the whole truth, and nothing but the truth, with the help of God. In the same way, with the help of God, we are commissioned to tell the full truth of God's revelation to the world. That includes not only the appeal to others to reconcile with God through Jesus but also the consequences if they refuse.

Faithful Gospel testimony warns of the peril of the Gospel for those who reject it, as well as the peace of the Gospel for those who accept it.

The Peril of the Gospel

Before we look closely at the text, briefly recalling Babylon's invasion and destruction of Jerusalem in 587 BC will enrich our understanding of John's vision. The Babylonians exiled the Jews who survived the invasion, removing them far from their homes and enslaving them once again. During the exile, God made a promise to his broken-hearted people. Through the prophet Isaiah, the Lord promised Good News, or a Gospel, to them. You may recognize these words:

> *How beautiful upon the mountains are the feet of him who brings good news, who publishes peace, who brings good news of happiness, who publishes salvation, who says to Zion, "Your God reigns."* (Isa. 52:7)

Sometimes we limit the Good News or Gospel to a message of God's forgiveness of sin, his love for the world, and the promise of everlasting life.

But the biblical authors describe the Good News as far greater in scope. For Isaiah's audience in exile, the Gospel promised that the God of Abraham reigned, not the gods of Babylon. And God's reign meant Good News to the exiles and included three elements.

First, the Lord would come to his people and set things right. Isaiah describes the Good News of God's arrival:

> *The voice of your watchmen—they lift up their voice; together they sing for joy; for eye to eye they see the return of the Lord to Zion.* (Isa. 52:8)

The Good News to the oppressed is bad news for the oppressor. With the larger meaning of the Gospel in mind, consider the words John recorded:

> *Then I saw another angel flying directly overhead, with an eternal gospel to proclaim to those who dwell on earth, to every nation and tribe and language and people. And he said with a loud voice, "Fear God and give him glory, because the hour of his judgment has come, and worship him who made heaven and earth, the sea and the springs of water."* (Rev. 14:6–7)

The angel's words, *"Fear God and give him glory,"* don't represent a second chance or one last pleading with humanity to repent. When judgment arrives, the offer of salvation to the unrepentant will cease. Instead, the angel's command to fear God and give him glory aligns with Paul's words:

> *At the name of Jesus every knee should bow, in heaven and on earth, and under the earth, and every tongue confess that Jesus Christ is Lord, to the glory of God the father.* (Phil. 2:10)[3]

On that day, "All will submit, all will confess, but not all will be saved."[4]

The second element of good news also promises the overthrow of Babylon. Isaiah commanded:

> *Go on up to a high mountain, O Zion, herald of good news... fear not; say to the cities of Judah, "Behold your God!' Behold the Lord comes with might, and his arm rules for him."* (Isa. 40:9–10)

Those in exile were assured of the destruction of the destroyers. Turning again to John, the second angel proclaims Babylon's demise:

> *Another angel, a second, followed, saying, "Fallen, fallen is Babylon the great, she who made all nations drink the wine of the passion of her sexual immorality."* (Rev. 14:8)

Centuries before John wrote these words, the actual city of Babylon (we often talk about Babylon as a metaphor for a much larger entity) fell to Persian invaders. With Babylon's fall, the Lord promised it would never be rebuilt (Isa. 13:19–22; Jer. 51:26, 64). So we are not waiting for the destruction of a literal city called Babylon.

Instead, even centuries after Babylon's fall, the city remained in Jewish memory as the "paradigm of wickedness, of idolatry, immorality, and sheer cruelty."[5] Babylon represents any and every institution, government, worldview, or people group that opposes the Lord's reign and oppresses his people. Babylon—the source of all the injustices, perversions, blasphemies, and oppressions that have wrecked so many lives—will be forever neutered of all influence, allure, and power on that day.

The final element of the good news promised punishment upon Israel's oppressors. The Lord assured his people that he would take from their hand *"the cup of staggering; the bowl of [his] wrath [they] would drink no more"*

(Isa. 51:22). The good news promised the removal of a cup, a common metaphor for God's wrath and anger (Ps. 11:6; 75:9, Isa. 51:17, 22; Jer. 25:15), from God's people. But the same good news promised Israel's oppressors a forced drink from the same cup: *"I will put it into the hands of your tormentors"* (Isa. 51:23). The third angel of John's vision repeats the same terrible promise:

> *And another angel, a third, followed them, saying with a loud voice, "If anyone worships the beast and its image and receives a mark on his forehead or on his hand, he also will drink the wine of God's wrath, poured full strength into the cup of his anger, and he will be tormented with fire and sulfur in the presence of the holy angels and in the presence of the Lamb. And the smoke of their torment goes up forever and ever, and they have no rest, day or night, these worshipers of the beast and its image, and whoever receives the mark of its name."* (Rev. 14:9–11)

We need to slow down and let this terrible picture do its work in our hearts. This dreadful description of the fate of those who die as enemies of Jesus should affect Christians. We see the ugly reality of hell and God's justice in casting men and women into its recesses. John tells us that those who drank the intoxicating wine of Babylon will drink wine prepared by God. Those who continue sipping Babylon's wine, suppressing what can be known about God (Rom. 1:18), and live and die rejecting Jesus will drink from the Lord's cup. The punishment will fit the crime.[6]

There is no such thing as a neutral disposition toward Jesus Christ. You either bow before him as Lord or you refuse his claims and so charge God with lying (1 John 5:10). The punishment will be just and without end: *"the smoke of their torment goes up forever and ever, and they have no rest, day or night"* (Rev. 14:11). There are no second chances for those who die as enemies of Christ, only *"a fearful expectation of judgment, and a fury of fire that will consume the adversaries"* (Heb. 10:27). And perhaps worst of all, will be the presence of Jesus Christ. All of these terrors and torments occur *"in the presence of the holy angels and in the presence of the Lamb"* (Rev. 14:10).

This description of hell may surprise us because its common description with preachers suggests a place where we are separated from God's presence. While Paul does describe the terror of punishment as being cast away *"from the presence of the Lord"* (2 Thess. 1:9), Paul also wrote on behalf of an omnipresent God.

The psalmist asked:

> *Where shall I go from your Spirit? Or where shall I flee from your presence? If I ascend to heaven, you are there! If I make my bed in Sheol, you are there!* (Ps. 139:7-8)[7]

No place in all of creation remains free from God's presence. God's creation includes hell, and his presence abides there, though not in mercy, patience, or offering redemption. One author writes "The damned will be in the presence of Christ forever, but that presence will be one of wrath and just indignation."[8] Once again, hell testifies to the justice of God. Those who wanted nothing to do with the mercy and the grace of God in this life will, in the next, have nothing to do with the grace and mercy of God. As Michael Horton summarizes, "Hell is not ultimately about fire, but about God... the real terror awaiting the unrepentant is God himself and his inescapable presence forever with his face turned against them."[9]

Like me, I would guess that you have people close to you who want nothing to do with Jesus. And this passage shows us the terrible things which await those who call God a liar and then must give an eternal account for themselves.

I can be tempted to look away from this scene. But I must not. And neither should you. Look long. Look hard even though a horrible picture rises to the surface. Because in the same image, we see God's love and the Gospel's peace.

The Peace of the Gospel

Where do we see the love of God here? We can sometimes talk so much about what Jesus did on the cross that we forget what he endured for his people. Think back to Jesus in the Garden of Gethsemane. Just before his arrest, Jesus entered the garden with his disciples, where sorrow, panic, and terror filled his soul. In his distress, he thought what he felt in his soul would kill him: *"My soul is sorrowful, even to death"* (Mark 14:34).

After he asked the disciples to pray for him, Mark tells us that Jesus fell on the ground and prayed (Mark 14:35). The language Mark uses suggests that Jesus repeatedly fell over and over, perhaps attempting to stand for prayer only to fall to the ground again and again.[10] What has happened?

Jesus knew all along that a cross lay before him over the horizon. And yet in the garden, the eternal Son of God became scared out of his mind. But the threat of death did not frighten him, nor the Romans who would pummel and dishonor his body. Instead, in the garden, looming just beyond the horizon, lay a terror indescribable—the wrath of his Father.

Remember his words in the garden: *"Remove this cup from me"* (Mark 14:36). John described the cup's contents as the wine of God's wrath, poured full strength by an angry God (Rev. 14:10). No wonder the body and soul of Jesus winced at the prospect of drinking this cup. In the garden, Jesus no longer simply talked about the cup. Instead, he began the awful task of drinking it down to the dregs.

Why did he do it? Why did the Father send him?

Because he loves you. Stare full into John's terrible description of what being in the presence of an angry God looks like, and you begin to see something of the *"breadth and length and height and depth"* of the love of Christ that surpasses all knowledge (Eph. 3:18–19). And that will move you to love God.

It will also move us to love others enough to warn them of what's coming and to invite them to flee to Jesus. We are called to love our neighbor as we love ourselves. We love our neighbors when we warn them about hell, though it may be awkward and, at times, uninvited. But love necessitates telling the whole truth.

Several years ago, I read an interview with a non-Christian who described love's often difficult requirements. The comments came from Penn Jillette—you probably know him as one half of the two-person magician act called Penn and Teller. Most of the talking is done by Penn, the tall guy. The shorter quiet guy, Teller, communicates through miming and nonverbals. Penn Jillette had this to say about people who share their faith, or proselytize:

> *I've always said that I don't respect people who don't proselytize. I don't respect that at all. If you believe that there's a heaven and a hell, and people could be going to hell or not getting eternal life, and you think that it's not really worth telling them this because it would make it socially awkward.... how much do you have to hate somebody to not proselytize?.... I mean, if I believed, beyond the shadow of a doubt, that a truck was coming at you, and you didn't believe that truck was bearing down on you, there is a certain point where I tackle you. And this is more important than that.*[11]

I've never been so convicted by the words of an atheist as I am by these. And it really comes down to love, doesn't it? If I know a cup of wrath awaits someone, love for them compels me to warn them and point them to Jesus Christ. For the joy set before him, the lover of my soul and yours drank the putrid cup of God's anger down to the dregs so that the wells of salvation would flow through and from him.

Unlike the cold, stone-faced Buddha statue in Sri Lanka that saved himself and not his people, the Lord Jesus Christ lost his life to give life to his. He drank a cup of poison to secure a cup of blessing for all who are thirsty. So drink again from the deep wells of salvation and then take Jesus to the thirsty people in your life.

Study Questions

1. Have you been taught that hell is a place of eternal torment separated from God's presence? How does God's presence in hell alter your understanding of this terrible destination? Read Philippians 2:10 and Revelation 14:10; how does this change your vision of eternity?
2. This dreadful description of the fate of those who die as enemies of Jesus should affect Christians. How does it affect you? How does it change you?
3. Read Mark 14: 34–36 and allow the terrible reality of being in the presence of God's wrath to settle on you. Does this stir fear or awe for the One who endured so much for you?
4. Read the comment from Penn Jilette. How does this sit with you? In what ways are you inadvertently not loving those around you by not telling them of what is to come? Pray for Christ to make you bold for him.

---

1. Gabriel Dabel, "Weary and Wary," *World Magazine*, February 5, 2005, 27.
2. There are four occurrences in Revelation similar in structure to vs. 12: *"Here is a call...."* (13:10, 18; 14:12; 17:9). In each saying, the introductory "Here" implies "Here is the appropriate response." See Dennis E. Johnson, *Triumph of the Lamb: A Commentary on Revelation* (Phillipsburg, NJ: P&RPublishing, 2001), 207.
3. See G.K. Beale, *The Book of Revelation: A Shorter Commentary* (Eerdmans, 2015), 300 for a discussion on the compulsory nature of this command.
4. J. A. Motyer, *The Message of Philippians* (Downers Grove, IL: IVP Academic, 1984), 96.
5. N.T. Wright, *Revelation for Everyone*, 128. See also 1 Pet. 5:13.
6. G.K. Beale, *The Book of Revelation: A Shorter Commentary*, 304.
7. Sheol sometimes refers simply to the grave (1 Kgs. 2:6, 9; Ps. 141:7)—in the sense that all men and women go there. At other times, it refers to the realm of the departed dead who know only despair—a place that the faithful do not go (Ps. 49: 13–15). The parallelism in Psalm 139:8 contrasting heaven with Sheol suggests the later use here.
8. Guy Prentiss Waters, *The Life and Theology of Paul* (Sanford, FL: Reformation Trust Publishing, 2017), 63.

9. Michael Horton, "Hell is Not Separation From God," Core Christianity, https://corechristianity.com/resource-library/articles/hell-is-not-separation-from-god/
10. John R. Donahue and Daniel J. Harrington, *The Gospel of Mark* (Collegeville: Liturgical, 2002), 408.
11. Recounted in Rico Tice, *Honest Evangelism* (The Good Book Company, 2015), 38.

26

JUDGMENT AND JUBILEE

REVELATION 14:14–15:4

The world of business leadership has a concept called the Stockdale Paradox.[1] The concept takes its name from Admiral Jim Stockdale, the highest-ranking officer in the "Hanoi Hilton" POW camp during the Vietnam War. For eight years, Stockdale endured torture from his captors and lived out his sentence suffering great injustice, with no prisoner's rights or set release date.

After eight terrible years, Stockdale came out of prison and wrote a book called *In Love and War*. Toward the end of his life, a journalist met with him to ask him about his time as a prisoner and how he pressed on through the most challenging days of imprisonment.

Stockdale said, "I never lost faith in the end of the story.... I never doubted not only that I would get out but also that I would prevail in the end." After a few moments, the interviewer asked about the prisoners who didn't make it. "Oh, that's easy," he said. "The optimists." Now completely confused, the journalist asked for clarification.

Stockdale explained that the optimists said: "We're going to be out by Christmas." And then Christmas would come, and Christmas would go. Then they'd say, "We're going to be out by Easter." And Easter would come, and Easter would go. And then they promised Thanksgiving, and then Christmas again, and then Easter again. Eventually, Stockdale lamented, the optimists "died of a broken heart."

Stockdale wasn't criticizing the very notion of optimism. Rather, he targeted the optimism that ignores reality and eventually leads to despair. In the world of business, the Stockdale Paradox argues that we should have confidence about the future while at the same time, we must confront the brutal facts of reality.

This principle works for the Christian life as well. But unfortunately, many live their lives with a baseless optimism about their eternal destiny. Several years ago, *The Atlantic Monthly* cited a study from the Barna Research Group showing that while 71 percent of Americans believe that some people will go to hell, just .005 percent (five one-thousandths of a percent) think they may spend eternity there.[2] While many believe in hell, few think it's a real or personal threat to them.

One man said to me, "If there is a God he'll let me into heaven. I'm a good man. I take care of my family. I've been faithful to my wife. My kids have never gone without." Many people entertain such unfounded optimism about the future, ignoring the brutal reality—they will stand before the judgment seat of God. And if they stand there apart from the safety of Jesus, they will eternally die of a broken heart.

On the other hand, the Christian looks forward to the coming judgment with confidence. John says elsewhere:

> Little children, abide in him, so that when he appears we may have confidence and not shrink back from him in shame at his coming. (1 John 2:28)

Do you have confidence as you look toward the judgment that is coming? Do you worry when you think about giving an account for your life?

In the passage before us, John sees the judgment in which everyone will participate. But then he sees another group of people who celebrate an eternal jubilee after the judgment. This vision gives confidence to those who follow Jesus while not ignoring that they, too, must stand before the judgment seat of God.

Judgment

The Gospel of Matthew records a parable Jesus told to explain what we should expect in this time before his return and what would happen when he does (Matt. 13:24–30, 36–43). The parable presents a farmer who sowed wheat seed into a field for a later harvest. But an enemy also planted weeds among the wheat seeds in the field. A house servant approached the farmer, asking if he should go into the field and destroy the weeds. The farmer objected:

> No, lest in gathering the weeds you root up the wheat along with them. Let both grow together until the harvest, and at harvest time I will tell the reapers, "Gather the weeds first and bind them in bundles to be burned, but gather the wheat into my barn." (Matt. 13:29–30)

Jesus explained the parable, identifying himself as the farmer who sowed the good seed. The field represents the world, and the good seed is the sons of the kingdom. The weeds picture the sons of the evil one, planted by the devil. And the two-fold harvest comes at the end of the age, which John observed:

> Then I looked, and behold, a white cloud, and seated on the cloud one like a son of man, with a golden crown on his head, and a sharp sickle in his hand. And another angel came out of the temple, calling with a loud voice to him who sat on the cloud, "Put in your sickle, and reap, for the hour to reap has come, for the harvest of the earth is fully ripe." So he who sat on the cloud swung his sickle across the earth, and the earth was reaped. (Rev. 14:14–16)

John sees Jesus Christ crowned and seated on a cloud.[3] John opened this book with the assurance that Jesus would come with the clouds and that every eye would see him (Rev. 1:7). As Jesus noted in his parable, the harvest at the end of the age would be two-fold: the sons of the kingdom and the sons of the devil would be gathered and separated. So far, John has seen the sons of the kingdom gathered to the Lord. The next group gathered are those who rejected the king and his kingdom:

> Then another angel came out of the temple in heaven, and he too had a sharp sickle. And another angel came out from the altar, the angel who has authority over the fire, and he called with a loud voice to the one who had the sharp sickle, "Put in your sickle and gather the clusters from the vine of the earth, for its grapes are ripe." So the angel swung his sickle across the earth and gathered the grape harvest of the earth and threw it into the great winepress of the wrath of God. And the winepress was trodden outside the city, and blood flowed from the winepress, as high as a horse's bridle, for 1,600 stadia. (Rev. 14:17–20)[4]

This scene shows the coming judgment and the full execution of God's wrath. A few details will help us see John's larger picture. First, the second harvest gathers a different group of people from the first harvest. The language John uses for the first harvest refers to grain ripened by drying, while the second harvest describes grapes ripened and full of juice.[5] Second, this imagery comes from the book of Joel, which describes the judgment coming upon sin: *"Put in the sickle, for the harvest is ripe. Go in, tread, for the winepress is full. The vats overflow, for their evil is great"* (Joel 3:13). Third, John saw the aftermath of the judgment. And the scene sobers us. Blood flowed as high as the horse's bridle for 1,600 stadia.

Blood measured to the horse's height was a Jewish idiom used to describe the destruction of an army.[6] The meaning of 1,600 stadia remains hard to nail down with certainty, though a few options exist. 1,600 is the sum of 40 squared, the traditional number of punishments. 1,600 may represent the comprehensive nature of punishment.

Alliteratively, 1,600 stadia, around 184 miles, corresponds to the length of Palestine from the northern to the southern border. John may be alluding to the Old Testament promise that while the city of God would be spared at the Lord's coming, the nations would be destroyed.[7] Regardless of what John's number refers to, we remember that we are studying an image that shouldn't be pressed to literalism. This bloody ocean covering the entirety of the land captures the awful reality of the coming judgment and destruction of those not committed to following Jesus.

Though not pictured here, John will later show us that everyone will stand before the judgment seat of Christ. John reports: *"I saw the dead, great and small, standing before the throne, and books were opened"* (Rev. 20:12). John saw an explicitly stated truth, one also found elsewhere in the New Testament. To the Corinthian Christians, Paul wrote, *"We must all appear before the judgment seat of Christ"* (2 Cor. 5:10). In Hebrews 10:30, we read, *"The Lord will judge his people."* To the young pastor Timothy, Paul said, *"I charge you in the presence of God and of Christ Jesus, who is to judge the living and the dead... preach the word"* (2 Tim. 4:1).

By what standard will everyone be judged? The standard will be the same for everyone: what has been revealed to them concerning God's will. Those who have more of God's revealed will have a greater responsibility to respond to it.[8] Those who only had the Old Testament revelation will be judged according to what they received. Those who have heard the complete revelation of God found in Jesus will be judged accordingly. Even those without the Old or New Testament have an awareness of their Creator from the created world and are responsible to respond. Paul wrote:

> For his invisible attributes, namely, his eternal power and divine nature, have been clearly perceived, ever since the creation of the world, in the things that have been made. So they are without excuse. For although they knew God, they did not honor him as God or give thanks to him, but they became futile in their thinking, and their foolish hearts were darkened (Rom. 1:20–21).

In other words, the Lord will not judge people based on what they don't know, but on what they do. And no one lacks complete knowledge of their Creator.

According to our knowledge of God, the Lord will assess our lived-out responses. So to the Corinthians, Paul wrote: *"For we must all appear before the judgment seat of Christ, so that each one may receive what is due for what he has done in the body, whether good or evil"* (2 Cor. 5:10).

Our deeds and words will be assessed:

> Nothing is covered up that will not be revealed, or hidden that will not be known. Therefore whatever you have said in the dark shall be heard in the light, and what you have whispered in private rooms shall be proclaimed on the housetops. (Luke 12:2–3)

In summary, every word, thought, and deed will come before the Judge of all the earth who gives to each what is owed.

On the one hand, the promise of judgment brings comfort to us. In a world troubled by holocausts, prisoner camps, human traffickers, corrupt politicians, and those who hurt children, there exists a profound comfort in knowing that the Lord will balance the books. Hollywood keeps making superhero movies because deep down, we long for the bad guys who get away with evil things to get the punishment for their evil. The coming judgment will satisfy the shared desire for a just and good world.

On the other hand, the brutal reality of judgment may strip us of confidence if we consider our hearts. When held up against what God requires of those who bear his image, I find I'm the bad guy in the superhero movie. I'm the villain who gets away with evil. And maybe you know this to be true of yourself. Paul tells us, *"None is righteous, no, not one... all have turned aside... no one does good, not even one"* (Rom. 3:10–12). Apart from Jesus, I've nothing to boast about in light of God's revelation to me. And yet, the Lord commands Christians to face that day confidently (1 John 2:28), because an eternal Jubilee approaches.

Jubilee

But for whom? By now, we know the answer, but notice how John wraps up this portrait of the time between the ascension and return of Jesus.[9] Remember how this section began. John saw a pregnant woman, who represents the people of God, who gave birth to a child who would rule the nations, a clear reference to Jesus Christ. A dragon also appeared on the scene and tried to kill the child, but the child was caught up to God and his throne, representing the ascension of Jesus.

The dragon then turned its attention to the woman, who ran into the wilderness to be nourished by God. The dragon tried to kill the woman with the help of two allies—a beast from the sea and another from the land. But the same child once caught up to God (Acts. 1:9–11) has returned, armed with a sickle.

With one swipe, he gathers his people to himself, and with another, he collects his enemies and crushes them in the winepress of God's wrath. Notice what has become of those gathered to Jesus. Standing seaside, they look back on the destruction of God's enemies:

> *And I saw what appeared to be a sea of glass mingled with fire—and also those who had conquered the beast and its image and the number of its name, standing beside the sea of glass with harps of God in their hands.* (Rev. 15:2)

This vision transports us from earth to heaven, where, once again, John views a sea of glass. John described the the first sea surrounding the throne of God as clear as crystal (Rev. 4:6). But now the clear sea mingles with fire, representing the judgment that has fallen upon the earth. Those who survived the judgment stand seaside with harp in hand singing of the power, justice, and sovereignty of God:

> *And they sing the song of Moses, the servant of God, and the song of the Lamb, saying, "Great and amazing are your deeds, O Lord God the Almighty! Just and true are your ways, O King of the nations! Who will not fear, O Lord, and glorify your name? For you alone are holy. All nations will come and worship you, or your righteous acts have been revealed."* (Rev. 15:3–4)

The mention of the song of Moses reminds us of the Exodus generation who sang seaside after fleeing from Pharoah and his armies (Ex. 15).

Recall a few details of that struggle. After the Passover event, where the lamb's blood spared the Jews from judgment, Pharaoh ordered them to leave (Ex. 12:31–32). And so, the Jews left Egypt and began their trek to the promised land via the wilderness (Ex. 12:37ff). After some time, the Lord told Moses that Pharaoh had changed his mind about letting Israel go and would soon bring his armies after him (Ex. 14:1–8).

Sure enough, the Egyptian army pursued Israel through the wilderness and got close enough to create panic in the Jewish ranks. But Moses commanded: *"Fear not, stand firm, and see the salvation of the LORD, which he will work for you today"* (Ex. 14:13). You know the rest of the story. Moses lifts his staff, and the waters of the sea divide, allowing Israel to pass through. And when God's people were safely on the other side, the same waters through which they had passed came back together to destroy Pharaoh and his army (Ex. 14:28).

With that struggle and deliverance in mind, we're prepared to understand the full portrait John has painted for us. Just as Pharaoh and his army pursued Israel through the wilderness, the dragon and his allies will pursue the Church during our "wilderness" period. And just as Israel passed through the same sea that consumed their enemies, the Church will also pass through the same sea of judgment that will destroy the dragon and his allies. The Exodus event includes a slain lamb, a chase through the wilderness passing through waters, and it ends with a seaside song of victory. This pictures another event. The Exodus story was a dim shadow of a more significant exodus, a more precious Lamb, and stunning deliverance of God's people through a better Moses (Heb. 3:1–6).

We can face the judgment with confidence so long as the blood of the better Passover Lamb covers us. The Lamb John described as the one *"who loves us and has freed us from our sins by his blood"* (Rev. 1:5). One of the most important aspects we must understand about the judgment to come concerns what it is not: the time to determine the eternal destination of those judged.[10]

We should not think of the judgment John describes as we think about the judgment process in our court systems. Human judges gather and investigate evidence before rendering a verdict. But the all-knowing God eternally comprehends all evidence both for and against all mankind, rendering investigation unnecessary. Additionally, the verdict upon humanity has already been handed down. Jesus informs us:

> *Whoever believes in [me] is not condemned, but whoever does not believe is*

condemned already, because he has not believed in the name of the only Son of God. (John 3:18)

Those who refuse to follow Jesus are already condemned and the *"wrath of God remains on him"* (John 3:36). So many people, even dear ones in my life, plan to stand before God's judgment and present evidence for admission to heaven. And yet, there will be no trial, no weighing of evidence, no counter-points. The world has already received the verdict upon those who refuse the Son. The judgment will seal the eternal consequences of the already-possessed verdict.

Christians also know the verdict that will be pronounced over them on that day. We already know the ruling that will be echoed as our thoughts, words, and deeds are set before the Lord: No condemnation! No condemnation! (Rom. 8:1). The loving and leading Lamb of God drowned in the sea of condemnation that you might stand seaside with the innumerable host who praise him for all eternity.

A friend of mine shared a story about one of the scariest days of his life, which involved his daughter on a family vacation. He owns a small cottage surrounded by giant oak trees tucked away in a remote section of the Ozark mountains. One of those trees leaned toward his cottage threatening damage to the home. So he hired a few local loggers to take it down. While the men worked outside, my friend instructed his children to stay inside the home. Everyone nodded in agreement, and the whole family resumed their everyday activities.

Sometime later, the family heard a terrifying scream coming from outside. A lumberjack yelled, "My, God. No!," and a tree crashed to the ground. My friend looked around the cabin to confirm the safety of all the kids and found them all, except his little girl. The family dashed outside, and what they saw forever changed them. Standing in the middle of a gigantic oak tree that had fallen on either side of her, his little girl stood smiling as though something fun had just happened.

One of the lumberjacks, with a face white as a ghost and red eyes, said, "She was in the right spot. Anywhere else, and this would've been tragic. She was in the right spot."

That's what it means to abide in Jesus today and on the coming day. The tree of God's judgment against our sin has fallen already. At the crucifixion of Jesus, God's wrath and fury descended and crushed the Savior so that, like that little girl, the falling tree of wrath would not touch us. On the day when we must all stand before the Judge, the only safe place and "right spot" will be in Jesus. And in him, we have confidence as we look forward to that day.

Study Questions

1. In what ways do you see baseless optimism regarding the future in the people around you? Have there been times that you've been guilty of the same thinking?
2. Compare the Exodus event with the seaside scene in John's vision. Discuss other Old Testament events that foreshadow New Testament developments.
3. One day, you will stand with the whole bride of Christ celebrating the power, justice, and sovereignty of God. How does this promised reality inform your life today? Your choices tomorrow? Your response to suffering?

---

1. The Stockdale Paradox is a concept developed in Jim Collins, *Good to Great* (New York, NY: HarperCollins, 2001), 83–87.
2. Cited in Raymond Cannata & Joshua Reitano, *Rooted: The Apostles' Creed*, 2nd ed. (White Blackbird Books, 2019), 109–110.
3. Some argue that this is an angel and not Jesus Christ (ex. David Aune, Leon Morris), but I find their arguments unpersuasive. Thomas Schreiner, who argues for Jesus here, suggests three important factors which should be considered. First, the title "son of man" occurs in 1:12–16 and is used for Jesus. Second, earlier in the book, Jesus is described as coming "with the clouds" (1:7), as is the figure seen here. And third, the being is seated on a cloud, and in Isaiah 19:1 (LXX), Yahweh is seated on a cloud. This points to the divine nature of the one described. See Thomas R. Schreiner, *The Joy of Hearing: A Theology of the Book of Revelation* (Wheaton, IL: Crossway, 2021), 113–114.
4. For the identification of the "city," see the chapter in this book on Revelation 11:1–14.
5. Dennis E. Johnson, *Triumph of the Lamb: A Commentary on Revelation* (Phillipsburg, NJ: P&RPublishing, 2001), 212.
6. G.K. Beale, *The Book of Revelation: A Commentary on the Greek Text* (Grand Rapids, MI: Eerdmans Publishing, 2013), 783.
7. There are many more options for mathematical arrangements leading to 1,600. For several options, see G.K. Beale, *The Book of Revelation: A Commentary on the Greek Text*, 782.
8. See Anthony A. Hoekema, *The Bible and the Future* (Grand Rapids, MI: Eerdmans Publishing, 1979), 259–260; Cornelis P. Venema, *The Promise of the Future* (Banner of Truth, 2021), 403–405.
9. Instead of abruptly ending the fourth portrait of the inter-advent period, John begins the fifth portrait in 15:1 only to break from it and return to the fourth for its conclusion in 15:2–4. We can think of section 15:1–4 as an overlap of the section which precedes it

(12:1–14:20) with that which follows (15:1–16:21). See G.K. Beale, *The Book of Revelation: A Shorter Commentary* (Eerdmans, 2015), 314–315.

10. See Anthony A. Hoekema, *The Bible and the Future*, 253–254. Another purpose of the judgment will be to reward believers, which Jesus speaks about in Matt. 25:14–30. For an excellent treatment on the complicated issues surrounding eternal rewards, see Cornelis P. Venema, *The Promise of the Future*, 405–419.

PART 5

THE SEVEN BOWLS 15:5–16:21

27

SEVEN BOWLS OUTPOURED (PART 1)
REVELATION 15:1, 5–16:7

A group of Christians in Wisconsin run a facility dedicated to serving boys and girls with Down syndrome and other developmental disabilities. This organization, called Shepherd's Ministries, provides a loving residential environment and a school that focuses on their unique residents' needs. But, most importantly, this ministry shares God's love with the boys and girls and encourages them to trust Jesus.

One afternoon, Joe Stowell, president of Cornerstone University, visited the facility to get a tour and meet with its founder and director, Bud Wood.[1] During the tour, Bud turned to Joe and said, "Hey, Joe, do you know what our biggest maintenance problem at Shepherd's is?" Joe had no idea and confessed as much. The director told him, "Dirty windows."

He explained that each day the children hear about Jesus' love for them and how he came to live and die for them. And that one day—maybe today, maybe tomorrow—Jesus would return and take them to their home, where they will be healed and complete. And so, every morning, every evening, and throughout the day, you could find children pressing their little hands and faces against the windows, looking to the sky, hoping that today is the day Jesus will come for them. Dirty windows remain the biggest maintenance problem at Shepherd's Ministries.

Every Christian ought to live with that kind of eager expectation for the return of our Lord. Each of us lives out the story we believe to be true. For some, The American Dream shapes their goals and strategies. Others, pursue the hope of living "happily ever after." The Book of Revelation portrays the incredible promise of Christ's return and the full arrival of God's kingdom. No better story exists than the one Revelation tells! And the more we rehearse these promises, the more we will joyfully anticipate his return.

With that in mind, when we turn to the seven bowls containing the wrath of God, our joyful anticipation may hit a speed bump. This challenging section of Revelation can make us uncomfortable and squirm when it's read aloud in church. While not the first nor the last time God's wrath surfaces in this book, this section stands apart from the others. Here we witness God's anger at sin poured out full strength on those who refuse to follow Jesus, leaving behind a chilling aftermath. We may be tempted to ignore such descriptions or explain them away. But however challenging the following descriptions may be, this vision inspires us to worship the Lord and anticipate Christ's second coming.

To that end, the seven bowls demonstrate how God's wrath will prepare a place for his people, will be perfectly just, and it will move us to praise him on the day John described.

Prepares a Place

First, remember that we've arrived at another transition point in this book. In the previous chapter, we noted that John overlaps the fourth and fifth portraits of the period between the ascension and return of Jesus. In Rev. 15:1, John introduced seven angels who will be given seven golden bowls containing the wrath of God (Rev. 15:7).

But then he broke away from those seven angels to focus our attention on an innumerable host of people standing seaside praising God for their safe deliverance from evil. In Rev. 15:5, our attention again shifts to the seven angels with seven golden bowls. But before we see the angels or the bowls, John tells us where the angels came from:

> *After this I looked, and the sanctuary of the tent of witness in heaven was opened, and out of the sanctuary came the seven angels with the seven plagues, clothed in pure, bright linen, with golden sashes around their chests.*

> *And one of the four living creatures gave to the seven angels seven golden bowls full of the wrath of God who lives forever and ever, and the sanctuary was filled with smoke from the glory of God and from his power, and no one could enter the sanctuary until the seven plagues of the seven angels were finished.* (Rev. 15:5–8)

It's essential to note that the angels come from the tent of witness or tabernacle, the place of God's unique presence among his people. So, it is the Lord who sends the bowl-carrying angels to carry out all that follows. But they're sent out in response to something—his people's prayers. Remember, we've already encountered these golden bowls. Back in Chapter 5, John stood in the throne room of God, and among the things he described were golden bowls *"full of incense, which are the prayers of the saints"* (Rev. 5:8). Remember also that under an altar, John saw the murdered saints who ask the Lord how long before he would judge the world (Rev. 6:8). The Lord commanded them to be patient.

Meanwhile, the Church continues to pray, filling up the golden bowls with incense. Every time you pray, *"Your kingdom come, your will be done, on earth as it is in heaven,"* and *"Come, Lord Jesus, come!"* incense mounts higher and higher in the bowls. The Lord never loses or forgets a single prayer, each one goes into the bowls. But the day will come when the last prayer ascends, the final Gospel invitation proclaimed, and the last of God's people gathered in (Rev. 6:11). And then the bowls, filled to the brim with incense, will be given to the angels to pour out upon the earth.

Through this action, a place will be prepared for God's people. John saw that the sanctuary could not be entered *"until the seven plagues of the seven angels were finished"* (Rev. 15:8).[2] Once emptied, these bowls will accomplish one of the great promises of the Holy Scriptures: God's dwelling place will be with his people (Lev. 26:21; Ezek. 37:27; Rev. 21:3).

Later in this book, with the arrival of the new heaven and the new earth, a voice will cry out, *"Behold, the dwelling place of God is with man"* (Rev. 21:3). John uses the same word for "dwelling place" in 21:3 as he does for "tent" in 15:5. Before the emptying of the bowls, no one can enter the tent of God's special presence. But after the bowls cleanse the earth from top to bottom, it becomes the arena where God dwells with his people.

You can see how this would have encouraged John's original audience. Like you and me, they were exhausted from living in a world tainted by evil, cruelty, corrupt governments, human trafficking, cancers, and irreparable relationships. And supreme among all frustrations is the separation we now experience from our Lord. The emptying of the bowls points to God's determination to cleanse the cosmos through and through so we will never be separated from him again.

Although the images associated with the bowls are horrible, the angels interrupt the narrative to affirm God's perfect justice in sending them.

Perfect Justice

As we look at the bowls themselves, we are ushered forward to the very end of the age. These seven bowls represent the fullness of God's wrath against sin, rebellion, and decay.[3] Like the first four trumpets, the first four bowls affect the same spheres of creation in the same sequence: earth, sea, rivers and streams, and the sky. But unlike the trumpets, which were limited to destroying only one-third of each sphere, the bowls bring about complete destruction. These bowls, then, signal the end of the present world.

A highly unpleasant description accompanies the first outpoured bowl:

> *Then I heard a loud voice from the temple telling the seven angels, "Go and pour out on the earth the seven bowls of the wrath of God." So the first angel went and poured out his bowl on the earth, and harmful and painful sores came upon the people who bore the mark of the beast and worshiped its image.* (Rev. 16:1–2)

Once again, just as we heard echoes of the Egyptian plagues in the seven trumpets, this bowl echoes the sixth plague upon Egypt that caused terrible sores to fall upon the people and animals (Ex. 9:9–10). John tells us the sores fell upon those whose bodies were branded with the mark of the beast on their right hand or forehead (see Rev. 13:16).

Recall that the mark of the beast symbolized the minds and deeds of those who live according to the thinking and behavior of the world. The punishment will fit the crime: those marked out as followers of the beast will be marked by the Lord with physical anguish.[4]

Now the second and third angels pour out their bowls into the sea and the rivers:

> *The second angel poured out his bowl into the sea, and it became like the blood of a corpse, and every living thing died that was in the sea. The third angel poured out his bowl into the rivers and the springs of water, and they became blood.* (Rev. 16:3–4)

Turning the sea and freshwater into blood echoes the first plague in

Egypt when the Nile's water was changed to blood and killed all the fish (Ex. 7:21). These bowls point to the removal of everything necessary to sustain life. In John's day, the sea was "Rome's worldwide web of trade and transportation."[5] So if everything in the sea is dead, this bowl signals total economic bankruptcy and worldwide famine.

The third bowl, which turns freshwater into blood, marks the last possibility of life continuing when God's wrath comes upon the earth. Even the life-giving waterways have been rendered lethal. These punishments seem severe and ferocious. Does the penalty for refusing to turn to Jesus fit the crime? Is this fair? Perhaps John's first audience had the same questions regarding the appropriateness of God's judgments. The sequences of outpoured bowls breaks with an angel addressing the appropriateness of God's actions:

> And I heard the angel in charge of the waters say, "Just are you, O Holy One, who is and who was, for you brought these judgments. For they have shed the blood of saints and prophets, and you have given them blood to drink. It is what they deserve!" (Rev. 16:5–6)

God's wrath should not be likened to the sinful wrath of men and women. Instead, as John Stott explains, God's wrath "is absolutely pure and uncontaminated by those elements which render human anger sinful."[6] Instead, Stott adds, "The wrath of God... is his steady, unrelenting, unremitting, uncompromising antagonism to evil in all its forms and manifestations."[7]

We may find ourselves startled at the full exercise of God's wrath because we are so accustomed to his ordinary course of action toward humanity: patience and long-suffering. Paul tells us that the Lord withholds his wrath to lead people to repent (Rom. 2:4–5). And because we are only familiar with the Lord's patience and long-suffering, we not only think we deserve it, but we also find ourselves surprised when these things are removed. The Bible does describe the Lord's patience and long-suffering, giving opportunities for repentance. But the Lord also reveals a limitation on these dispositions toward those who refuse his son. As a result, a terrible, steady opposition to evil builds, which God will one day unleash, consuming his adversaries with a fury of fire (Heb. 10:27).

Donald Grey Barnhouse once likened the patience and wrath of God to the Hoover Dam. He recounts his first experience seeing the Hoover Dam and being impressed by its ability to hold back miles and miles of the

Colorado River. As he looked at the dam, he thought about God's patience. He said:

> The first time there ever was a sin committed, the wrath of God was stored up against that sin. As more men lived upon the earth, and as their hearts grew more wicked... the store of wrath grew greater and greater, held back by the patience of God, which lies across the valley of his judgment like a dam across the river.[8]

Now and then, he continues, God has stooped down "to dip his hand into the pent-up flood" to pour a few drops of wrath upon some especially vicious rebellion. But a day will come—which John saw in these bowls—when the patience of God will have run its course, the dam will be removed, and a deluge of perfect justice and unimaginable terror will be unleashed upon this world and those who are enemies of Christ.

God's perfect justice will be terrible news for some but exhilarating for others. If you, by faith, cling to Jesus, God has joined you to one who stood before the dam of God's patience. While Jesus hung on a cross with outstretched arms, a deluge of furious, watery wrath drowned him. As I study these bowls representing God's just and holy judgments, at the end of the day my question is not, "How can I reconcile the ferocity of these things with what I know about God?" Instead, a nearly indescribable mystery fills my mind: Why did Jesus suffer these bowls for me? The answer, of course, points to his love for me. His love for you. Before the flood of God's wrath took the life of our Savior, he cried out in agony, *"My God, my God, why have you forsaken me?"* (Matt. 27:46) so that those same words would never find a place on our lips.

These bowls will prepare a place for God's people. They'll magnify the holy justice of God. And once outpoured, will move us to praise him.

Praise to the Lord

The angels aren't the only ones to speak up as the bowls of God's wrath fall upon the world. John also heard a voice coming from the altar: *"And I heard the altar saying, "Yes, Lord God the Almighty, true and just are your judgments!"* (Rev. 16:7)

Remember, the martyrs cried out to God for justice from under the altar (Rev. 6:10). They asked the Lord "how long" before he would make things right. The Lord gave them white robes, representing their coming vindication. He told them to rest a little longer until the total number of God's people were safely home. But now, with the pouring out of the bowls, the period of waiting has come to an end. God is making all things right. In response, John hears the people of God, each and every one gathered safely to the Lord, praising the Lord that this day has come. If you're a Christian, these words will be yours on that dreadful day of terror: *"Yes, Lord God the Almighty, true and just are your judgments"* (Rev. 16:7)!

As I consider that coming day, I can think of many reasons I'll be prompted to praise God. All of the evil things done throughout history that have gone unpunished and unresolved will finally be fully addressed. But at the same time, many things come to mind that make the thought of praising God on this day difficult, if not impossible. I have people very close and dear to me that want nothing to do with Jesus. And Revelation describes terrible things that await those who refuse him. My heart breaks even as I write these words. How will I praise God on that day when I know of loved ones who have already passed away rejecting God's offer of pardon?

I remember R.C. Sproul telling a story from his days as a seminary student in which he struggled to reconcile his grief over lost loved ones with the promise of heavenly bliss.[9] He said one of his fellow students asked the professor, "If I go to heaven and find that my mother's not there but that she's in hell, how can I possibly be happy in heaven?"

The professor looked at the student and said, "Young man, don't you know that when you get to heaven you'll be so purified from sin, so sanctified by the Holy Spirit, that you'll be much more concerned about the glory of God than you will be about the well-being of your mother?" Dr. Sproul said there was an audible gasp from the students in the class. No one could believe what the professors said. But as the years went by, he recognized the accuracy of the professor's point. Each and every one of us sins. At present, we have far more in common with fellow sinners than with God in his perfection and holiness. As a result, our concerns now favor those like us.

But when we finally stand healed in Jesus' presence, we will be changed. Our interests and our comforts now dominate our concerns. But then, on that day when we sing from the altar, we'll be so in love with the Lord and the glory and vindication of Christ we'll be able to rejoice even in these bowls. Our chief concern on that day will be the glory of God, not our comfort.

I am not there yet, and I suspect you may still struggle here as well. But God promises us that he will wipe every tear from our eyes when we see him (Rev. 21:4). And what God wipes away will never return.

Christian, stay the course. Set your eyes on Jesus, who has ascended into the clouds, and from there, will come again to set things right (Acts 1:11).

If you have never come to Jesus for rescue, fall before him and receive his mercy. He will welcome you with joy, pardon all your sins, and drink these bowls down for you. To your tired soul, he says, *"Come to me, all who labor and are heavy laden, and I will give you rest"* (Matt. 11:28).

Study Questions

1. "Each of us lives out the story we believe to be true." Consider this statement. What story shapes your hopes, dreams, and goals? If a stranger looked at your life, what story would they suggest you believe is true?
2. God's wrath is never uncontrolled rage that causes him to act out of accord with his moral perfection. Because all we've known of the Lord is patience and long-suffering, we tend to believe we deserve these things. Admit your honest response to these descriptions of God's wrath. Do you flinch? Object? Cry out that it isn't fair? Are you comforted by it? Ask the Lord to align your response to his word.
3. Consider the indescribable mystery the author sets before us: Jesus suffered these bowls for us. How does your heart respond to this? How should it shape your life?
4. How do you reconcile grief over loved ones who want nothing to do with Jesus with the promise of your heavenly bliss? Spend some time with the Lord confessing your struggle to make full sense of these things, and ask for the peace that surpasses all understanding.

---

1. See https://www.youtube.com/watch?v=s5gj9nBq26I
2. Dennis Johnson notes, "the unapproachability of the cloud of God's glory not only conveys his utter holiness but also draws our attention to the terminus of his creatures' exile from his holy presence." See Dennis E. Johnson, *Triumph of the Lamb: A Commentary on Revelation* (Phillipsburg, NJ: P&R Publishing, 2001), 218.
3. Three reasons suggest these bowls occur at the end of history. First, we're told that *"the wrath of God is finished"* after the bowls are emptied (Rev. 15:1). Second, there is a correspondence between the first four trumpets and the first four bowls in terms of the sphere of influence and sequence: earth, sea, rivers and springs, and sky. But while the trumpet devastation is limited to one-third of each sphere, the bowls' destruction is total. Third, earlier in Revelation, God is identified as the one *"who is and who was and who is to come"* (Rev. 1:4, 8). But after the third bowl is poured out, the future orientation (*"who is to come"*) is dropped. This omission suggests that the Holy One has now come.

4. See G.K. Beale, *The Book of Revelation: A Shorter Commentary* (Eerdmans, 2015), 330.
5. Dennis E. Johnson, *Triumph of the Lamb: A Commentary on Revelation* (Phillipsburg, NJ: P&R Publishing, 2001), 226.
6. John R. W. Stott, *The Cross of Christ* (Downers Grove, IL: InterVarsity Press, 1986), 105–106.
7. Ibid, 173. See also Richard D. Phillips, *Revelation* (Phillipsburg, NJ: P&R Publishing, 2017), 445, who cites Stott and many others along these lines.
8. Donald Grey Barnhouse, *Man's Ruin* (repr.; Grand Rapids, MI: Eerdmans, 1991), 1:227–228.
9. This story is recounted in R. C. Sproul, *Luke: An Expositional Commentary* (Orlando, FL: Reformation Trust, 2020), 372–373.

28

SEVEN BOWLS OUTPOURED (PART 2)
REVELATION 16:8–21

What do you do when you get discouraged in your faith? Maybe you've been praying for someone to turn to Jesus, but it doesn't look like that will happen. Perhaps you've prayed and labored to heal a fractured relationship, but nothing seems to help. Maybe you feel unused by the Lord. Perhaps you look back on your life with loads of regret wishing you could have done things differently. So what do you do when you find yourself in these situations?

You know the name of John Bunyan, author of *Pilgrim's Progress*. You may also be aware that he knew what it felt like to fall into these times of deep discouragement, frustration, and doubt.

But he also knew the solution. He wrote the answer into his best-known book. In one scene, Christian, the main character, travels to the Celestial City when he loses his concentration and falls into a swampy area called the Slough of Despond, or what we might call the Swamp of Despair.

Christian tried over and over to free himself from the swamp, but the more he worked, the more he sank. But then someone named Help comes along and asks Christian if he can free himself from the slough. Christian responds that he cannot.

The helper tells Christian there are solid stones, like steps, which have been placed throughout the swamp so pilgrims who fall in can make their way out. Then Help reaches out his hand to Christian; Christian grabs it, sets his foot on a stone, and he stands up from the slough.

The Slough of Despond pictures those times when Christians fall under deep conviction of sin and feel themselves sinking in discouragement. You may know the feeling of the swamp of pessimism. Your affection or zeal for Jesus isn't what it used to be, and you can't get it back. Your public witness for Christ has gone from courageous to cowardly, and you don't know what to do. Perhaps you've fallen back into an old sin you thought was forever done away with, and you wonder what hope you have. From time to time, we all fall into a swamp of discouragement.

But in Bunyan's story, Christian placed his weight on solid stones, and he got out. The stones represented the promises of God and were set there by the Lord himself.

There are stones of promise in these last four bowls that can uphold the weight of anyone seeking the Lord Jesus. And we're commanded to step on them today. The two stones of promise are the mercy and might of the Lord. Stand on these promises, and your foot will never slip.

The Mercy of the Lord

As we return to the bowls, remember these events will happen at the end of history. Bowl one, which poured out painful sores upon those who bore the mark of the beast, represented the physical torment that will fall upon those who refuse to turn to Jesus. The second bowl, turning the sea into blood and killing all sea life, pointed to complete economic devastation and worldwide famine conditions. The third bowl, turning all freshwater into blood, rendered life-giving waters lethal. Those bowls represent the helpless estate of anyone who refuses to turn to the Lord.

Turning to bowls four and five, any optimism one might have of surviving the judgment of God apart from Christ ebbs away:

> *The fourth angel poured out his bowl on the sun, and it was allowed to scorch people with fire. They were scorched by the fierce heat, and they cursed the name of God who had power over these plagues. They did not repent and give him glory. The fifth angel poured out his bowl on the throne of the beast, and its kingdom was plunged into darkness. People gnawed their tongues in anguish and cursed the God of heaven for their pain and sores. They did not repent of their deeds.* (Rev. 16:8–11)

The fourth bowl poured out upon the sun that scorches people with fire comes from several Old Testament passages that describe the coming judgment accompanied by fire. One example from Ezekiel threatens:

> *I shall gather you and blow on you with the fire of my wrath, and you will be melted in the midst of it.... and you will know that I, the Lord, have poured my wrath on you.* (Ezek. 22:21–22. See also Jer. 7:20)

Intended to give life and light, the sun turns into an instrument to burn and destroy.

The fifth bowl, which causes darkness to descend upon the beast's kingdom, also pictures judgment. You'll recall that the beast represents the Satanically-inspired, man-centered kingdoms of this world that deny Christ and persecute his people. For now, the beast has been given the authority it uses to do terrible things. But John sees the day when God's wrath will neuter the beast of any power and control, plunging it into darkness. And there in the dark, those condemned gnaw away at their tongues. This is a picture of hell, described elsewhere by Jesus as a place of outer darkness and gnashing of teeth (Matt. 22:13; 25:30).[1]

Notice the response of those inflicted by these terrible judgments. After bowls four and five, we're told these terrible judgments will not move people to turn to the Lord. Instead, they double down and curse the name of God. We might have expected that upon seeing the God they so long suppressed in their hearts, they would turn to him and cry out for mercy. Or something along the lines of "Now I know you exist! I want to serve you."

But we see something else here. We witness hearts digging in their heels and acknowledging God, only to curse him. There are at least two reasons for their response. The first comes from the lips of Jesus:

> *And this is the judgment: the light has come into the world, and people loved the darkness rather than the light because their works were evil. For everyone who does wicked things hates the light and does not come to the light, lest his works should be exposed.* (John 3:19–20)

It's not a lack of knowledge that leads people to refuse the summons to follow the Lord. Jesus tells us there's an inner hostility toward the Lord, which explains the refusal. That hostility has no room for anyone telling them how to live or think. In their natural state, people hate being told who they must forgive and who they must love. Those who love darkness prefer to decide how to use their body and whom they may or may not marry. Jesus tells us that by nature, people love darkness.[2]

We also don't read of repentance on this day because the mercy of God has been withdrawn. When anyone turns away from sin and to the Lord, the origin of the new behavior traces back to God's mercy working through his Spirit (2 Tim. 2:25). No one repents on this coming day because God's mercy toward the rebellious, the fuel for repentance, has expired.

If you have not turned to Jesus, you have cause right now to praise the Lord. The mercy-absent day John describes has yet to come. So with outstretched arms, today Jesus mercifully still summons us, *"Come to me, all who labor and are heavy laden, and I will give you rest"* (Matt. 11:28). But if you've never come to Jesus, I must also warn you. If you resist the Lord saying, "Maybe I'll turn to God later," you may be in danger. God's mercy-filled heart grants repentance as a gracious gift, and therefore he's not obligated to offer mercy on your timetable. God owes us swift justice, not mercy. So today, don't harden your heart if you hear his voice calling you to turn to him.

There's also encouragement for those who have turned their hearts to Jesus. The mercy of God is a stone of promise for us to stand on as well. We might think this doesn't need stating, but sometimes we entertain strange caricatures of the Lord regarding his mercy. We think he's happy to show us mercy to forgive our sins and put us in a relationship with him, but once there, he becomes tight-fisted with his kindness. We begin to reason: "It was one thing to sin against the Lord when I was an unsaved enemy, but it's another thing to sin as an adopted child. I knew better than to have run to that sin. I have the Holy Spirit in me!"

And we begin to think that God's ways are like our ways and his thoughts like ours. We will forgive people once or twice, but it becomes too much for us at some point. Relationships have limits and established boundaries; restoring the relationship can be difficult if not impossible when those boundaries are broken. That's how human relationships function.

And when we assume that God's actions mirror our own, it keeps us from going to him when we sin. John Calvin captures this truth by writing: "There is nothing that troubles our consciences more than when we think that God is like ourselves." The consequence of projecting human-like limitations upon God's mercy, Calvin continues, creates people who "do not venture to approach to him and flee from him as an enemy, and are never at rest."[3]

But God tells you to stand on this stone of promise today—I am not like you. My ways are not your ways. Remember what the Lord told Moses when Moses effectively asked him: What are you like? What is your glory? What makes you tick? The Lord answered by proclaiming his name, saying, *"The LORD, the LORD, a God merciful and gracious, slow to anger, and abounding in steadfast love and faithfulness"* (Ex. 34:6). That speaks to his activity of showing mercy and, coupled with what Micah wrote, reveals his eagerness to show mercy:

> *Who is a God like you, pardoning iniquity and passing over transgression for the remnant of his inheritance? He does not retain his anger forever because he delights in steadfast love.* (Mic. 7:8)

Slow to anger.
Abounding in mercy.
Delights to forgive.

And none of this is because he makes little of our sin—looking at these terrible bowls of judgment dispels that idea. Instead, he delights in showing mercy because it magnifies his Son. His anger moves at a glacial pace. On the other hand, his mercy strikes like lightning. He delights in his Son. And he delights in those who make much of him. In God's mercy, we have a strong stone of promise by which to regain our footing. The promise of God's might will encourage the Church as we come to the sixth bowl.

The Might of the Lord

The promise of God's might will encourage the Church as we come to the sixth. This bowl shows terrible things ahead for the Church of Jesus Christ. But in the seventh bowl, the power and might of the Lord deliver the church.

Before we look at the text itself, it's helpful to recognize an Old Testament background against which we should see John's description. There are numerous Old Testament passages that foretell a conflict at the end of history, in which God gathers the nations against Israel for a final confrontation. In Zechariah, for example, the Lord says, *"I will gather all the nations against Jerusalem to battle"* (Zech. 14:2; See also Zeph. 3:8–20; Ezek. 38:2–9). In that same book, we read: *"All the nations of the earth will gather against [Jerusalem]"* (Zech. 12:3).

The Jews anticipated an actual war that would end all wars and occur at the end of the age. We must note that this is not a war of nation against nation. Instead, the war foretold in the Scriptures describes nations gathering against the Lord's people.[4] John describes this end-of-the-age conflict in the sixth bowl:[5]

> *The sixth angel poured out his bowl on the great river Euphrates, and its water was dried up, to prepare the way for the kings from the east. And I saw,*

coming out of the mouth of the dragon and out of the mouth of the beast and out of the mouth of the false prophet, three unclean spirits like frogs. For they are demonic spirits, performing signs, who go abroad to the kings of the whole world, to assemble them for battle on the great day of God the Almighty. (Rev. 16:12–14)

We'll come back to the drying of the Euphrates shortly. But for now, notice the kings of the whole world described in such a way as to echo the foretold promises of a final, worldwide conflict against the Lord's people. They gather together, having been persuaded by the false trinity—the dragon, the beast, and the false prophet—that eliminating God's people will lead to a better world.

John introduced this conflict and the world's answer to the problem of Christians in Chapter 11. There, John saw the two witnesses, who represent the church, who testified to the power of the Gospel and called the world to repent. But after the two witnesses finished their testimony, the beast that rises from the bottomless pit made war on the two witnesses and killed them. The sixth bowl presents the same conflict, but from another angle and with different details.

In addition to a well-known conflict that was coming, the Old Testament also records a famous place called Megiddo, where many battles occurred in the Bible. One of the most notable confrontations in the book of Judges, between Barak and Sisera, occurred in Megiddo (Judg. 5:19) as did the battle between the righteous King Josiah and Pharaoh Neco (2 Kgs. 23:29). By John's time, Megiddo had become proverbial for the place where evil nations attacked righteous Israelites.[6] In the same way that locations of conflict in the United States, like the Alamo or Bull Run, later took on symbolic value, and so did Megiddo in the Jewish mind. This explains why John places this end-time conflict in Megiddo: *"And they assembled them at the place that in Hebrew is called Armageddon"* (Rev. 16:16).

Behind the English word "armageddon" two Hebrew words combine to form Mount of Megiddo. In a literal sense, no mention of any mountain in Megiddo can be found in the Old Testament or anywhere in Jewish literature. This suggests that the location of the end-time battle uses the symbolic value Megiddo held in the Jewish mind versus an attempt to pinpoint an exact geographical location.[7]

One more background detail, and then we'll try to put all these pieces together. In addition to a well-known war at the end and a famous place of battle, in the Jewish mind, no greater enemy existed than Babylon. John has already introduced Babylon, and in the seventh bowl, it surfaces again. But, as we've noted, the Persians destroyed the city of Babylon centuries before John's day. And when Babylon fell, the Lord promised that it would never be rebuilt (Jer. 50:39–40; 51:24–6; Isa. 13:19–22). And yet in the Jewish mind, Babylon lived on as the supreme symbol of wickedness, idolatry, cruelty, and oppressor of God's people.

The record of Babylon's literal destruction may be alluded to in John's description. Surrounding the ancient city were brick walls soaring forty feet high and spacious enough to accommodate racing chariots on top. Through the city's center ran the river Euphrates, supplying water and protection from outside enemies. Many assumed the city would remain impenetrable from outside forces.

But in 539 BC, Cyrus the Persian approached Babylon and laid siege against the city. Unable to get through the thick brick walls, he diverted the waters of the Euphrates into a nearby marsh. This tactic dried up the river bed, enabling his men to enter the city and bring it to an end.[8]

Let's put these pieces together so a bigger picture emerges. A decisive conflict comes at the end of the age when the world has had enough of God's people and decides to destroy them. Three entities will work together: the dragon, the beast, and the false prophet.

The dragon represents Satan, who will inspire the world's nations to gather against the church. Nothing in John's description suggests a conflict including tanks, planes, or other items of traditional warfare. Remember, Armageddon describes a conflict not between nations, but the nations against Christ's church. Instead of conventional war, this conflict may start with a worldwide body of politicians who gather and create legislation to silence and penalize those who follow Jesus. Or, in the words of John, those who lack the mark of the beast will be targeted (Rev. 13:15–17).

What will trigger the beginning of this end-time conflict? Perhaps the world will fatigue with the church's testimony of a coming judgment, the need for repentance, a refusal to bow down to some governmental edict regarding the definition of marriage, or gender issues. I can only speculate here. But behind the war, a dragon released for a short time to do his worst will be instrumental (Rev. 20:3).

Assisting in the march to war will be the false prophet or those who promote the silencing of the church. Help may come from the media, the university classroom, local city councils, and sadly, even within the church. People will lobby for compromise with the beastly legislation. Like in the plains of Megiddo, the world will gather against the church. And, for a time, they will succeed.

Returning to the two witnesses who represented the Church in

Chapter 11, the world killed them. We know that this false trinity will succeed in silencing the Church. John observed the world celebrating the death of the two witnesses and even exchanging gifts because they were no longer tormented by the message of sin, judgment, and repentance coming from the two witnesses (Rev. 11:7–10).

The death of the two witnesses presents us with a sober truth reinforced by the vision of Armageddon: the church's path to glory must first go through a cross. Just as our Lord embraced a cross before he was crowned in heaven, the Church has a cross-shaped future that precedes its glory.

If we didn't know the end of the story, our stomachs might get twisted in knots here. But we do see the end of the story. Imagine sitting in a movie theater watching a film when the story turns for the worse, and you become quite upset. Imagine that a friend who has already seen the movie leans over and says, "Don't worry. I've seen this movie. Everything turns out great." Jesus is that friend who has seen the end of the movie and leans into our midst today to encourage us:

> *Behold, I am coming like a thief! Blessed is the one who stays awake, keeping his garments on, that he may not go about naked and be seen exposed!* (Rev. 16:15)

Like that friend in the theater, Jesus leans in to assure of his coming. So, don't be afraid. Don't silence your witness. And don't try to blend in to avoid being hated for him. Like a thief, he will come upon a world that thinks it will triumph over his church. But they are not safe:

> *The sixth angel poured out his bowl on the great river Euphrates, and its water was dried up, to prepare the way for the kings from the east.* (Rev. 16:12)

Remember, the actual city of Babylon looked to the Euphrates to keep it safe. But when Cyrus drained the river, the city fell. In the same way, God will remove everything that protects and nourishes the spiritual city of Babylon. They think they gather to put an end to the Church, but in reality, the Lord will gather them for destruction. The Lord will manifest his power in the seventh bowl:

> *The seventh angel poured out his bowl into the air, and a loud voice came out of the temple, from the throne, saying, "It is done!" And there were flashes of lightning, rumblings, peals of thunder, and a great earthquake such*

as there had never been since man was on the earth, so great was that earthquake. The great city was split into three parts, and the cities of the nations fell, and God remembered Babylon the great, to make her drain the cup of the wine of the fury of his wrath. And every island fled away, and no mountains were to be found. And great hailstones, about one hundred pounds each, fell from heaven on people; and they cursed God for the plague of the hail, because the plague was so severe. (Rev. 16:17–21)

The seventh bowl is the end of the movie. Those who hate and malign the Church cannot win. And those who love the Lord Jesus cannot lose.

Just as the crucifixion looked like a victory for evil, we know that the victory was short-lived. Three days later, God's power raised Jesus from the dead, triumphant over sin, death, and hell.

So too, the Church will suffer. On the horizon, a cross waits for the church. But the victory of evil will be short-lived. God will come in power to destroy the destroyers and at the same time give his people their longed-for inheritance.

Therefore, be bold. Be courageous for Jesus. Don't compromise! Don't adopt a victim mentality, nor retreat to lick your wounds. Christian, we're on the winning side. Don't retreat from the fight. Set your feet afresh on the solid stone of God's mercy, with the full assurance that he will deliver you in his might.

Study Questions

1. Consider what stones of promise the Lord has given to stabilize your footing and bring you out of the slough of despair. Are there other promises you've found helpful, not mentioned in this chapter? Take some time to write them down; it can be helpful to keep a box, bowl, envelope, or some other means of storage of the Lord's promises to you to be recalled as often as needed.
2. Mercy is a stone of promise for the people of God to stand upon. In what ways is the Lord's mercy different than ours? What dangers occur when we think God is like us?
3. As the terror of these bowls and the wrath and justice they carry is poured out, with the seemingly defeated witnesses, you may be tempted to despair—what a hopeless picture we see before us. But, take heart! Bowl 7 shows us the end of the story.

In what ways is this a comfort to you, Christian? How does Bowl 7 encourage you?

4. The might of God that raised Jesus from the dead is at work in Bowl 7. Jesus shows us that he sees the end of this story, and we are promised that we are on the winning side. Pray for courage and strength as you stand firm on the stones of God's mercy and might.

---

1. There is also a probable allusion to the Egyptian plague of darkness (Ex. 10:21–23).
2. The fifth bowl of darkness is another example of the punishment fitting the crime: for those who love darkness, darkness is their eternal reward.
3. John Calvin, *Commentary on the Prophet Isaiah*, vol. 4, trans. William Pringle (repr., Grand Rapids, MI: Baker, 2003), 169.
4. Vern S. Poythress, *The Returning King: A Guide to the Book of Revelation* (P&R, 2000), 157.
5. This conflict is the same one already portrayed in 11:7–11 and appears again in 19:19–21; 20:8–10.
6. G.K. Beale, *The Book of Revelation: A Shorter Commentary* (Eerdmans, 2015), 346.
7. See Ibid. 346–347 for other challenges to a literal read of Megiddo.
8. The Lord threatened Babylon's downfall, including drying up the Euphrates. See Isa. 11:15; 44:27, 50:2; 51:10.

PART 6

THE FALL OF BABYLON 17:1–19:21

29

BEAUTY? AND THE BEAST

REVELATION 17:1-18

The well-known English journalist Malcolm Muggeridge spent much of his life as an agnostic but later converted to Christianity. Throughout his life, he kept detailed diaries recording events surrounding his journalism career.

One story tells of a time when Malcolm made a terrible decision that resulted in receiving a profound gift. While covering a story in India, Malcolm left his residence to swim in a nearby river. As he approached the water, he noticed a woman in the river bathing. She looked attractive, and thinking that she was probably a prostitute, he entered the water with the intent of giving her business. But as he swam toward the woman, thoughts of another woman filled his mind.

Malcolm was married and had never been unfaithful to his wife. But he reasoned that no one would ever know about this encounter. So he decided to go for it and swam and swam, trying to out-swim his conscience while at the same time entertaining how satisfying this encounter would be.

But the meeting was anything but pleasurable. As he drew near the woman, who turned around to greet her visitor, what he saw made his heart drop. The woman was not a prostitute but a leper. Weeping sores, peeling scabs, and white and yellow blotches covered her face. Additionally, the disease had consumed the flesh and cartilage of what had once been a nose, leaving behind only two small nostrils.

As Malcolm tried to process the scene before him, the woman grinned at him, revealing a toothless smile. Now in shock and disgust, he initially characterized the woman as a vile creature. But upon further reflection, his contempt centered upon himself and not upon the poor woman. His own heart was foul.[1]

Muggeridge received a gift that day. That encounter pictured the emptiness and folly of trying to fill the Christ-shaped void in our hearts with the pleasures of this world. The Lord created us for the glory and enjoyment of Jesus Christ. But as we often sing together, our hearts are "prone to wander, Lord I feel it. Prone to leave the God I love."[2]

The Lord Jesus gives us a gift in the vision before us to bring us back from wandering. The image shows us the folly and danger of running to the world's offer of comfort, identity, value, and safety. But it also shows us the incomparable worth of what we have in Jesus.

Two characters dominate this chapter's vision—a beast and a prostitute. While we've already encountered the beast, the prostitute is new, though she has the familiar name of Babylon. These characters are enemies of the Church and wield their powers to lure Christians away from faithfulness to Jesus. The prostitute promises joy through seduction, while the beast promises safety through the threat of violence. Joy and safety: two things everyone wants. This vision exposes the world's temporary and superficial joy and safety as counterfeits of the joy and safety offered by Jesus.

Before we look at these two characters, we should note how Chapter 17 relates to the seven bowls we studied. Recall that Bowl 6 showed us the dragon, beast, and false prophet working together at the end of history to make war on the Church in a place called Armageddon. But once assembled, an angel poured out the seventh bowl, ushering in the final judgment that destroys Babylon's city.

As we come to chapters 17:1–19:21, again, we find Babylon, the dragon, beast, and the false prophet engaged in an end-of-the-age conflict with the Lord and his church. So, it's best to understand the following few chapters as another portrait of the time between the ascension and return of Jesus. But instead of covering the whole time period, this portrait focuses on the final conflict already alluded to in this book.

Returning to our chapter, we noted that two characters use their skills to allure us away from trusting the Lord. John begins with the seductive prostitute who lures her victims with counterfeit joys.

Counterfeit Joy

John witnessed the destruction of Babylon with the seventh bowl. Now, the angel who held the bowl comes to John and essentially says, "Let me show you in more detail what Babylon is like and how the Lord will destroy her":

> Then one of the seven angels who had the seven bowls came and said to me, "Come, I will show you the judgment of the great prostitute who is seated on many waters, with whom the kings of the earth have committed sexual immorality, and with the wine of whose sexual immorality the dwellers on earth have become drunk." And he carried me away in the Spirit into a wilderness, and I saw a woman sitting on a scarlet beast that was full of blasphemous names, and it had seven heads and ten horns. The woman was arrayed in purple and scarlet, and adorned with gold and jewels and pearls, holding in her hand a golden cup full of abominations and the impurities of her sexual immorality. And on her forehead was written a name of mystery: "Babylon the great, mother of prostitutes and of earth's abominations." (Rev. 17:1–5)

In our study, we've already encountered the city of Babylon as the preeminent symbol of wickedness, cruelty, and oppression. Babylon stands for the world in rebellion against God. Men and women, institutions, and governments who don't give honor and glory to God but seek those things for themselves constitute Babylon. John describes Babylon as a city and a prostitute, which we'll later see compared and contrasted with another city and another woman.

As a city, John observed Babylon seated on many waters in verse 1: *"Come, I will show you the judgment of the great prostitute who is seated on many waters."* Then in verse 15, we're told these waters represent peoples of every country, in every time period, who live in hostility toward the Lord: *"And the angel said to me, 'The waters that you saw, where the prostitute is seated, are peoples and multitudes and nations and languages."* (Rev. 17:15). The city also has power over innumerable people: *"And the woman that you saw is the great city that has dominion over the kings of the earth."* (Rev. 17:18)

As soon as John takes in the image of Babylon as a city, the Spirit transports him to the wilderness, where he contemplates Babylon as a seductive prostitute:

> *And he carried me away in the Spirit into a wilderness, and I saw a woman sitting on a scarlet beast that was full of blasphemous names, and it had seven heads and ten horns. The woman was arrayed in purple and scarlet, and adorned with gold and jewels and pearls, holding in her hand a golden cup full of abominations and the impurities of her sexual immorality. And on her forehead was written a name of mystery: "Babylon the great, mother of prostitutes and of earth's abominations." And I saw the woman, drunk with the blood of the saints, the blood of the martyrs of Jesus. When I saw her, I marveled greatly.* (Rev. 17:3–6)

John describes Babylon as a woman of outward beauty who allures men and women away from fidelity to the Lord with offerings of the world's fleeting pleasures. Consider how this image of worldliness, pictured as a seductive prostitute, would have impacted John's first audience. Remember from our study of the seven churches how the early Christians tried to navigate living out their faith in a hostile environment. For example, those regarded as good citizens of the Roman Empire honored the emperor with the titles of lord and god. But, of course, Christians couldn't do that.

They also couldn't attend pagan feasts that honored local deities. Faithfulness to Jesus had economic consequences for some in John's first audience. If they didn't go along with the crowds, they could no longer buy or sell in the marketplace (Rev. 13:17). For others, faithfulness meant losing freedom, reputation, and networking opportunities.

And you'll recall, false teachers came along teaching a way of compromise. "It's just incense," we can imagine them saying, "God knows what's in your heart. And it's okay to call Caesar 'lord.' It's just words. Don't you want to keep your job?" I'm sure you can appreciate how tempting such teachings may have been to the little churches living under the watchful eye of Rome.

But John saw what was behind the compromising proposals: a seductive prostitute offering quick pleasures. Consider just a few of the momentary pleasures she offers. We all want to be accepted. No one of sound mind wants to be hated, mocked, or reviled in this world. The prostitute says, "Drop the Jesus stuff, and I'll love you." That's the offer of joy in acceptance.

She also offers immediate satisfaction in comfort, wealth, luxury, and ease. She's dressed head to toe in the finest clothing. Purple and scarlet were both colors of royalty in the first century.[3] The finest gold, jewels, and pearls covered her clothing. She stands for the comfort, ease, reputation, and economic well-being that come at the expense of faithfulness to Jesus.

To be clear, she often offers good things. But they come on her terms, "Come to me," she invites us, "but leave behind talk about sin, judgment, redemption, the wrath of God, slain lambs, and holy living." And like Christ, she too holds out a cup saying, "Take. Drink." But her cup does not hold the blood of one who loves us, but, in John's words, her cup contains "abominations and the impurities of her sexual immorality" and the blood of God's people (Rev. 17:4, 6). Even if this image of a prostitute is new to us, the allure of her offers is not. I know the inner appeal of keeping my faith silent around people hostile toward Jesus. Acceptance brings joy, and the prostitute says, "You can have it right now!" I also know the appeal of changing the subject when someone asks me about hot-button issues like abortion, homosexuality, and gender issues.

I like comfortable conversation like anyone else, and the prostitute says, "Change the subject." Many Christians know a public faith can harm their business, income, and networking opportunities. The prostitute says, "You gotta make money while you can. Living for Jesus will hurt the bottom line."

You know the voice of the prostitute as well. We all have areas where the Lord calls us to surrender to him, but it involves taking up a cross. And when we grimace under the imagined weight of trusting the Lord, the prostitute offers a quick fix with counterfeit joy.

How can we solve this? Determining to abstain from seeking joy, comfort, and acceptance will not work. The Lord created us for these things and never forbids us to seek them. Instead, he commands that we find them in the right place. Remember, John describes Babylon as a city and a prostitute offering joy. John's visions show us that the lasting joy, comfort, and acceptance that we're created for can only be found in a particular city and with a particular woman. Later in John's vision, an angel holding the seven bowls invites John to see a different woman: *"Come, I will show you the Bride, the wife of the Lamb"* (Rev. 21:9).

With this invitation, we would be forgiven if we expected John to view and describe the Bride, the wife of the Lamb with a number of expected human female attributes. Instead, John beholds and describes not a human, but a city: *"the holy city Jerusalem, coming down out of heaven from God"* (Rev. 21:10). Just as John pictures the world in rebellion with two metaphors—a city and a prostitute—those who comprise the people of God are likewise pictured as a woman and a city.

We'll look in more detail at that vision later, but let's appreciate John's description of the Bride of Jesus, his city. Like the prostitute, precious stones, pearls, and gold adorn Jesus' bride (Rev. 21:18–21). Like the prostitute, the bride of Jesus wears glorious attire. And, like the prostitute, who has a name on her forehead associating her with immorality and abominations, the bride of Jesus also has a name on her forehead associating her with God himself (Rev. 17:5; 22:4). Bearing God's name on her forehead, the bride possesses eternal safety, mutual belonging, and perfect acceptance.

But that's not just a picture of the future; it represents our present reality. The same love, acceptance, belonging, and security pictured on that day we possess already through our union with Jesus. Jesus calls us to live now in light of what we already have. Therefore, let the beauty, grace, and love of Jesus for you fill your mind so that the offers of the prostitute will not compare. In Jesus, we find the joy in acceptance our hearts long for and the eternal safety that the beast, who re-enters the scene, counterfeits through threats of violence.

Counterfeit Safety

We've already encountered this beast numerous times. First mentioned in Chapter 11, the beast received the power to slay the two witnesses representing the Church (Rev. 11:7–8). In Chapter 13, John saw the same beast rise out of the sea bearing crowns on ten horns, with seven heads covered with blasphemous names (Rev. 13:1). Then again, in the sixth bowl, this same beast, along with the dragon and false prophet, make war upon the Church at the place called Armageddon (Rev. 16:13).

The image of a beast coming out of the sea comes from the book of Daniel. Recall that Daniel saw four beasts coming out of the sea, which the Lord later explained represented four man-centered kingdoms that resist the reign of God and persecute his people (Dan. 7:1–28). But the beast of John's vision (Rev. 13:1–2) blended Daniel's four oppressive kingdoms into one (i.e., the beast has a leopard's head, bear's feet, and the mouth of a lion). As noted in an early chapter, this merging of Daniel's four beasts into one suggests that the beast of John's vision represents not just the Roman Empire of his day but all the oppressive, man-centered empires throughout history. That same beast of previous chapters returns in the present vision, but this time it has a jockey:

> *And he carried me away in the Spirit into a wilderness, and I saw a woman sitting on a scarlet beast that was full of blasphemous names, and it had seven heads and ten horns.* (Rev. 17:3)

While this may be a strange image at first glance, our studies together help us to understand its essential meaning. The beast-riding prostitute gives the reader an unforgettable image of how Satan uses the seductive appeal of worldliness (the prostitute) in tandem with the threat of violence (the beast) to woo the Church into compromise. And when John sees these two terrible forces working together, he marvels. Perhaps the sight bewildered and frightened the disciple.

Just then, an angel speaks to encourage and explain to John what he saw:

> When I saw her, I marveled greatly. But the angel said to me, "Why do you marvel? I will tell you the mystery of the woman, and of the beast with seven heads and ten horns that carries her. The beast that you saw was, and is not, and is about to rise from the bottomless pit and go to destruction. And the dwellers on earth whose names have not been written in the book of life from the foundation of the world will marvel to see the beast, because it was and is not and is to come. (Rev. 17:6–8)

The angel explains that the beast, representing a man-centered, oppressive empire, will soon rise from the bottomless pit. Remember, John has already described this story in Chapter 11. There, a beast that "rises from the bottomless pit" killed the two witnesses representing the Church (Rev. 11:7). According to that vision, toward the end of history, Satan will use the instrument of the state to punish and silence the church. The same plot line played out in the sixth bowl, which, when poured out upon the earth, revealed the dragon, the beast, and the false prophet waging war against Christ's people at Armageddon (Rev. 16:12–16). In our chapter, John describes the same future conflict from a fresh angle.

I wish this fresh insight were clear and easy to understand, but it's far from either. Verses 9-11 are typically acknowledged as the most difficult in Revelation to understand, and when we read them, we understand why:

> This calls for a mind with wisdom: the seven heads are seven mountains on which the woman is seated; they are also seven kings, five of whom have fallen, one is, the other has not yet come, and when he does come he must remain only a little while. As for the beast that was and is not, it is an eighth but it belongs to the seven, and it goes to destruction. (Rev. 17:9–11)

What will we make of these seven heads, which picture seven mountains and seven kings? Do these seven kings represent Roman emperors? Some have argued that when John recorded this vision, five emperors had fallen, one remained during John's life, and another emperor would come. This approach comes with many problems. Others suggest the seven kings represent seven world empires. For example, if you count back to Egypt, the first oppressor of God's people, then add Assyria, Babylon, Persia, and Greece, you come to five. Rome would be the sixth, with another final empire to come. But this approach also contains difficulties.[4]

The simple and more consistent approach treats this number seven as a symbol. "Seven" or "seventh" occurs forty-five times outside this passage, and it always has a figurative expression meaning fullness or completion.[5] So seven kings point to the totality of anti-Christian governments throughout history. John sees that five heads have died, the sixth is alive, but one worse has not yet come. John puts in picture form what he writes elsewhere: *"Children, it is the last hour, and as you have heard that antichrist is coming, so now many antichrists have come. Therefore we know that it is the last hour"* (1 John 2:18; see also 1 Cor. 10:11, 2 Thess. 2:3–7). This vision communicates that the beast's days are limited. Five out of seven have already fallen. And while John would say that he lived at the end of the age, he also understood that history would climax with evil's desperate stand against the Lord and his church.

If that wasn't enough to make us scratch our heads, verse 11 presents another puzzle to solve: *"As for the beast that was and is not, it is an eighth but it belongs to the seven, and it goes to destruction"* (Rev. 17:11). Grammaticality, this verse makes our heads spin! John seems to be saying that within the last conflict to come with the seventh head, there will be such an embodiment of satanic power working in the state that this oppressor will be unlike any before.[6] The eighth king probably refers to the antichrist John writes about elsewhere (1 John 2:18, 22; 4:3; 2 John, 7), and the "the man of lawlessness" of Paul's letter (2 Thess. 2:3,8) who will champion the cause of ridding the world of Jesus's people.

The final embodiment of evil will enlist help:

> *And the ten horns that you saw are ten kings who have not yet received royal power, but they are to receive authority as kings for one hour, together with the beast. These are of one mind, and they hand over their power and authority to the beast.* (Rev. 17:12–13)

Ten is another number used in this book to symbolize completion or totality.[7] Horns in the Bible represent strength. The ten horns represent an unprecedented level of oppression and persecution of the Church coming for the church. As we've seen previously, a cross stands on the horizon for the Church of Jesus.

But this must not drive us to fear. And not because I think these events remain far off in the future. I don't know when this will happen. But I do know that those who study religious persecution tell us that more Christians were killed for their faith in the twentieth century than combined in the previous nineteen centuries.[8]

I also know that I have witnessed a seismic shift of attitude toward Christians in my life as a disciple. Not long ago, Christians could share their faith publicly without much social consequence. Not everyone believed what Christianity taught, of course. But until recently, those who rejected Christianity concluded that Christians were strange, a little kooky perhaps, and pitiful people who embrace fairy tails.

But I believe that has changed. As our culture addresses critical issues that it regards as non-negotiable—such as sexual identity, abortion, and gay marriage—the pushback against Christians has become more aggressive. If you are out of line with the latest societal non-negotiable, you are considered not simply foolish but a bigot—a person of hatred.

In my twenty years of ministry, I have witnessed a shift in our culture's patience for the church. The societal cost my children will have to pay for living publicly for Jesus may be much greater than I've had to pay. I must prepare them for this, and you must also prepare your children and grandchildren.

But at the same time, we don't move them to fear. On the contrary, we point them to the proper place of safety: the Lamb of God:

> *They will make war on the Lamb, and the Lamb will conquer them, for he is Lord of lords and King of kings, and those with him are called and chosen and faithful."* (Rev. 17:14)

At the end of history, Jesus wins, and so do those sheltered in him. A cross waits for the church, but so does a resurrection. Until then, God honors the Bride by commanding her to walk the same path to glory as her crucified and risen Savior.

Not long ago, I read about an encounter between Tertullian, one of the early church fathers, and a congregant listening to one of his sermons. Tertullian lived at a time when some Christians made a living working in explicitly pagan trades. For example, Christian painters and sculptors were sometimes employed to beautify pagan temples with their skills. Tertullian taught that Christians ought to have nothing to do with such things.

One man challenged Tertullian, saying, "You don't understand. I have to make compromises here and there. After all, I must live!" Tertullian responded with a question: "Must you?"[9]

Tertullian taught that the Christian has only one "must"—he must be faithful to Jesus and follow him, come what may, wherever he leads. Turn from the seduction of the prostitute and the threats of the beast. Lean into Jesus' care. He alone offers us lasting joys and eternal safety.

Study Questions

1. "There is joy in acceptance." Have you ever compromised your faithful witness for fear of losing the approval of your peers?
2. How does the Lord tell us to fight the allure of the prostitute? In what ways does our present description as the bride and a city inform how we live today?
3. Can you think of times when the tandem working of the beast and the prostitute was evident in church history? Do you feel "the state" working to silence the Church in your own life?
4. In what ways has our culture shifted regarding its feelings and thoughts toward Christians? How do we prepare ourselves, our kids, and our grandkids, for the potentially great cost of following Christ?

---

1. This story is recounted in Ian Hunter, *Malcolm Muggeridge: A Life* (Toronto: Totem, 1981), 40.
2. Robert Robinson, "Come Thou Fount of Every Blessing" (1758).
3. William Hendriksen, *More than Conquerors* (Baker Books, 1998), 169. Yet the scarlet also points to her alliance with the red dragon (12:3), whose color points to the shedding of the martyr's blood.
4. For an examination of the problems associated with a historical approach to the seven kings, see Dennis E. Johnson, *Triumph of the Lamb: A Commentary on Revelation* (Phillipsburg, NJ: P&R Publishing, 2001), 248–250.
5. See G.K. Beale, *The Book of Revelation: A Shorter Commentary* (Eerdmans, 2015), 366–367. See also Dennis E. Johnson, 250–251, for a symbolic approach toward a solution.
6. G.K. Beale, *The Book of Revelation: A Shorter Commentary*, 370.
7. Ibid., 246.
8. https://www.christianity.com/church/church-history/timeline/1901-2000/modern-persecution-11630665.html
9. James Montgomery Boice, *Seven Churches, Four Horsemen, One Lord: Lessons from the Apocalypse* (Philipsburg, NJ: P & R Publishing, 2020), 111.

30

COME OUT, MY PEOPLE

REVELATION 18

You are probably familiar with the legendary Greek king and hero Odysseus. One tale recounts a method he used to fight temptation. While sailing home from the Trojan Wars, Odysseus travels past an island filled with dangerous creatures called sirens. The sirens were known for singing beautiful songs from their island home to ships that passed by. The sirens sang to allure vessels close to the island where, just under the water's surface, jagged rocks would rip open the bottom of the ship, and the sirens would destroy all on board.

The Greeks believed no one could hear the sirens' song and turn away. Odysseus devised a plan involving putting beeswax in the ears of his crew so they could not hear the sirens, but he wore none. He wanted to listen to the siren song and believed he could resist. But as a precaution, he was tied to the ship's mast so he could not jump overboard, and he forbade the crew from untying him no matter how much he protested.

You know how the story goes: they sail past the island, Odysseus hears the sirens' song, becomes convinced that they are not dangerous, and demands to be untied. But his crew followed orders and didn't untie him until they were out of earshot of the sirens. In the end, Odysseus made a wise decision. His grit and determination to resist were no match for the seductive appeal of the sirens.

A less familiar story of mythology centers around a man named Orpheus, a skilled musician, who also had to sail past the same siren-filled island. The accounts differ because when Orpheus heard the sirens' song, he drew out a lyre and played his own music. He and the crew regarded the melody coming from his instrument as far more beautiful and appealing than anything the sirens could offer.

As I think of those two stories and the different methods for dealing with temptation, I hear echoes of what we know about ourselves. Sometimes, like Odysseus, with resolve and determination, we turn away from things we know are dangerous to our souls. But often, we give in because some joy is better than none. But Jesus doesn't simply tell us to turn away from sin, he, like Orpheus, sings a better and more alluring song, with the familiar lyric, "Come to me." Only he can satisfy the joy God designed our hearts for.

In the previous chapter, an angel told John that he would show him the judgment of Babylon, portrayed as a beautiful prostitute and representing human societies in rebellion against the Lord. In Chapter 18, the overthrow of Babylon is detailed. Amid the vision, a voice will cry, *"Come out of her, my people, lest you take part in her sins"* (Rev. 18:4). But that call to leave Babylon is also an invitation to come to a better city and to serve a better spouse.

Better City

We'll appreciate what this chapter pictures for us if we first return to the very beginning of the Bible, where God set the goal of creation: to magnify his glory. The Lord's command to Adam and Eve was to *"Be fruitful and multiply and fill the earth and subdue it"* (Gen. 1:28). Imagine hearing that command as Adam and Eve: "Fill the earth."

They likely understood that the Garden in Eden was not intended to remain in a static situation. Instead, the goal of the Creator is to fill the earth through Adam's offspring, who, reflecting the image of God, would cover the entire world.[1] We both know that Adam failed. The earth descended into chaos. The Lord sent a flood sparing only Noah and his kin. But when Noah and his family left the ark, the original creation plan was restated: *"Be fruitful and multiply and fill the earth"* (Gen. 9:1). This shows us that the goal remains to fill the earth with God's glory.

Not long after Noah received this renewed command, a group of his descendants defied the order to fill the earth for the glory of God. Assembling in a city, they built a tower that they thought would reach the heavens to bring glory to themselves and prevent dispersion across the earth. We know this building as the Tower of Babel. We also know that the Lord came down, confused everyone's languages, and forced them to disperse.

Many people left the area; some stayed behind. Those who remained built an empire known as Babylon. Over time, the city grew in wealth and prosperity, and one of its kings described the city as Babylon the Great, constructed for the glory of man (Dan. 4:30). That city became a symbol of human society in rebellion against the Lord. As a symbol, Babylon represents any entity, government, people group, or worldview that rejects the Lord and seeks glory for itself.

In this chapter, we glimpse the futility of man's plan to center himself in the universe, seeking his glory. An angel announces that spiritual Babylon is doomed:

> *After this I saw another angel coming down from heaven, having great authority, and the earth was made bright with his glory. And he called out with a mighty voice, "Fallen, fallen is Babylon the great! She has become a dwelling place for demons, a haunt for every unclean spirit, a haunt for every unclean bird, a haunt for every unclean and detestable beast."* (Rev. 18:1–2)

Babylon, the seductive and beautiful prostitute stripped of her prosperity, gross materialism, and a man-centered, Christ-denying pursuit of its own glory, is revealed for what it truly is: a dwelling place for foul, dark spirits. The same foul aim of Satan, who seeks to wrestle God from his throne for his own glory, fills the hearts of Babylon's citizens.

If you live outside of obedient trust in Jesus, you are a citizen of Babylon. If your goal in life is to strive to do all you can for your name, comfort, family, some social cause, or a political party, you do so against the will of your Creator. The Lord created you to seek and reflect his glory. Building our lives around ourselves makes us like those who tried to build a tower to reach high up to heaven. In a probable allusion to that same tower project aimed for the heavens, the angel tells us the only thing citizens of Babylon have heaped up to heaven is their rebellion: *"For her sins are heaped high as heaven, and God has remembered her iniquities"* (Rev. 18:5).

When citizens of spiritual Babylon are brought to account for their rebellion, the man-centered experiment will be over in a moment:

> *For this reason her plagues will come in a single day, death and mourning and famine, and she will be burned up with fire; for mighty is the Lord God who has judged her.* (Rev. 18:8)[2]

When Babylon the prostitute falls, her clients will grieve. But their grief doesn't include pity for her. Instead, they only mourn the loss of her services. The kings of the earth are the first to mourn —those who derived power from her:

> *And the kings of the earth, who committed sexual immorality and lived in luxury with her, will weep and wail over her when they see the smoke of her burning. They will stand far off, in fear of her torment, and say, "Alas! Alas! You great city, you mighty city, Babylon! For in a single hour your judgment has come."* (Rev. 18:9–10)

Those who found their significance in having power and authority over others will lose it all. Human authority is a gift from God to establish and maintain order (Rom. 13:1). But authority becomes tyranny when used for selfish, self-glorifying purposes instead of bringing honor to God and good to those governed. And the Lord promises to topple every tyrant.

A second group, the merchants of the earth who built their lives around luxurious living, will also lose it all:

> *And the merchants of the earth weep and mourn for her, since no one buys their cargo anymore, cargo of gold, silver, jewels, pearls, fine linen, purple cloth, silk, scarlet cloth, all kinds of scented wood, all kinds of articles of ivory, all kinds of articles of costly wood, bronze, iron and marble.* (Rev. 18:11–12)

Nothing is inherently evil about gold, silver, and precious jewels. In fact, the first mention of gold and precious stones in the Bible comes in the description of the land of Eden (Gen. 2:12). Also, these same precious materials describe the New Jerusalem (Rev. 21:11–21). The problem is turning good gifts from God, given to bless others and honor the Lord, into instruments of self-indulgence and self-glory. As we resume the list of things the merchants grieve, we find at the end what they are willing to sacrifice to get what they want:

> *... cinnamon, spice, incense, myrrh, frankincense, wine, oil, fine flour, wheat, cattle, and sheep, horses and chariots, and slaves, that is, human souls.* (Rev. 18:11–13)

Tragically, even human souls find a spot in the list of commodities the merchants use and abuse for their own glory. When you worship the things of luxury, they become an idol. And "when you worship idols, the idols demand sacrifices."[3] Rome prospered in part due to its horrific use of free human labor. Still today, some men and women enjoy a high standard of living made possible by the countless souls laboring in sweatshops and human trafficking. In the words of our Lord, many people labor day in and day out to gain the whole world but forfeit their own souls (Mark 8:36). And those who gave everything for the things of this world will, in the end, lose it all.

John hears one more group of people grieving. This time it's the sea merchants who sought their significance and security in the accumulation of wealth:

> *And all shipmasters and seafaring men, sailors and all whose trade is on the sea, stood far off and cried out as they saw the smoke of her burning, "What city was like the great city?" And they threw dust on their heads as they wept and mourned, crying out, "Alas, alas, for the great city where all who had ships at sea grew rich by her wealth! For in a single hour she has been laid waste.* (Rev. 18:17–19)

Those heard crying aloud over Babylon's fall are those who built their lives around accumulating wealth. Wealth and the pursuit of it shaped their hopes and identities and gave them a sense of security and value. When the shipmasters rose each morning from bed, they didn't labor for heaven's treasures but those which moth and rust destroy (Matt. 6:19–20).

The angel then acts out[4] the moment when the Lord seizes all power, luxury, and wealth from the hands of those who sought it so desperately and lost it all in a moment:

> *Then a mighty angel took up a stone like a great millstone and threw it into the sea, saying, "So will Babylon the great city be thrown down with violence, and will be found no more; and the sound of harpists and musicians, of flute players and trumpeters, will be heard in you no more, and a craftsman of any craft will be found in you no more, and the sound of the mill will be heard in you no more, and the light of a lamp will shine in you*

> *no more, and the voice of bridegroom and bride will be heard in you no more, for your merchants were the great ones of the earth, and all nations were deceived by your sorcery. And in her was found the blood of prophets and of saints, and of all who have been slain on earth."* (Rev. 18:21–24)

As I read these words, I see a millstone descending to the bottom of the sea, and as it makes its journey to the bottom, an angel announces all that Babylon loses. Like six hammer strikes, we hear that the city of man is no more. Music is no more. Creativity is no more. Industry is no more. Light is no more. Relationships are no more.

And don't miss the contrast between the "no mores" of Babylon and those of the New Jerusalem, where there are no more tears, no more death, no more mourning, crying, or pain.[5] Above all, no more separation from the one who loves us and spilled his blood to bring us into a better kingdom.

Jesus calls us with a voice from heaven saying, *"Come out of her, my people, lest you take part in her sins, lest you share in her plagues"* (Rev. 18:4).

This exile from Babylon is not a matter of changing zip codes. Some within the early church took passages like this literally and moved out of the cities into desert areas to live in caves. They thought they were leaving Babylon behind when, in truth, Babylon went with them. Babylon is in the heart of us all.

But we also don't leave Babylon once by walking an aisle or saying the "sinner's prayer." The call to leave Babylon comes daily. Your Savior calls you out of the city of man every day because you are now a citizen of the kingdom Jesus brought into the world at his first advent and will bring it to its fullness at his second. Until that time, Christians live as exiles, not at home in Babylon. We await another city founded on better ethics. Therefore, we turn from the values of Babylon. What does that look like?

Consider how the kings of Babylon used their power and authority contrasted with our Lord. Babylon's kings used their authority to secure personal comfort and safety. How did the Lord Jesus use his power and authority? Remember his words:

> *For this reason the Father loves me, because I lay down my life that I may take it up again. No one takes it from me, but I lay it down of my own accord. I have authority to lay it down, and I have authority to take it up again. This charge I have received from my Father."* (John 10:17–18)

The source of all power and authority used both to bring glory to God and good to others.

Each of us has been given a measure of authority: Some have authority in the church, others in the workplace, some in government, and every parent has authority in the home. Leaving Babylon means leaving behind the way the world uses authority—for itself—and exercising it for God's glory and the good of others. You belong to a better kingdom.

Think also of the merchants and seafarers who mourn the loss of luxuries and wealth. What does it look like for us to come out of Babylon concerning luxuries and wealth? Again, we don't want to follow those in the early church who left all their possessions behind and lived a life of extreme asceticism, thinking that was the only way to serve God. We serve a God who gives us gifts to enjoy, share with others, and to magnify his glory.

As people belonging to a better kingdom, think about the one who founded it. We serve a God who gave us the world. And he gave a garden to Adam. And to Adam, he gave a wife. And when they sinned, he gave them the promise of a Redeemer. Surely, the Lord gave all these things with a cheerful heart. And while the New Testament does not prescribe a percentage of one's wealth to give away, it does address the attitude of the giver. Like the One in whose image we are made, cheerfulness should fill the Christian's heart when they give, not reluctance or compulsion (2 Cor. 9:7).

Ten percent may be too much for a young family, while the same percentage may be far too low for a bachelor. I'm convicted on this matter because, as a young bachelor, I thought the first ten percent was the Lord's and the rest was all mine. But none of it was "all mine." It belongs to the Lord. I'm simply a steward of his resources.

We gather now in the name of the One who came to give his life for you and me. Meditate on this. I find it impossible to look at the face of Jesus and say to him, "You get only this much, the rest is mine." Instead, looking at the face of Jesus moves us to give generously and with cheerfulness, which thrills the heart of God (2 Cor. 9:6–7). For he, too, is a cheerful giver. So much so that he gave us his Son, who is a better spouse than Babylon.

Better Spouse

We'll be brief on this point as it becomes far more explicit in the next chapter. But even the description of Babylon as a prostitute and describing the pursuit of wealth, power, and luxury as sexual immorality points us to

Christ. Did that strike you as odd to describe those who run after money, power, and luxury as being guilty of sexual immorality?

It's odd only if we don't know the kind of relationship God desires of us and for us. There are many ways in which the Lord relates to his people. Sometimes he does so as our Creator. At other times, as our King or our Shepherd. But perhaps most moving of all is when he calls himself our Husband. Think of those words from Isaiah: *"Fear not... for your Maker is your husband... the LORD has called you like a wife deserted and grieved in spirit"* (Isa. 54:4–5). Elsewhere, the Lord says, *"As the bridegroom rejoices over the bride, so shall your God rejoice over you"* (Isa. 62:5).

Does it move your spirit to hear that the Lord wants that kind of relationship with you? Of all human relationships, none are more intimate, comprehensive, or sacred than marriage. And from the opening pages of the Bible, the Lord communicates that he desires that kind of relationship with his people. Consider how the Bible begins with the first Adam, wed to his bride in a garden, in the immediate presence of God. That first marriage was a dim picture of the marriage God, from eternity past, planned for the second Adam and his Bride, celebrated in the garden to come. Human marriage gives us the clearest picture of the relationship God desires for and with his people.

When we see the marriage relationship forming the backdrop for how the Lord relates to his people, the description of sin as sexual immorality makes perfect sense. Turning away from the Lord, our Husband, and seeking the pleasures of Babylon constitutes not merely breaking a rule, but running to a counterfeit lover. And nothing makes me want to flee Babylon more than hearing the alluring song of my Savior, who says, "I am the Lord your God. A mighty one who will save you! I will rejoice over you with gladness and quiet you with my love. Over you, I will exalt with loud singing."[6] Can you, by faith, hear his voice? *"Come out of her, my people!"* And can you see in Jesus a better spouse than Babylon?

Did you notice how those who mourn the death of the prostitute stand far off from her (vv. 10, 15, 17)? Afraid of getting consumed themselves, they stand at a distance as Lady Babylon dies. What a contrast to Jesus, who saw our suffering and the torment to come and, in his first advent, said, "I go for my wife, and I'll pay anything to save her." At his second advent, he will say to her, *"Rejoice and exult... for the marriage of the Lamb has come!"* (Rev. 19:7). Until then, he sings to us, *"Surely, I am coming soon"* (Rev. 22:20). And the Spirit and Bride say, *"Amen. Come, Lord Jesus!"* (Rev. 22:17, 20).

Study Questions

1. How do you deal with and fight temptation? Do you tend toward resolve and determination, muscling your way toward avoiding what you know is dangerous to your soul? How is the call of Christ different?
2. The Lord and Babylon seek to fill the earth with their glory. How do you see Babylon working and striving today in the world? In what ways do you see Babylon in your own heart?
3. When Babylon the prostitute falls, her clients grieve, not for her, but for losing what she gives them. Where do you see yourself in the three groups outlined here? Do you resonate with the kings who seek significance in having power and authority over others? Or the merchants who build your lives around luxurious living and earthly comfort? Or the sea merchants, who seek their worth and security in accumulating wealth?
4. Consider the "no mores" contrasted above. Does this reorient your energy and thoughts from temporary joys to eternal pleasures?
5. Jesus tells you, "Behold, I'm coming for my wife, and I will pay anything for her." How does this gentle tenderness of the One who loves and bled for you change your heart and mind? How will you respond to him today?

---

1. See G.K. Beale, *The Temple and the Church's Mission* (InterVarsity Press, 2004), 81–121 for more on this theme.
2. This may allude to the punishment of burning with fire prescribed for women of priests found practicing prostitution. See Lev. 21:9.
3. N.T. Wright, *Revelation for Everyone* (Louisville, IL: Westminster John Knox Press, 2011), 164.
4. This event echoes an event from the book of Jeremiah (51:63). There, Jeremiah ordered his servant to tie a book containing judgments against Babylon to a stone and to throw it into the Euphrates, symbolizing the city's coming destruction.
5. I owe this excellent insight to Nancy Guthrie. See Nancy Guthrie, *Blessed: Experiencing the Promise of the Book of Revelation* (Wheaton, IL: Crossway, 2022), 198.
6. Lightly adapted language from Zeph. 3:17.

31

THE MARRIAGE SUPPER OF THE LAMB

REVELATION 19:1–10

A friend recently took his two girls to a theme park in Orlando. At this particular attraction, they have a section called Old Town that recreates historic architecture, automobiles, and even characters dressed in outfits from the early twentieth century. All these things combine to make visitors feel like they've been transported back in time.

As my friend and his daughters took in the sights and sounds of the 1920s, a limousine rolled up, and a young woman dressed as a flapper girl from the Roaring Twenties emerged. She wore a sequin-covered dress, her hair was bobbed short, and her neck hosted several pearl necklaces. Heavy layers of cosmetics covered her face. But the most prominent feature of her outfit was a dramatic ostrich-feather boa worn around her shoulders.

Impressed with how accurate this flapper woman appeared, my friend looked down at his two girls to gauge their response, which was different from what he expected. Both of the girls struggled not to laugh at the woman. "What are you laughing at?" he asked them.

"She looks funny, Daddy. Look at that old car! And she has silly feathers on her shoulders. And she's wearing so much makeup." My friend then tried to explain that this woman would have been the envy of all her friends back in the day.

But the girls didn't care. She still appeared goofy in their eyes. Then, within a few moments, he noticed something else. Far above the streets of Old Town, an airplane was skywriting with smoke a simple sentence: "Smile. Jesus loves you." Directing the girl's attention to the message, they both smiled, and one said, "Jesus loves me."

My friend later reflected that the events of that day illustrated a profound message. Like the flapper girl, many give their lives to pursue the things of this world, believing they will find lasting joy, value, identity, and meaning in them. People labor long and hard to look a certain way, have a certain level of wealth, or find acceptance with a particular group.

In the end, those things which seem so important at the moment are later laughed at by children. But if we set our minds on the things above (Col. 3:2), like the skywriter with the simple but enduring truth that Jesus loves you, we find that for which our hearts long.

One of the purposes of the Book of Revelation is to help us see the present world for what it is and to set before us the world to come. Many of those who begin with Jesus do not endure to the end because they've set their hearts on this world. As Jesus warned in the parable of the sower (Mark 4:1–20), some begin with Jesus, only to abandon him when trials or persecution come. Others start with Jesus but get distracted in the pursuit of wealth and comfort.

The Book of Revelation reveals the folly of leaving or being diverted away from Jesus for the stuff or the approval of the world. Because, as John tells us in another place, *"the world is passing away along with its desires"* (1 John 2:17) which he witnessed with the fall of Babylon in the last chapter. But the Lord promises another world, upon which we are to set our minds. The vision before us fixes our attention upon a future wedding and the appropriate response of those in attendance.

The Coming Wedding

In the previous chapter, John described the downfall of Babylon, a symbol of the world in rebellion against God and intoxicated with the pursuit of pleasures and possessions. Babylon was portrayed as a prostitute laboring to allure the people of God to her fleeting pleasures at the expense of faithfulness to Jesus. With her demise, three categories of people mourned her absence. The kings of the earth lamented their loss of power. The land merchants wept for the lack of luxury she provided. And the sea merchants, who built their lives around wealth accumulation, also grieved. Those who derived their meaning, value, and joy in the things of the earth grieved that the end had come. But among the mourners, another voice says, *"Rejoice over her, O heaven, and you saints and apostles and prophets, for God has given judgment for you against her!"* (Rev. 18:20).

Turning to Chapter 19, those called to rejoice at the fall of Babylon do so:

> *After this I heard what seemed to be the loud voice of a great multitude in heaven, crying out, "Hallelujah! Salvation and glory and power belong to our God, for his judgments are true and just; for he has judged the great prostitute who corrupted the earth with her immorality, and has avenged on her the blood of his servants."* (Rev. 19:1–2)

Those spared from God's wrath sing over the prostitute's destruction.[1] The choir consists of an innumerable host of people from all tribes, tongues, and nations brought together into one voice and personified under one description: they are the Bride of the Lamb (Rev. 19:7). In contrast to the unholy, temporary beauty of the prostitute, an eternally glorious woman enters the scene shouting "Hallelujah" over the seductress' destruction.[2]

In contrast to those who mourned the death of the prostitute, the bride of Jesus celebrates her fall. She rejoices because her prayer, *"Your kingdom come; your will be done, on earth as it is in heaven,"* (Matt. 6:10) has materialized. But her song lacks petty vindictiveness and smug gloating. Instead, praises to the Lord fill her heart because evil has not had the final word. She sings because the misery, exploitation, greed, injustice, human slavery, and violence pervasive in our world have collapsed under God's strong hand. The bride sings because her husband has defended the honor of God's name by not leaving evil unpunished.[3]

The twenty-four elders and the four living creatures accompany the Bride's song, adding their own "Hallelujah!" to the hymn (Rev. 19:4–5). John hears the Bride's voice once again:

> *Then I heard what seemed to be the voice of a great multitude, like the roar of many waters and like the sound of mighty peals of thunder, crying out, "Hallelujah! For the Lord our God the Almighty reigns. Let us rejoice and exult and give him the glory, for the marriage of the Lamb has come, and his Bride has made herself ready.* (Rev. 19:6–7)

The Bride sings not only because the Kingdom of God has come in its fullness but also because the day she's longed for since she first heard of the Savior's love has arrived: It's her wedding day! So she sings, *"For the marriage of the Lamb has come, and his bride has made herself ready"* (Rev. 19:7).

We'll appreciate the end-time wedding of Christ to his people by returning to the very beginning of the Bible, where we see this has been God's plan from the start. So think about the beginning of Genesis and the creation of the heavens and the earth.[4] God created Adam in his image and placed him in a garden. The honor of bearing God's image made Adam a son of God. This language may startle us, but in Luke's genealogy of Jesus, he traces the line of Christ back to Adam, whom he calls *"the son of God"* (Luke 3:38). God placed his son in a garden with dominion over it (Gen. 1:26). Moving forward to the end of Genesis 2 (Gen. 2:18–24), God gave his son a bride to rule over creation with him.

Putting these pieces together, we have a new creation and a holy couple in a sacred place under God's holy law. Adam, the created son of God, failed to rule over creation and instead brought sin and misery into the world.[5] But the Lord never abandoned the plan for a son of God, ruling with his bride in a holy place under the sacred law of God.

Instead, before the first son of God and his bride were expelled from the garden, the Lord promised that another Son of God would come to undo the curse brought upon creation and his Bride (Gen. 3:15). Everything that follows from Genesis 3 unfolds the Lord's plan to re-establish a new creation with a Son of God and his bride in a holy place and under the holy law of the Lord. The theologian Geerhardus Vos often likened the first three chapters of Genesis to a seed that grows to full flower throughout the rest of the Scriptures. We might say that God encoded all of the DNA of his eternal purposes in Scripture's opening pages: a son of God with his bride as a holy couple in a holy place under the holy law of the Lord.

As we move from the Garden, the Lord's original purpose continues to echo throughout the Old Testament. But now, the Lord is the husband, and the people of Israel are called the bride. Through Isaiah, the Lord says, *"Your maker is your husband, the LORD of hosts is his name"* (Isa. 54:5). And again, *"As the bridegroom rejoices over the bride, so shall your God rejoice over you"* (Isa. 62:5; see also Hosea 2:19–20). These descriptions of the Lord as husband and Israel as the bride suggest what is later made explicit: the first marriage pictured the relationship the Lord desires with and for his people (Eph. 5:31–32).

Even though the Lord is the husband, the Old Testament tells the story of a terrible, one-sided marriage. Except for a few rare instances, the Jews did not live under God's holy law. Therefore, they were not holy people, and the land was not a holy place.

But God's original purpose revealed in the first garden could not be thwarted. He sent another Son of God, a second Adam, into the world. And when the eternal Son of God performed his first miracle, it was not at a funeral, synagogue, or temple.

Instead, not accidentally, he begins at a wedding (John 2:1–12). The Son of God had come for his Bride. But before they could be a holy couple, he had to live, die, and be raised for her.

Returning to the garden, we find an echo of what the true Son of God would have to do to make his Bride holy. Recall that when Adam and Eve sinned, they fled in terror from the Lord, covered with fig leaves to conceal their shame and guilt. But then something remarkable happens.

The Lord comes to the leaf-covered couple and gives them garments made from animal skins (Gen. 3:21). But the couple had already covered themselves with leaves. Why did the Lord cover them with animal skins?

First, it communicates that their actions were far more severe than they thought. *"The wages of sin is death"* (Rom. 6:23) and not the death of a plant. Blood must be spilled.[6]

And second, the Lord showed them that he would provide garments to cover their shame. Like the innocent animal who died to cover our guilty parents, the Son of God—the Lamb of God—would die to cover his Bride's shame and guilt.

Putting these things together, we see a story that begins with a son of God who failed to love the Lord and his bride. The Lord exiled the holy couple from the garden. The story continues to develop when the true Son of God comes to live and die for his guilty Bride:

> *that he might sanctify her, having cleansed her by the washing of water with the word, so that he might present [her] to himself in splendor, without spot or wrinkle or any such thing, that she might be holy and without blemish.* (Eph. 5:25–27)

And the story ends with the Son of God wed to his cleansed bride, living as a holy couple, in a holy place, and under the holy law of God.

In all of these details, we shouldn't treat them as trivia or as an interesting lens through which to see the story of the Bible. Instead, this should melt our hearts, lift our heads, and strengthen our knees to run the race set before us with vigor and zeal. As those who look forward to what God has planned from the very beginning, we live now as those who lean into the reality of that coming day.

The Present Engagement

We have yet to be married to Christ. Instead, those who love Jesus live as those betrothed to him. Paul wrote to the Corinthian Christians, saying, *"I betrothed you to one husband, to present you as a pure virgin to Christ"* (2 Cor. 11:2). The Jewish culture regarded betrothal much as our culture considers a wedding engagement, but with far more legal ramifications.[7]

The betrothal event included exchanging promises to marry in front of witnesses. During this pre-marriage phase, the woman legally belonged to the groom, and the couple were considered husband and wife. Those betrothed could not be uncoupled except through divorce (Matt. 1:19). The second stage of the process, the marriage ceremony itself, would come later. But until then, the bride-to-be would ready herself for her husband.

In our chapter, the wedding has come, and the Bride sings that she has prepared herself for this day:

> *Let us rejoice and exult and give him the glory, for the marriage of the Lamb has come, and his Bride has made herself ready; it was granted her to clothe herself with fine linen, bright and pure"—for the fine linen is the righteous deeds of the saints.* (Rev. 19:7–8)

Instead of fig lives and animal skins, bright and pure fine linen adorns this bride. Her righteous deeds now cover her once naked and ashamed state (Gen. 3:7). Describing the Bride covered with her righteous deeds does not suggest that she has in some way contributed to her salvation through obedience. Nor does it indicate that her salvation results from a cooperative effort between God and man. In the words of Jonah, *"Salvation belongs to the Lord"* from beginning to end (Jon. 2:9).[8]

Instead, this vision fits nicely with what our Lord tells us in the parable of the sower. When the seed of the Gospel goes deep into the soil of the heart, a harvest of fruit results (Mark 4:20). The righteous deeds covering the Bride do not cause or contribute to her salvation. But those same righteous deeds give evidence that she has truly entrusted herself to the Groom.

What does the evidence of loving Jesus look like? Love for Jesus results in a growing love for other people, possessing a deep-seated joy in the soul, and seeking peace whenever possible. It also manifests a growth in patience, kindness, and goodness. Becoming more faithful, gentle, and self-controlled.

You may recognize this list as the one Paul gave in the book of Galatians (Gal. 5:22–23). These righteous deeds are described as fruit growing up from the heart in which the Gospel seed has found a home.

This inventory does not represent a to-do list for those seeking salvation, but the behavioral and attitudinal outcome of those who already possess it.

The Bride hears the Groom say, *"Come out of [Babylon], my people, lest you take part in her sins, lest you share in her plagues"* (Rev. 18:4) and she responds by saying, "I will love, obey, and honor you, in sickness and in health, forsaking all others, as long as we both shall live." Until the Bride sees her groom face to face, she will stumble many times along the way (Jas. 3:2). But her life's trajectory grows with love and obedience to her Savior as she prepares for the coming day.

The preparation looks the same regardless of your present relationship with Jesus. If you're not a Christian, you must turn away from sin and to Jesus. If you are a Christian, but you don't see a lot of evidence of the fruit of the Spirit, you too must turn to Jesus. He is the vine, and we are the branches. Apart from him, we can do nothing (John 15:5).

And as we run to him, let this image of a coming wedding day shape your heart. The Father gave us his Son not simply to secure pardon from sin or to provide us with a place in heaven. Nor did Jesus come to ensure the reunion with loved ones where death no longer reigns, and tears are wiped away. All wonderful things, to be sure.

Above all else, the Father gave up his Son so that we might be part of a holy couple, living in a holy place, and under the holy law of God. Jesus is not a means to some other end. He is the end. The Father has given us the very same one in whom is all of his delight: the glorious, incomparable, and infinitely marvelous Son of God.

John heard the Bride singing on the wedding day to come. And while we wait, an angel speaks to us in the present:

> *Write this: Blessed are those who are invited to the marriage supper of the Lamb." And he said to me, "These are the true words of God.* (Rev. 19:9)

You have an invitation to the marriage supper of the Lamb! When we turn to Jesus, we RSVP for the event surpassing all others declaring, "Yes, I will be there!"

But should you come, it will not be as an audience member or a wedding party member. You will be the Bride. The Groom will dress you in white and crown you with the gift of everlasting life. But your focus will not be upon your dress or your crown. It will be the face of your dear Savior that will forever thrill your heart. Until then, prepare your heart and mind to see him.

Study Questions

1. Journal a list of items that may fall into the category of things we think are important today but may be later laughed at by children. Now, evaluating the list, are your priorities in the right order? Meditate on this truth: "The world is passing away along with its desires."
2. What details does the author say should "melt our hearts, lift our heads, and strengthen our knees to run the race set before us"? How are these details an encouragement to you?
3. John shows us that we prepare for the wedding by living for the groom now. Reread what the evidence of loving Jesus looks like; do you see these things in your life? Is anything on this list convicting to you? Take these observations to the Lord in prayer today.
4. The Fruit of the Spirit is not a list of things to do as much as it is a list that describes what occurs in the life of those who love Jesus. Knowing this, how can we grow in such things? If we do not see a lot of evidence of the fruit of the Spirit, the answer is to turn to Jesus, respond to his word, draw near in prayer, and partake in the Lord's Supper. Apart from him, we can do nothing. Journal ways you can draw nearer to him this week.

---

1. Dennis E. Johnson, *Triumph of the Lamb: A Commentary on Revelation* (Phillipsburg, NJ: P&R Publishing, 2001), 260.
2. Revelation 19 contains the only use of *Hallelujah* in the New Testament. *Hallelujah* combines the verb *hallel*, meaning "praise," with the name of God *Yah*, short for *Yahweh*.
3. G.K. Beale notes that the bride also praises the Lord for his justice, demonstrating that His people were in the right all along and the world's verdict against them was wrong. See G.K. Beale, *The Book of Revelation: A Shorter Commentary* (Eerdmans, 2015), 394.
4. For an extensive examination of some of the ideas present here, see Dr. Jonathan Gibson's Session 3—God's Kingdom in a New Creation: The Beginning of the Greatest Story Ever Written, at https://faculty.wts.edu/lectures/back-to-the-beginning-genesis-1-2/.
5. The Westminster Confession of Faith, Shorter Catechism Q. 17.
6. Lev. 17:11 states, *"For the life of the flesh is in the blood, and I have given it for you on the altar to make atonement for your souls, for it is the blood that makes atonement by the life."*
7. See Robert H. Stein, *Luke: An Exegetical and Theological Exposition of Holy Scripture* (Nashville, TN: B&H Publishing, 1992), 82.
8. Ultimately, the fine linen wedding garment is given to the bride by her groom, as the background in Isaiah 61:10 makes clear: *"I will greatly rejoice in the LORD; my soul shall exult in my God, for he has clothed me with the garments of salvation; he has covered me with the robe of righteousness, as a bridegroom decks himself like a priest with a beautiful headdress, and as a bride adorns herself with her jewels."*

32

THE MACABRE SUPPER OF DEFEAT

REVELATION 19:11-21

Years ago, there was a Bible College in Uganda filled with students who lived through the murderous regime of Idi Amin, one of the most brutal tyrants in world history. Many of the students bore in their bodies reminders of his brutality. Some were missing their hands. Others lacked an arm or an eye. Several students  had cherry-red scars on their backs, shoulders, and faces from old machete wounds. They were forced to live through one of the darkest periods of African history. However, at this college, these students gathered together to study the Bible and to bring the light of Jesus to their villages.

During a lecture on the return of Jesus Christ, a professor quoted these words from Paul's first letter to the Thessalonians, *"For the Lord himself will come down from heaven with a commanding shout, with the voice of the archangel, and with the trumpet call of God."* (1 Thess. 4:16). One student asked, "What will the Lord shout?" The question stumped the professor. He'd never thought about the content of what Jesus would shout, but Paul did write that Jesus would give a cry of command at his return.

The professor finally admitted that he didn't know. He then solicited thoughts from the other students in class. The accumulated suffering that those students had endured begged for an answer. What will the Lord say when he returns? One student suggested, "I think he will shout, 'Enough!'"[1]

We don't know what Jesus will say, but I like the student's suggestion. Enough!

When Christ returns, it will be a day of accounting. There won't be discussion, debate, or second chances. When he comes, his light will drive out darkness. His truth will banish all lies. His goodness will incinerate and punish all wickedness. On that day, every knee will bow down in worship to Jesus. Some knees will be forced to bend, while others will do so with joy-filled willingness. But all will bend, acknowledging that he is King of kings and Lord of lords (Phil. 2:9–11; Rev. 19:16).

While we don't hear Jesus shout anything in this passage before us, we do see him. We see him as The Word of God who doesn't appear to need to say anything at all! He shows up, and the day of evil deeds and dark plans is no more.

The vision John has of Jesus is unsettling at first glance. As we'll soon discover, John sees not the "Gentle Jesus, meek and mild"[2] as he is toward the broken-hearted sinner. Instead, John sees Jesus as the living, breathing nightmare from which unrepentant men and women will never awake.

But while it's not the picture of Jesus we often think of, it is nevertheless him. And if we let this vision work in our hearts and minds, we'll discover that those who have been sinned against and those who have sinned need this vision.[3]

Those Sinned Against

Before we look at the text, let's review some of the characters we have encountered in John's vision. In Chapter 12, we met a dragon—representing Satan—and a pregnant woman. The woman embodies the people of God. She gave birth to the Christ child, whom the dragon attempts and fails to kill. The child was caught up to heaven, a picture of the ascension of Jesus, and the dragon turned his attention to trying to destroy the woman. To aid the dragon, he summoned two beasts, one from the sea and one from the earth (Rev. 13:1–18). The beast from the sea represents man-centered governments in rebellion against the Lord, while the beast from the earth points to those who promote allegiance to the state even at the cost of fidelity to Jesus.

Then, we were introduced to a prostitute called Babylon (Rev. 17:1–18). She represents the seductive allure of the world which labors to entice Christ's followers away from him and into its grip. The strange images show us the nature of the time between the ascension and the return of Jesus Christ.

Satan will pursue the Church during this period, using the state and its champions to do his bidding. All the while, the present world and its offer of affluence and pleasures will call out to Christ's people like a prostitute offering quick and easy satisfaction.

One by one, the dragon, the beasts, and the prostitute are set before us as real and external threats. But now they begin to fall. In reverse order, the enemies of the Church get escorted off the stage.

Chapter 18 saw the fall of Babylon, the prostitute who was burned alive. Chapter 19 pictures the destruction of the two beasts, who are also burned alive in the lake of fire (Rev. 19:20). Chapter 20 will show the dragon, Satan himself, thrown into the lake of fire to be tormented day and night forever and ever (Rev. 20:10).

Clearly, the tide of the war has shifted in favor of the woman chased by the dragon, harassed by the beasts, and solicited by the prostitute. John now sees why. The child caught up to heaven in Chapter 12 has returned:

> *Then I saw heaven opened, and behold, a white horse! The one sitting on it is called Faithful and True, and in righteousness he judges and makes war. His eyes are like a flame of fire, and on his head are many diadems, and he has a name written that no one knows but himself. He is clothed in a robe dipped in blood, and the name by which he is called is The Word of God. And the armies of heaven, arrayed in fine linen, white and pure, were following him on white horses. From his mouth comes a sharp sword with which to strike down the nations, and he will rule them with a rod of iron. He will tread the winepress of the fury of the wrath of God the Almighty. On his robe and on his thigh he has a name written, King of kings and Lord of lords.* (Rev. 19:11–16)

This is a very different image of Jesus than we are accustomed to. There are a number of contrasts between the Jesus we read about in the gospel and the Jesus who returns to the earth. He isn't mounted on a donkey, a beast of burden, as he was when he entered Jerusalem (Matt. 21:1–11). This time, he rides upon a white horse, the familiar symbol of military victory.[4]

When Jesus came to the earth, he ended his life wearing a crown of twisted thorns pressed down into his scalp (Matt. 27:29). John now sees crowns piled high upon Jesus' head, representing the absolute, comprehensive authority the Father has given to him to judge and to make war.

Looking at his robe, John tells us it's covered with blood. But whose blood is it? We might be forgiven if our first thought is that the blood must belong to Jesus, shed for the sins of his people. But as we've found in other places of this book, our understanding of Revelation's images is enhanced by looking at the Old Testament.

In the Book of Isaiah, the prophet wrote of the day when the Lord would judge the nations (Isa. 63:1–6). Isaiah describes seeing a figure dressed in crimsoned garments coming from enemy nations. As he wonders at the identity of this strange figure, the figure identifies himself as the Lord.[5] Why, then, Isaiah asks, are you dressed in red? Why do you look like you've been stomping grapes in a winepress? Isaiah receives the bone-chilling answer. The Lord's clothing is spattered red with the blood of his enemies. He explains, saying:

> *I trod them in my anger and trampled them in my wrath; their lifeblood spattered on my garments, and stained all my apparel. For the day of vengeance was in my heart, and my year of redemption had come. (Isa. 63:3–4)*

The first coming of Jesus resulted in the spilling of his own blood and the destruction of his body. The events of his return could not be more different:

> *From his mouth comes a sharp sword with which to strike down the nations, and he will rule them with a rod of iron. He will tread the winepress of the fury of the wrath of God the Almighty. On his robe and on his thigh he has a name written, King of kings and Lord of lords. (Rev. 19:15–16)*

And finally, when Jesus came for the first time, he celebrated a meal with his disciples in which he was pictured as the object to be consumed. At his return, he will oversee another feast. But it will be a very different meal:

> *Then I saw an angel standing in the sun, and with a loud voice he called to all the birds that fly directly overhead, "Come, gather for the great supper of God, to eat the flesh of kings, the flesh of captains, the flesh of mighty men, the flesh of horses and their riders, and the flesh of all men, both free and slave, both small and great." And I saw the beast and the kings of the earth with their armies gathered to make war against him who was sitting on the horse and against his army. And the beast was captured, and with it the false prophet who in its presence had done the signs by which he deceived those who had received the mark of the beast and those who worshiped its image. These two were thrown alive into the lake of fire that burns with sulfur. And the rest were slain by the sword that came from the mouth of him who was*

sitting on the horse, and all the birds were gorged with their flesh. (Rev. 19:17–21)[6]

Few images are more disturbing to me than birds feasting on human flesh, but it does serve several purposes. First, it presents a picture of complete loss and eternal death.[7] In one sense, Jesus returns to judge and "make war," but we see no battle. He simply shows up, and that's the end. There's no dialogue, discussion, or second chances. He returns to judge and make war.

Second, this image functions as a macabre parody of the feast of the marriage supper of the Lamb just described in the previous section. The horrible image of this chapter suggests that, in the end, there are only two options. We will either feast with Jesus at the marriage supper of the Lamb, or the Lamb will offer us up to be feasted upon.

I'm reminded of something C.S. Lewis wrote: "There are only two kinds of people in the end: those who say to God, 'Thy will be done,' and those to whom God says, in the end, '*Thy* will be done.'"[8] In other words, some say, "I will come to the marriage supper!" while others say, "I'd rather be the supper."

Finally, this image encourages the people of God. How so? Millions and millions of Christians have suffered terribly in and for Jesus' name. And every one of them has a desire for justice. Remember the martyrs' cry in Chapter 6, "*O Sovereign Lord, holy and true, how long before you will judge and avenge our blood on those who dwell on earth?*" (Rev. 6:10). This image assures the Lord's people that he will address every wrong ever done to them. In our present age, people often get away with terrible things because they have political, vocational, or family connections. How can Jesus instruct his people not to seek revenge or to repay evil for evil? This image reminds us that vengeance belongs to the Lord (Rom. 12:19). Without this image of Christ soaked in the blood of his enemies, you cannot relinquish your anger or surrender your desire for revenge.[9] But if you believe in the perfect judgment of God, you are free from the burden of trying to make things right on your own.

I saw how this plays out in real-time once while visiting Rwanda. I was there to lead a conference on theology for a group of local pastors, and during a break in class, I toured the countryside with one of the students. During our travels, I noticed several concrete pads dotting the landscape. Some were the size of a basketball court, while others appeared large enough to serve as a foundation for a home.

So I asked the driver what function the concrete pads served. I suspected they might be foundations for a future building project, but I was mistaken. Each concrete structure was a mass grave from the Rwandan Genocide of 1994.

In three months, 800,000 Rwandans were killed, and many of the bodies were bulldozed into holes in the ground and covered with concrete pads. As we traveled in silence, my stomach turned as more and more mass graves appeared in town after town.

The driver finally broke the silence saying, "Many of those who did this to us are still alive. Most of them never went to prison or were punished in any way for what they did. And sometimes I get so angry I want to hurt them."

What could I say to him? Thankfully, I didn't need to say anything because he broke the silence again: "But God will make all things right." I was there to teach, and I left having learned what giving vengeance to God looks like.

We find this image of Jesus so disturbing because we have not suffered for his name like many of our brethren through the centuries and as many still do around the world. When your idea of suffering for Jesus is not finding a church that caters to your musical preferences or doesn't provide your family with all your felt needs, a blood-soaked Jesus is highly irrelevant and even off-putting.

But if you've watched your husband's throat get slit open for Jesus or your wife and daughters made victims of human trafficking, this image of Jesus becomes precious. But even if we've not or not yet seen and experienced such atrocities for Jesus, this image remains valuable and necessary for us. Retaliation must never be our goal, but instead, we endeavor to love our enemies and pray for the very ones who malign us. On what basis can we do any of those things? Paul helps us here: *"Beloved, never avenge yourselves, but leave it to the wrath of God, for it is written, 'Vengeance is mine, I will repay, says the Lord'"* (Rom. 12:19).

So instead of gnashing our teeth in despair, rage, and fury, we can rest in the vengeance of God, pictured for us in the blood-soaked Warrior King, who calls you his friend.

This image assures those who've been sinned against that Christ will execute perfect justice upon his return. And just as important, this image of perfect justice gives assurance to those who have sinned.

Those Who Have Sinned

When you hear that Jesus will return and bring perfect justice upon everyone, does it cause your heart to rejoice? Or perhaps worry a bit? John looked into the eyes of Jesus and described them as flames of fire, representing not only his holy gaze but also his ability to peer beyond the surface of outward behavior to the heart's inner motives. Jesus will judge not just the person we present on social media or to the rest of the watching world. Instead, Jesus will assess the real you. The person you are when no one is looking. Jesus said:

> *Nothing is covered up that will not be revealed, or hidden that will not be known. Therefore whatever you have said in the dark shall be heard in the light, and what you have whispered in private rooms shall be proclaimed on the housetops.* (Luke 12:2–3)

And yet John tells us elsewhere that when Jesus appears, we may have confidence and not shrink from him in shame (1 John 2:28). How can one be exposed as a sinner on that day and at the same time not shrink away in shame with the promise of his appearing? The answer comes when we take our eyes off of ourselves and place them on the One John saw atop the white horse and called "Faithful and True" (Rev. 19:11). Jesus will be faithful and true to his promises, not only to return to expose and punish sin in the rebellious but also to vindicate his name and his people.[10]

Listen to what John says in one of his letters about the faithful and true Savior: "*If we confess our sins, he is faithful and just to forgive us our sins and to cleanse us from all unrighteousness*" (1 John 1:9). We'll find a truckload of comfort in that promise if we slow down and listen to it.[11] Notice the promise does not say that if we confess our sins, God is merciful, patient, or willing to give us another chance—all accurate descriptions of God, but not what John wrote.

Instead, the confidence the repentant sinner has on the day of judgment finds support in this: God's faithfulness and justice. That is, if you trust in Jesus Christ and at the judgment the Lord refuses to forgive you, God would be guilty of injustice. How could that be?

Consider this line of reasoning. The Bible tells us that the wages of sin is death (Rom. 6:23), meaning, God's justice owes death to sinners. But when Jesus died, he died not for himself but for his sinful people. Jesus said he came not "*to be served but to serve, and to give his life as a ransom for many"* (Matt. 20:28; Mark 10:45). On the cross, the justice of God toward your sin and mine was fully met. [12]

Do we start to see what John means when he says, *"If we confess our sins, he is faithful and just to forgive us our sins and to cleanse us of all unrighteousness?"* While we don't often think of the unbending, uncompromised justice of God as a comfort to us, perhaps we should. Because of what the Savior has already done and will complete upon his return, our hearts are buoyed in hope by the justice of God. God's justice now demands our full acquittal on the coming day.

What a Gospel! God has given us strong assurances of his grace, mercy, and even his justice which are all now for us in Jesus.

What hope we have. And at the same time, what a sober warning that ought to be on our hearts and lips for those in our lives who know little of the Savior and the terrors of what is coming if they refuse his advances. Someone has done the math and determined that roughly 13 percent of Jesus's preaching and teaching focused on hell and judgment.[13] As those called to be his witnesses, I don't know that we need to talk about hell and judgment 13 percent of the time when we talk about Jesus. But faithfulness requires that we not shy away, explain away, or avoid speaking of such things. You have been given this vision of the returning, conquering King for your sake and others.

I'll close with the words from a sermon of one of history's greatest preachers, Charles Spurgeon. May his words fill us both with boldness for the Savior and love for our neighbor:

> Oh, my brothers and sisters in Christ, if sinners will be damned, at least let them leap to hell over our bodies; and if they will perish, let them perish with our arms about their knees, imploring them to stay, and not madly to destroy themselves. If hell must be filled... let not one go there unwarned and unprayed for.[14]

Study Questions

1. Consider the consequences of being "free from the burden of trying to make things right on your own." What would that look like in your life?
2. Do you find these images of a blood-soaked Jesus and the "supper of God" disturbing and unsettling, or the assurance of justice to come? Why might we be disturbed instead of encouraged by this?

3. Our author poses a question at the top of the second point in this chapter. Take a moment to answer it honestly: When you read that Jesus is coming back and will execute perfect justice upon all men and women, does it cause your heart to rejoice or perhaps worry a bit?
4. When Jesus appears, John tells us we may have confidence and not shrink away in shame. How can this be? Flesh out this statement: Because God is infinitely determined to exercise justice without compromise, the sinner has hope.
5. This terrifying vision is good news for those who have been sinned against and for those who have sinned. How does this shape our thinking, change our witness, and affect our daily lives?

---

1. This story is recounted in Ben Patterson's *God's Prayer Book: The Power and Pleasure of Praying the Psalms* (Tyndale Momentum, 2008), 184–185.
2. Charles Wesley, "Gentle Jesus, Meek and Mild" (1742).
3. Treating this vision under these two headings is inspired by the excellent treatment of God's judgment in Raymond Cannata & Joshua Reitano, *Rooted: The Apostles' Creed*, 2nd Ed. (Baltimore, MD: White Blackbird Books, 2019), 107–120.
4. Dennis E. Johnson, *Triumph of the Lamb: A Commentary on Revelation* (Phillipsburg, NJ: P&R Publishing, 2001), 119.
5. In the Isaiah passage, the crimsoned-covered figure notes that he is alone (63:3). In John's vision, the armies of heaven accompany Jesus (Rev. 19:14). The identity of those with Jesus is a matter of some discussion amongst commentators. Some think the armies consist of heavenly angels, while others suggest that it consists of Christ's people. The parallel reference in 17:14, *"The Lamb will overcome them... and those who are with Him are the called and chosen and faithful,"* suggest the latter option. See G.K. Beale, *The Book of Revelation: A Shorter Commentary* (Eerdmans, 2015), 413.
6. This battle is the same climactic end-time surge of evil we've examined in Rev. 16:14, 16, 17:14, and will return to in 20:7–10. Once again, John is giving us a fresh angle on an already-visited event.
7. I also suspect there is an ironic reversal of dominion pictured in the birds feasting on men. In the beginning, God gave man dominion over the earth, which included *"the birds of the heavens"* (Gen. 1:28). But in the end, the birds *"that fly directly overhead"* (Rev. 19:17) will have dominion over the wicked.
8. C. S. Lewis, *The Great Divorce*, Chapter 9 (1946). Italics original.
9. Raymond Cannata & Joshua Reitano, *Rooted: The Apostles' Creed*, 117.
10. G.K. Beale, *The Book of Revelation: A Shorter Commentary*, 409.
11. I'm indebted to Tim Keller for the following insight into the justice of God. See Tim Keller, *Encounters with Jesus: Unexpected Answers to Life's Biggest Questions* (Penguin Group, 2013), 127–148.
12. The word used for the satisfaction of God's wrath is "propitiation." See Rom. 3:25; Heb. 2:17; 1 John 2:2, 4:10.
13. Found in Mark Jones, *Knowing Christ* (Banner of Truth, 2016), 195.
14. Charles Spurgeon, "The Wailing of Risca" (1861)

PART 7

THE NEW JERUSALEM, THE GREAT CONSUMMATION, AND EPILOGUE 20:1–22:5

33

ONE BOUND, COUNTLESS EMBOLDENED

REVELATION 20:1-10

September 8, 1998, is one of the most important dates in history if you are a St. Louis Cardinals fan. That evening, the crowd anticipated that Mark McGwire would hit his 62nd home run of the year, passing Roger Maris' record of 61 home runs in a single season. One of my friends, a diehard Cardinals fan, secured tickets just a few rows behind home plate and attended the game, hoping to witness baseball history.

Unfortunately, McGwire's first at-bat did not go well; he grounded out to end the inning. After that, the game's pace slowed, so my friend decided to make his way to the concession stand to secure some fresh roasted peanuts. He reasoned that he had enough time to get a snack and return to his seat to witness McGwire's second at-bat.

Many other fans thought the same, and the lines for the concession stand were long. And then, while he was in line, he heard the crack of a bat and the crowd roaring. So he dashed out of the line for peanuts back into the stadium, only to see Mark McGwire rounding second base. Unfortunately, he'd just hit his 62nd home run, and my friend missed it.

Today there is a famous picture of McGwire's record-breaking home run. It shows McGwire's follow-through and the ball launching off his bat headed toward the left field wall. In that famous photo, you should see my friend in the seats, a few rows behind home plate. But he's not there. Instead, at the moment when baseball history was being made, he was somewhere behind the pictured crowd, standing in line, distracted with his pursuit of peanuts.[1]

In our study of Jesus' letters to the seven churches, we found that many churches were distracted from their pursuit of Jesus. Some were consumed with the quest for wealth (Rev. 3:14–22). Others concealed their witness for Christ because they were absorbed with the desire to maintain a good reputation with the Romans (Rev. 2:12–17). Others still were inattentive to their love for Jesus, which had grown cold (Rev. 2:1–7).

From time to time, we all find ourselves distracted from pursuing Jesus and sharing him with others. The things of the world have their allure, and we can find ourselves in autopilot mode with Jesus. Perhaps we're not denying him, but we also aren't making much of him. It's easy to find ourselves distracted. It's also easy to find ourselves discouraged as we see so much evil and rampant injustice in the world. At times it can look and feel like the kingdoms of man hold all the power, and the Kingdom of God limps along.

John shares this vision with a group of people who no doubt also felt overwhelmed and discouraged at times. As the small group of Christians in Asia Minor tried to live faithfully for Jesus in the shadow of the mighty Roman Empire, they must have felt some skepticism about some of the images in this book. How could the mighty Roman Empire ever fall? How could the kingdom of man, which seems to hold all the power, ever give way to the Kingdom of our Lord and of his Christ? We've repeatedly seen the answer to those questions throughout this book, and this chapter is no exception.

This vision of the binding of Satan reminds us that we are on a side that cannot lose, and we bring Christ to a dying world that cannot win. Therefore, there is no excuse for cowardice or retreat. Instead, we take the battle to the enemy. And to encourage us along those lines, we see the restrictive binding of Satan, which should embolden us to press on in our testimony before the world.

Satan Bound

Chapter 20 begins the last of John's portraits of the time between the ascension and return of Jesus. I believe this chapter begins a new portrait because of the way Chapter 19 ended with the complete and eternal destruction of Christ's enemies at an end-time conflict.[2] And yet in this chapter, John witnesses and offers another description of an end-time conflict. But we encounter not a new or different conflict, but the same one we've examined in Chapters 11, 16, and 17. Chapter 20 offers a fresh vantage point of a familiar coming conflict. But before John describes the battle, he describes the binding of our great enemy:

> *Then I saw an angel coming down from heaven, holding in his hand the key to the bottomless pit and a great chain. And he seized the dragon, that ancient serpent, who is the devil and Satan, and bound him for a thousand years, and threw him into the pit, and shut it and sealed it over him, so that he might not deceive the nations any longer, until the thousand years were ended. After that he must be released for a little while.* (Rev. 20:1–3).

This is not the first time that John describes Satan as *"that ancient serpent."*[3] This title invites us to return to the garden in Eden when Satan first made his appearance in the form of a serpent. He came to deceive and destroy the peace and purity of God's covenant with our first parents. And he was successful.

The serpent duped Adam and Eve, bringing sin, misery, and death into creation. But remember, God's response was not merely reactionary. Instead, he went on the offensive. He declared war on the serpent and those who follow him.

God promised in Genesis 3:15 that through a man, described as a skull-crushing warrior, he would restore all that was lost and destroy the destroyer. The rest of the Old Testament tells us how God went about that program through one particular group of people who traced their ethnicity back to Abraham, a man whose name means *"father of a multitude of nations"* (Gen. 17:5).

But in the Old Testament, we don't see the non-Jewish nations calling Abraham their father. Instead, God worked through the one nation of Israel, while the other nations dwelt in darkness, living under the spell of satanic influence, resulting in all types of idolatry and myth. But the Lord promised through Isaiah that he would send his servant to be *"a light for the nations"* (Isa. 42:6) and that salvation would *"reach to the ends of the earth"* (Isa. 49:6).

Stated another way, when the Lord's servant comes, Satan's present stranglehold on the nations will be undone. Put another way still, we can say that Satan will be bound and unable to stop the salvation of the Lord from reaching the ends of the earth. In the vision before us, John saw and described the moment restriction fell upon Satan and his influence.

The question we bring to this text pertains to the timing of the binding of Satan. Has the binding already occurred or should we look for something yet to come? The New Testament tells us it has already happened. Matthew's Gospel records that once when Jesus healed a demon-oppressed man, he was accused by the Pharisees of casting out demons by the power of Satan. Jesus responded that he was not in league with Satan asking, *"How can someone enter a strong man's house and plunder his goods, unless he first binds the strong man? Then indeed he may plunder his house"* (Matt. 12:29). Jesus effectively says, "I've come into Satan's house—the sinful world over which Satan had terrible sway—and I've bound him up. Now I'm taking from him the souls he kept imprisoned in ignorance." Matthew and John both use the same word (Greek *deō*) for binding the strong man and the serpent. On another occasion, several Greeks approach Jesus requesting a meeting with him. Again, we have to appreciate how significant this would have been. Greeks prided themselves on wisdom, and they wanted to hear from a Jewish rabbi. When the disciples told Jesus that these men representing the nations wished to speak with him, he immediately began speaking about his death and a judgment upon Satan. He said:

> *Now is the judgment of this world; now will the ruler of this world be cast out. And I, when I am lifted up from the earth, will draw all people to myself."* (John 12:31–32)

Once again, the verb Jesus used for the casting out of Satan in John 12 is derived from the same root as the word used in Revelation 20:3 for Satan thrown into the pit.[4]

To the Greeks coming to Jesus, we can add the wise men from the East who worshiped Jesus at his birth. To the wise men, add the Romans, Samaritans, Ethiopians, and those from modern-day Europe, all confessing Jesus as the Christ and heirs to the promises made to Abraham. This happened because the people who walked in darkness had seen a great light. And they could now see the light because the prince of darkness had been bound and cast out of the earth.

Therefore, the scene John describes represents not a future event but something that Jesus said has already occurred. We should be clear about what this binding does and does not mean. The binding of Satan does not suggest total inactivity or even influence. The Bible warns us that Satan still blinds the minds of unbelievers (2 Cor. 4:4), prowls around like a roaring lion (1 Pet. 5:8), and is someone who needs to be resisted (Jas. 4:7).

As Hendriksen notes:

> A dog securely bound with a long and heavy chain can do great damage within the circle of his imprisonment. Outside that circle, however, the animal can do no damage and can hurt no one.[5]

Sadly, Satan, like a violent dog on a leash, remains active and brings destruction wherever possible. But the binding of Satan does mean two things. First, he cannot prevent the spreading of the Gospel anymore.[6] John alludes to this in verse 3 when describing the binding of Satan as an inability to keep the nations deceived. Satan no longer has any permitted authority over those who walk in darkness. Instead, all authority now belongs to Jesus, whose parting command to his disciples was to go into all the world to *"make disciples of all nations"* (Matt. 28:18–19). Second, a bound Satan cannot yet gather the nations together to try to destroy the Church:

> *And when the thousand years are ended, Satan will be released from his prison and will come out to deceive the nations that are at the four corners of the earth, Gog and Magog, to gather them for battle; their number is like the sand of the sea. And they marched up over the broad plain of the earth and surrounded the camp of the saints and the beloved city, but fire came down from heaven and consumed them, and the devil who had deceived them was thrown into the lake of fire and sulfur where the beast and the false prophet were, and they will be tormented day and night forever and ever.* (Rev. 20:7–10)

We'll return to the thousand years in a moment. For now, we are told again of the same end-time conflict we've studied numerous times. In Chapter 11, we considered the two witnesses destroyed by the beast at the end of history. In Chapter 16, we examined how the dragon will convince the nations to gather against the Church in the battle of Armageddon. In Chapter 17, we observed one final, terrible manifestation of the beast that will arise at the end to make war on the Lamb.

And now John tells us of that same conflict but from another angle. Satan will gather the nations, this time called Gog and Magog, to wage war on the Church. These titles of Gog and Magog go back to the Book of Ezekiel, which describes a mysterious alliance of nations who, at the end of the ages, will try to destroy the people of God.[7] But for now, Satan cannot launch his last effort to destroy the Church, as Jesus has yet to free him from his imprisonment (Rev. 20:7).

John tells us the unbinding of Satan will come at the end of a thousand-year period. We've become accustomed to treating numbers in this book symbolically. The number 1,000 is often used in Scripture for a large and complete number.[8] For example, the Lord tells us he owns *"the cattle on a thousand hills"* (Ps. 50:10) and that one day in the courts of the Lord *"is better than a thousand elsewhere"* (Ps. 90:4).

Satan will be bound for the perfect, complete amount of time. After that, he will be released to rally the nations against the Church. At this point, the dragon, the last character in the cast of miserable enemies of the Church, will be escorted off-stage to join the beast and the false prophet in the lake of fire and sulfur (Rev. 20:10). But until then, though active in the world, Satan remains bound and unable to stop the forward progress of the Gospel to all nations.

Emboldened Saints

This revelation should encourage us today just as it would have encouraged the first audience. And John gives us another encouragement by showing us what occurs in heaven while we wait to see our Savior:

> *Then I saw thrones, and seated on them were those to whom the authority to judge was committed. Also I saw the souls of those who had been beheaded for the testimony of Jesus and for the word of God, and those who had not worshiped the beast or its image and had not received its mark on their foreheads or their hands. They came to life and reigned with Christ for a thousand years. The rest of the dead did not come to life until the thousand years were ended. This is the first resurrection. Blessed and holy is the one who shares in the first resurrection! Over such the second death has no power, but they will be priests of God and of Christ, and they will reign with him for a thousand years.* (Rev. 20:4–6)

Remember the situation for the first group of Christians who received this letter from John. The Romans demanded allegiance to the emperor that Christians could not give. At the time of writing, some were going to be imprisoned for their faith (Rev. 2:10), and others had already faced the executioner's sword for refusing to betray Jesus (Rev. 2:13). The Church must have felt feeble and puny compared to the overwhelming power of the beastly Roman Empire.

But John sees that nothing could be further from the truth. Verses 4–6 show us what happens in the heavenly realms during this long, complete period before Jesus returns. Those who have suffered for Jesus on the earth go to be with him to reign in heaven.

John observed many thrones and the souls of those who have fought the good fight and have finished their race. They took hold of eternal life, and now they reign in heaven with Jesus. Theologians sometimes make a distinction between the Church militant and the Church triumphant. The Church militant comprises those engaged in the battle against the world, the devil, and their own flesh. The Church triumphant refers to those who have run their course and now dwell in the presence of the Lord.

It's the triumphant Church John sees and describes here. And what a contrast to what we see with our eyes when we bury a loved one who trusts the Lord! We see a lifeless body placed in a coffin and lowered into the cold earth.

But John sees them as living beings—though their bodies lay in the ground until the Lord raises them at his return, their souls go to be with Jesus.[9] And those with the Lord not only live, they reign with Jesus (2. Tim. 2:11–12). They are more alive than ever! You may remember that great quote from the evangelist D. L. Moody. He said:

> Some day you will read in the papers that D. L. Moody, of East Northfield, is dead. Don't you believe a word of it! At that moment I shall be more alive than I am now. I shall have gone up higher, that is all; out of this old clay tenement into a house that is immortal.[10]

"More alive" is an apt description of what happens when we go to be with the Lord. Sometimes we talk about being with Jesus as entering our eternal rest and going where there is no pain, mourning, or death. All that is true, but our entrance into eternal rest isn't an entry into eternal idleness. Nor just simply watching from the bleachers as Jesus carries out his purposes in the world.

John sees the beloved departed on thrones and reigning with Jesus (Rev. 20:4). The exact nature of this co-reigning with Jesus has yet to be made known to us. Whether these saints simply agree with Jesus' judgments or make their own has not been revealed.[11] But we know that they marvel at God's infinite wisdom and justice as he carries out his purposes on earth. They ever sing:

> *Great and amazing are your deeds, O Lord God the Almighty! Just and true are your ways, O King of the nations!* (Rev. 15:3)

Do you see how this vision would have emboldened John's first audience as they watched friends and relatives losing jobs, income, and even their lives for Jesus? In this vision, they learned that suffering for Christ on this side of death results in reigning with him on the other side. Every Christian who watched the beastly Roman Empire grind their fellow Christians into the dirt, now sit on thrones, reigning with Jesus. I suspect it energized their testimony as they lived in the cold, menacing shadow of the Roman Empire.

It should likewise embolden us. We belong to something so much greater than simply believing in Jesus so that we can go to heaven when we die. Jesus teaches us that his Kingdom, in which you hold your citizenship, cannot fail:

> *this gospel of the kingdom will be proclaimed throughout the whole world as a testimony to all nations, and then the end will come.* (Matt. 24:14)

Jesus assures us that the Church will fulfill the Great Commission. All the nations will hear about Jesus. And we have the high dignity of being called to participate. Every time we pray and send missionaries to unreached or under-reached people groups, we participate in an endeavor that must succeed. When you invite someone to church, Bible study, or give the reason for your hope in Jesus to a non-Christian, none of those things function apart from God's promise to fill the earth with the knowledge of the glory of the Lord, as the waters cover the sea (Hab. 2:14).

God has involved you in a program so much more history-making than a guy in St. Louis hitting a baseball over a wall. Jesus has bound Satan, your faith proves it. You're in a kingdom that cannot fail.

I used to work for a man who ran a ministry in Ukraine. He loved telling the story of an old, run-down church building purchased in Ukraine. A group of Christians bought the building, which had sat vacant for years because the Soviet Union shut down churches and turned many of them into public toilets.

However, after the Soviet Union dissolved, many Christian groups began restoring the buildings to their former glory. During one such renovation, while men made repairs on the roof, one of them noticed something familiar-looking in a gutter. He soon realized it was the cross that once adorned the church's steeple. When the Soviets took this church, they hacksawed the cross off the top and tossed it aside, and the cross slid down into the gutter, where it remained obscured for years. The workers decided to clean the cross and return it to its place atop the church.

As my friend recounted the story, he would often smile, saying, "The men who raised their fists saying, 'God is dead! We will conquer the world!' Where are they now? They are gone. The Soviet Union is no more. They tried to stop the kingdom of God. But, like that cross in the gutter, obscured and weak looking for a time, the Kingdom of God was still there."

Be bold in your witness. You don't serve a defeated King but one who has triumphed, bound Satan, and today gathers to himself men and women, boys and girls from all the nations. Take your place in battle as a member of the Church militant until you sit on a throne above with the Church triumphant.

Study Questions

1. In the opening illustration, we meet a man who misses something substantial due to his "pursuit of peanuts." Consider the things that are distracting you today from your pursuit of Jesus. What are the "peanuts" in your life that take your focus off Jesus?
2. The binding of Satan is "not a future event but something that Jesus said has already been accomplished." How does this differ from how you may have been previously taught or may have once understood it? What are the implications of this, and how does it encourage us?
3. John sees many thrones and the souls of those who have fought the good fight and finished their race. How does this vision make us bold in our witness and have joy in our suffering?
4. Consider that when you die, you will live and reign with Jesus. Do you believe you will be "more alive" on that day? Take the time to journal and pray for the Lord to settle this reality into your heart and shape your life and choices today.

---

1. My friend is also my former pastor, the Rev. Dr. George Robertson. He recalls this story in a sermon found at https://www.thegospelcoalition.org/podcasts/word-of-the-week/the-dignity-of-causality/.

2. Giving a complete defense of the millennial view presented here (amillennialism) falls outside of the scope of the present work. For a full defense of this view, the reader is encouraged to consult additional sources. Among the resources, I suggest the following: for a brief introduction, William Hendriksen's, *More Than Conquerors* is among the best. I would also add Vern Poythress' *The Returning King* as an accessible introduction to Revelation. For a more thorough defense of amillennialism, one could do no better than G.K. Beale's longer and shorter commentaries regularly referenced in this book. Additionally, Anthony A. Hoekema's *The Bible and the Future* contains an excellent chapter devoted to Chapter 20 of Revelation. Another helpful resource especially dealing with the relationship between Revelation Chapters 19 and 20 is Cornelis P. Venema, *The Promise of the Future* (Banner of Truth, 2000. Reprint 2021), 296–339.
3. See Rev. 12:9. The use of the same four names in Chapter 12 (dragon, ancient serpent, the devil, and Satan) utilized here again in Chapter 20 suggests a return to the same event, but from another perspective.
4. In John 12:3, "cast out" translates the Greek *ekballō* while in Rev. 20:3, "threw," in Greek, is *ballō*.
5. William Hendriksen, *More than Conquerors* (Baker Books, 1998), 125.
6. Venema helpfully notes, "Those who are members of the new covenant church of Jesus Christ are apt to forget the greater richness of saving blessing that has been poured out upon the nations of the earth in these last days. The light of the gospel that has shone among the nations of the earth in the present age contrasts vividly with the darkness in which the nations dwelt during the period of the old covenant." See Cornelis P. Venema, *The Promise of the Future*, 318–319.
7. Ezek. Chapters 38–39. For an extended discussion on John's use of Ezekiel's prophecy, see G.K. Beale, *The Book of Revelation: A Commentary on the Greek Text* (Grand Rapids, MI: Eerdmans Publishing, 2013), 1021–1031.
8. 1,000 is also the cube of 10, the number of completion. See Leon Morris, *Revelation* (Grand Rapids, MI: Eerdmans, 1984), 235.
9. John calls the soul going to be with Jesus the "first resurrection" (v. 5), which implies a second resurrection involving a renewed body. See 1 Cor. 15:22–23.
10. These words are found in Moody's autobiography. See https://www.christianitytoday.com/ct/2018/february-web-only/billy-graham-viral-quote-on-death-not-his-d-l-moody.html.
11. See Anthony A. Hoekema, The Bible and the Future (Grand Rapids, MI: Eerdmans, 1994), 230.

34

THE GREAT WHITE THRONE
REVELATION 20:11–15

If you follow professional baseball, you know the name Ted Williams. He played for the Boston Red Sox and is regarded as one of the league's all-time greatest hitters. But when Williams died in 2002, Ted's children began a public disagreement about what to do with their father's body.

One of the children insisted that her father's final wish was to be cremated and his ashes scattered off Florida's coast. Other children produced documents showing that their father wanted to have his body frozen with liquid nitrogen and preserved in a stainless-steel tomb.

After a short court battle, the court gave the body to those who wanted to freeze their father, and they sent it to a facility in Scottsdale, Arizona, where it remains to this day, frozen solid.

Why did they freeze his body? The children said it gave them hope. Hope that someday, through scientific advances, their father's body could be reanimated and brought back to life. Ted's daughter later wrote, "Our father knew we needed something to hold onto for hope and comfort... and if [freezing his body] was the answer, then the solution was simple."[1]

I don't mean to ridicule the Williams family. Rather this story illustrates the human desire for something beyond the grave. Every worldview makes an argument for how history will end.

Raised in the Chicago Public School system, I learned that the universe began as a product of time, plus matter, plus chance, plus energy. Energy will one day dissipate into non-energy, and everything will eventually fade into nothingness. Many people share this worldview today. And yet, as the

Williams family demonstrates, there remains something deeply unsettling about that worldview. A longing exists within us all for more to the story. Revelation 20 shows us that death doesn't have the final say; there is more to the story. As we come to this familiar scene, three things serve to buoy up the comfort and hope of Christ's people. First, John sees the beginning of the renewal of creation. Second, he witnesses the resurrection of the body. And, finally, he perceives God's glory in salvation and damnation.

The Renewal of Creation

Let's set the scene: the end of the symbolic 1,000 years, representing the time between the ascension and return of Jesus has arrived. The beast of the sea, the beast of the earth, and Satan, the parody of the holy Trinity, have been cast into the lake of fire to be tormented *"day and night forever and ever"* (Rev. 20:10). Now comes the event promised in the book of Hebrews *"it is appointed for man to die once, and after that comes judgment"* (Heb. 9:27). But before we see the judgment of mankind, John describes a throne, one seated upon it, and creation fleeing away:

> *Then I saw a great white throne and him who was seated on it. From his presence earth and sky fled away, and no place was found for them.* (Rev. 20:11)

John doesn't tell us who sits on the throne, but the Scriptures tell us elsewhere that Jesus himself will judge the world. In John's gospel, he records Jesus saying,

> *For the Father judges no one, but has given all judgment to the Son, that all may honor the Son, just as they honor the Father.* (John 5:22–23)

Likewise, Paul told the Athenians that God has fixed a day when he will judge the world by a man whom he has appointed and raised from the dead (Acts 17:31).[2] Christ is seated on a white throne representing his victory, purity, and holiness.

But before he calls people to account, notice what happens to the creation: *"From his presence earth and sky fled away, and no place was found for them"* (Rev. 20:11). In one of John's early visions, when Christ entered into the judgment of men and women, they were described as desiring to flee from the presence of the one seated on the throne (Rev.

6:15–17). In this vision, creation, cursed because of man's sin (Gen. 3:17), now flees from the Lord's presence

But this doesn't signal the end of creation, nor the destruction of the world. Peter tells us that a purification of creation is coming (2 Pet. 3:10, 12; Acts 3: 21). That is to say, God will not destroy creation, but he'll renew it. Additionally, Paul personifies creation as a pregnant woman who, during labor, longs for the day when it will be free from its present turmoil (Rom. 8:19–21). A woman in labor wishes not for her death but for the present struggle of childbirth to pass so that she might enjoy her child. So, in the same way, Paul tells us that the creation *"waits with eager longing for the revealing of the sons of God"* (Rom. 8:19).

John witnesses the end of creation's birth pains. In the next chapter, we'll see the liberation for which it longs. What a glorious hope and inheritance we have, Christian! Jesus promises his people will inherit the earth for all eternity (Matt. 5:5). This earth, but renewed. It will be free from hurricanes, tornadoes, droughts, viruses, and cancer cells, which stop beating hearts. Post-judgment, creation will serve its original purpose as the setting in which God and man dwell together in mutual love, service, and enjoyment, a world without end.[3] But John sees more than just the renewal of the earth. He also sees the resurrection of our bodies.

The Resurrection of the Dead

When we think of the resurrection from the dead, our thoughts typically turn first to Jesus Christ, who, on Easter morning, was raised body and soul from death. But we should not isolate the resurrection of Jesus's body from our own resurrection. Paul asserted that Easter morning gives us a glimpse of the greater resurrection to come (1 Cor. 15:20, 23). Paul termed the raising of Jesus as "the firstfruits," which you'll recall from our earlier study, was an agrarian term for the earliest crop that preceded the fuller, larger harvest to come later. So when we think about the resurrection of Jesus from death to life, his resurrection points to a massive, humanity-wide bodily raising to come. In a very real sense, God has already begun the renewal of creation in the resurrected body of Jesus Christ.[4] Most Christians know that the Bible teaches that we will spend eternity in physical bodies. Not all, however, are aware that even those who die in rebellion against the Lord will also be raised bodily from the dead for eternal life.[5] Consider these words from Daniel:

> *And many of those who sleep in the dust of the earth shall awake, some to everlasting life, and some to shame and everlasting contempt.* (Dan. 12:2)

Jesus echoes this universal resurrection in John's gospel:

> *An hour is coming when all who are in the tombs will hear his voice and come out, those who have done good to the resurrection of life, those who have done evil to the resurrection of judgment.* (John 5:28–29; see also Acts 24:15)

Regardless of their relationship with Jesus, every person will be raised bodily for eternal life.[6] John describes the moment that both Daniel and Jesus spoke about:

> *And I saw the dead, great and small, standing before the throne, and books were opened. Then another book was opened, which is the book of life. And the dead were judged by what was written in the books, according to what they had done. And the sea gave up the dead who were in it, Death and Hades gave up the dead who were in them, and they were judged, each one of them, according to what they had done.* (Rev. 20:12–13)

Though everyone will live in a resurrected body for eternity, the contrast between where and how it will be spent could not be more significant. Jesus promises that the meek will inherit the new heavens and the new earth with imperishable, glorious, and powerful bodies (1 Cor. 15:42–43). But those who die in rebellion against Jesus will be bodily raised for eternity to face unimaginable, unending physical and spiritual torment:

> *Then Death and Hades were thrown into the lake of fire. This is the second death, the lake of fire. And if anyone's name was not found written in the book of life, he was thrown into the lake of fire.* (Rev. 20:14–15)

God's faultless justice once again manifests itself here with punishment befitting the crime. Those who sinned against the Lord in body and soul will be punished not as immaterial beings but as those who have a resurrected body which, with their souls, will suffer the unending wrath of God.

While we may wince at such a thought or try to avoid the clear teaching regarding an indescribably terrifying and eternal hell, we must bow our heads and accept that it is true. We might wish for an end to the punishment with time.

Yet we must acknowledge that Scripture speaks not of temporary punishment but eternal.[7] And no one in Scripture speaks about hell as frequently or in as much detail as our Lord Jesus Christ, whose depth of human feeling and compassion for humans none could deny. Jesus knew the terrors of an eternal hell; after all, he'd created it. And on the cross, he experienced it. As acquainted as Jesus was with the terror of unending misery, he pleaded with people to embrace life, not eternal death (John 5:40). He pleads with us still today.

Those who refuse his offer will be thrown into the presence of an angry God and might wish for an end to the suffering. But John says that Death and Hades[8] were thrown into the lake of fire (see 1 Cor. 15:26). On that day, death and the cessation of existence would be a mercy to those who are found guilty before God. But John sees here not a day of mercy to the rebellious, but a day of perfect justice, carried out by an eternal God.[9]

Regardless of their relationship with Jesus, everyone will be raised bodily and live eternally. But as this vision makes clear, not everyone will share the same destination. Some will know unending suffering, weeping, and gnashing of teeth (Matt. 8:12; 13:42, 50; 22:13; 24:51; 25:30). Others will know glory, harmony, and perfect communion with God, creation, and the rest of the Lord's people. And by now, it shouldn't surprise us that how and where we will spend eternal life depends entirely upon one's relationship with Jesus Christ. And one of the purposes of the judgment is to reveal the final destiny of each person and to display God's glory through it all.

The Revelation of Destinies and the Glory of God

Returning to the vision, as the Lord sits upon the throne of judgment, with every human raised to stand before him, John sees two sets of books:

> *And I saw the dead, great and small, standing before the throne, and books were opened. Then another book was opened, which is the book of life. And the dead were judged by what was written in the books, according to what they had done. And the sea gave up the dead who were in it, Death and Hades gave up the dead who were in them, and they were judged, each one of them, according to what they had done... And if anyone's name was not found written in the book of life, he was thrown into the lake of fire.* (Rev. 20:12-13, 15)

One set of books contains a record of each person's life. Every word, deed, and motive of the heart now concealed, will on that day, be exposed in the light (Matt. 12:36; 25:35–40).[10]

Consider what it might look like to give an account for what the Bible calls sin. Imagine if, in thought, word, or deed, you failed to image the God who made you just five times a day, a *very* conservative estimate. That would come to 35 crimes against the Lord in just one week, around 140 crimes in a month, and 1680 crimes over just one year. Now imagine you live just thirty years. The books would contain over 50,000 acts of rebellion and hostility against God's authority and existence for which you would have no defense. And that's just five sins a day, which I sometimes commit just on my drive to work!

The thought of this can overwhelm us, and if we take this to heart, we cry out with the psalmist, *"If you, O LORD, should mark iniquities, O Lord, who could stand?"* (Ps. 130:3). Some, on that day, will not be left standing when they are given what their deeds are owed.

Yet some will stand. Their names are in a different book:[11] *"And if anyone's name was not found written in the book of life, he was thrown into the lake of fire."* (Rev. 20:15)

This isn't the first time we've come across the Book of Life in Revelation. Jesus spoke about this book in Rev. 3:5. Also, in Chapter 13, we were told that God wrote people's names in this book before *"the foundation of the world"* (Rev. 13:8; see also 17:8). This book contains not deeds but the names of those for whom the Lamb has shed his blood. The only hope we have of standing on that day lies here. Either we'll stand alone in our guilt before God, representing ourselves, or the Lamb of God and his righteousness will represent us.

Is your name written in the Book of Life? Are we able to know that our name will appear in the book on that day? Thankfully, we need not guess or cross our spiritual fingers. Have you placed your faith in Christ? I don't mean, do you believe in Jesus? But have you placed your faith in Jesus?

What's the difference between belief and faith? I heard an old story as a boy that points to the answer. The story concerns a man named Jean Francois Gravelot, better known as "The Great Blondin," so named for his blonde hair. Blondin was a famous tightrope walker who lived just before the American Civil War.

Blondin's fame came in 1859 when he was the first to cross Niagara Falls while walking on a tightrope. Crowds gathered from the United States and Canada to witness the Great Blondin cross the Niagara multiple times: sometimes on foot, at times on a bicycle, and even blindfolded. Once, a crowd gathered to watch Blondin traverse the Falls, but first, he yelled out to the multitude, "Do you believe I can walk across these falls using only a tightrope?"

"Yes! We believe!" answered the crowds.

"Do you believe I can do so while carrying a man on my back?"

"Of course," the crowd cheered. He was the Great Blondin, after all!

Finally, Blondin asked, "Which of you will volunteer to be the one I carry?"

The eager and vocal crowd now went silent. As the story goes, only one person, his manager, volunteered and climbed on Blondin's back, who then carried him across the falls. The crowds knew and even believed great things about Blondin. But only one in the crowd trusted him.[12]

That's the question the Bible asks us from cover to cover: is your trust in Christ? When Jesus commands hard things, do you trust him? When Jesus calls you to take up the cross, do you trust him and do so? Do you trust him when he calls you to love unlovable people, forgive unforgivable things, and befriend the unfriendly? And when you fail at these things, as we all do from time to time (James 3:2), do you trust him when he says, *"Repent and believe in the gospel"* (Mark 1:15)? Or do you find reasons why such things don't apply to you? If you trust him, you do so because the Father of our Lord Jesus wrote your name in that book long before he created the world.

And therefore, you can face this day with eager hope and deep comfort. But we might wonder how that can be. Will the sins of Christ's people be publicly exposed on that day?[13] Scripture consistently affirms this. Jesus assures us:

> *Nothing is covered up that will not be revealed, or hidden that will not be known. Therefore whatever you have said in the dark shall be heard in the light, and what you have whispered in private rooms shall be proclaimed on the housetops.* (Luke 12:2–3)

How, then, do we square the exposure of all our sins on that day with the Bible's promises of the bliss that we'll know at the coming of the Lord Jesus? Two answers help us understand. First, Christians will have been changed when they stand at the judgment (1 John 3:2). It will not be our comfort and interests which will ultimately concern us on that day. Our hearts will be so sanctified and free from self-interest that our supreme aim will be the glory and vindication of Jesus Christ. It seems, too, that our consciences will demand that our sins be set before Jesus.[14] We all know the burden our hearts feel when we have sinned against someone we love, but perhaps they are unaware of the transgression. In those situations, we often want to tell the other person how we've violated them because love compels us not to keep it buried. On that day when our hearts are focused on the glory and vindication of Jesus, perhaps we'll desire that all violations against God be set before our Lord.

The second reason we face the exposure of our sin with comfort and hope is the purpose for which it will be done: to magnify the glory of God in salvation. Remember, judgment will not occur to determine where people will spend eternity.[15] God isn't gathering evidence and then deciding based on what happens when the books are opened. He has already pronounced the verdict upon humanity. Jesus said:

> *Whoever believes in [me] is not condemned, but whoever does not believe is condemned already because he has not believed in the name of the only Son of God.* (John 3:18)

We already know the verdict that awaits both Christians and non-Christians. So the purpose for which Christ will set our sins before us is not to determine eternal life or death. Instead, it will be to magnify God's glory and righteousness in both salvation and damnation![16] Think again about that scenario of the person who sinned five times a day, 35 times a week, 140 times a month, over thirty years. Imagine now as those fifty thousand-plus crimes against Jesus are put on public display. The Christian will hear Jesus say over each one, "No condemnation. No condemnation" (Rom. 8:1).

At that moment, we will for the first time truly comprehend the width, length, height, and depth of the love of Jesus for us. Therefore, no inconsistency exists between the exposure of our sin and the promised bliss of that day. As John Murray wrote:

> It is against the gravity of [our] sins that [our] salvation in Christ will be magnified, and not only the grace but the righteousness of God will be extolled in the consummation of [our] redemption.[17]

Far from being a day designed to shame and embarrass the people of God openly, its design will magnify the glory of Jesus and bring your joy in him to its zenith.

There's a question in the Heidelberg Catechism which captures the issue for us. It asks, "What comfort is it to you that Christ will come to judge the living and the dead?" It doesn't ask, "How terrified are you that Christ will come to judge," but rather, "What comfort is it to you?" Answer:

"The one who comes to judge is the same person who came to be judged for my sake and has removed all curses from me."[18]

What a Savior we serve! What great confidence, hope, and comfort we have as we look forward to the coming judgment. Until then, let us make it our aim to please him and to summon others to embrace the One seated on the throne, in whom life, comfort, and hope are found.

Study Questions

1. Consider the promise of a renewed creation instead of the popular notion that heaven is a place of immaterial existence. Does this change the way you look at the future? Does Jesus's promise that the meek will inherit the earth mean more to you after studying this passage from Revelation?
2. The Lord will raise everyone's body and soul to live eternally in one of two destinations. In what ways do you shy away from speaking of this reality with your friends and neighbors?
3. On the day that you stand before the Lamb and he opens the books, you can face it with great comfort and hope. What are the two reasons this hope will be possible?
4. Take some time this week to commit to memory this point from the Heidelberg Confession and ask the Lord to make it a comforting reality for you.

---

1. https://www.bostonherald.com/2014/05/19/ted-williams-daughter-why-we-froze-dad/
2. It is true that the One seated on the throne in Revelation is typically God the Father (Chs. 4–5; 6:16, 19:4; 21:5), and Dan. 7:9–10, where the Ancient of Days is seated on the throne, forms the backdrop for this vision. But there is no need to split hairs here. Insisting on the Father or the Son is fruitless. While Scripture repeatedly attributes the judgment to the Father (Matt. 18:35; 2 Thess. 1:5; Heb. 11:6), he accomplishes this work through Christ, to whom all judgment has been given. See Herman Bavinck, *Reformed Dogmatics, Volume 4: Holy Spirit, Church, and New Creation*, edited by John Bolt (Grand Rapids, MI: Baker Academic, 2008), 700.
3. For more on this theme, see Thomas R. Schreiner, *Romans* (Grand Rapids, MI: Baker Academic, 1998), 432–441.
4. For a discussion on Christ as the beginning of the new creation, see G.K. Beale, *The Book of Revelation: A Commentary on the Greek Text* (Grand Rapids, MI: Eerdmans Publishing, 2013), 298; Vern S. Poythress, *The Returning King: A Guide to the Book of Revelation* (P&R, 2000), 93.
5. John Murray writes: "The disembodied state is not the final state. Neither bliss nor woe can be complete until the integrity of personal life is restored by resurrection." See John Murray, *Collected Writings of John Murray, Volume Two: Select Lectures in Systematic Theology* (Carlisle, PA: Banner of Truth, 2009), 402.

6. Paul tells us that those who are alive when the Lord returns will be caught up to meet him in the air (1 Thess. 4:15-17) with bodies changed from perishable to imperishable (1 Cor. 15:51–53). While Paul's focus falls upon the blessed hope of the Christian, we can only assume that non-Christians who are alive at the Lord's coming will also, at that time, be given an immortal body in which they will stand for judgment.
7. For a treatment of the eternality of hell, see Herman Bavinck, *Reformed Dogmatics*, 708–714.
8. *Hades* is a term used throughout Scripture to refer to the realm of the dead. Some suffer in Hades while others, also in Hades, are in the presence of the Lord. The equivalent term we might use here is the afterlife, where some suffer, and others do not. Hades represents the temporary realm of disembodied persons that will, at the resurrection of the just and unjust, be abolished. For more on Hades, see Anthony A. Hoekema, *The Bible and the Future* (Grand Rapids, MI: Eerdmans, 1994), 92–108.
9. Bavinck notes: "The eternal life [the Lord] imparted to us presupposes an eternal death from which he has saved us." Herman Bavinck, *Reformed Dogmatics*, 713.
10. These opened books are an allusion to the throne room scene in Daniel 7, where the Ancient of Days is seated on a throne, *"and the books were opened"* (Dan. 7:10).
11. This book is an allusion to Daniel 12: *"your people shall be delivered, everyone whose name shall be found written in the book"* (Dan. 12:1).
12. Saving faith is typically categorized as having three necessary elements: knowledge, assent, and trust. Question 72 of the Westminster Larger Catechism asks, "What is justifying faith?" The answer captures all three elements: "Justifying faith is a saving grace, wrought in the heart of a sinner by the Spirit and the word of God, whereby he, being convinced of his sin and misery, and of the disability in himself and all other creatures to recover him out of his lost condition, not only assenteth to the truth of the promise of the gospel; but receiveth and resteth upon Christ and his righteousness, therein held forth, for pardon of sin, and for the accepting and accounting of his person righteous in the sight of God for salvation."
13. Theologians debate whether the sins of believers will be brought forth on that day. Some argue that such an act would war against the very promises of the new covenant, which assure us that God has "forgotten" all of our sins (Heb. 8:12), having cast them "behind his back" (Isa. 38:17). Nevertheless, the consistent testimony of Scripture is that believers will stand in the judgment with both the "good" and "bad" presented (2 Cor. 5:10. See also 1 Cor. 3:10–15).
14. On this, see John Murray, *Collected Writings of John Murray, Volume Two: Select Lectures in Systematic Theology*, 414.
15. See the chapter covering Rev. 14:14–15:4.
16. Although not mentioned here, the Bible indicates that another purpose of the judgment will be to bestow various rewards to God's people, e.g., Luke 19:12–19; 1 Cor. 3: 10–15; 2 Cor. 5:8-10. As there will be gradations of rewards for the people of God, so too will gradations of punishment be given to those outside of Christ, e.g., Matt. 10:15; Luke 12:47–48. For a discussion of rewards, see Anthony A. Hoekema, *The Bible and the Future*, 262–264; John Murray, *Collected Writings of John Murray, Volume Two: Select Lectures in Systematic Theology*, 416–17.
17. John Murray, *Collected Writings of John Murray, Volume Two: Select Lectures in Systematic Theology*, 414–415.
18. This paraphrases a longer question and answer to the catechism's question 52.

35

ALL THINGS SUPERABUNDANTLY NEW

REVELATION 21:1–8

One of the most enjoyable baseball games I've ever witnessed was Game Seven of the 2016 World Series between the Chicago Cubs and the Cleveland Indians. It's still strange to remember that game with joy because if you were with me that night, you would have seen a man having a miserable time. The game went well for the Cubs through the eighth inning, and the 108-year World Series drought appeared to be ending.

But then everything started to fall apart. Poor pitching by the Cubs and good bats for the Indians shifted the game's momentum, and it seemed that the Lovable Losers, as Chicago fans call the Cubs, were facing yet another year of frustration. And so was I.

Text messages started to explode on my phone. Some came from well-wishers lamenting the situation, others from my friends in Ohio capitalizing on my misery. And as the game went on, I got irritable, frustrated, and angry.

But then something remarkable happened. The Lord, in his kindness, opened the windows of heaven, and an unexpected rainstorm fell, creating a game delay that cooled the bats of the Indians. And after a few more innings, the Cubs rallied and won. A simple rainstorm ended the longest drought in MLB history.

Here's what I've found since that night: whenever I see rerun clips from that tortuous game, I can endure the ups and downs because I know how it ends. Knowing how the game ends shapes how I now see every bad pitch, strikeout, and missed opportunity in the highlights. The ending gives meaning to the whole.

These final two chapters of the book of Revelation function much in the same way. John's first audience suffers things far more terrible than a lousy baseball game, and so will you. Perhaps you have health problems. It could be relational pain that you experience, a cold marriage, wandering children, or lost friendships. Perhaps you feel aimless right now, unused by the Lord, and wondering how it all fits together. Maybe you're honest enough to confess that you struggle with a besetting sin that sometimes appeals more to you than obedience to the Lord.

God gives us these final chapters, showing us the astonishing joys that await those who don't give up and give in to the world. Jesus promised us a world where troubles will find us. But seeing how the story ends enables us to press on and fight on with hope.

John strains his pen to show us the lasting treasures that await those who love Jesus. The Christian looks forward to a rich inheritance and restored intimacy with the Lord.

Rich Inheritance

In the previous chapter, John witnessed the earth and sky flee from the presence of the Lord as he called everyone to stand before the judgment seat. Those whose names were not found in the Book of Life will dwell in the lake of fire, a most dreadful eternal inheritance (see also Rev. 21:8). John's attention now shifts to the inheritance awaiting those in the Lamb's Book of Life. Jesus promised his people that they would inherit the earth (Matt. 5:5). John sees the promise kept:

> *Then I saw a new heaven and a new earth, for the first heaven and the first earth had passed away, and the sea was no more. And I saw the holy city, new Jerusalem, coming down out of heaven from God, prepared as a bride adorned for her husband.* (Rev. 21:1–2)

As a little boy in Sunday School, I distinctly remember my boredom with descriptions of eternity. Teachers taught us about an endless existence of floating around on clouds and playing harps. As a little guy at the time, going to heaven meant the end of baseball, which sounded more like an eternal life of punishment!

Thankfully, the Lord promises a far richer inheritance than an eternal, immaterial existence.[1] The meek shall inherit the earth. What earth? This one, but different. John describes the earth and heavens as "new." What does John mean by calling them "new"?

Suppose I told you I had a new hat. I might mean a few things by that. Perhaps I just bought a hat that I previously didn't own. In that sense, it would be new to me.

Now suppose I show you that same hat and tell you that it had been previously misshaped, filthy, and full of holes. But after taking it to a professional for cleaning and repair, I say, "Look at my new hat!" I'm not claiming that the hat didn't exist before, but that it's been restored, beautified, and returned to its original purpose.

Just as we sometimes use the word "new" differently, the Greeks did too. Here's the point: when John describes the inheritance promised to the people of God, he uses the word that points to a restored, beautified, and wholly transformed new heaven and new earth.[2] I wince now when I hear Christians say they'd like to see the world before they die, as though there isn't this glorious promise of a new heavens and earth given to us. I suspect I'm not the only one who had been taught that my eternal home with Jesus was off somewhere in the clouds versus on a renewed and restored earth.

While we look forward to the fulfillment of this promised inheritance, we praise God even now because, in many ways, the world will not be the same. There's a glorious discontinuity between the earth as we know it now and the one we'll know then. The renewal of the heavens and the earth will not be a cosmic "do over" or a simple return to Eden.[3] Our inheritance will be breathtakingly different from our world and even the world as Adam knew it in the garden:

> *He will wipe away every tear from their eyes, and death shall be no more, neither shall there be mourning, nor crying, nor pain anymore, for the former things have passed away." And he who was seated on the throne said, "Behold, I am making all things new." Also he said, "Write this down, for these words are trustworthy and true."* (Rev. 21:4–5)

The promise of the "former things" passing away carries so much comfort for us. Unlike the world of Genesis 1, in the one to come, there will be no more trees carrying the threat of death (Gen. 2:17). Instead, there will only be the Tree of Life, signifying life evermore (Rev. 22:2). Our bodies will no longer break down, sag, and weaken with age. Instead, they will be like Christ's resurrection body: imperishable, glorious, and brimming with life.

And when we see Christ, we shall be like him (1 John 3:2), forever free from sin and its terrible consequences. Poverty, pain, fear, hunger and thirst, injustice, racism, weakness, dishonor, and corrupt politicians will all be cast out of the earth. That's what I believe John means when he describes the new earth, writing, *"the sea was no more"* (Rev. 21:1).

Remember, Revelation uses symbols to communicate eternal truths. Throughout the book, the seas of the earth are places of chaos, evil, and judgment.[4] From the sea, the beast emerges (Rev. 13:1), and upon its waters, merchants transport slaves to fund their luxurious lifestyle (Rev. 18:13). And under its surface, the sea serves as an abode for the dead (Rev. 20:13).

But no such things find a place in the new heavens and the new earth! Indescribable blessings characterize the rich inheritance awaiting Christ's Bride. Holiness, glory, full adoption, eternal life, and complete conformity to the will of God will permeate the cosmos. And supreme amongst all these blessings: we shall see the face of the Lord Jesus and stare into the eyes of the One who loves us and has freed us from our sins by his blood (Rev. 1:5).

John will show us this blessed reunion in a moment, but first, consider the kindness of our God in showing us this future inheritance. This promise awaits future fulfillment to be sure, but with it, he gives us a present proof that he will renew the earth and give it to his Son and his Bride.

We all like proof that substantiates big claims. The promise of a restored heaven and earth certainly qualifies as an enormous promise! And the Lord props up our weak faith by giving us proof that he will surely deliver on his promise. So what's the proof?

Paul tells us it's our trust in Jesus. Let me explain.

Paul wrote to the Roman Christians, assuring them that as we wait for the renewing of all of creation, including our bodies, we have *"the firstfruits of the Spirit"* within us (Rom. 8:23). We've encountered this term "firstfruits" already.[5] The firstfruits functioned as a small ingathering of crops that pointed toward a more extensive harvest to come. The Bible tells us that the Holy Spirit within us is the *"first pledge of blessings that are still to come."*[6] In other words, your faith in Jesus, brought about by the Spirit of God, is the Father's promise to you that the renewal and re-creation he's already begun in you, he'll bring to completion on the day John witnessed in his vision.

Christian, the Spirit of God at work within you is the Father's vow that the healing, acceptance, and forgiveness your heart longs for in Jesus will all be yours. Do you see the kindness and mercy of God to you? We need this, particularly when we barely limp along the path of obedience and only have enough faith to say, "I believe! Help my unbelief!" Even if just a mustard seed of faith rattles around in your heart, the Ancient of Days stands behind that seed, with the vow to keep every promise made to you in Jesus Christ. And supreme among God's promises is that we will be with our Savior.

Restored Intimacy

We've seen many images and symbols in John's Revelation: elders on thrones, a lamb holding a scroll, seals broken, four horses released, trumpets blowing, plagues falling, and beasts coming out of the sea and the land. The list goes on: a dragon chasing a woman, people with marks on their foreheads and hands, a prostitute drunk on blood, and martyrs crying out for justice. But the realization of all the visions comes to fruition before John's eyes. The disciple sees the holy city, the new Jerusalem coming down from heaven. But before he describes the city, which he'll do shortly, he's interrupted by a voice:

> *And I heard a loud voice from the throne saying, "Behold, the dwelling place of God is with man. He will dwell with them, and they will be his people, and God himself will be with them as their God.* (Rev. 21:3)

Two things come together in this pronouncement. The first is a well-known promise found numerous times in the Bible: I will dwell with my people. For example, in the book of Ezekiel, speaking about an everlasting covenant with his people, the Lord promised: *"My dwelling place shall be with them, and I will be their God, and they shall be my people"* (Ezek. 37:27).

Over and over again,[7] the Lord asserts his desire: I want to be with my people. One writer has called God's stated desire to be with his people as "the golden thread woven into the fabric of Scripture from beginning to end… it is the thread of God's abiding love toward his covenant people."[8] And can you doubt this captures his desire when you consider that he didn't spare his own Son but gave him up for you? Let that golden thread bind up your broken heart today. He desires to be with you.

In addition to a well-known promise, John hears the voice alluding to the tabernacle's well-known structure. Although hidden behind our English words, in the original Greek the voice says, "The tabernacle of God is with man. He will tabernacle with them." Recall that God's unique presence dwelt among his people in the mobile tent called the tabernacle.

But the tabernacle's design also kept people from getting too close to God's special presence. Only Moses and the High Priest could enter the most sacred room of the tabernacle. And little changed once the tabernacle became the brick-and-mortar structure in Jerusalem. Gentiles could only come so close to the holiest room. Jewish women could come a little closer, and Jewish men closer still. But the innermost rooms were still reserved only for priests.

For the first time since the fall, John sees God and his people living under one roof. All the protective barriers and safeguards preventing approach have been removed. In the next chapter, we'll be told that there's no temple in the new heaven and earth (Rev. 21:22). As we'll see, the entire cosmos becomes where God and man dwell together. Never again will we be outside of the immediate presence of our God. Instead, we'll be so close that, like a compassionate mother who stoops down to comfort a child, the Lord will dry our tear-soaked eyes.

If that were not enough, the Lord's love and desire for his people escalates in the way he describes the eternal relationship he has with his people:

> *And he said to me, "It is done! I am the Alpha and the Omega, the beginning and the end. To the thirsty I will give from the spring of the water of life without payment. The one who conquers will have this heritage, and I will be his God and he will be my son."* (Rev. 21:6–7)

"You will be my son." Did we read that right? This may cause us to scratch our heads and re-read that promise, especially if we know the origin of these words. This language echoes a promise to David about an individual who comes from his line and with whom the Lord would have a unique relationship: *"I will be to him a father, and he shall be to me a son"* (2 Sam. 7:14; Ps. 89:26–27).

The Scriptures point to Jesus Christ as the one who fulfills this role. If we've any doubt, both at the baptism of Jesus (Matt. 3:17) and when he was transfigured before the disciples (Matt. 17:5), the Lord speaks from heaven over both events saying, *"This is my beloved Son,"* pointing to Jesus. And yet, the promise here, using the same language, applies to all who are untied to Jesus: you are my Son. This same language shows up in other places in the New Testament. Consider Paul's words to the Galatians: *"in Christ Jesus you are all sons of God, through faith"* (Gal. 3:26. See also Gal. 4:5–6). Likewise to the Christians in Rome, Paul wrote: *"All who are led by the Spirit of God are sons of God"* (Rom. 8:14).

How do we understand this promise made to an individual, "he will be my son," that is applied now to all who follow him? The answer lies in what Paul calls union with Christ. Our faith in Jesus consists of more than mental knowledge of, assent to, and trust in Jesus. Instead, our faith brings about a true union with Jesus. What does it mean to be united to the Son?

We could summarize union with Christ saying what he possesses, you possess, and vice versa. The relationship of human marriage dimly reflects the union we have with Jesus Christ (Eph. 5:31–32). The two become one. We've all been to weddings where we have heard that famous line, "All that I am, I give to you. And all that I have, I share with you."

Do you see the astounding mercy, patience, and indescribable love Jesus has for you? He didn't come into the world simply to save you from God's wrath, as necessary as that is. Nor simply to forgive your sin and promise eternal life in a renewed heaven and earth. All wonderful and glorious promises to be sure!

So in love with you, and so loving, he came to live, die, and be raised for you to share with you his status: that you might be a son of God. Christ came for you and me so that we might share in the same relationship he has had with the Father from eternity. What was the Father doing before he created the world through the Son? He loved the Son with infinite, eternal, and unchangeable zeal (John 17:5). What will the Father do in the new heavens and the new earth? He will love you with the same unchangeable zeal he's always had for his only begotten Son.

Though Jesus will always and forever be God's unique, divine Son, those for whom he died will share in all the rights and privileges of sonship.[9]

Standing before the Holy Trinity, I long to hear, *"Well done, good and faithful servant"* (Matt. 25:23). And I suspect that would be enough to satisfy me forever! But the depths of the Lord's love go deeper than treating us only as a faithful servant. You will be as loved, treasured, and desired as the very Son of God. Can you even imagine a love so great and a grace so immeasurable and so divine? The sinner who knows who their depravity, apart from Jesus, blushes with embarrassment to hear such things. But there remains no "apart from Jesus" for those united to him.

You may be familiar with the name Brennan Manning, the Christian writer probably best known for his book *The Ragamuffin Gospel*. However, you may not know that Brennan was not his birth name—it was Richard Xavier Francis Manning. But later in life, he entered the priesthood, and when instructed to adopt the name of a saint, he chose the name of his best friend: Ray Brennan. These two men knew one another from their earliest days and did everything together. They attended the same classes in grade school, bought a car together as teenagers, double-dated in high school, and even joined the army together, fighting side by side in the Korean War.

One night the two of them sat in a foxhole reminiscing about the good old days back in Brooklyn. Suddenly a live grenade lobbed by a North Korean soldier landed right at their feet. Ray spotted it first and immediately threw himself on top of it. It detonated instantly. His stomach smothered the explosion, killing him instantly but preserving his friend's life.

Later, when instructed to take the name of a saint, Manning didn't think twice about taking the name of his late best friend. As a priest and public speaker, Manning's travels took him back to Brooklyn, where he once visited Ray's mother. As they shared a cup of tea, Brennan somewhat flippantly asked, "I wonder if ol' Ray loved me as much as I loved him?"

With tears in her eyes, Ray's mother looked at Brennan and, with a finger in his face, said, "How can you ask such a thing? What more could he have done for you?"

Brennan later said that he suddenly imagined himself standing at the foot of the cross asking a similarly dumb question, "Does God really love me?" And then he imagined Mary, also at the foot of the cross, pointing to Jesus and saying, "How can you ask such a thing? What more could he have done for you?"

And so the Spirit comes to us, putting his finger upon our hearts, asking, "How can you ever doubt the love of God? Look at the inheritance that awaits you. Look at the desire he has to be with you. And then look at the cross, where you see what it cost him to make it all possible. What more could he have done?" Setting that kind of love before you will strengthen you to keep running the race until you cross the finish line, where the Son of God waits to welcome you and crown you with his unshakable love.

Study Questions

1. How does the above description of eternity as a restored heavens and earth differ from what you previously understood? In what ways are you most looking forward to this rich inheritance?
2. What's the proof that this renewed earth is your inheritance?
3. God desires to be with you. Do you find this "golden thread" woven throughout Scripture comforting? Perhaps it's a bit

difficult to believe? How does it urge you toward honoring the Lord with your life?

4. This promise that he will be our God and we will "be God's son" is not an outdated usage of male nouns that needs contemporary updating. Instead, it perfectly describes our inherited sonship through union with Christ. Take some time to tease out the meaning and implications of this promise.

5. Reread the last paragraph of this chapter slowly to yourself, journal your response, and pray for the Lord to make these promises ever present, informing and molding your life.

---

1. See Isaiah 65:17–18; 66:12, which serves as the background of John's description.
2. The Greek word *kainos*, meaning "qualitatively new," generally differs from *neos*, meaning "not previously in existence." John uses the first term in Revelation and never the second. See G.K. Beale, *The Book of Revelation: A Shorter Commentary* (Eerdmans, 2015), 464; and Simon Kistemaker, *Revelation*, New Testament Commentary (Grand Rapids: Baker, 2001), 554–555. Bavinck sums up the matter brilliantly, "God's honor consists precisely in the fact that he redeems and renews the same humanity, the same world, the same heaven, the same earth that have been corrupted and polluted by sin." See Herman Bavinck, *Reformed Dogmatics, Volume 4: Holy Spirit, Church, and New Creation,* edited by John Bolt (Grand Rapids, MI: Baker Academic, 2008), 717.
3. For a chapter-length treatment of this theme, see Michael D. Williams, *Far As the Curse Is Found: The Covenant Story of Redemption* (Phillipsburg, NJ: P&R Publishing, 2005), 271–302.
4. For a discussion on the sea in God's throne room, see the chapter above on Rev. 4:1-11, ft. nt. 10.
5. See the chapters covering Rev. 14:1–5 and 20:11–15.
6. See Thomas R. Schreiner, *Romans* (Grand Rapids, MI: Baker Academic, 1998), 438.
7. See, for example, Gen. 17:7; Ex. 6:7; Lev. 26:12; Ezek. 11:20; 2 Cor. 6:16.
8. Simon Kistemaker, *Revelation*, New Testament Commentary (Grand Rapids, MI: Baker, 2001), 557.
9. The Westminster Shorter Catechism Question 34 asks, "What is adoption?" Answer: "Adoption is an act of God's free grace, whereby we are received into the number, and have a right to all the privileges of the sons of God."

36

HERE COMES THE BRIDE

REVELATION 21:9-27

Henry Gunther was the name of an American soldier with the sad honor of being the last man to die in World War I. Before getting drafted into the Army, Henry lived a comfortable life in Baltimore, looking forward to marrying a woman he loved and building a life with her. Unfortunately, that dream was interrupted by a draft that took Henry to a place he didn't want to go (France) to fight in a war he didn't support.

While on duty, Henry wrote a letter to a friend back in Baltimore complaining about life in the trenches and urging him not to sign up for duty. Somehow, senior officials intercepted and read that letter, which immediately demoted Henry multiple ranks down to private. Around the same time, Henry's fiancée decided to break off their engagement because of his shameful demotion.

Henry's peers immediately noticed a change in their fellow soldiers. No longer a cheerful and social man, Henry grew depressed and withdrawn. Henry remained a broken man up to the final day of World War I, also known as Armistice Day, when the end of all hostilities was scheduled for November 11th at 11 am.

On that day, at 10:44 am, a trench runner came to Henry's regiment with the order to hold their position. Only sixteen minutes remained until the end of all hostilities, and then they could all go home. Until then, they were to maintain their position and wait. Which is why what happened next surprised not only his fellow soldiers but also his German enemies.

With a fixed bayonet on his rifle, Henry climbed out of the trench and approached a German roadblock staffed with heavily armed men. As he charged forward, the voices of his friends begged him to stop, as did the voices of his German enemies who, with broken English, warned him not to come any closer.

But Gunther continued. The Germans sent a few warning shots over Gunther's head to show him they meant business, but Henry continued to charge. When he came too close to the roadblock, a burst of fire from a German machine gun lodged a bullet in Henry's left temple, killing him instantly. Time of death: 10:59 am. One minute before the official end of all hostilities.

Henry's fellow soldiers and numerous historians have since wrestled with trying to understand what Henry was thinking. What was behind his decision to disobey the order to hold position and wait and instead charge forward into a certain death?

Finally, years later, family members back in Baltimore provided some answers. They possessed Henry's correspondence letters filled with words from a man consumed with shame. Having been demoted by the army and dumped by his fiancée, he felt useless and worthless. So when Henry heard that there were just sixteen minutes left until the end of the war, he reasoned he had sixteen minutes left to make his life matter.[1]

Henry Gunther set a sad example of one's identity driving one's behavior. What we think of ourselves will shape how we respond to the ups and downs of everyday living. Henry saw himself through a filter of failure and in one last act of desperation, he sought redemption.

It's important to know who we are if we are to live lives of faithfulness to Jesus Christ. What do you see when you look in the mirror? Someone who can't live up to other people's expectations? Someone who is never content? Perhaps you see someone who worries all the time. Maybe the political landscape or how much money you have or don't have makes you anxious. Is that who you are?

You may see yourself through a filter of your sin. The person in the mirror shows you a man or woman who, in your estimation, cannot be very attractive to the Lord. What we think of ourselves drives the lives we live. Thankfully, the Lord doesn't leave us to our imaginations when it comes to understanding ourselves. If you love Jesus, you've been united to him, and that relationship must shape how you see yourself.

In this vision, John describes what God sees when he looks upon those in union with his son. We are not invited to decide if we agree with his assessment but rather to trust it and let it shape our lives until we see him. John describes a community eternally safe in the Lord and of immense value to him.

Eternally Safe

In the last section, John described the new heavens and earth where God dwells with his people in a renewed and invigorated creation. In this section, John gets a closer look at the things to come. You may recall from our study in Chapter 17, that an angel approached John and invited him to come and behold a woman. The angel transported John to a wilderness where he saw a seductive prostitute representing a city (Babylon). The prostitute symbolizes the world in rebellion against God.

John now sees a different woman, who he, likewise, describes as a city. But this woman, far from the wilderness, dwells on a great high mountain,[2] which the Scriptures often associate as a place of God's dwelling (Ex. 19:3; Isa. 2:2; Ps. 48:1–2, Matt. 14:23; Luke 6:2; Rev. 14:1).

> *Then came one of the seven angels who had the seven bowls full of the seven last plagues and spoke to me, saying, "Come, I will show you the Bride, the wife of the Lamb." And he carried me away in the Spirit to a great, high mountain, and showed me the holy city Jerusalem coming down out of heaven from God.* (Rev. 21:9–10)

We shouldn't be surprised at what we read here at this point in our study. After hearing about a woman, the Bride, the wife of the Lamb, John sees a city. This pattern of hearing one thing and seeing another occurs several times in Revelation. In Chapter 5, John heard about a Lion from the tribe of Judah, but when he looked for a lion, he saw a lamb. In Chapter 7, John hears about 144,000 people who will survive the judgment, but it's an innumerable number when he looks at the group. And, as we just noted, in Chapter 17, John hears about a prostitute but then describes a city.

In these cases, we are not forced to pick one or the other (Jesus exists as a Lion and a Lamb) because both images represent the same entity. So too here, the Bride of Jesus and the holy city of Jerusalem picture the same thing.[3] As we listen to John's description, the city's eternal safety stands out as one of its most striking characteristics.

John piles up image after image to show the Church they are safe in God's care. John describes an enormous wall with angel-protected gates[4] surrounding the city:

> *It had a great, high wall, with twelve gates, and at the gates twelve angels, and on the gates the names of the twelve tribes of the sons of Israel were inscribed—on the east three gates, on the north three gates, on the south three gates, and on the west three gates.* (Rev. 21:12–13)

In the ancient world, walls protected its citizens from harm. The thicker and higher the walls, the better. In verse 17, John records that the walls measured 144 cubits. Once again, John uses a symbolic number to convey a spiritual truth. As we've seen previously, the Lord utilizes the number 12 as a number of completion. 144 is a multiple of 12, signifying the complete and total safety in the Kingdom of God.

Ancient cities also built strong gates into the walls for protection, which would be closed at night, forbidding enemies' entrance under the cloak of darkness. But the gates of the city that John sees will never close. There's no need (Isa. 60:11). In this city, there dwells no thieves, murderers, terrorists, beasts of the land and the sea, nor the dragon that inspired them all.

It's hard to imagine a world where you don't lock your doors, worry about terrorism, face natural disasters, or hear of new viruses or strong nations toppling over weaker ones. The nightly news thrives on our fears and present vulnerabilities. But don't let them. The city of man will not survive the judgment. Our current fears and vulnerabilities have an expiration date.[5] While we may be physically vulnerable in this world, the Lord sees us as eternally secure through his son. Consider the words of Paul:

> *Who shall separate us from the love of Christ? Shall tribulation, or distress, or persecution, or famine, or nakedness, or danger, or sword?.... No, in all these things we are more than conquerors through him who loved us. For I am sure that neither death nor life, nor angels nor rulers, nor things present nor things to come, nor powers, nor height nor depth, nor anything else in all creation, will be able to separate us from the love of God in Christ Jesus our Lord.* (Rom. 8:35–39)

John's first audience needed this image of eternal safety just as we do. The churches addressed at the beginning of this book were threatened with all sorts of terrible things if they didn't comply with governmental demands and expectations. Satan (whom John saw as a dragon) labored to dull and even extinguish the church's public witness through the government and the propaganda of the religious cults of the day (viewed as the beast of the sea and the beast of the land).

But Jesus shores up his bride's confidence with this image, a reassurance of her genuine and ultimate security.[6] Sometimes, our eyes only see things that make us physically vulnerable like cancer, terrorism, persecution, and other threats. But should that cause us to live in fear? Should we live as those always concerned about what's over the horizon or around the corner? Have you only one life to live, one that ends with your body buried in the dirt?

Or do we live as those who believe that in the face of those physical vulnerabilities, none of them can separate us from the love of God in Christ Jesus our Lord? We are more than conquerors through him who loves us. Therefore, we should live boldly and publicly for Jesus, knowing that whatever takes our mortal life only serves to deliver us into the presence of our Savior (2 Cor. 5:6–8; Phil. 1:23). John saw the eternal safety of God's people and, just as gloriously, the exquisite value the Lord places upon them.

Immense Value

It would be far too sterile only to see safety and security in John's description, as though he saw a glorified Fort Knox. Before John describes the city's safety, he labors to capture the radiant beauty and infinite value of the Bride of Jesus. Christian, this means that John will describe what God sees when he looks at those in union with his Son. Do you see yourself only through the filter of your sin? Do you define yourself by your successes or failures in the business world? God shows us what he sees, and he doesn't do it for purely academic purposes. He intends to shape our hearts through this description.

John records his first impression of the city, describing its gleaming shine, reflecting the radiant beauty and infinite worth of God himself. For all of the other details that follow, the glory of God reflected upon the city seems to have impressed John the most:

> *And he carried me away in the Spirit to a great, high mountain, and showed me the holy city Jerusalem coming down out of heaven from God, having the*

glory of God, its radiance like a most rare jewel, like a jasper, clear as crystal. (Rev. 21:10–11)

If you go back to Rev. 4:3, John described the radiance emanating from the throne of God. He recorded that the One on the throne appeared like jasper and other precious stones. As we come to this chapter, the same radiance once confined to the throne room of God now describes the entire city that *"shines with the reflected glory of God himself."*[7]

This description makes sense when we remember that the Lord of Glory indwells his people and covers them with the beauty of his holiness.[8] When we read through the Gospels, we get a glimpse of the glory of God when Jesus and a few disciples went up on a mountain, and Jesus' appearance changed *"his face shone like the sun, and his clothes became white as light"* (Matt. 17:1–2). Those present saw a glimpse of the radiant glory the Son had with the Father before being veiled by human flesh. And to that same radiant glory, the Son returned at his ascension (John 17:5). And as we see here, the glory of Jesus—beautiful in holiness and purity—describes his people.

Notice how the Lord pictures his people through some of the city's finer details. Twelve gates allow entry into the city, each inscribed with the names of the sons of Israel (Rev. 21:12). The city's wall rises up from twelve foundations, each bearing the name of the apostles of the Lamb (Rev. 21:14). The gates and foundations remind us that this city comprises all those from the Old Testament who looked forward to the coming of the Messiah and those from the New Testament era to the return of Christ who looks back in faith to him who has come.[9] John sees in picture form what Paul assured the church:

> *You are fellow citizens with the saints and members of the household of God, built on the foundation of the apostles and prophets, Christ Jesus himself being the cornerstone, in whom the whole structure, being joined together, grows into a holy temple in the Lord.* (Eph. 2:19-21. See also 1 Pet. 2:5)

What a glorious thought! You and I share the same citizenship in the city of God as Abraham, Moses, the Hebrew midwives, David, Solomon, Ruth, Isaiah, Matthew, Mark, Luke, John, and Paul. Each and every one of these celebrities of the faith, like you, is made beautiful in radiant glory by the righteousness of Jesus. As John continues to describe the Bride and city, some of the other details suggest he also sees a temple of astronomical proportions:

> *The city lies foursquare, its length the same as its width. And he measured the city with his rod, 12,000 stadia. Its length and width and height are equal.* (Rev. 21:16)

Before we consider the numbers and their significance, note John describes the city as a cube: *"its length and width and height are equal"* (Rev. 21:6). This shape points to something far more than an interesting detail. Those whose minds were steeped in the Old Testament would have made a connection between John's description of the city and the most sacred room in Jerusalem, which also formed a perfect cube: the Holy of Holies (1 Kg. 6:20).

Not only does the shape of the city suggest temple imagery, but so do the stones adorning its foundation. The twelve precious stones on the foundation of the wall mirror the stones that adorned the breastplate of the High Priest of Israel.[10] Remember, the High Priest alone could enter the Holy of Holies, and only once a year. When there, he wore a breastplate of twelve precious stones, each representing a tribe of Israel. This Old Testament, jewel-covered outfit provided a picture of what Christ, our High Priest, does. He has ascended into the holy place in heaven where he bears us on his heart and presents us to the Lord not in our sin but in his beauty.

Another detail suggesting temple imagery is the famous streets of gold, which match the golden floors of Solomon's temple (1 Kg. 6:30).[11]

Now we return to the measurement of the city equaling 12,000, by 12,000, by 12,000 stadia. Cooperating with John's symbolic use of numbers in this book, twelve represents a number of completion, while one thousand signifies a large number, signifying fulfillment. So perhaps we are to understand the measurement to suggest that the entire renewed cosmos will be a Holy of Holies where God's special presence dwells.[12] The Glory of God, no longer contained in a cube-shaped room in Jerusalem, will cover the earth as the waters cover the sea (Hab. 2:14)

How do these details of the coming city shape how we live now? First, it shows us the wonders of God's grace toward us through Jesus. I know how dark and vile my heart and actions are at times. I am often stained with pride, lust, envy, materialism, crooked motives, and half-truths. If I were to design something for the high priest to wear on his breast as an accurate picture of me, I wouldn't choose a precious stone. Instead, a piece of coal or petrified dung would do. But I am no longer my own, and neither are you. The Lord Jesus bought us with his own blood and covered us with his own beauty.

Secondly, shake from your mind this idea that the Lord tolerates you or that you have been made merely acceptable to him. The Lord describes his Bride as something he treasures. The Lord promised through Isaiah that his people would *"be a crown of beauty in the hand of the* LORD*... you shall be called My Delight Is in Her... for the* LORD *delights in you... as the bridegroom rejoices over the bride, so shall your God rejoice over you"* (Isa. 62:3–5). Astonishingly, we are not presented as some charity case here. Instead, almost beyond belief, Christ's people make his heart sing. He delights in us.

Do you see yourself in union with Jesus? Are you laboring under a cloud of suspicion that the Lord tolerates you, or do you trust him when he says he delights in those who love his Son? When you think of the Lord, does an image of an ever-demanding and rarely-pleased lawgiver come to mind? Or do you trust that through the grace of Jesus, the Lord rejoices over you with gladness, and exults over you with loud singing (Zeph. 3:17)?

This vision shows that God delights in those who love his Son and pursue God's design for us. The city radiates with the glory of the holiness of God. Though this vision shows us the Bride's future state of complete holiness before the Lord, God wills that we pursue a life of holiness now (1 Thess. 4:3). But what do we mean by holiness? The words "holy" and "holiness" sometimes come across as cold, stuffy words pursued by people who lived long ago in monasteries.

At other times, the pursuit of holiness sounds like a set of rules one follows if one want to go to heaven. But when someone asked Jesus what one command summarizes God's will for us, he answered with these words: *"You shall love the Lord your God with all your heart and with all your soul and with all your mind"* (Matt. 22:34–38). God wills above all things that we should pursue and grow in our love for him. Remember, Jesus told the unloving crowds, *"If God were your Father, you would love me"* (John 8:42).

Those who pursue holiness then, are those who pursue greater love for the Lord Jesus Christ. Love for Jesus, of course, will affect how we conduct our lives. Jesus said, *"If you love me, you will keep my commandments"* (John 14:15). But holiness begins and ends with love for Jesus. The Puritan John Owen wrote that the fundamental part of being made in the image of God begins with a delight in the Son and that "nothing renders us so like unto God as our love unto Jesus Christ, for he is the principal object of his love."[13]

The Father has eternally delighted in the Son and wills that you would find your supreme delight in him as well. We might like to think God's supreme desire for us involves uninterrupted success in finance, relationships, or our vocation. But if that were so, he would be holding back from us the very object of his own supreme desire: the Son of God. And knowing that shapes how we respond to trial and sorrow. Every heartache, distress, persecution, and letdown sent from the Lord serves to drive us deeper into the arms of our Savior, where we find the delight our hearts long for. And when those hard times come, and they will, we have this vision that reminds us that we are eternally safe in God's care and of eternal value to him.

An old story tells of a woman who had for years heard that the Lord refines his people as a silversmith refines metal, but she didn't understand what that meant. So she made her way to a local silversmith to ask about the process of refining metal. The silversmith explained when silver arrives in his shop, it is filled with impurities called dross. To ensure the highest quality of silver, the dross must be removed. He explained that impurities can be removed from silver by heating it until it liquefies, causing dross to rise to the surface, which can then be skimmed off.

But, he warned, if the metal overheats, it will destroy the silver. The woman then asked, if the silver needs to be hot enough to liquefy but not overheated, how do you know when all the dross is out? "I have a trick," he said. "I know the silver is ready when I look at it and see my reflection."

Christian, the Lord will sometimes walk us through valleys that disappoint, discourage, and disorient us. But rest assured. The Lord wills in all these not your destruction, but your growth in affection for his son.

Study Questions

1. What we think of ourselves will shape how we respond to the ups and downs of everyday living. Take a moment to assess what you see in the mirror honestly. What drives you? How does this agree or differ from what the Lord says is true of who you are?
2. Of these images that God gives John to convey our eternal safety with Him, which one strikes you as most comforting and why?
3. Do you struggle with the idea that the Lord only tolerates you? Or that you've simply been made acceptable to him? Why is this? What feeds this lie, and how can we fight it?

4. How do you see the world respond to trial and sorrow? Now, consider how you react to the same. Are these two answers drastically different? Whether yes or no, answer why.
5. One of the most prominent, clear, and understated ways we witness as Christians is how we respond to suffering, trial, and sorrow. Take some time to meditate on your witness in this area; do you have space for praise, need for confession, or both?

---

1. For more on Henry Gunther, see https://www.history.com/news/world-war-i-armistice-last-american-death.
2. The tie here to Ezekiel 40 is unmistakable. John, like Ezekiel, was brought to a high mountain where he could see and describe a city that was a temple. However, there are similarities and differences in what they see appropriate to their time in redemptive history. For a treatment of the Ezekiel background of John's vision, see G.K. Beale, *The Book of Revelation: A Commentary on the Greek Text* (Grand Rapids, MI: Eerdmans, 2013), 1065–1071.
3. Properly speaking, the New Jerusalem cannot be reduced to a description of God's covenant people though it is here called the wife of the Lamb. Instead, the Scriptures present the New Jerusalem as the place where God's immediate presence dwells with his people. For a discussion of the New Jerusalem as a place, presence, and a people, see Richard Bauckham, *The Climax of Prophecy: Studies in the Book of Revelation* (Edinburgh: T&T Clark, 1993), 132–143. On this point, see also Herman Bavinck, *Reformed Dogmatics, Volume 4: Holy Spirit, Church, and New Creation*, edited by John Bolt (Grand Rapids, MI: Baker Academic, 2008), 719.
4. An angel at the gate, keeping it open, may be an allusion to and reversal of the cherubim-guarded entrance to the garden of Eden forbidding entry. See Gen 3:24.
5. Nancy Guthrie, *Blessed: Experiencing the Promise of the Book of Revelation*, (Chicago, IL: Crossway, 2022), 231.
6. The angel's measuring of the temple in 21:5 is also an image of safety. As we noted in our treatment of Revelation 11:1–14, Ezekiel Chapters 40–48 present detailed measurements of the temple city, which point to the Lord's promise of his abiding and protecting presence. See also G.K. Beale, *The Book of Revelation: A Shorter Commentary* (Eerdmans, 2015), 215.
7. Richard Bauckham, *The Climax of Prophecy: Studies in the Book of Revelation*, 134.
8. Dennis E. Johnson, *Triumph of the Lamb: A Commentary on Revelation* (Phillipsburg, NJ: P&R Publishing, 2001), 309.
9. The twelve open gates on all sides of the city allow entrance to *"every tribe and language and people and nation"* (Rev. 5:9).
10. At least eight of the stones listed are identical to those that adorned the High Priest. Because the ancient writers were somewhat vague in their descriptions of precious stones, precise identification is sometimes difficult. John's descriptions of the other four stones are rough equivalents. See G.K. Beale, *The Book of Revelation: A Shorter Commentary*, 486; Dennis E. Johnson, *Triumph of the Lamb: A Commentary on Revelation*, 314–315.
11. In Rev. 22:4, John saw the name of God on the foreheads of those in the city. This is a probable allusion to the practice of placing the name of the Lord on the high priest's forehead in the Old Testament (Ex. 28:36-38), creating one more allusion to the city's temple-like description wherein all have unrestricted access to the Lord.

12. An interesting detail about the measurement of 12,000 stadia unfolds if we were to treat this number literally. 12,000 stadia (or about 1,500 miles), in height and width, represents the size of then then-known world of John's day. See G.K. Beale, *The Book of Revelation: A Shorter Commentary*, 483.
13. John Owen, "Christologia," in *The Works of John Owen,* ed. William H. Goold, 24 vols. (1850–1855; republished, Edinburgh: Banner of Truth, 1965–1991), 1:146.

37

THEY WILL SEE HIS FACE
REVELATION 22:1-5

One of my favorite movies is the 1997 Italian film *Life Is Beautiful*, which tells the story of a Jewish father and his little boy, both prisoners in a Nazi concentration camp. The father hides their true situation to protect his son from the nightmare around them. He tells his son that they have been brought to the camp to play a complicated game of hide and seek, which, if played well, would result in a prize at the end: a full-sized tank. The father assured his son that the first person to get one thousand points would win the tank, a prize most little boys would love to have.

The rules of the game were simple. The father explained that if the boy complained of hunger or cried for his mother, he would lose points. On the other hand, the boy could earn points by successfully hiding whenever he saw a Nazi enter the barracks: twenty-five points if he could hide from one guard, fifty points if there were two.

Over time, the little boy gets better and better at hiding and suppressing complaints about hunger and missing his mother. So good was he at the "game" the guards didn't even know the little boy was there. Whenever the boy would get discouraged, his father would remind him of the prize awaiting him if he didn't give up. A tank. And not a toy tank, but a real tank he could ride in.

I'll tell you in a moment how that movie ends, but for now, consider the similar technique of the father in that movie to one of the purposes of the book of Revelation. Far from being a book fashioned to confuse or terrorize Christians, its design is to comfort God's people with his promises to motivate them to persevere in faith until we see the Lord. The father in *Life Is Beautiful* kept before his son's eyes the promise of a future reality that would be his if he could make it to the end. John does the same thing in this final glimpse of the holy city, the new Jerusalem, where God and his people dwell together for all eternity.

In the last section, John described the new heavens and earth with language reminding us of the temple in the earthly Jerusalem. The renewed world is in the shape of a perfect cube, just like the cube-shaped holy of holies in the temple. The same precious stones adorning the foundation of the new city match those worn on the breast of the temple's high priest. And the gold-covered streets of the city remind us of the golden floors of Solomon's temple.

In this last glimpse of the city, a final image emerges, taking us back to the beginning of the Bible when God and man dwelt in a garden. But in this garden, the Bride of Christ will see her Groom's face.

Garden

As noted a few chapters back, the Bible begins and ends in a garden. A few of John's details point us in this direction.[1] First, we know that the original garden sat atop a mountain. The book of Ezekiel tells us that the Garden of Eden was on *"the mountain of God"* (Ezek. 28:14). Additionally, we know that a river flowed out of Eden, suggesting it was higher in elevation than the surrounding areas.

With this in mind, we recall that an angel carried John away in the Spirit to a *"great, high mountain"* to see the city (Rev. 21:10).[2] Additionally, a river flowed through the first garden (Gen. 2:10), just as John describes a river running through the center of the city (Rev. 22:1).[3] Moses also tells us that the finest gold and precious stones filled the land of Eden (Gen. 2:11–12), just as John described the renewed earth with a foundation adorned with priceless stones and gold-covered streets. And finally, the Tree of Life (Gen. 2:9), one of the best-known features of the original garden finds a home in the renewed earth, bearing fruit year-round (Rev. 22:2).[4]

We might say that the Tree of Life bookends the Bible. References to this tree only occur in Genesis and Revelation, and both in a garden.[5] The Tree of Life thus connects the world's creation to the recreated world to come.

The Bible provides few details about the Tree of Life, but its name suggests that its fruit functioned as an edible, tangible symbol of unending life with the Lord. And in so long as Adam and Eve obeyed the Lord, they could eat from the tree that nourished their bodies and souls.

But we know how the story goes. In the garden, there stood another tree from which Adam and Eve were forbidden to eat: the Tree of the Knowledge of Good and Evil. This tree represented the authority to decide between what is good and evil, an authority that belonged to God alone. This is why they were forbidden from eating from the tree and why what happened was so horrific. When our first parents took from that tree, they were saying to God and each other that they would determine based on their own judgment, the nature of good and evil.[6]

It sounds so matter-of-fact: "*She took of its fruit and ate, and she also gave some to her husband who was with her, and he ate*" (Gen. 3:6). But their decision to determine right from wrong apart from the Lord's counsel brought disaster upon creation.

I see a lot of myself in my first parents. I suspect you do as well. We still choose forbidden fruit over our Creator. I came across a prayer from a Puritan not long ago that poetically captures what happened in the garden and still happens today:

> *You placed us in Paradise, and we continued in your favor until we disrupted your counsels, disappointed your purposes, and sold our glorious, gracious God for an apple. O write it! O brand it on our foreheads forever: for an apple once we lost our God, and still, today, lose him for no more: for money, for meat, for temporary pleasures.*[7]

I love and hate that line: we sold our God for an apple. Still today, we sell him for no more; for money, sex, power, and image, we lose our God. Do you remember the Lord's response to being sold off for a piece of fruit? Moses tells us that God acted with swift justice and mercy:

> *Then the LORD God said, "Behold, the man has become like one of us in knowing good and evil. Now, lest he reach out his hand and take also of the tree of life and eat, and live forever—" therefore the LORD God sent him out from the garden of Eden to work the ground from which he was taken.* (Gen. 3:22–23)

We see the justice of God in expelling the man and woman from the garden. They forfeited God's promise of life, so he removed access to the tree that promised life on the condition of obedience. But we also see the glorious mercy of the Lord. Scholars often note that the Lord doesn't finish his sentence in verse 22, represented by a dash indicating strong emotion. It's as though the thought of humanity eternally confirmed in his rebellious state was unthinkable and even unspeakable for the Lord.[8]

Upon observing, John beholds a garden abundant with Trees of Life, which serves as a testament to the magnificence of God's grace. John probably didn't just see one Tree of Life but a whole grove of them!

There are a few reasons this may be the case. The first is that John's vision echoes Ezekiel's vision when he too describes the city of God. Like John, Ezekiel also saw a river in a city. And on either side of the river, Ezekiel observed *"all kinds of trees for food"* whose leaves do not wither and are used for healing (Ezek. 47:12). Ezekiel saw groves of trees on the banks of the river and it's possible John did too.

Additionally, it's hard to imagine how one tree could grow on both sides of a river, implying that John observed many trees of life.

And finally, John's language suggests[9] that he used "Tree of Life" as a collective description of many trees, much like we do when we refer to a grove of oak or pine trees. We say things like, "The hill is covered with pine" or "I walked through the oak grove." The singular words "pine" and "oak" function collectively for numerous pine and oak trees.

Why make this point? Because John describes not a mere return to the garden and a Tree of Life. Instead, the one tree in the first garden has become a whole grove of trees in the escalated paradise of the second garden. That singular Tree of Life in the beginning, representing life, peace, and communion with God and with fellow man, has become a grove of innumerable trees as far as John's eye could see, all planted along the life-giving waters coming from the throne of God and of the Lamb.

Think about the prospect set before us here. When God put Adam and Eve in the garden, he gave them a task that no other creature had: to have dominion and rule over creation.

God gifted to his image-bearers the task of mirroring his creative action, love for beauty, and design. Our rule included the care and cultivation of creation such that it would benefit every person and *"everything that has the breath of life"* (Gen. 1:30) and all to the glory of the One we mirror.

And that last point is crucial. Our dominion labors under the guidance of the Creator, which excludes exploiting the earth's resources for selfish purposes and the veneration of creation such that we cannot use it. [10] Instead, the rule given to his image-bearers served to cultivate and care for the earth while reflecting the One who cares for all of creation, not just human beings.

And if Adam and Eve had ruled in such a way, they would have lived and flourished in the immediate presence of God and with access to the Tree of Life. But we know they blew it. They failed to serve and rule over creation as designed and were expelled from the garden.

But what do we see in this vision before us? A garden restored, the curse removed, Trees of Life covering the city as far as the eye can see, and the people of God recommissioned to serve, rule, and reign over creation:

> *No longer will there be anything accursed, but the throne of God and of the Lamb will be in it, and his servants will worship him.... And night will be no more. They will need no light of lamp or sun, for the Lord God will be their light, and they will reign forever and ever.* (Rev. 22:3, 5)

We can hardly be bored with the thought of eternal life if we understand what's happening here! The Lord has placed us back in a garden of superabundance and reissues the charge to reign over creation.

As I think of how I now cultivate and keep my little piece of soil here in South Florida, I get excited about what lies ahead. When I moved into my home a decade ago, under-watered brown grass and a few pitiful shrubs made up the landscape. Today, I have mango trees imported from India, bamboo from China, a palm tree from Madagascar, and a floss silk tree from South America. Large Oak and Gumbo Limbo trees now cast shade and relief over stretches of green grass. A hedge of cocoplums now brims with life offering shelter to bunnies, butterflies, and birds of all sorts. I like to think of my yard as a little garden, arranged in such a way as to highlight the wisdom, creativity, goodness, and love of our Lord.

Now imagine, as we saw in the last chapter, that God intends to make the entire universe a garden. And you will be part of that eternal, joy-filled labor. But think of a cosmos-wide garden as having more than just trees and flowers but also works of art, literature, song, and dance, and all of it to the glory of our Lord.

We're approaching an area where the Bible does not give us the details we may long to have. But this much we know about the garden to come: Our Groom, the Lord Jesus Christ, will be there!

Groom

> *No longer will there be anything accursed, but the throne of God and of the Lamb will be in it, and his servants will worship him. They will see his face, and his name will be on their foreheads.* (Rev. 22:3–4)

"They will see his face." Such a brief statement that carries with it the unimaginable joy, peace, and love for which the Lord designed our hearts.

In the Old Testament, seeing God's face was nothing less than a death sentence. The Lord warned even Moses that he could not see his face and live (Ex. 33:20, 34:29–45; Num. 12:8). The Lord permitted Moses to see only his back while shielded at the same time by his hand. And later, when the high priest would enter the Holy of Holies that one special day of the year, he couldn't enter before first making sure the smoke of incense engulfed the room, lest he look directly at the manifestation of God's glory above the mercy seat (Lev. 16:13). But on that day, in the garden to come, "no protection is now needed against the 'consuming fire' of God's blazing holiness, for no trace of sin" remains in his people.[11]

Consider again that quote from the Puritan who prayed, "O write it! O brand it on our foreheads forever: for an apple once we lost our God, and still, today lose him for no more." But praise the Lord, John sees not sin on the Bride's forehead, but the name of her Lord (Rev. 22:4). As we saw early in this book, when the Lord seals his name on someone's forehead, they bear the mark of God's treasured possession, and consequently, they are safe from his wrath. And the Bride knows why God treasures her and has spared her from his wrath. Though we sold our God for a piece of fruit and lost access to the Tree of Life, the beloved Groom of the Church came to embrace a tree that would bring him death.

While the Bible begins and ends with a tree in a garden, sandwiched between Genesis and Revelation another Tree, another Adam, and another garden emerges (John 19:41). In this garden, on that Tree, the second Adam lovingly took upon his brow the name of "Sinner" to place his Father's holy name on yours.

The Bible also begins and ends with a garden wedding. The first Adam was wed to his bride in the presence of God in a garden. In the garden to come, the second Adam, having been cursed and crushed on a tree, will welcome his Bride to take and eat from the Tree of Life and to be his forever. There, he will crown her with life everlasting, dress her in robes of beauty, and welcome her to rule with him. But it will not be the robes of beauty or crowns of righteousness that will steal her attention. It will be his face.

There is a face now seated at the right hand of the Father that bears eyes of love into which you one day will peer. And you will do so, Christian, because of God's love for you. Do you know that love today?

If so, live as one engaged to be the Lord's. Have you wandered away from that love or wonder if it's still available? If so, know this—*"the steadfast love of the Lord never ceases, and his mercies never come to an end; they are new every morning"* (Lam. 3:22–23).

I began by telling you about the movie *Life is Beautiful*. Let me tell you how it ends. Remember, to keep his young boy's hope alive, the father created a game that promised the grand prize of a tank if his son accumulated enough points.

Toward the movie's end, the Nazi soldiers become aware that the Allied Forces will soon arrive to liberate the camp. To cover their tracks, the Nazis rounded up prisoners, executing most of them and forcing survivors onto trains. Before long, the camp appeared empty. Eerily empty. All except for the little boy, still hiding, hoping he'd accumulated enough points to win the game.

But eventually, he realized he alone remained in the concentration camp. As he tried to make sense of his situation, the sound of heavy machinery broke the silence and the earth started rumbling under his feet. When he turned toward the sound of the loud rolling noise, he saw a full-sized tank driven by the Allied Forces who'd come to save him.

The boy's eyes grew large, his jaw dropped open, and once the tank rolled to a stop, the boy shouted, "It's true!" He'd won the game.

Christian, we long for the day when our faith will be sight. On that day, we will see the garden, the jewels adorning the city, and the streets covered with gold. But supreme above all, we will see the face of Jesus. And perhaps we'll say at that moment, "It's true! It's true! It's really true." Jesus commands us to live in the reality of these truths now.

Study Questions

1. What we think of ourselves will shape how we respond to the ups and downs of everyday living. Take a moment to assess what you see in the mirror honestly. What drives you? How does this agree or differ from what the Lord says is true of who you are?
2. Of these images that God gives John to convey our eternal safety with Him, which one strikes you as most comforting and why?
3. Do you struggle with the idea that the Lord only tolerates you?

Or that you've simply been made acceptable to him? Why is this? What feeds this lie, and how can we fight it?
4. How do you see the world respond to trial and sorrow? Now, consider how you react to the same. Are these two answers drastically different? Whether yes or no, answer why.
5. One of the most prominent, clear, and understated ways we witness as Christians is how we respond to suffering, trial, and sorrow. Take some time to meditate on your witness in this area; do you have space for praise, need for confession, or both?

---

1. For a book-length treatment on how the tabernacle and temple were designed to reflect the garden of Eden and the entire cosmos, see G.K. Beale, *The Temple and the Church's Mission* (InterVarsity Press, 2004).
2. See also Ezekiel 40:2, where the prophet is likewise brought to a *"very high mountain, on which was a structure like a city"* to describe what he saw.
3. This same river was seen and described by three Old Testament prophets. Joel saw it before the exile (Joel 3:18), Ezekiel while in exile (Ezek. 47:1–9), and Zechariah after the return to the promised land (Zech. 14:8).
4. Twelve has been used repeatedly in Revelation for a number of completion or the fullness of redemption. The twelve kinds of fruit that appear every month point to the abundant provision of life for those who dwell in this garden. See G.K. Beale, *The Book of Revelation: A Shorter Commentary* (Eerdmans, 2015), 499.
5. The Book of Proverbs references the Tree of Life metaphorically four times (3:18; 11:30; 13:12; 15:4).
6. On the point of the Hebrew "knowing" meaning "to choose" see, Geerhardus Vos, *Biblical Theology: Old and New Testaments* (Eugene, OR: Wipf and Stock, 2003), 30.
7. This prayer comes from George Herbert, who spoke these words before a sermon. I've lightly adapted the language for ease of reading. For the original, see https://ccel.org/ccel/herbert/temple2/temple2.xli.html.
8. See C. John Collins, *Genesis 1–4: A Linguistic, Literary, and Theological Commentary* (Phillipsburg, NJ: P&R Publishing, 2006), 175.
9. The definite article "the" is absent in verse 2 before *"tree of life,"* which may suggest a collective meaning. See G.K. Beale, *The Book of Revelation: A Shorter Commentary*, 498.
10. For an excellent treatment of God-like dominion which neither exploits nor venerates creation, see Christopher Watkin, *Biblical Critical Theory: How the Bible's Unfolding Story Makes Sense of Modern Life and Culture* (Zondervan Academic, 2022), 83–106.
11. Christopher Watkin, *Biblical Critical Theory: How the Bible's Unfolding Story Makes Sense of Modern Life and Culture*, 562.

38

"SO WHAT?"

REVELATION 22:6-21

An old story about Dr. Robert Rayburn, Covenant Theological Seminary's founding president, gets told often. In the early days of the seminary, one of Dr. Rayburn's responsibilities was instructing fresh divinity students in the art of preaching a sermon.

The legend retold over sixty years to incoming students concerns how Dr. Rayburn would conduct himself in those preaching classes. As a student would preach his sermon, Dr. Rayburn sat in the back of the room, arms crossed, often with a scowl. His upset face indicated that he had one pressing question for the preacher. Sometimes, the young preachers satisfied Dr. Rayburn, but more times than not, students failed to answer the one question he had in mind.

What was the question? Two simple words: So what? You can imagine how heartbreaking those two words would have been if you'd poured over ancient languages, considered various theological issues tied to the text and the history of interpretation, and packaged it all to be presented in thirty minutes or less.

The point of Dr. Rayburn's "So what?" was not to dismiss all the young preacher's work. Instead, the threat of hearing that question reminded the student that if their sermon doesn't address the person in the pew by providing hope to the hopeless, warning to the rebellious, comfort for the lonely, and direction for the aimless, they have not yet preached. They've only given a lecture. A lecture instructs students about the Bible's truths. But a sermon provides those same truths and calls for a response.

Dr. Rayburn has now gone to be with Jesus, but an oil painting of him hangs in the seminary chapel. And while I never met him, whenever I passed by his representation, I would imagine him asking me, "So what?"

In this last section of Revelation, we come to the "so what?" of the whole book. Far from being merely a book of riddles to solve or images demanding interpretation, the Revelation of Jesus Christ calls us to action!

One author writes, "Scripture is not a passive cadaver waiting for curious medical students to dissect it in their quest for information."[1] But sadly, Revelation sometimes provides only a playground for the curious and imaginative:

- What does 666 mean?
- What is the mark of the beast?
- Who rides on the white horse?

All good questions, and I hope we've gotten some answers, but if we stop there, we miss the "so what?" of the whole book. In fact, Jesus makes his desires clear by pronouncing a blessing upon those who hear and keep the words of this book (Rev. 1:3; 22:7). As we listen in now to the last recorded words of Jesus in this last book of the Bible, what does he call us to do? He commands us to turn from counterfeits, trust in his care, and take from the waters

Turn From Counterfeits

Throughout our study, we've been reminded that faithfulness to Jesus Christ requires a long, hard battle against many foes. The world, the devil, and our flesh continually pull us toward compromise, apathy, and idolatry. While Christians long to have Christ as the supreme object of their worship, they nevertheless battle against a heart that is, in the famous words of John Calvin, a "perpetual idol factory."[2] But this book has called us away from any acceptance, favor, joy, or safety that comes at the expense of honoring Christ as supreme. These temporary pleasures are counterfeits from which we must flee.

Even John himself possessed a heart prone to giving priority of place to creation when its full devotion belonged to Christ alone. We might have expected John's response to seeing and hearing these heavenly visions of Christ to end this book forever changed and at the feet of Jesus. But John falls prey to his own fallible heart and misplaces his worship:[3]

> *I, John, am the one who heard and saw these things. And when I heard and saw them, I fell down to worship at the feet of the angel who showed them to me, but he said to me, "You must not do that! I am a fellow servant with you and your brothers the prophets, and with those who keep the words of this book. Worship God."* (Rev. 22:8–9)

John's heart was not yet fully healed of its proneness to wander at the time of this vision. Today, Jesus has fully healed John of his fallible heart, as he will heal yours when you see him (1 John 3:2). Until then, we must remain on the watch against anything that serves as counterfeit replacements for Christ himself.

When we studied the letters to the churches in the opening pages of this book, we saw that some churches suffered persecution for their faith, as do many worldwide today. In such situations, people may be tempted to turn to counterfeit offers of safety and approval. Being vocal for Christ will sometimes lead to losing friends, business opportunities, some social circles, and, tragically sometimes the loss of family. In the face of such threats, we may be tempted to give in a little here and there. Be less public with our witness. Only speak of Jesus if asked.

Perhaps out of the fear of loss, you have gone silent in your witness for Jesus. But this book has shown us that the temporary approval of the city of Babylon can not compare with the eternal applause of God himself. Don't live for a slap on the back from the temporary city of Babylon. Live for the one who says to his own, *"Well done, good and faithful servant"* (Matt. 25:23).

Other churches, such as the one in Sardis, suffered not from persecution but—strange as it sounds—because of the lack of local pressures against the church. These Christians had fallen into a spiritual coma, neither denying Jesus outright nor making much of him either. Under no local threats, they fell into a spiritual slumber from which Jesus commanded them to wake.

And then there was the church in Laodicea, vigorously pursuing the accumulation of wealth and comforts. Both Sardis and Laodicea wandered not because of persecution but prosperity. Both churches had lost the plot, forgetting they were no longer their own, but belonged to another. But Christ was not through with them. He stood at the door, knocking. He still stands at the door, offering true riches that moth and rust can't destroy (Matt. 16:19–21).

Jesus has shown us that he will undo and renew this world. Therefore, the wise live for the world to come and not for the one that will flee from his presence at the judgment. Jesus pronounces a blessing upon those who hear and take heed to this counsel.

The wise will also recognize the urgency of prioritizing Christ above things because his coming is always at hand. In verse 6, we're told that the things shown in this book must *"soon take place."* In verse 7, Jesus says, *"I am coming soon."* Verse 10 warns us that *"the time is near."* And lest we miss the nearness of Jesus's return, Jesus's final words make it clear: *"He who testifies to these things says, 'Surely I am coming soon'"* (Rev. 22:20).

What do we make of these statements about the soon-to-be coming of Jesus and the nearness of the time, given that over two thousand years have passed since John wrote them down? For example, how do we understand the words of verse 10: *"And he said to me, 'Do not seal up the words of the prophecy of this book, for the time is near.'"*

The Old Testament background to these words helps us understand the nearness of Jesus's return. Over seven hundred years before John saw his vision, the prophet Daniel received a similar one. Daniel had many questions about his vision, but the Lord told him to shut the book he was writing and *"seal the book until the time of the end"* (Dan. 12:4, 9).

The Lord instructed Daniel to seal the book until the time of the end, while John received the opposite command of not sealing the book because the end had arrived.[4] From Revelation's perspective, the end times had already come upon the world and with it, the nearness of the Messiah's return. To this book, we could add Peter's claim in his Pentecost sermon that the coming of the Spirit upon those assembled indicated that the *"last days"* had arrived (Acts 2:17). The author of Hebrews also classifies his own time as the *"last days"* (Heb. 1:2), just as Paul describes the same period as *"the end of the ages"* (1 Cor. 10:11), which John labels the *"last hour"* (1 John 2:18). I think we can safely conclude that the writers of the New Testament believed they lived and wrote in the last days.

But we should be clear about what the label "last days" does and does not mean. Describing our time as the "last days" offers a description of the character of our times versus a description of time as measured by a clock.[5] Christopher Watkin offers a helpful comment, writing:

> The "last days" are so-called because no further epochal event in salvation history remains before the final judgment. "Last" is not a comment on how long these days continue but on where they come in the story.[6]

We might liken our times to the last chapter in a novel. A last chapter may be very long or it may be short, but no chapter follows the last one.

Even if that chapter were much, much longer than those that went before it, it would still be the last chapter.

Put another way, when Jesus speaks about coming "soon" he speaks of the next major event to occur in God's plan of redemption. Commentator G.K. Beale is also instructive here:

> After Christ's death and resurrection and Pentecost, the next significant event in God's salvation scheme is the final coming of Christ.[7]

Jesus may return in ten days, ten years, or ten thousand years from now. God alone knows the precise timing of Christ's return. Even so, he will return. And Christ calls us to live in light of this certainty and to make it our constant aim to turn from the temporary god-substitutes of this world to the eternal, true, and living God.

And until you see Jesus face to face, you can trust him with every part of your life.

Trust in Christ

I hope that through our study of this book together, you have become bolder in your witness for Jesus and more confident of his care for you. In my youth, preachers and teachers used passages from Revelation to scare me away from things like microchips forced into people's foreheads and wrists, and barcodes on cereal boxes placed there by politicians secretly in league with Satan. Revelation only frightened and confused me.

But Jesus gifts us this Revelation for the opposite purpose. It serves to shore up our confidence in the Lord we serve. Indeed, we live in a world hostile to our faith. We'd miss much of Revelation if we ignored the ugly reality of Satan, who uses the beasts of the sea and land to trample on Christians. We'd be foolish to pretend that there isn't an alluring appeal to living in and for Babylon, presented as a seductive prostitute, offering all the pleasures and comforts our heart desires, and all of this for the low price of your soul.

But even with the world, the devil, and our sinful flesh waging war against our fidelity to Christ, he remains greater than them all. He remains a more faithful and trustworthy harbor where we may dwell safely until our faith becomes sight. Consider the name by which he refers to himself in verse 13: "*I am the Alpha and the Omega, the first and the last, the beginning and the end.*"[8] The use of the first and last letter of the alphabet was an ancient figure of speech for the Lord's complete control over history, from the beginning to the end, and the totality of everything in between.[9] When it comes to hope-filled assurances, there's nothing quite like the promise held within that name for Christians.

God makes many promises to his people. And the promise to work all things together for the good of those who love him remains sweetest among the many (Rom. 8:28). In taking the name of Alpha and Omega, Jesus assures us of his commitment to bring light out of dark times, good out of the bad, and joy will be the result of all sorrows.

And behind this amazing promise, the Scriptures paint a portrait not of a God who, like an emergency room surgeon, takes a bad situation and does all that he can to fix it. Instead, our sovereign Lord reflects the architect or city planner who has ordained the means just as much as he's ordained the end. He doesn't simply promise to bring sunshine after the storm. Instead, the Alpha and the Omega sends the storm into our world, and at his word, the clouds part and let the sunlight he's ordained break through.

Do you see how important this single title would have been to the first audience that heard it and for those who suffer terribly for Jesus today? As the Alpha and the Omega, Jesus can promise that no storm, trial, disappointment, or setback is purposeless, hopeless, or random. Christ works in our lives, "not despite dark days, difficult trials, and broken hearts, but through them. Such circumstances are the raw material he uses to form and shape his good plans, his perfect purposes."[10]

The assurance of his sovereign, purposeful rule over our short lives makes all the difference as we pilgrim to the house of the Lord, where there awaits oil for our heads and cups overflowing with wine. But every pilgrim on the way must also pass through the valley of the shadow of death. However, we fear no evil because a Good Shepherd accompanies us, carrying a rod and staff, held by hands bearing puncture wounds received in love.

This means that Christ calls us to trust him, whether we can now see the good assured to us or if we must lean into his promises by faith alone. And our faith finds nourishment further still in verse 16, where we're reminded of the love that brought the Son of God into the world:

> *I, Jesus, have sent my angel to testify to you about these things for the churches. I am the root and the descendant of David, the bright morning star.* (Rev. 22:16)

The first description of our Lord as the root and descendant of David reminds us of God's promise to raise a mighty, just, and wise king from

David's line (Isa. 11:1, 10). As told through Isaiah, this King will have the Spirit of the Lord upon him (Isa. 11:2); and with the words of his mouth, he'll slay the wicked from the earth (Isa. 11:4), gather people from all the nations (Isa. 11:10), and fill the earth with the knowledge of the Lord as the waters cover the sea (Isa. 11:9).

But first, this same King would have to lose his life for his bride. And we know what brought Christ into this world for us. Do you remember that opening praise John offered to Jesus before any of his visions started? John said, *"To him who loves us and has freed us from our sins by his blood... be glory and dominion forever and ever"* (Rev. 1:5–6).

I am not a grammar nerd, but I cannot get over John's present tense for the love of Jesus. He loves us. He loves me. Christian, he *loves* you. Not *loved* me, but *loves* me still. Though I have given him innumerable reasons to cease loving me, he cannot deny himself (2 Tim. 2:13). He is love and loves me still.

He is also the *"bright morning star"* (Rev. 22:16). Two assurances come to us through this title. First, Jesus will one day stand as the undisputed champion of God's people. You may recall from our earlier study the Old Testament figure named Balaam, the false prophet hired by a pagan king to curse Israel. Whenever Balaam tried to curse Israel, God would fill his mouth with blessings for his people. One of those forced blessings promised that a star would rise from out of Israel, and his enemies would fall before him (Num. 24:17–18).

In calling himself the bright morning star, Jesus declares that the night of darkness and the temporary reign of evil will cease when he returns. But we find another assurance packed into that title for the Church. Before the dawning of a new day, if you look into the night sky the bright morning star often sits on the horizon with the promise of the sun's soon rising. When Balaam spoke of the star that would arise out of Israel, he said, *"I see him, but not now; I behold him, but not near"* (Num. 24:17). Though the Lord Jesus was far away in Balaam's day, in John's day and our own, the coming of the morning star "is near" (Rev. 22:10).

And while we wait, we're invited to take from the waters.

Take From the Waters

Before the Lord invites us to drink from the waters, he gives a warning:

> *I warn everyone who hears the words of the prophecy of this book: if anyone adds to them, God will add to him the plagues described in this book, and if*

> *anyone takes away from the words of the book of this prophecy, God will take away his share in the tree of life and in the holy city, which are described in this book.* (Rev. 22:18–19)

A wayward world has received a sacred deposit of truth through the revelation of God in the person of Jesus and recorded in the Holy Scriptures. This revelation comes from a jealous God (Ex. 20:5), zealous for his glory and the good of his people. Those who tamper with God's invaluable word invite his fury and wrath upon themselves. Any who presume to take away the call to obedient, faithful living to Christ will have their access to the blessings described in this book taken from them. And any who would presume to improve the message through additional requirements or declaring, "thus sayeth the Lord" when the Lord has not spoken, will have added to him the horrific curses of this book. Once again, we see the justice of God in this warning. The punishment will fit the crime. Those who take from this word will have life taken from them. Those who add to it will receive the horrors contained within these pages.

Jesus has repeatedly called us to turn from sin and to find hope through him. He warns those who remain unchanged by his summons of the dangers of their present situation:

> *Blessed are those who wash their robes, so that they may have the right to the tree of life and that they may enter the city by the gates. Outside are the dogs and sorcerers and the sexually immoral and murderers and idolaters, and everyone who loves and practices falsehood.* (Rev. 22:14–15)

Your robes must be washed, or you will not enter the city.

But how do we get these required washed robes? If Jesus warns that certain types of people and behaviors, such as liars and the sexually immoral, idolaters, and cowards, have no place in the city, we might expect that strenuous efforts of personal devotion to Jesus clean our robes and keep them so. That's certainly what many in the church believe, and it has led to no shortage of those who've added to the Gospel all sorts of manufactured requirements that ensure entrance into eternal life.

But thankfully, the Lord hasn't left our assurance of salvation to fickle people. John has already told us how the robes we need get washed. In an earlier vision, he described an innumerable multitude of people, dressed in white robes, washed with the blood of the Lamb (Rev. 7:14).

What an odd, beautiful, and memorable image: white robes, washed clean, with the Lamb's blood. The same one who warns us of our need for washed robes provides them at no cost:

> *The Spirit and the Bride say, "Come." And let the one who hears say, "Come." And let the one who is thirsty come; let the one who desires take the water of life without price.* (Rev. 22:17)

Are you thirsty? Jesus invites not the righteous, the consistent, or the responsible but the thirsty. No matter what kind of person you've been, what you've done, or for how long you have done it, the Lord offers living waters that quench parched souls. And if you take your thirst to him, you'll find that the wells of salvation never run dry.

As we come to the end of our study, I'm reminded of another ending in a different book that has always deeply moved me. I've read C. S. Lewis's *The Chronicles of Narnia* to each of my four children several times. When I reach the final paragraph of the last book, I fight back tears. At the story's end, the children and Aslan, the Christ figure of Narnia, come together once again and we read:

> As [Aslan] spoke he no longer looked to them like a lion, but the things that began to happen... were so great and beautiful that I cannot write them. And for us, this is the end of all the stories... but for them, it was only the beginning of the real story. All their life in this world and all their adventures in Narnia had only been the cover and title page: now at last they were beginning Chapter 1 of the Great Story which no one on earth has read: which goes on forever: in which every chapter is better than the one before.[11]

So we arrive at the end of the Bible; but not the end of our story. The end of this book holds out the promise of a new and better day. It ends with less the feel of a going-out-of-business sale and more of a grand reopening gala, one where God recreates the cosmos, dwells with his people, and his glory covers the earth as the waters cover the sea.[12]

All of our life now prepares us for Chapter 1 of the Greatest Story ever told, which goes on forever, and every chapter is better than the last. Until then, Jesus says to you, *"Come to the waters."* And the thirsty respond, "Amen. Come, Lord Jesus!"

Study Questions

1. "So what?" As we come to the end of this glorious book, the goal is to be shaped by what we've come to understand. Take some time to meditate on how this trek through Revelation has shaped you.
2. Consider what Christ offers but people seek in other people or possessions. Where do you see your heart seeking counterfeits, being prone to wander, or simply not making much of Christ?
3. Many of us thought the book of Revelation was simply terrifying and confusing. We now see that its purpose is to shore up our confidence in the Lord we serve. What are some ways this book has opened up to you in this study?
4. How does the title of Alpha and Omega, the truth of God's sovereignty, bring assurance to you?
5. What comforts are offered through the other titles in this chapter: the Root and Descendant of David, and the Bright Morning Star?
6. "No matter what kind of person you've been, or what you've done, or for how long you have done it, the Lord offers living waters that quench parched souls." Pray in thanksgiving and adoration, and if needed, return to the One who calls thirsty people to come to him.

---

1. Dennis E. Johnson, *Triumph of the Lamb: A Commentary on Revelation* (Phillipsburg, NJ: P&R Publishing, 2001), 334.
2. John Calvin, *Institutes*, 1.11.8.
3. This is the second time John offered inappropriate worship to an angel (Rev. 19:10).
4. The Daniel background of verse 10 also informs how we understand the cryptic words of vs. 11: *"Let the evildoer still do evil, and the filthy still be filthy, and the righteous still do right, and the holy still be holy."* After Daniel was told to seal up the book until the end (Dan. 12:4), the Lord assured him that *"Many shall purify themselves and make themselves white and be refined, but the wicked shall act wickedly. And none of the wicked shall understand, but those who are wise shall understand"* (Dan. 12:10). John is indicating in 22:11 that what was predicted in Daniel's day—that the wise will respond and the obstinate will refuse to heed this book's warnings—is being fulfilled in his own.
5. Dennis E. Johnson, *Triumph of the Lamb: A Commentary on Revelation*, 35.
6. Christopher Watkin, *Biblical Critical Theory: How the Bible's Unfolding Story Makes Sense of Modern Life and Culture* (Zondervan Academic, 2022), 460.
7. G.K. Beale, *The Book of Revelation: A Shorter Commentary* (Eerdmans, 2015), 516. Beale further writes, "Whether this occurs in one year or five thousand, it could still be referred to as 'near' since it is the next *major* event in the decretive order of God's redemptive plan," 516 (italics original). Beale's emphasis upon the return of Christ as the next major event allows for minor events to precede Christ's return, such as those

mentioned in 2 Thess. 2:3–4, 8 (a great apostasy, and the revealing of the man of lawlessness). For more on these preceding events, see Anthony A. Hoekema, *The Bible and the Future* (Grand Rapids, MI: Eerdmans, 1994), 129–136.
8. God, the father, has been referred to as *"the Alpha and the Omega"* twice in Revelation (1:8; 21:6) and *"the beginning and the end"* (21:6). Here, in 22:13, all three titles come together in Christ to highlight his deity.
9. G.K. Beale, *The Book of Revelation: A Shorter Commentary*, 471.
10. Tim Challies, *Seasons of Sorrow: The Pain of Loss and the Comfort of God* (Zondervan Reflective, 2022), 88.
11. C.S. Lewis, *The Chronicles of Narnia: The Last Battle* (New York: Scholastic, 1995), 210–211.
12. Christopher Watkin, *Biblical Critical Theory: How the Bible's Unfolding Story Makes Sense of Modern Life and Culture* (Zondervan Academic, 2022), 549–550.

ABOUT WHITE BLACKBIRD BOOKS

White blackbirds are extremely rare, but they are real. They are blackbirds that have turned white over the years as their feathers have come in and out over and over again. They are a redemptive picture of something you would never expect to see but that has slowly come into existence over time.

There is plenty of hurt and brokenness in the world. There is the hopelessness that comes in the midst of lost jobs, lost health, lost homes, lost marriages, lost children, lost parents, lost dreams, loss.

But there also are many white blackbirds. There are healed marriages, children who come home, friends who are reconciled. There are hurts healed, children fostered and adopted, communities restored. Some would call these events entirely natural, but really they are unexpected miracles.

The books in this series are not commentaries, nor are they crammed with unique insights. Rather, they are a collage of biblical truth applied to current times and places. The authors share their poverty and trust the Lord to use their words to strengthen and encourage his people.

May this series help you in your quest to know Christ as he is found in the Gospel through the Scriptures. May you look for and even expect the rare white blackbirds of God's redemption through Christ in your midst. May you be thankful when you look down and see your feathers have turned. May you also rejoice when you see that others have been unexpectedly transformed by Jesus.

ALSO BY WHITE BLACKBIRD BOOKS

A Year With the New Testament: A Verse By Verse Daily Devotional

All Are Welcome: Toward a Multi-Everything Church

The Almost Dancer

Birth of Joy: Philippians

Carrying Casseroles on Motorcycles

Choosing a Church: A Biblical and Practical Guide

Christ in the Time of Corona: Stories of Faith, Hope, and Love

Co-Laborers, Co-Heirs: A Family Conversation

The Crossroads of Adultery: A Journey of Repentance and Faith

Doing God's Work

Driven By Desire: Insatiable Longings, Incredible Promises, Infinite God

EmbRACE: A Biblical Study on Justice and Race

Ever Light and Dark: Telling Secrets, Telling the Truth

Everything Is Meaningless? Ecclesiastes

Faithful Doubt: Habakkuk

Grace-Centered Economics: A Biblical Theology of Economics

Heal Us Emmanuel: A Call for Racial Reconciliation, Representation, and Unity in the Church

Hear Us, Emmanuel: Another Call for Racial Reconciliation, Representation, and Unity in the Church

How to Speak a Sermon: So That People Will Listen

The Organized Pastor: Systems to Care for People Well

Our Heads on Straight: Sober-mindedness—A Forgotten Christian Virtue

Plunder: Unearthing Truth for Marketplace and Ministry Leadership

Questions of the Heart: Leaning In, Listening For, and Loving Well Toward True Identity in Christ

Rooted: The Apostles' Creed

Single-Handedly Blessed

A Sometimes Stumbling Life

To You I Lift Up My Soul: Confessions and Prayers

Urban Hinterlands: Planting the Gospel in Uncool Places

Follow storied.pub for titles and releases.

Made in the USA
Columbia, SC
06 September 2024

41952697R00209